VIEW OF THE CENTENNIAL CELEBRATION AT LITCHFIELD, CT., 1851.—FROM THE RESIDENCE OF MRS. MORSE, WEST ST.

LITCHFIELD COUNTY,

CENTENNIAL CELEBRATION,

Held at Litchfield, Conn.,

13TH AND 14TH OF AUGUST, 1851.

HARTFORD:
PUBLISHED BY EDWIN HUNT, NO. 6 ASYLUM ST.
1851.

STEAM PRESS OF
GEORGE D. JEWETT,
26 STATE STREET, HARTFORD.

CONTENTS.

MEETING OF THE BAR.

At a meeting of the Bar of Litchfield County, held January 8th, 1851, the following Resolution was adopted, viz.:

Whereas, during the present year a century will elapse since the organization of this County; and, whereas, the subject of a Centennial Celebration of that event has been under consideration, therefore

Resolved, That Messrs. Phelps, Seymour, Hubbard, Hall, Hollister, Harrison, and Foster, be a Committee to call a meeting of the citizens of the County to consider that subject, and to take such order therefor, by the appointment of a Committee of Arrangements, or otherwise, as shall be deemed best.

The Committee appointed under the foregoing resolution, in pursuance thereof, do, therefore, hereby call a meeting of the citizens of the County, to be held at the Court House, on Wednesday, the 19th day of February, 1851, at 10 o'clock in the forenoon, to take into consideration the subject of said Centennial Celebration, and to make the needful preliminary arrangements. And the Committee respectfully request a general attendance of gentlemen friendly to the object, from every town in the County, in order that a Committee of Arrangements from each town may then be appointed.

C. B. PHELPS, *Chairman*.

Meeting of the Citizens

OF

LITCHFIELD COUNTY.

At a meeting of the citizens of Litchfield County, convened pursuant to a call of the Committee, at the Court House in Litchfield, February 19th, 1851, for the purpose of making preparations for a *Centennial Celebration* of the organization of the County:

The meeting was called to order by Charles B. Phelps, Chairman of the Committee, and on motion, Origen S. Seymour, Abijah Catlin, and Gideon H. Hollister, were appointed a Committee to nominate officers of the meeting.

The Committee made the following Report which was unanimously accepted:

FOR PRESIDENT,

WILLIAM M. BURRALL.

FOR VICE PRESIDENTS,

DAVID S. BOARDMAN,
SETH P. BEERS,
ERASTUS LYMAN,
RUSSEL C. ABERNETHY,
CHARLES B. PHELPS,
DANIEL B. BRINSMADE,
JOHN BOYD,
SAMUEL W. GOLD,
ALEXANDER H. HOLLEY.

FOR SECRETARIES.

ROGER H. MILLS,
EDWARD CARRINGTON,
JULIUS B. HARRISON,
EDWARD W. ANDREWS.

The following Resolutions were adopted on report of a Committee appointed for the purpose:

Whereas, we have now entered on the one hundredth year since the organization of the County of Litchfield, and as during this period thousands of the sons and daughters of the County have emigrated to other States and countries, many of whom are still living and occupying prominent positions in public stations, professions, and occupations, who, as well as others, would rejoice to return and visit the homes of their childhood, and we would rejoice to meet and welcome them:

Resolved, That for this purpose a CENTENNIAL CELEBRATION shall be held at Litchfield, on Wednesday and Thursday, the 13th and 14th days of August, 1851, and that a Committee of Arrangements from the different towns in the County be appointed; also, a Central Committee, to make the necessary and suitable arrangements for the occasion.

Resolved, That among the public exercises there be a Sermon, Oration, and Poem; a Public Dinner, and other social entertainments, at which there will be delivered, by invitation of the Committee of Arrangements, short Addresses and Poems suited to the occasion.

Resolved, That the Committee shall make the invitation of attendance as general through the public papers, and as particular by letter, as possible, and that the general arrangements for the celebration be made public through the newspapers and otherwise, as early as possible.

The following persons were then appointed a

CENTRAL COMMITTEE.

SETH P. BEERS,
JONATHAN LEE,
DAVID C. SANFORD,
HOLBROOK CURTIS,
ORIGEN S. SEYMOUR,
G. H. HOLLISTER,
ROBBINS BATTELL,
EDWIN B. WEBSTER,
WILLIAM H. THOMPSON.

The following named gentlemen were appointed from their respective towns as a

COMMITTEE OF ARRANGEMENTS.

LITCHFIELD — SAMUEL CHURCH,
" GEORGE C. WOODRUFF,
" DAVID L. PARMELEE,
" WILLIAM BEEBE,
" HUGH P. WELCH,
" JONATHAN BUEL.

BETHLEM,........JOHN C. AMBLER,
" JOSHUA BIRD,
" PHILO H. SKIDMORE.
BARKHAMSTED,...LESTER LOOMIS,
" HIRAM GOODWIN,
" PELEG SHEPARD,
" CORNWELL DOOLITTLE.
CANAAN, ...WILLIAM M. BURRALL,
" SAMUEL F. ADAM,
" HARLEY GOODWIN,
" FITCH FERRIS,
" CHARLES HUNT.
COLEBROOK, ...EDWARD A. PHELPS,
" REUBEN ROCKWELL,
" EDWARD CARRINGTON,
" ABIRAM CHAMBERLIN.
CORNWALL,......BENJAMIN SEDGWICK,
" FREDERICK KELLOGG,
" GEORGE WHEATON,
" EDWARD W. ANDREWS,
" H. MILTON HART.
GOSHEN,..........JOSEPH I. GAYLORD,
" LAVALETTE S. PERRIN,
" LEWIS M. NORTON,
" HORATIO N. LYMAN,
" LAMONT STREET.
HARWINTON,......TRUMAN KELLOGG,
" ABIJAH CATLIN,
" PHINEAS W. NOBLE.
KENT,...........WELLS BEARDSLEY,
" JOHN M. RAYMOND,
" PETER W. MILLS,
" HENRY I. FULLER,
" ASHBEL FULLER.
NEW HARTFORD,..HERMON CHAPIN,
" JAMES F. HENDERSON,
" JARED B. FOSTER,
" THOMAS WATSON.
NEW MILFORD,...DAVID S. BOARDMAN,
" PERRY SMITH,
" ORANGE MERWIN,
" GEORGE TAYLOR,
" ROYAL I. CANFIELD.
NORFOLK,.........MICHAEL F. MILLS,
" WARREN CONE,
" E. GROVE LAWRENCE,
" ORRIN TIBBALS,
" SAMUEL D. NORTHWAY.
PLYMOUTH,........EPHRAIM LYMAN,
" ELISHA JOHNSON,
" TERTIUS D. POTTER,
" EDWARD LANGDON.
ROXBURY,.........MYRON DOWNS,
" HERMON B. EASTMAN,
" AARON W. FENN.
SALISBURY,.......JONATHAN LEE,

SALISBURY,.......ROBERT N. FULLER,
" SAMUEL C. SCOVILLE,
" DONALD J. WARNER.
SHARON,.........ANSEL STERLING,
" CHARLES F. SEDGWICK,
" JOHN COTTON SMITH,
" WILLIAM T. KING.
TORRINGTON,.....LORRAIN THRALL,
" GEORGE D. WADHAMS,
" CHARLES B. SMITH,
" ANSON COLT.
WARREN,........GEORGE STARR,
" CHARLES CARTER,
" GEORGE P. TALLMADGE.
WASHINGTON......ITHIEL HICOX,
" WILLIAM MOODY,
" REMUS M. FOWLER,
" DAVID C. WHITTLESEY.
WATERTOWN,.....MERRIT HEMINWAY,
" LEMAN W. CUTLER,
" WILLIAM B. HOTCHKISS,
" HOLBROOK CURTIS,
" JOHN DE FOREST,
" NATHANIEL WHEELER.
WINCHESTER,.....WM. S. HOLABIRD,
" LEMUEL HURLBUT,
" JOHN BOYD,
" JEHIEL COE.
WOODBURY,......NATHANIEL B. SMITH,
" CHARLES B. PHELPS,
" WILLIAM COTHREN,
" CHARLES H. WEBB,
" ELIJAH SHERMAN,
" GARWOOD H. ATWOOD.

At a meeting of the Central Committee on the 26th of February, 1851, the Hon. Samuel Church, of Litchfield, a native of Salisbury, was selected to deliver the Oration; Rev. Horace Bushnell, D. D., of Hartford, a native of Litchfield, the Sermon, and the Rev. John Pierpont, LL. D., of Medford, Mass., a native of Litchfield, the Poem, and on being notified of their appointments immediately signified their acceptance.

On the 22d of March the Chairman of the Central Committee issued to the Committees of the several towns the following

CIRCULAR.

"LITCHFIELD, March 22d, 1851.

GENTLEMEN: — Having received several communications in relation to the approaching Centennial Celebration, from the Town Committees, making enquiries as to the nature and duties expected from them, we take the liberty of making a few suggestions on that subject.

Invitations have been prepared, and will soon be printed, to be addressed to the emigrants from the County, requesting their attendance at the celebration. Copies of these invitations will be sent you in a few days, for you to direct to such natives of your town as you may choose to send to, and we would recommend that thorough enquiry be made, so that the invitations may be sent to all who ought to be invited.

We also respectfully request you to procure Portraits and other relics of the past, illustrative of former manners and modes of life, to be forwarded some few days before the festival, so that they may be properly arranged for exhibition.

We further take the liberty of suggesting, that it may be well to have gatherings of the natives of each town, in the towns where they belong, before the days of the general meeting at Litchfield. In the event that this suggestion should be adopted, the Committee of the Town will, of course, act as a Committee of Reception and Arrangement, in regard to it.

And we would also suggest, that they select an individual, who may come prepared to make some remarks in the name and behalf of your town, when called on by the presiding officer of the day; and let the name of such individual be seasonably furnished to the Central Committee.

The Committee will be happy to receive any short *Poem*, suitable to be read or sung at the meeting.

Individuals, who cannot attend in person, are requested to forward to the Committee a *sentiment*, to be read on the occasion.

The gentleman who delivers the Address wishes information on the topics embraced in the following questions, and, therefore, requests of you an early answer; to be addressed to the Hon. Samuel Church, at this place, viz.:

1. At what time was the settlement of your town commenced?
2. What is the date of the Charter of the town?
3. What Indians inhabited the place at the time of its settlement, their character, &c.?
4. What was the name and character of the first minister of the town and his immediate successors?
5. General and field officers, chaplains, and captains in the war of the American Revolution?
6. Notices of distinguished lawyers, divines, physicians, or authors?
7. Judicial officers and members of Congress, natives of your town?
8. Other distinguished men natives of your town?
9. Origin and present condition of manufactures of the town?
10. Agricultural condition of the town?
11. Any miscellaneous matters worthy of notice?

Respectfully yours,

SETH P. BEERS, *Chairman Central Com.*

On the 22d of May the Central Committee prepared the following letter of invitation to emigrants from the County, caused about fifteen hundred copies to be printed and distributed to the Committees of the several towns, to be by them directed and forwarded to the emigrants from their respective towns:

LETTER OF INVITATION.

LITCHFIELD, May 22d, 1851.

DEAR SIR: — You have, perhaps, noticed in the newspapers, that a Centennial Celebration of the County of Litchfield, is to be held at this place on the 13th and 14th of August next.

At this celebration we expect a large gathering of those who have emigrated from this County to other parts of the United States, and to other lands.

Measures have been taken to render the occasion interesting. An address is expected from the Hon. Judge Church, a poem from the Rev. John Pierpont, and a sermon from the Rev. Horace Bushnell.

It is hoped that many will avail themselves of this occasion to re-visit the homes of their fathers and to revive the associations of their childhood.

Your own attendance is respectfully requested.

Yours truly,

SETH P. BEERS,
JONATHAN LEE,
DAVID C. SANFORD,
HOLBROOK CURTIS,
WM. H. THOMPSON,
ORIGEN S. SEYMOUR,
GIDEON H. HOLLISTER,
ROBBINS BATTELL,
EDWIN B. WEBSTER,
} *Central Com.*

A general invitation was also given through the public papers printed in the village, and in other papers in this and other States, requesting all to attend. And lest there might be some not notified or invited, the Committee gave the following further notice through the papers, which was continued down to the time of the celebration:

GENERAL INVITATION.

The proceedings of a meeting of the citizens of this County, in February last, having been published in hand-bills, in both of the newspapers in this village, and in many other papers in this and other States, and the Central Committee having given notice by circular, to the Committee of each town, in addition to about fifteen hundred special invitations by letter, to emigrants from the County, requesting their attendance, it is hoped and presumed that it has come to the knowledge of all.

Lest there be some individuals who have not received notice, you are requested to publish the *Circular Letter of Invitation*, which was issued in May last, and hope every native of the County will consider it as specially addressed to him.

If, (as has been represented,) the Committee in some of the towns have not yet sent out to the emigrants from their town, the printed invitations which were early forwarded to them for that purpose, it is requested that no time be lost in doing it.

To the above was appended the Circular Letter of Invitation.

On the 4th of July the Chairman of the Central Committee issued the following Circular to all the Town Committees to meet them at Litchfield, the 18th of July; pursuant to which, a meeting was held and the following proceedings had:

CIRCULAR.

To the Town Committee of the Town of ——: The Central Committee for the approaching Centennial Celebration desire to meet the Town Committees, for the purpose of completing the necessary arrangements for the occasion, and propose that such meeting be held at the Mansion House, in Litchfield, on Friday, the 18th day of July, at 11 o'clock, A. M., at which time a full attendance is requested, in order that the final arrangements may then be made.

Per Order of the Central Committee,

S. P. BEERS, *Chairman.*

MEETING OF THE CENTRAL AND TOWN COMMITTEES.

At a meeting of the Central and Town Committees, held at Litchfield, on Friday, the 18th inst., for the purpose of making arrangements for the County Centennial Celebration, John Boyd, Esq., of Winchester, was called to the Chair. Robbins Battell, of Norfolk, was appointed Clerk.

Hon. S. P. Beers, Chairman of the Central Committee, made a full statement of what had been accomplished by the Committee, and wished to lay the subject of other arrangements before the meeting, for their advice and action.

After consultation, it was

Voted, That the large tent owned by the corporation of Yale College, be procured, and if hereafter thought necessary, the smaller college tent, also.

Voted, To procure the services of a good band of music.

Voted, To dispense with a public dinner.

Voted, That we approve of the project of an Encampment for the male inhabitants of the County not residing in the immediate vicinity of Litchfield, while we look to the citizens of Litchfield to provide sleeping accommodations for the females, and for friends from out of the County.

Voted, To appoint the following Committee to make arrangements for the Encampment: John Boyd, of Winchester, Peter W. Mills, of Kent, William Cothren, of Woodbury, Charles Adams, of Litchfield, Robbins Battell, of Norfolk.

Voted, To raise eight hundred dollars to defray the expenses of the celebration.

Voted, To appoint Edwin Webster, of Litchfield, Treasurer of the funds raised by last resolve.

Voted, To appoint Major-General William T. King, of Sharon, Marshal, on the occasion of our celebration.

Voted, To invite the Sheriff and his deputies to be on duty for the preservation of good order.

Voted, To authorize the Central Committee to employ such additional police force as they may deem necessary.

Voted, To request the Central Committee to see that accommodations are provided for horses.

Voted, To request the Town Committees to procure the loan of old family portraits, to be exhibited at the court room in Litchfield.

JOHN BOYD, *Chairman.*

R. BATTELL, *Clerk.*

MARSHALS.

Maj. General Wm. T. King, Marshal for the day, immediately appointed twenty-two Assistant Marshals, one from each town in the County, viz.:

Litchfield, Col. Wm. F. Baldwin; Harwinton, Abijah Catlin, Esq.; Colebrook, Gen. Edward A. Phelps; Norfolk, Col. Robbins Battell; Goshen, Gen. G. Cook; Salisbury, Col. Nathaniel Benedict; Sharon,

Andrew Lake, Jr. Esq.; Washington, A. J. Center, Esq.; New Milford, Col. J. C. Smith; Kent, Maj. P. W. Mills; Winchester, Roland Hitchcock, Esq.; Woodbury, Charles H. Webb, Esq.; Torrington, Rufus W. Gillett, Esq.; Bethlem, Samuel Bird, Esq.; Cornwall, Col. Dwight Pierce; Plymouth, Seth Thomas, Jr., Esq.; New Hartford, Capt. Wm. T. Nash; Canaan, Walter Cowles, Esq.; Roxbury, Col. Albert Hodge; Barkhamsted, Col. Justin L. Hodge; Watertown, Col. Wm. B. Hotchkiss; Warren, Maj. E. Carter. The Marshals will wear as a badge, a sash of red.

On the 21st of July, the Committee of Arrangements, for the town of Litchfield, prepared and published the following suggestions to their citizens:

TO THE CITIZENS OF LITCHFIELD.

The approaching Centennial imposes upon you some important duties; and that these duties may be effectively performed, the Town Committee beg leave to make you some suggestions.

I. At a meeting held on the 17th inst., of the Central Committee, in connection with the committees of the several towns, (an account of which meeting is published in the newspapers,) it was resolved to raise $800 to defray public expenses, to wit: Band of music, erection of seats, tents, and tables, printing, &c. Three hundred dollars of this expense is allotted to be raised by the town of Litchfield, and will, we doubt not, be readily and cheerfully subscribed.

II. It is expected of every citizen of the town, that he will, at his own house, on the days of the occasion, exercise a most liberal hospitality.

1st. By entertaining his own family friends, emigrants from this town.

2d. By inviting his friends and acquaintances from other parts of the county. And this hospitality is invoked in favor not only of man and woman kind, but stable and barn room must be provided for horses and carriages of our friends.

III. It is expected of the Ladies, that very ample provision will be made in each house to accommodate for a single night all of their own sex who may be here on the occasion; and a little exertion on the part of each householder, will secure this important object. It is very easy to put up in every room of the house, several beds. All the old bedsteads must be set up, and may easily be furnished for a night with clean straw beds Mr. Bulkley is ready to set up at a small expense, in every house, such extra bedsteads as may be required.

A communication in the Enquirer implies a doubt, whether this duty will be thoroughly met. We trust, for the credit of our hospitable town, that this doubt is wholly groundless. A failure here would involve us in overwhelming disgrace. The celebration is in honor of the county which bears our name, and of which this is the honored Capitol, famed in the past, for talent, worth, generosity and hospitality. Let us not show ourselves unworthy of our past history.

It is expected that each town will provide mainly its own eatables; but it is presumed that every family here will keep set at all hours of the day, a table for the entertainment of such friends as may not be otherwise provided.

These suggestions are made, not only for the people of the village, and its immediate vicinity, but all the houses in the town ought to be prepared in like manner.

SAMUEL CHURCH,
DAVID L. PARMELEE,
GEORGE C. WOODRUFF,
WM. BEEBE,
HUGH P. WELCH,
JONATHAN BUEL,
} *Town Committee of Litchfield.*

LITCHFIELD, July 21st, 1851.

The Central Committee residing in Litchfield, appointed a meeting of themselves, to be held each day for two or three weeks previous to the celebration.

The Park in the West street, was selected for the exercises, near the center of which was erected the large tent belonging to Yale College, with large additions, over which floated the National flag. Beneath the covering was arranged the stand for the speakers, officers, and others. In front and around it, were long rows of substantial seats sufficient to accommodate from three to four thousand persons. Other tents surrounded it, with their flags bearing the names of the towns whose citizens erected and occupied them. Many other tents were erected in different parts of the village.

The Sheriff had selected several special deputies to be on duty for the preservation of order. Twenty members of the "Bacon Guards," were selected to perform duty through each night. A sub-committee was appointed to be in constant attendance to provide accommodations for visitors and their horses as they should arrive.

General Daniel B. Brinsmade, of Washington, was designated as President of the day.

General R. C. Abernethy, of Torrington; Charles B. Phelps, Esq., of Woodbury; Roger H. Mills, Esq., of New Hartford; John Buckingham, Esq., of Watertown, and Hiram Goodwin, Esq., of Barkhamsted, as Vice Presidents.

A programme of the exercises was printed in handbills and published in the village papers. And agreeably thereto, a procession was formed on Wednesday, at 10 o'clock, A. M., in front of the Mansion House, under the direction of General King, Marshal of the day, and his Assistants, in the following order, viz:

Band of Music, from the Watervliet Arsenal, N. Y.

Governor Seymour, and General Brinsmade, President of the day.

Vice Presidents.

Orators of the day and Poet.

Clergy.

Central Committee of Arrangements.

Town Committees.

Emigrant Sons, &c., of the County.

Odd Fellows, Cadets of Temperance, &c.

Citizens at large.

The procession marched from the Mansion House, through a part of the East street, thence up North street, and returning, entered the Pavilion in the west Park, at about 11 o'clock.

The audience being seated as far as practicable, the exercises were opened with vocal music by the Litchfield County Musical Association, who sang with fine effect the following Psalm, to the tune of Old Hundred, viz.:

1

"Be thou, O God! exalted high;
And, as thy glory fills the sky,
So let it be on earth displayed,
Till thou art here, as there, obeyed.

2

O God, my heart is fixed—'tis bent,
Its thankful tribute to present;
And, with my heart, my voice I'll raise
To thee, my God, in songs of praise.

3

Thy praises, Lord, I will resound
To all the listening nations round;
Thy mercy highest heaven transcends,
Thy truth beyond the clouds extends.

4

Be thou, O God, exalted high;
And, as thy glory fills the sky,
So let it be on earth displayed,
Till thou art here, as there, obeyed."

PRAYER.

A fervent and impressive prayer was offered to the throne of Divine Grace, by the Rev. George A. Calhoun, of Coventry, a native of Washington, in nearly the following words, viz.:

Almighty God, our heavenly Father; our fathers' God, and our God: we recognize Thee as the God of the earth, and of the heavens; swaying an undivided sceptre, controlling the worlds which revolve in the heavens, and the falling sparrow, and numbering the hairs of our head. We rejoice in the manifestations of thy love, mercy, and grace, unto us. We bless Thee for the institutions of our fathers, and that it pleased Thee to cast our lot in a land so highly favored, to give us our birth in a commonwealth so highly blessed, and in a portion of it so signally favored of Thee. And we bless Thee, that the institutions of our fathers have been continued to the present time, and that Thou hast allowed us, natives of this County, to assemble from different towns, counties, and states, for the purpose of celebrating this Centennial Anniversary of this County's organization, and to mingle together our praises, and our supplications, to Thee, around the sepulchres of our fathers. O, grant us Thy presence and Thy smiles on this occasion. We pray, that God, of His infinite mercy, would look down upon us, and bestow upon us His favor; lifting upon us the light of His countenance, and enabling all of us, connected by birth with this County, to pursue that course of conduct in life, which, through thy grace, shall secure the favor of heaven, and perpetuate the privileges which we enjoy to future generations.

Wilt thou, Almighty God, smile on the services of this occasion. May they be to the praise and glory of Thy name. And may Thy grace be magnified in richly blessing this great collection of natives of the same State, and of the same County. And may we all be enabled to live in such a manner, as to be prepared to meet together in the *great assembly*, and celebrate Thy praise in an undying song.

Regard in mercy, Our Heavenly Father, all the inhabitants of this State, and of this nation. Prosper all interests, civil, literary, religious, and charitable, of the land; and show mercy, grace, and salvation, to all the dying children of men. And hasten that blessed period, when the light of the moon shall be as the light of the sun, and the light of the sun shall be sevenfold, as the light of seven days. And to the Father, the Son, and to the Holy Spirit, shall be the glory forever. AMEN!

ADDRESS,

DELIVERED AT LITCHFIELD, CONN.,

ON THE OCCASION OF THE

CENTENNIAL CELEBRATION, 1851.

BY

JUDGE CHURCH.

JUDGE CHURCH'S ADDRESS.

The Hon. Samuel Church, LL. D., Chief Justice of the State, was then introduced to the audience, who commenced the delivery of his Oration. When about half through a recess was taken until 2 o'clock, P. M., when the address was resumed and finished, — occupying about two hours and a half, which is as follows:

Fellow-Citizens:

I have no leisure now to offer apologies for my unadvised consent to appear before you, in this position, on the present occasion. Declining years, and the constant pressure of other duties, should have excused me.

My residence of sixty-six years from my nativity in this County, and an acquaintance of half a century, of some intimacy, with the events which have transpired, and with the men who have acted in them here, and having been placed within traditional reach of our early history, I suppose, has induced the call upon me to address you. In doing this, I shall make no drafts upon the imagination, but speak to you in the simple idiom of truthful narrative.

Among the most ancient and pleasant of New England usages, has been the annual gathering of children and brethren around the parental board on a Thanksgiving day. The scene we now witness reminds me of it. Litchfield County,—our venerable parent, now waning into the age of an hundred years, has called us here, to exchange our mutual greetings, to see that she still lives and thrives, and hopes to live another century.

A little display of vanity on the part of such a parent, thus surrounded by her children, may be expected; but speaking by me, her representative, it shall not be excessive. She must say something of herself—of her birth and parentage—of her early life and progress, and of the scenes through which she has passed. She may be indulged a little in speaking of the children she has borne or reared, and how they have got along in the world. To tell of such as she has lost, and over whose loss she has mourned; and in the indulgence of an honest parent's pride, she may boast somewhat of many who survive, and who have all through this wide country made her name and her family respected.

We meet not alone in this relation, but we come together as brethren, and many of us after long years of separation and absence, to revive the memories and associations of former years.

Some of you come to visit the graves of parents and friends—to look again into the mansions where the cradle of your infancy was rocked, or upon the old foundations where they stood—to look again upon the favorite tree, now full grown, which your young arms clasped so often in the climbing, or upon the great rock upon and around which many a young gambol was performed. You come to enter again, perhaps, the consecrated temples at whose altars the good man stood who sprinkled you with the waters of baptism, and from whose lips you learned the lessons which have guided your footsteps in all your after life.

These are but some of the pages in the history of early life, which it is pleasant after the lapse of years to re-peruse. And now, if the spirits of these dead can pierce the cloud which hides our view of heaven, they look down with a smile of love upon your errand here; and when you shall leave us on the morrow, many of you will feel in truth, as did the patriot Greek, "moriens reminiscitur Argos."

A stranger who looks upon the map of Connecticut, sees at its north-west corner a darkly shaded section, extending over almost the entire limits of this County, indicating, as he believes, a region of mountains and rocks—of bleak and frozen barrens.* He

* Litchfield County is the large Northwestern county of Connecticut; averaging about thirty-three miles in length, with about twenty-seven miles in breadth; bounding North on Berkshire County, Mass., and West on New York. The present number of towns is twenty-

turns his eye from it, satisfied that this is one of the waste places of the State—affording nothing pleasant for the residence of men. He examines much more complacently the map of the coast and the navigable streams. But let the stranger leave the map, and come and see! He will find the mountains which he anticipated —but he will find streams also. He will find the forests too, or the verdant hill-sides where they have been; and he will see the cattle on a thousand hills, and hear the bleating flocks in many a dale and glen, and he will breathe an atmosphere of health and buoyancy, which the dwellers in the city and on the plain know little of. Let him come, and we will show him that men live here, and women too, over whom it would be ridiculous for the city population to boast: a yeomanry well fitted to sustain the institutions of a free country. We will show him living, moving men; but more than this, we will point out to him where, among these hills, were born or reared, or now repose in the grave, many of the men of whom he has read and heard, whose names have gone gloriously into their country's history, or who are now almost every where giving an honorable name to the County of Litchfield, and doing service to our State or nation.

The extensive and fertile plains of the Western country may yield richer harvests than we can reap; the slave population of the South may relieve the planter from the toil experienced by a Northern farmer; and the golden regions of California may sooner fill the pockets with the precious metals;—and all this may stand in strong contrast with what has been often called the rough and barren region of Litchfield hills. But the distinguishing traits of a New England country, which we love so well, are not there to give sublimity to the landscape, fragrance and health to the mountain atmosphere, and energy and enterprise to mind and character.

Not many years ago, I was descending the last hill in Norfolk in a stage-coach, in company with a lady of the West, whose for-

---

two. The towns of Hartland and Southbury which originally belonged to it, were annexed to other counties more that 40 years since.

The surfaee of the County is hilly, some parts mountainous, and is the most elevated County in the State. It is watered by numerous lakes, and by the Housatonic, Naugatuck, and Shepauge Rivers, furnishing much valuable water-power, which is extensively used by the thriving manufacturing establishments. The Housatonic and Naugatuck Railroads pass through the County on the vallies of the streams bearing those names.

mer residence had been in that town. As we came down upon the valley of the Housatonic, with a full heart and suffused eyes, she exclaimed, "Oh, how I love these hills and streams! How much more pleasant they are to me than the dull prairies and the sluggish and turbid waters of the Western country." It was an eulogy, which if not often expressed, the truth of it has been a thousand times felt, before.

Our Indian predecessors found but few spots among the hills of this County, which invited their fixed residence. Here was no place for the culture of maize and beans, the chief articles of the Indian's vegetable food. Their settlements were chiefly confined to the valley of the Housatonic, with small scattered clans at Woodbury and Sharon. The Scaticoke tribe, at Kent, was the last which remained among us. It was taken under the protection of the Colony and State; its lands secured for its support. These Indians have wasted down to a few individuals, who, I believe, still remain near their fathers' sepulchers, and remind us that a native tribe once existed there.

We now see but little to prove that the *original* American race ever inhabited here. It left no monuments but a few arrow-heads, which are even now occasionally discovered near its former homes and upon its former hunting grounds,—and a sculptured female figure made of stone, not many years ago was found in this town, and is now deposited at Yale College.

There are other monuments, to be sure, of a later race of Indians; but they are of the white man's workmanship,—the quit-claim deeds of the Indians' title to their lands! These are found in several of the Towns in the County, and upon the public records, signed with *marks uncouth*, and names unspeakable, and executed with all the solemn mockery of legal forms.—These are still referred to, as evidence of fair purchase! Our laws have sedulously protected the minor and the married woman from the consequences of their best considered acts; but a deed from an Indian, who knew neither the value of the land he was required to relinquish, nor the amount of the consideration he was to receive for it, nor the import or effect of the paper upon which he scribbled his mark, has been called a fair purchase!

The hill-lands of this County were only traversed by the Indians as the common hunting grounds of the tribes which inhabited the valleys of the Tunxis and Connecticut rivers on the eastern, and the valley of the Housatonic on the western side.

The first settlers of this County did not meet the Indian here in his unspoiled native character. The race was dispirited and submissive—probably made up of fugitives from the aggressions of the early English emigrants on the coast,—the successors of more spirited tribes, which, to avoid contact with the whites, had migrated onward toward the setting sun. These Indians were like the ivy of the forest, which displays all its beauties in the shade, but droops and refuses to flourish in the open sunshine.

Previous to the accession of James II. to the throne of England, and before our chartered rights were threatened by the arrival of Sir Edmund Andros, the territory now comprising the County of Litchfield was very little known to the Colonial Government at Hartford. The town of Woodbury, then large in extent, had been occupied some years earlier than this, by Rev. Mr. Walker's congregation, from Stratford. The other parts of the County were noticed only as a wilderness, and denominated the *Western Lands*. Still it was supposed, that at some time they might be, to some extent, inhabited and worth something. At any rate, they were believed to be worth the pains of keeping out of the way of the new government of Sir Edmund, which was then apprehended to be near. To avoid his authority over these lands, and to preserve them for a future and better time of disposal, they were granted, by the Assembly of the Colony, to the towns of Hartford and Windsor, in 1686,—at least, so much of them as lay east of the Housatonic river. I do not stop to examine the moral quality of this grant, which may be reasonably doubted; and it was soon after followed by the usual consequences of grants, denominated by lawyers, *constructively* fraudulent—dispute and contention.

Upon the accession of William and Mary, in 1688, and after the Colony Charter had found its way back from the hollow oak to the Secretary's office, the Colonial Assembly attempted to resume this grant, and to reclaim the title of these lands for the Colony. This was resisted by the towns of Hartford and Windsor, which relied upon the inviolability of plighted faith and public grants. The towns not only denied the right, but actually resisted the power of the Assembly, in the resumption of their solemn deed. This produced riots and attempts to break the jail in Hartford, in which several of the resisting inhabitants of Hartford and Windsor were confined.

It would be found difficult for the Jurists of the present day, educated in the principles of Constitutional Law, to justify the Assembly in the recision of its own grant, and it can not but excite a little surprise, that the politicians of that day, who had not yet ceased to complain of the mother country for its attempts, by writs of quo warranto, to seize our charter, should so soon be engaged, and without the forms of law, too, in attempts of a kindred character against their own grantees. No wonder that resistance followed, and it was more than half successful, as it resulted in a compromise, which confirmed to the claimants under the towns the lands in the town of Litchfield and a part of the town of New Milford. The other portions of the territory were intended to be equally divided between the Colony and the claiming towns. Thus Torrington, Barkhamsted, Colebrook, and a part of Harwinton, were appropriated to Windsor; Hartland, Winchester, New Hartford, and the other part of Harwinton, were relinquished to Hartford; and the remaining lands in dispute, now constituting the towns of Norfolk, Goshen, Canaan, Kent, Sharon and Salisbury, were retained by the Colony. These claims having at length been adjusted, the western lands began to be explored, and their facilities for cultivation to be known.

Woodbury, as I have before suggested, by several years our elder sister in this new family of towns, began its settlement in 1674. The Church at Stratford had been in contention, and the Rev. Mr. Walker, with a portion of that Church and people, removed to the fertile region of Pomperauge, soon distinguished by the name of Woodbury, and then including, beside the present town, also the region composing the towns of Southbury, Bethlem and Roxbury.

Pomperauge is said to have felt some of the effects of Philip's war—enough, at least, to add another to the many thrilling scenes of Indian depredation, so well drawn by the author of Mount Hope.

New Milford next followed in the course of settlement. This commenced in 1707. Its increase of population was slow until 1716, when Rev. Daniel Boardman, from Wethersfield, was ordained as the first minister. This gentleman was the ancestor of the several distinguished families and individuals of the same name, who have since been and now are residents of that town. His influence over the Indian tribe and its Sachem in that vicinity, was powerful and restraining, and so much confidence had this good man and his family in the fidelity of his Indian friends, it is said, that when his lady was earnestly warned to fly from a threatened savage attack, she coolly replied, that she would go as soon as she had put things to rights about her house, and had knit round to her seam needle! The original white inhabitants were emigrants from Milford, from which it derives its name.

Emigrants from the Manor of Livingston, in the New York Colony, made Indian purchases and began a settlement at Weatogue, in Salisbury, as early as 1720. After the sale of the township in 1737, the population increased rapidly,—coming in from the towns of Lebanon, Litchfield, and many other places, so that it was duly organized in 1741, and settled its minister, Rev. Jonathan Lee, in 1744.

The first inhabitants of Litchfield came under the Hartford and Windsor title, in 1721, and chiefly from Hartford, Windsor and Lebanon. This territory, and a large lake in its south-west section, was known as Bantam. Whether it was so called by the Indians, has been doubted, and is not well settled.

The settlement of the other towns commenced soon after, and progressed steadily, yet slowly. The town of Colebrook was the last enrolled in this fraternity, and settled its first minister, Rev. Jonathan Edwards, in 1795. Rev. Rufus Babcock, a Baptist minister, had, for some time before this, resided and officiated in the town.

One general characteristic marked the whole population; it was gathered chiefly from the towns already settled in the Colony, and with but few emigrants from Massachusetts. Our immediate ancestors were religious men, and religion was the ruling element; but it would be a mistake to suppose that it absorbed all others.

I shall not detain you with an eulogium on Puritan character. This may be found stereotyped every where—not only in books and speeches, but much more accurately in its influence and effects, not in New England alone, but throughout this nation. Our American ancestors were Englishmen, descendants of the same men, and inheritors of the same principles, by which Magna Charta was established at Runny-mede.—They were Anglo-Saxons, inspired with the same spirit of independence which has marked them every where, and especially through the long period of well defined English history, and which is destined in its further developments to give tone and impress to the political and religious institutions of Christendom. So much has been said and written of the Puritans, I have sometimes thought that some believe that they were a distinct race, and perhaps of a different complexion and language from their other countrymen; whereas, they were only Englishmen, generally of the Plebian caste, and with more of the energies and many of the frailties and imperfections common to humanity. If our first settlers here cherished more firmly the religious elements of their character than any other, the spirit of independence to which I have alluded developed another—the love of money, and an ingenuity in gratifying it.

Since the extent and resources of this County have been better known, the wonder is often expressed, how such an unpromising region as this County could have invited a population at first; but herein we misconceive the condition of our fathers. Here, as they supposed, was the last land to be explored and occupied in their day. They had no where else to go, and the growing population of the east, as well as the barren soil of the coast, impelled them westward. Of the north, beyond the Massachusetts Colony, nothing was known; only Canada and the frozen regions of Nova Scotia had been heard of. On the west was another Colony, but a different people; and still beyond, was an unknown realm, possessed by savage men, of whom New England had seen enough; and not much behind this, according to the geography of that day, was the Western Ocean, referred to in the Charter. A visible hand of Providence seems to have guided our fathers' goings. Had the valley of the Susquehanna been known to them then, they would but the sooner have furnished the history of the massacre of Wyoming.

If there were here the extensive and almost impenetrable everglade of the Green-Woods, the high hills of Goshen, Litchfield and Cornwall, and heavy forests every where—these were trifles then in the way of a New England man's calculation, and had been ever since the people of the May Flower and the Arabella and their descendants had been crowding their way back among the forests. These, and a thousand other obstacles, were surmounted, with hardly a suspicion that they were obstacles at all, and every township began ere long to exhibit a well ordered, organized society.

This was no missionary field, after the manner of modern new settlements. Every little Colony, as it became organized and extended from town to town, either took its minister along with it, or called him soon after. He became one with his people, wedded to them almost by sacramental bonds, indissoluble. A Primus inter pares, he settled on his own domain, appropriated to his use by the proprietors of every town, and he cultivated with his own hands his own soil, and at his death was laid down among his parishioners and neighbors in the common cemetery, with little of monumental extravagance to distinguish his resting place. The meeting-house was soon seen at the central point of each town, modestly elevated above surrounding buildings, and by its side the school-house, as its nursling child or younger sister, and the minister and the master were the oracles of each community. The development of the Christian man, spiritual, intellectual and physical, was the necessary result of such an organization of society as this.

The original settlers of this County were removed two or three generations from the first emigrants from England, and some of the more harsh peculiarities of that race may well be supposed, ere this time, to have become modified, or to have subsided entirely. If a little of the spirit of Arch-Bishop Laud, transgressing the boundaries of Realm and Church, had found its way over the ocean, and was developed under a new condition of society here, it is not to be wondered at; it was the spirit of the age, though none the better for that, and none the more excusable, whether seen in Laud or Mather—in a Royal Parliament, or a Colonial Assembly.

Less of these peculiarities appeared in Connecticut than in Massachusetts; and at the late period when this County was settled, the sense of oppression inflicted by the mother country, whether real or fancied, was a little forgotten, and of course neither Quakers, Prayer Books nor Christmas were the object of penal legislation. A more tolerant, and of course a better spirit, came with our fathers into this County, than had before existed elsewhere in the Colony, and, if I mistake not, it has ever since been producing here its legitimate effects, and in some degree has distinguished the character and the action of Litchfield County throughout its entire history, as many facts could be made to prove.

Before the year 1751, this territory had been attached to different Counties—most of it to the County of Hartford; the towns of Sharon and Salisbury to the County of New Haven; and many of the early titles and of probate proceedings of several of the towns, before their organization or incorporation, may be found on the records of more early settled towns. The first settlements of estates in Canaan are recorded in Woodbury, and many early deeds are on record in the office of the Secretary in Hartford.

In 1751, the condition of the population of these towns was such as to demand the organization of a new County, and the subject was extensively discussed at the town meetings. As is always true, on such occasions, a diversity of opinions as well as the ordinary amount of excited feeling existed, regarding the location of the shire town. Cornwall and Canaan made their claims and had their advocates—but the chief contest was between Litchfield and Goshen. The latter town was supposed to occupy the geographical center, and many persons had settled there in expectation that that would become the fixed seat of justice, and, among others, Oliver Wolcott, afterward Governor of the State. But at the October session of the General Court in 1751, the new County was established with Litchfield as the County Town, under the name of Litchfield County.

Litchfield County, associated with the thought of one hundred years ago! A brief space in a nation's history; but such an hundred years!—more eventful than any other since the introduction of our Holy Religion into the world. This name speaks to us of home and all the hallowed memories of youth and years beyond our reach,—of our truant frolics, our school boy trials, our youthful aspirations and hopes; and, perhaps, of more tender and romantic sympathies; and many will recall the misgivings, and yet the stern resolves, with which they commenced the various avocations of life in which they have since been engaged. And from this point, too, we look back to ties which once bound us to parents, brothers, companions, friends—then strong—now sundered! and which have been breaking and breaking, until many of us find ourselves standing, almost alone, amidst what a few years ago was an unborn generation.

Litchfield County! Go where you will through this broad country, and speak aloud this name, and you will hear a response, "That is my own, my native land." It will come from some whom you will find in the halls of Legislation, in the Pulpit, on the Bench, at the Bar, by the sick man's couch, in the marts of Trade, by the Plow, or as wandering spirits in some of the tried or untried experiments of life. And sure I am, that there is not to be found a son of this County, be his residence ever so remote, who would not feel humbled to learn that this name was to be no longer heard among the civil divisions of his native State.

The usual officers, made necessary by the erection of the new County, were immediately appointed by the General Court. William Preston, Esq., of Woodbury, was the first Chief Justice of the County, and his Associates were John Williams, Esq., of Sharon, Samuel Canfield, of New Milford, and Ebenezer Marsh, of Litchfield. Isaac Baldwin, Esq., was the first Clerk, and the first Sheriff was Oliver Wolcott, of whom I shall speak again. The County Court, at its first session in December of the same year, appointed Samuel Pettibone, Esq., of Goshen, to be King's Attorney, who was, within a few years, succeeded by Reynold Marvin, Esq., of this village, and these two gentlemen were all in this County, in this capacity, who ever represented the King's majesty in that administration of criminal justice.

The tenure of official place in the early days of the Commonwealth, was more permanent than since party subserviency has in some degree taken the place of better qualifications. The changes upon the bench of the County Court were not frequent. The office of Chief Judge, from the time of Judge Preston to the time of his successors, who are now alive, have been John Williams, of Sharon, Oliver Wolcott, Daniel Sherman, of Woodbury, Joshua Porter, of Salisbury, Aaron Austin, of New Hartford, also a member of the Council, and Augustus Pettibone, of Norfolk. I can not at this time present a catalogue of Associate Judges. It has been composed of the most worthy and competent citizens of the County—gentlemen of high influence and respect in the several towns of their residence.

In the office of Sheriff, Governor Wolcott was succeeded by Lynde Lord, David Smith,* John R. Landon, Moses Seymour, Jr., and Ozias Seymour, of this village, and the successors of these gentlemen are still surviving.

Mr. Marvin was succeeded in the office of State's Attorney, by Andrew Adams, Tapping Reeve, Uriah Tracy, Nathaniel Smith, John Allen, Uriel Holmes, and Elisha Sterling, whose successors, with a single exception,† still survive.

Hon. Frederick Wolcott succeeded Mr. Baldwin in the office of Clerk, and this place he held, undisturbed by party influences, for forty years, and until nearly the time of his death in 1836.

The common Prison first erected was a small wooden building, near the late dwelling house of Roger Cook, Esq., on the north side of East street. This stood but a few years, and in its place a more commodious one was built, nearly on the same foundation. The present Prison was built in 1812, and essentially improved within a few years. The first Court House stood on the open grounds a little easterly from the West Park, and may still be seen in the rear of the buildings on the south side of West street. It was a small building, but in it were often witnessed some of the most able efforts of American eloquence. In this humble Temple of Justice, Hon. S. W. Johnston of Stratford, Edwards of New Haven, Reeve, Tracy, Allen, and the Smiths of this County, exhibited some of the best essays of forensic power. The present Court House was erected in 1798.

The early progress of the County presents but a few incidents of sufficient note to retain a place in its traditionary history. The apprehension of savage incursions had passed away, and the people were left undisturbed to carry out, to their necessary results, what might have been expected from the spirit and enterprise which brought them hither. The old French War, as it has

* This gentleman was the father of Junius Smith, LL. D., formerly a distinguished merchant in London, and one of the projectors of Steamship Ocean Navigation, and now engaged in the culture of the Tea Plant in South Carolina.

† Leman Church, Esq., of Canaan.

since been called, disturbed them but little. Some of the towns in the County, moved by a loyal impulse, and a legitimate hatred of France, as well as hostility to Indians in its service, furnished men and officers in aid of some of the expeditions to the northern frontier.

The pioneers here were agriculturists. They came with no knowledge or care for any other pursuit, and looked for no greater results than the enjoyment of religious privileges, the increase of their estates by removing the heavy forests and adding other acres to their original purchases, and with the hope, perhaps, of sending an active boy to the College. Of manufactures, they knew nothing. The grist-mill and saw-mill, the blacksmith and clothier's shops,—all as indispensable as the plow and the axe,—they provided for as among the necessaries of a farmer's life.

Thus they toiled on, till the hill-sides and the valleys every where showed the fenced field and the comfortable dwelling. The spinning wheel was in every house, and the loom in every neighborhood, and almost every article of clothing was the product of female domestic industry. Intercourse with each other was difficult. The hills were steep, and the valleys miry, and the means of conveyance confined to the single horse with saddle and pillion, with no other carriage than the ox-cart in summer and the sled in the winter. The deep winter snows often obstructed even the use of the sled, and then resort was had to snow-shoes. These were made of a light rim of wood bent into the form of an ox-bow, though smaller, perforated and woven into a net work with thongs of raw-hide, leather or deer skin, and when attached to the common shoe enabled the walker to travel upon the surface of the snow. Four-wheeled carriages were not introduced into general use until after the Revolution. Ladies, old and young, thought no more of fatigue in performing long journeys over the rough roads of the County, on horseback, than the ladies of our times in making trips by easy stages, in coaches or cars.

The County Town constituted a common center, where the leading men of the County met during the terms of the Courts, and they saw but little of each other at other times. The course of their business was in different directions. The north-west towns found their markets on the Hudson River—the southern towns at Derby and New Haven—and the eastern ones at Hart ford. In the mean while, and before the breaking out of the war of the Revolution, nearly every town had its settled Pastor, and the schools were every where spead over the territory.

No manufacturing interest was prevalent in the County at first. The policy and laws of the mother country had discouraged this. But the rich iron mine which had been early discovered in Salisbury, and the iron ore found in Kent, could not lie neglected. Iron was indispensable, and its transportation from the coast almost impracticable. The ore bed in Salisbury had been granted by the Colonial Assembly to Daniel Bissell of Windsor, as early as 1731, and produces a better quality of iron than any imported from abroad or found elsewhere at home.

The manufacture of bloomed iron in the region of the ore, commenced before the organization of the County. Thomas Lamb erected a forge at Lime Rock, in Salisbury, as early as 1734,—probably the first in the Colony. This experiment was soon extensively followed in Salisbury, Canaan, Cornwall and Kent, and there were forges erected also in Norfolk, Colebrook and Litchfield. The ore was often transported from the ore beds to the forge in leathern sacks, upon horses. Bar iron became here a sort of circulating medium, and promissory notes were more frequently made payable in iron than in money.

The first Furnace in the Colony was built at Lakeville, in Salisbury, in 1762, by John Hazleton and Ethan Allen of Salisbury, and Samuel Forbes of Canaan. This property fell into the hands of Richard Smith, an English gentleman, a little before the war of the Revolution. Upon this event he returned to England, and the State took possession of the furnace, and it was employed, under the agency of Col. Joshua Porter, in the manufacture of cannon, shells and shot, for the use of the army and navy of the country, and sometimes under the supervision of Governeur Morris and John Jay, agents of the Continental Congress; and after the war, the navy of the United States received, to a considerable extent, the guns for its heaviest ships, from the same establishment.

It will not be any part of my purpose to become the Ecclesiastical historian of the County. This duty will be better performed by other pens. And yet, the true character and condition of a people can not be well understood without some study of their religious state.

I have already suggested, that there was here a more tolerant and better spirit than existed among the first emigrants to Plymouth and Massachusetts. The churches were insulated, and in a manner shut out from the disturbing causes which had agitated other portions of the Colony. I do not learn from that full and faithful chronicler of religious dissensions, Dr. Trumbull, that there was in this County so much of the metaphysical and subtle in theology, as had produced such bitter effects at an earlier time, in the churches at Hartford, New Haven, Stratford and Wallingford. The Pastors were men of peace, who had sought the retired parishes over here in the hills and valleys, without much pride of learning, and without ambitious views. The influence of the Pastor here was paternal; the eloquence of his example was more potent than the eloquence of the pulpit. It might be expected, that by such a Clergy, a deep and broad foundation of future good would be laid,—a fixed Protestant sentiment and its legitimate consequence, independent opinion and energetic action.

There was here, also, very early, another element which modified and liberalized the temper of the fathers, who had smarted, as they supposed, under the persecutions of an English home and English laws. A little alloy was intermixed in the religious crucible, which, if it did not, in the opinion of all, render the mass more precious, at least made it more malleable, and better fitted for practical use. There was not in this County an universal dislike of the Church of England. We were removed farther back in point of time, as I have said, from the original causes of hostility. We were Englishmen, boasting of English Common Law as our birthright and our inheritance, and into this was interwoven many of the principles and usages of English Ecclesiastical polity. This respect for the institutions of the mother country, though long felt by some, was first developed in the College, and extended sooner and more widely in this County than any where else; so that congregations worshiping with the Liturgy of the English Church were soon found in Woodbury, Watertown, Plymouth, Harwinton, Litchfield, Kent, Sharon and Salisbury, and were composed of men of equal intelligence and purity of character with their neighbors of the Congregational Churches. And yet, enough of traditional prejudice still remained, uncorrected by time or impartial examination, often to subject the friends and members of the Church of England to insult and injustice. Some of it remains still, but too little to irritate or disturb a Christian spirit.

The spirit of emigration, that same Anglo-Saxon temperament which brought our ancestors into the County, and which constantly pushes forward to the trial of unknown fortune, began its manifestations before the Revolution, and sought its gratification first in Vermont. Vermont is the child of this County. We gave to her, her first Governor, and three Governors besides; as many as three Senators in Congress, and also many of her most efficient founders and early distinguished citizens,—Chittendens, Allens, Galushas, Chipmans, Skinner and others. The attitude assumed by Vermont in the early stages of the Revolutionary War, in respect to Canada on the north and the threatening States of New York and New Hampshire on either side, was peculiar and delicate, and demanded the most adroit policy to secure her purpose of independence. In her dilemma, her most sagacious men resorted to the counsels of their old friends of Litchfield County, and it is said that her final course was shaped, and her designs accomplished, by the advice of a confidential council, assembled at the house of Governor Wolcott in this village.

Perhaps no community ever existed, with fewer causes of disturbance or discontent than were felt here, before the complaints of British exaction were heard from Boston. But the first murmurings from the East excited our quiet population to action, and in nearly every town in the County, meetings of sympathy were holden, and strong resolves adopted, responsive to the Boston complainings. The tax on tea and the stamp duty were trifles. The people of this County knew nothing of them, and probably cared no more. The principle of the movement was deeper—more fundamental; the love of self-government—"the glorious privilege of being independent!" The excitement was general throughout the County. Individuals opposed it, and from different, though equally pure motives. Some supposed resistance to the laws to be hopeless at that time, and advised to wait for more strength and resources; others were influenced by religious considerations, just as pure and as potent as had influenced their fathers aforetime; others had a deeper seated sense of loyalty, and the obligations of sworn allegiance. But the County was nearly unanimous in its resistance to British claims, and saw in them the commencement of a Colonial servitude, degrading, and threatening the future progress of the country, in its destined path to wealth and glory. I believe no individual of distinction in the County took arms against the cause of the country.

Our remote position from the scenes of strife and the march of armies, will not permit me to speak to you of battle-fields, of victories won or villages sacked any where in our sight. We were only in the pathway between the different wings of the American army. I have no means of determining the amount of force in men or money furnished by this County in aid of the war. From the tone of the votes and resolves passed at the various town-meetings, and from the many officers and men, Continental and militia, who joined the army, I may venture the assertion, that no county in New England, of no greater population than this, gave more efficient aid in various ways, or manifested by its acts, more devoted patriotism.

Sheldon's was, I believe, the first regiment of cavalry which joined the army. It was raised in this County chiefly, and commanded by Col. Elisha Sheldon of Salisbury. The services of this regiment have been favorably noticed by the writers of that day, and on various occasions called forth the public thanks of the Commander-in-Chief. Among other officers attached to it, was Major Benjamin Tallmadge, afterwards and for many years a distinguished merchant and gentleman of this village, and, for several sessions, a valuable member of Congress in the Connecticut delegation. Major Tallmadge distinguished himself by a brilliant exploit against the enemy on Long Island, for which he received the public approbation of General Washington; and through the whole struggle, this officer proved himself a favorite with the army and the officers under whom he served. Besides these, several other officers of elevated as well as subordinate rank, were attached to the Continental army, from this County. Among them were Col. Heman Swift of Cornwall, Major Samuel Elmore of Sharon, Col. Seth Warner of Woodbury, Major Moses Seymour of Litchfield, Major John Webb of Canaan, Capt. John Sedgwick and Edward Rogers of Cornwall, Col. Blagden and Major Luther Stoddard of Salisbury, and many others not now recollected.

Contributions in support of the war were not confined to the payment of heavy taxes, but voluntary aid came from associations and individuals in every town. The aggregate can not be computed,—if it could, it would show an amount, which, rich as we now are, I think could not be demanded of our citizens for any cause of patriotism or philanthropy without murmurs, and perhaps, resistance.

Nor was the Patriot spirit confined to men and soldiers,—it warmed the bosoms of wives, mothers and sisters, in every town. An equestrian statue of the King, of gilded lead, before the war, had stood upon the Bowling Green in New York. As soon as the news of the signing of the Declaration of Independence reached New York, this was missing. Ere long it was found at the dwelling-house of Hon. Oliver Wolcott, in this village, and in time of need was melted down into the more appropriate shape of forty thousand bullets, by the daughters of that gentleman and other ladies, and forwarded to the soldiery in the field. Other ladies still, and in other towns, were much employed in making blankets and garments for the suffering troops.

I have no means of determining the number of killed and wounded soldiers belonging to this County.

Mr. Matthews, the Mayor of the city of New York, was for some time detained in this village, a prisoner of war, and it is said that his traveling trunk, and some parts of his pleasure carriage, still remain in possession of the Seymour family. Governor Franklin, the Royal Governor of New Jersey, and a son of Dr. Benjamin Franklin, was confined as a prisoner of war in our jail which was often used to detain English prisoners as well as Tories.

Although the treaty of peace brought peace to other parts of the State, it did not bring it to the whole of this County. One town was left,—not to the continued and merciless inroads of British soldiers and savage Indians, as before, but to the unjust oppressions of Pennsylvania,—Westmoreland, better known to the readers of Indian tragedy by the name of *Wyoming*. Its history is one of melancholy interest. This territory is in the valley and region of the Susquehanna River, and included the present flourishing village of Wilkesbarre. Its extent was as broad as this State. It was supposed to be embraced within our chartered limits, and such was the opinion of the most eminent counsel in England and in the Colony. Under this claim, a company associated about the year 1754, by the name of the Susquehanna Company, and purchased the Indian title to the country, for two thousand pounds, New York currency. This was a voluntary movement,—a people's enterprise, unsanctioned by any direct Legislative act, but unforbidden, and probably encouraged. Within a few years, a settlement was effected upon the choice lands of the Susquehanna, chiefly by emigrants from the counties of Windham and New London, with several from this County, among whom was John Franklin of Canaan, the brother of the late Silas Franklin, Esq., of that town, a gentleman whose fortune and history were closely interwoven with the fortunes of that colony. The Authorities of Pennsylvania, though claiming under a later Charter, opposed this settlement, and kept up a continual annoyance until the breaking out of the war with England, and even then sympathized but little with our people there, under the dreadful afflictions which that event brought upon them.

Sad indeed was the condition of the colonists of Wyoming!—persecuted by their Pennsylvania neighbors, and left defenceless to the ravages of British troops and their savage allies! The Legislature of this Colony recognized this interesting band of its own children, and incorporated them into a township, by the name of Westmoreland, in 1774, and annexed it to the County of Litchfield. They would have been protected from the aggressions of Pennsylvania, if the war of the Revolution had not prevented, and the *good Friends* of that Commonwealth would have been compelled to doff the Quaker a while, or quietly to have left our fellow-citizens in peace. Under the protection of their parent power, this little colony now looked for security. They were a town of the Connecticut Colony, organized with Selectmen and other ordinary Town Officers, and semi-annually sent their Deputies to the General Court at Hartford and New Haven; chose their Jurors to attend the Courts of this County, and their Justices of the Peace were magistrates of the County of Litchfield, and all writs and process, served there, were returnable to the Courts of this County, and remain now upon our records. But their security was transient; the war of the Revolution brought down upon them a combined force of British Provincials and Tories, from Pennsylvania, New Jersey and New

York, and a large body of Indians, commanded by Brant, a celebrated chief. This whole force was directed by Col. John Butler, of infamous memory.

I have no leisure to describe, in its details, the progress of the tragedy of the Wyoming massacre. Cols. John Franklin and Zebulon Butler were conspicuous in their efforts to avert the sad destiny of the citizens. It was in vain. The battle opened on the 3d day of July, 1778, and it closed with the entire destruction of the settlement. Men, women and children, whether in arms or defenceless, were devoted to the bayonet and scalping knife, and such as were so fortunate as to escape, were driven away, houseless and homeless, many of them to be dragged from their hiding places to the slaughter, and others to escape after many perils by the way. That massacre was without a likeness in modern warfare, and a stain upon the English character, for which English historians have found no apology.

"Accursed Brant! he left of all my tribe
Nor man, nor child, nor any thing of living birth;
No,—not the dog that watch'd my household hearth
Escaped that night, upon our plains,—all perished!"

Men, maidens, widowed mothers and helpless infants, flying from this scene of death, are remembered by many still living, passing on foot and on horseback through this County, back to their friends here and to the eastern towns. Such was the fate of a portion of the citizens of our own County. Nine years Wyoming had been a part of us, and after the war was over, Pennsylvania renewed her claims and her oppressions. Our Pilgrim fathers could recount no such afflictions! Our jurisdiction ceased in 1782, after a decision by a Board of Commissioners; but a great portion of those who had survived the conflict with the Indians, gathered again around the ruins of their former habitations, and still refused submission to the claims of Pennsylvania. Col. Franklin was the master spirit of resistance, and upon him fell the weight of vengeance. He was arrested, imprisoned, and condemned to death as a traitor. After a long confinement in jail, he was at length released, and survived many years, and was a respectable and influential member of the General Assembly of Pennsylvania, from the County of Luzerne.

The result of the compromise of our claim to the town of Westmoreland, was the acknowledgment, by Congress, of the claim of Connecticut to the Western Reserve, from which has been derived the School Fund of the State.

The war of the Revolution had ceased, and left us an exhausted people. The extravagant hopes of many were disappointed: they felt the present pressure, but anticipated none of the future prosperity and glory in reserve. This disappointment, in a neighboring State, had produced open resistance to the laws,—rebellion! It was a contagious spirit, and such as municipal lines could not confine. Much was feared from it here. A spark from that flame in Berkshire county had flown over into Sharon. One Dr. Hurlbut, an emissary of Shay's, visited that town, in the spring of 1787, to enlist men in his cause. He made some impression. The General Assembly was then in session, and took efficient measures to prevent the spread of the treasonable contagion. Col. Samuel Canfield, of New Milford, and Uriah Tracy, of this village, were sent to suppress it. Several individuals were arrested and imprisoned in the jail of this County; but, as the disturbance in the sister State subsided, the advocates of resistance to the laws were disheartened, the prosecutions were finally abandoned, and these disciples of the treasonable doctrine of resistance were permitted to go at large, punished enough by the contempt which followed them.

Although the resources of our citizens had been consumed by a wasting war and a bankrupt government, the elasticity of our former enterprise was not relaxed. Released, now, from Colonial dependence, and free to act without foreign restrictions, the energies of our citizens soon recovered all they had lost. A Constitution of Government, uniting the former Colonies into a great nation, was proposed to the State for adoption; and, in January, 1787, a convention of delegates from the several towns met at Hartford to consider it. The votes of the delegates from this County, upon this great question, stood, twenty-two in the affirmative, and nine in the negative. The negative votes were from Cornwall, Norfolk, and Sharon. Harwinton, New Hartford, and Torrington were divided.

No portion of the country sooner revived under the new impulse, given by the establishment of a National Constitutional

Government, than this County. Our resources were varied. Our soil was every where strong on the hills and by the streams. Various sections possessed their peculiarities of production. Wheat was a staple of the western towns. Dairy products were yielded in abundance in the northern and central regions; and, in almost every location, every species of grass, fruit, and grain, indigenous to any northern latitude, by reasonable culture, was found to flourish. We were rich in the most useful mineral in the world, and our streams of purest water afforded privileges every where for converting our ores into iron and our forests into building materials. But we had more—that, without which, all these were worthless; we had an industrious, and what was better, an *economical* and an intelligent yeomanry. We had a few slaves, to be sure; not enough of these, nor enough of a degraded foreign population to render the toil of our own hands, in the fields, or of our wives or daughters, in the kitchen or the dairy, dishonored or disgraceful. Our people were Native Americans! And here is the secret of our prosperity and progress.

In 1784 the first newspaper press was established in this County by Thomas Collier, and was continued under his superintendence for more than twenty years. It was called the "Weekly Monitor." It was a well conducted sheet, and it is refreshing now, after the lapse of many years, to look through its columns, as through a glass, and see the men of other days, as they have spoken and acted on the same ground on which we stand. Mr. Collier was an able writer, and his editorial efforts would have done honor to any journal. It is a Litchfield monitor now, and whoever shall look over its files will see, at a glance, the great changes which have been introduced, in later days, into all the departments of business and of social and political life.

Then, the intercourse between the several towns in this County and the market towns was slow and difficult. The Country merchants were the great brokers, and stood between the farmer and the markets. They received all his produce and supplied all he wished to buy. The thrifty farmer, on settlement, received his annual balance from the merchant. This enabled him to increase his acres. He did not invest it in stocks; of these he knew nothing, except such as he had seen attached as instruments of punishment, to the whipping post in every town.

The merchants, thus employed, almost all became wealthy. A broken merchant in the County was seldom heard of. Among the most successful and respectable of these gentlemen, whom I now recollect, were Julius Deming and Benjamin Tallmadge, of this town; Tallmadge, of Warren; Bacon, of Woodbury; Leavitts', of Bethlem and Washington; Starr, Norton, and Lymans', of Goshen; Battel, of Norfolk; King, of Sharon; Holley, of Salisbury, and Elijah Boardman, of New Milford, afterwards a highly respectable Senator in the Congress of the United States. At that time, Derby was the chief market town for many of the merchants in the southern towns of the County.

The age of Turnpike Roads commenced about the year 1800, and no portion of the country was more improved by them than this County. Before this, a journey through the Green Woods was spoken of as an exploit,—a region now accommodated by the most pleasant road in the County. The roads constructed, about the same time, from New Haven to Canaan, from Sharon to Goshen, and from Litchfield to Hartford, changed very much the aspect of the County and its current of business, and if they have not been profitable to stockholders, they have been invaluable to the people.

The spur given to agriculture by the wars following the French Revolution was felt in every thing. If our farmers have failed in any thing, it has been in a proper appreciation of their own calling. They have yielded a preference to other employments, to which they are not entitled. If we are to have an Aristocracy in this country, I say, let the farmers and business men, and not our idlers, be our Princes!—not such as are ashamed of their employments and withdraw their sons from the field and their daughters from domestic labor. I would have no such to rule over me. But, in spite of some such false notions, agriculture has kept pace even with other branches of industry in the County, as the appearance of our farms and the thrift of our farmers attest. Much of this may be attributed to an Agricultural Society, which was formed here several years ago, and has been well sustained until this time.

I have alluded to the condition of manufactures as it was before the Revolution—limited to iron and confined to the furnace in Salisbury and a few forges in that vicinity; to which may be added, the manufacture of maple sugar, to some extent by the farmers in some of the towns.

Even a few years ago, this County was not believed to be destined to become a manufacturing community. During the Revolutionary War, Samuel Forbes, Esq., commenced a most important experiment in Canaan—the manufacture of nail rods. Before this, nails were hammered out from the bar iron—a slow and expensive process. There was a slitting-mill in New Jersey, in which nail rods were made, but the machinery was kept hidden from public inspection. Forbes wished to obtain a knowledge of it, and for this purpose employed an ingenious mechanic and millwright, Isaac Benton, of Salisbury. Benton, disguised as a traveling mendicant, obtained admission to the mill, and so critically, and without suspicion, marked the machinery and its operation, as to be able immediately to make such a model of it as to construct a mill, of the same sort, for Forbes. This was the foundation of his great fortune in after life. He afterwards erected another slitting-mill in Washington, (now Woodville.) By these he was able to supply the great demand for this article. This was a great improvement upon the former mode of nail-making, but was itself superseded, some years afterwards, by the introduction of cut nail machinery. Esquire Forbes, as he was afterwards familiarly called by every body, may justly be deemed the pioneer of the manufacturing interests in this County. His efforts were confined, generally, to the working of iron. His forge he extended, and accommodated to the manufacturing of anchors, screws, and mill irons. He introduced this branch of the iron business into this County, if not into the State. It was not long after followed by those enterprising manufacturers, Russell Hunt & Brothers, at South Canaan, by whom the largest anchors for the largest ships of the American Navy were made.

The manufacture of scythes by water-power, was commenced in this County first at Winsted, by Jenkins & Boyd, in 1794. These enterprising gentlemen, with the brothers Rockwell, soon extensively engaged in various branches of the manufacture of iron and steel in Winsted and that vicinity, from which originated, and has grown up to its present condition, one of the most flourishing manufacturing villages in the State.

The furnace, in Salisbury, continued for many years in most successful operation under its active proprietors, and especially its last owners, Messrs. Holley & Coffing, by whose energy and success, the iron interest, in Salisbury, has been most essentially promoted; and it has extended into the towns of Canaan, Cornwall, Sharon, and Kent. Ames' works, at Falls Village, are not equalled by any other in the State.

In speaking of the iron interest, I cannot but allude again to the Salisbury iron ore, which is found in various localities in that town. It stands superior to any other for the tenacity of the iron which it produces, with which the armories of Springfield and Harper's Ferry are supplied, and from which the chain cables and best anchors for the Navy are made. And I am confident, if the machinery of the steam vessels and railroad cars were made exclusively from this iron, and not from a cheaper and inferior material, we should know less of broken shafts and loss of life in our public conveyances.

Paper was first made in this County, at the great Falls of the Housatonic, in Salisbury, by Adam & Church, as early as 1787, and soon after in Litchfield. The first carding-machine erected, I think, in this .State, was built at the great falls in Canaan, about 1802. Previous to this time, wool was carded only by females, at their own firesides.

A general manufacturing policy was suggested by the measures of government, and not long after a more extensive experiment was made in the manufacture of woolen cloths by the late Gov. Wolcott, and his brother Hon. Frederick Wolcott of this place, than had been made in this County before; and although the trial was disastrous to its projectors, it was the parent of the subsequent and present prosperity of the village of Wolcottville.

The same policy has spread into almost every town in the County, and has not only extended the manufacture of iron, from a mouse trap to a ship's anchor, but has introduced, and is introducing, all the various branches of manufactures pursued in this country; and of late, the elegant manufacture of the Papier Mache. Plymouth, New Hartford, Norfolk, Woodbury, as well as the towns before mentioned, have felt extensively the beneficial effects of this modern industrial progress, so that our County may now be set down as one of the first manufacturing Counties in the

State; and this confirms what I have said, that here are all the varied facilities of profitable employment, which can be found in any section or region of this country. Our young men need no longer seek adventure and fortune elsewhere! Neither the desire of wealth, nor the preservation of health and life, should suggest emigration.

As soon as the war was over, and the Indians subdued into peace, our people rushed again to Vermont, and to the Whitestown and Genesee countries, as they were called; so that, in a few years, let a Litchfield County man go where he would, between the top of the Green Mountains and Lake Champlain, or between Utica and the Lakes, and every day he would greet an acquaintance or citizen from his own County.

And then followed the sale and occupation of the Connecticut Western Reserve. Many of its original proprietors were our citizens; and among them, Messrs. Boardman, of New Milford; Holmes, Tallmadge, and Wadsworth, of Litchfield; Starr and Norton, of Goshen; Canfield, of Sharon; Johnston, Church, and Waterman, of Salisbury. For a time it seemed as if depopulation was to follow. The towns of Boardman, Canfield, Tallmadge, Johnson, Hudson, and several others on the reserve, were soon filling up with the best blood and spirit of our County; and since then, we have been increasing the population of other parts of the States of New York and Ohio, as well as of Michigan, Illinois, and Indiana, so that now there is not one of us who remain, who has not a parent, a brother, or a child, in New York, Vermont, or the States of the West. And we believe that these children of our own raising, have transmitted the impress and image of Litchfield County, to the general condition of society where they have gone, and that they have fixed there a moral likeness which proves its parentage. This emigrating propensity has characterized the Saxon race in all times of its history; and it is still at work, scattering us into every corner and climate, and away to dig for gold and graves in the barrens of California! Notwithstanding this exhausting process of emigration, our population which, in the year 1800, was 41,671, has increased to the number of 46,171.

I do not know that before the Revolution there was a public Grammar School in the County. The preparatory studies of young men, intended for a collegiate course, were prosecuted with private instructors — generally, the Clergy; and this course was pursued still later.

Among the clergymen of the County most distinguished as instructors, and in *fitting* young men for college, as it was called, were Rev. Daniel Farrand, of Canaan, Ammi R. Robbins, of Norfolk, Judah Champion, of Litchfield, and Azel Backus, D. D., of Bethlem. This last named gentleman was afterwards President of Hamilton College.

Soon after the war, Academies were instituted, and among the first and best of them was the Morris Academy in the parish of South Farms, in this town, which was commenced in 1790, by James Morris, Esq. Esquire Morris was no ordinary man. He was a distinguished graduate of Yale College, and an active officer in the Revolutionary Army. His learning was varied and practical, and under his direction the Morris Academy became the most noted public school of the County, and so continued for many years. This excellent gentleman died in 1820, aged 68 years. An Academy at Sharon, not long after, acquired a deserved reputation, under such instructors as John T. Peters, Elisha Sterling, and Barzillai Slosson. Many years afterwards an Academy was conducted in Ellsworth Society, in the same town, under the superintendence of Rev. Daniel Parker, which soon attained a high reputation.

Our relative position in the State, and the controlling influence of the cities, have left us without College, Asylum, or Retreats; but our district schools have been doing their proper work, so that Judge Reeve remarked while alive, that he had never seen but one witness in Court, born in this County, who could not read. And these schools have not only made scholars, *but school-masters*, and these have been among the best of our indigenous productions, and have found a good market every where. When Congress sat in Philadelphia, a Litchfield County man was seen driving a drove of mules through the streets. A North Carolina member congratulated the late Mr. Tracy upon seeing so many of his constituents that morning, and enquired where they were going, to which he facetiously replied, that they were going *to North Carolina to keep school.*

A new tone to female education was given by the establishment of a Female Seminary, for the instruction of females in this village, by Miss Sarah Pierce, in 1792. This was an untried experiment. Hitherto the education of young ladies, with few exceptions, had been neglected. The district school had limited their course of studies. Miss Pierce saw and regretted this, and devoted herself and all of her active life to the mental and moral culture of her sex. The experiment succeeded entirely. This Academy soon became the resort of young ladies from all portions of the country — from the cities and the towns. Then, the country was preferred, as most suitable for female improvement, away from the frivolities and dissipation of fashionable life. Now, a different, not a better practice, prevails. Many of the grandmothers and mothers of the present generation were educated as well for genteel as for useful life, in this school, and its influence upon female character and accomplishments was great and extensive. It continued for more than forty years, and its venerable Principal and her sister assistant now live among us, the honored and honorable of their sex.

Before this, and as early as 1784, a Law School was instituted in this village. Tapping Reeve, then a young lawyer from Long Island, who had commenced the practice of his profession here, was its projector. It is not known whether in this country, or any where, except at the Inns of Court at Westminster, a school for the training of lawyers had been attempted. No Professorships of Law had been introduced into American Colleges; nor was the Law treated as a liberal science.

Before this, the law student served a short clerkship in an attorney's office, — studied some forms and little substance, and had within his reach but few volumes beyond Coke's & Wood's Institutes, Blackstone's Commentaries, Bacon's Abridgment, and Jacob's Law Dictionary; and, when admitted to the Bar, was better instructed in pleas in abatement, than in the weightier matters of the Law. Before this, too, the Common Law, as a system, was imperfectly understood here and in our sister States. Few lawyers had mastered it. The reputation of this institution soon became as extensive as the country, and young men from Maine to Georgia sought to finish their law studies here.

Judge Reeve conducted this school alone, from its commencement until 1798, when, having been appointed to the Bench of the Superior Court, he associated with him, as an instructor,

James Gould, Esq. These gentlemen conducted the school together for several years, until the advanced age of Judge Reeve admonished him to retire; after which, Judge Gould continued the school alone until a few years before his death. It may be said of Judge Reeve, that he first gave the Law a place among liberal studies in this country, — that "he found it a skeleton, and clothed it with life, color, and complexion." This school gave a new impulse to legal learning and it was felt in the Jurisprudence as well as in the Legislation of all the States.

A new subject of study, not known in any other country, had been presented to the legal student here, — the Constitution of the United States and the Legislation of Congress. Uniformity of interpretation was indispensable.

At this institution students from every State drank from the same fountain, were taught the same principles of the Common and Constitutional Law; and these principles, with the same modes of legal thinking and feeling and of administration were disseminated thoughout the entire country. More than one thousand lawyers of the United States were educated here, and many of them afterwards among the most eminent Jurists and Legislators. Even after Judge Gould's connection with the school, an inspection of the catalogue will show, that from it have gone out among the States of this Union, a Vice President of the United States, two Judges of the Supreme Court of the United States, forty Judges of the highest State Courts, thirteen Senators, and forty-six Representatives in Congress, besides several Cabinet and Foreign Ministers.*

* LITCHFIELD LAW SCHOOL. — At a late dinner of the Story Association of the Cambridge Law School, the famous Litchfield Law School was adverted to. The whole passage will be interesting to the former pupils of that institution, and to the friends of its celebrated teachers.

Judge Kent gave —

The first-born of the law schools of this country — the Litchfield Law School. The Boston bar exhibits its rich and ripened fruits. By them we may judge of the tree and declare it good.

Charles G. Loring, Esq., replied. He began with expressing his regret that there was no other representative from the Litchfield Law School to respond to the complimentary but just notice of that institution.

I do not remember, said he, to have ever been more forcibly reminded of my younger days, than when looking around upon our young friends in the midst of whom I stand. It recalls the time when I, too, was a student among numerous fellow students. It will, probably, be news to them and many others here, that thirty-eight years ago, which to many here seems a remote antiquity, there existed an extensive Law School in the State of Connecticut, at

I have said that this school gave a new impulse to legal learning in this country. Soon after its establishment, and not before, reports of judicial decisions appeared. Ephraim Kirby, Esq., an able lawyer of this village, published the first volume of Reports of Adjudged Cases, in this country, — a volume which deserved and received the approbation of the profession here and elsewhere. This was soon followed by Reports in Massachusetts and New York.

Standing at this point of time, and looking back over the events of an hundred years, we would recall, not only the scenes which have transpired, but revive our recollections of the men

---

which more than sixty students from all parts of the country were assembled, — every State then in the Union, being there represented. I joined it in 1813, when it was at its zenith, and the only prominent establishment of the kind in the land.

The recollection is as fresh as the events of yesterday, of our passing along the broad shaded streets of one of the most beautiful of the villages of New England, with our ink-stands in our hands, and our portfolios under our arms, to the lecture room of Judge Gould— the last of the Romans, of Common Law lawyers; the impersonation of its genius and spirit. It was, indeed, in his eyes, the perfection of human reason — by which he measured every principle and rule of action, and almost every sentiment. Why, Sir, his highest visions of poetry seemed to be in the refinement of special pleading; and to him, a *non sequitur* in logic was an offence deserving, at the least, fine and imprisonment — and a repetition of it, transportation for life. He was an admirable English scholar; every word was pure English, undefiled, and every sentence fell from his lips perfectly finished, as clear, transparent, and penetrating as light, and every rule and principle as exactly defined and limited as the outline of a building against the sky. From him, Sir, we obtained clear, well-defined, and accurate knowledge of the Common Law, and learned that allegiance to it was the chief duty of man, and the power of enforcing it upon others his highest attainment. From his lecture room we pass to that of the venerable Judge Reeve, shaded by an aged elm, fit emblem of himself. He was, indeed, a most venerable man, in character and appearance — his thick, gray hair parted and falling in profusion upon his shoulders, his voice only a loud whisper, but distinctly heard by his earnestly attentive pupils. He, too, was full of legal learning, but invested the law with all the genial enthusiasm and generous feelings and noble sentiments of a large heart at the age of eighteen, and descanted to us with glowing eloquence upon the sacredness and majesty of law. He was distinguished, Sir, by that appreciation of the gentler sex which never fails to mark the true man and his teachings of the law in reference to their rights and to the domestic relations, had great influence in elevating and refining the sentiments of the young men who were privileged to hear him. As illustrative of his feelings and manner upon this subject, allow me to give a specimen. He was discussing the legal relations of married women; he never called them, however, by so inexpressible a name, but always spoke of them as, "the better half of mankind," or in some equally just manner. When he came to the axiom that "a married woman has no will of her own;" this, he said, was a maxim of great theoretical importance for the preservation of the sex against the undue influence or coercion of the husband; but, although it was an inflexible maxim, in theory, experience taught us that practically it was found that they sometimes had wills of their own — MOST HAPPILY FOR US.

We left his lecture room, Sir, the very knight errants of the law, burning to be the defenders of the right and the avengers of the wrong; and he is no true son of the Litchfield School who has ever forgotten that lesson. I propose, Sir -

The Memories of Judge Reeve and Judge Gould, — among the first, if not the first founders of a National Law School in the United States — who have laid one of the corner stones in the foundation of true American patriotism, loyalty to the law. — *Boston Atlas.*

who have acted in them. Memory cannot raise the dead to life again; yet it may bring back something of their presence,— shaded and dim, but almost real;— and through the records of their times we may hear them speak again. To some of these I have made allusion. I would speak of others.

The allusion to the Law School of the County suggests to me a brief notice, also, of the legal profession here, and of its most distinguished members, as well as a further allusion to others of the sons of Litchfield County, distinguished in other professions and employments of life. In speaking of these I must confine myself to the memory of the dead. And here, I feel, that I am under a restraint, which, on any other occasion, I would resist. I feel this chain which binds me, the more, as I look around on this gathering and see some here, and am reminded of others — so many, who have contributed, by splendid talents and moral worth, to make our name a praise in the land. As the representative of the County, I would most gladly do them living homage before you all. I regret that I have had so brief an opportunity to make this notice as perfect as it should be, — a favorite theme, if I could but do it justice.

I have not been able to learn much of the Lawyers who practiced in this territory before the organization of the County in 1751. Samuel Pettibone, Esq., of Goshen, and Reynold Marvin, Esq., of Litchfield, (a native of Lyme,) are all of whom I can speak.

Mr. Pettibone lived to a great age and died in reduced circumstances, in 1787. Mr. Marvin was respectable in his profession, and was King's Attorney at the time of the Revolution. His residence was at the dwelling of Dr. William Buel, in this village.

Among the Lawyers of the new County who appeared in its Courts, were Mr. Thatcher, of New Milford, Hezekiah Thompson and Edward Hinman, of Woodbury, Mr. Humphrey, of Norfolk, John Canfield, of Sharon, Andrew Adams, of Litchfield, Mr. Catlin, of Harwinton, and Joshua Whitney, of Canaan. Of these, Messrs. Canfield and Adams became distinguished at the Bar and in public life. Mr. Canfield was the son of Samuel Canfield, of New Milford, one of the Associate Judges of the County. He was appointed a member of Congress under the

4

Confederation, but died before he took his seat. We can appreciate his character when informed that he was the chosen colleague of Johnson, Ellsworth, and Trumbull. Mr. Adams succeeded Mr. Marvin as State's Attorney. He was esteemed an eloquent advocate, and his reputation at the Bar was distinguished. He was well versed in theological studies, and in the absence of his minister, often officiated in the pulpit. He was a member of the Continental Congress, and after the Revolution, became an Associate, and then Chief Justice of the Superior Court.

Before the Revolution there were but few eminent lawyers in the County, and professional gentlemen from abroad attended our courts and were employed in the most important causes. Among these were Thomas Seymour, Esq., of Hartford, and Hon. Samuel W. Johnson, of Stratford, then standing at the head of the Connecticut Bar. A colonial condition was, as it ever will be, unfavorable to the development of forensic talent.

The change in the state of this Bar, after the War, and especially after the settlement of the government, was sudden and great; and, within a few years after this event, no County in the State and but few in other States, could boast of a Bar more distinguished for legal talent and high professional and moral excellence, than this. Reeve, Tracy, Allen, Kirby, Strong of Salisbury, Smith of Woodbury, Smith and Canfield, of Sharon, are names which revive proud recollections among the old men of the County. And while these gentlemen stood before our courts, there came to their company a younger band, destined, with them, to perpetuate the high standing of the profession here;—Gould, Sterling, of Salisbury; Benedict, Ruggles, Boardman, Smith, of Litchfield; Slosson, Southmayd, Swan, Pettibone, and afterward, Miner, Williams, Bacon, and others.

Tapping Reeve was a native of Long Island, and a distinguished graduate of Nassau Hall, New Jersey, and a tutor in that college. He commenced practice here in 1783, and was one of the most learned lawyers of the day in which he lived. He loved the law as a science, and studied it philosophically. He considered it as the practical application of religious principle to the business affairs of life. He wished to reduce it to a certain, symmetrical system of moral truth. He did not trust to the inspiration of genius for eminence, but to the results of profound and constant study, and was never allured by political ambition. I seem, even now, to see his calm and placid countenance shining through his abundant locks, as he sat, poring over his notes in the lecture room, and to hear his shrill whisper, as he stood when giving his charge to the jury. He was elevated to the Bench of the Superior Court in 1798, and to the office of Chief Justice in 1804, and retired from public life at the age of seventy years, and died in 1827. He published a valuable treatise on Domestic Relations, and another on the Law of Descents.

Gen. Uriah Tracy was a native of Norwich, and one of the first of the pupils of Judge Reeve. As a jury advocate he obtained a high distinction. His wit was pungent and his powers of oratory uncommon. He was a politician, often a member of our own Legislature; for several years a member of Congress, and he died in 1807, while a member of the Senate of the United States, in which body he was eminently distinguished.

Col. Adonijah Strong, the father of the late Hon. Martin Strong, was unique in genius and manner, of large professional business, sound practical sense, and many anecdotes of his sayings and doings are still remembered and repeated in the County.

Hon. Nathaniel Smith, of Woodbury, a native of Washington, commenced life under discouraging circumstances. He had neither fortune nor the prospect of any, nor early education, to stimulate him. Like many other New England boys, he fought his way to eminence; and eminent he was; and I cannot tell by what process he became so. He, too, was one of the early members of the Law School here. He was not a man of many books. He seemed to understand the law, as did Mansfield and Marshall, by intuition, and to have acquired the power of language by inspiration. His was a native eloquence, yet chaste, and "when unadorned, adorned the most." I think he was one of the most profound lawyers and judges of this country. He was a member of the Council, a member of Congress, and was elevated to the Bench of the Superior Court in 1806.

Hon. Nathan Smith was a younger brother of Nathaniel Smith, and though born and reared in this County, his professional and public life was passed in New Haven County, but he often appeared at this Bar. He was less profound than his brother, more ardent, and perhaps more effective as a jury lawyer. He died, while a Senator in Congress, in 1835.

Hon. John Allen was a native of Massachusetts and instructed by Mr. Reeve, and for several years held a commanding position at this Bar.

Hon. John Cotton Smith, of Sharon, was the son of Rev. Cotton Mather Smith, of that town. A graduate of Yale College and of the Litchfield Law School, he soon took a prominent place by the side of Tracy and Nathaniel Smith at the Bar of the County. He was known as a fluent speaker, and of easy and graceful address; he became a popular advocate. For several sessions of the Legislature of the State he was speaker of the House of Representatives. In Congress he sustained an enviable reputation as a presiding officer. Upon retiring from Congress he was soon placed upon the Bench of the Superior Court, from which he was promoted to the office of Governor of the State. From this he retired, and from public life, in 1817. The remainder of his life was spent in doing good, either as President of the American Bible Society, or in discharging the duties of a virtuous citizen in his native town, until his death in 1845.

Hon. James Gould was a native of Branford, a graduate and a tutor of Yale College. He pursued his professional studies with Judge Reeve, and, soon after coming to the Bar of this County, he became associated with him as an instructor of the Law School. Judge Gould was a critical scholar, and always read with his pen in his hand, whether Law book, or books of fiction or fancy, for which he indulged a passion. In the more abstruse subjects of the law, he was more learned than Judge Reeve, and, as a lecturer, more lucid and methodical. The Common Law he had searched to the bottom, and he knew it all—its principles, and the reasons from which they were drawn. As an advocate, he was not a man of impassioned eloquence, but clear and logical, employing language elegant and chaste. He indulged in no wit, and seldom excited a laugh, but was very sure to carry a listener along with him to his conclusions. With his brethren, his intercourse was always courteous, and with his younger ones, kind and affectionate. He never gave offense. In his arguments, he resorted to no artifice, but met the difficulties in his way fully in the face, and if he could not overcome them, he yielded without irritation. He was appointed an Associate Judge of the Superior Court in 1816, and retired from the Bench to private life soon after. Judge Gould published an able treatise on the Law of Pleading, in which he was governed by the truth of Lord Coke's saying, "he knoweth not the law, who knoweth not the reason thereof." His volume has received flattering approval from the most learned Jurists in this country and England. Judge Gould died in 1838.

Noah B. Benedict was the son of Rev. Noah Benedict, of Woodbury, a gentleman of no precocity of intellect or genius, and his first appearance at the Bar did not promise the eminence which he afterwards acquired. He studied, and the Law was the chief subject of his study. He aspired to no higher place than distinction in his profession. He engaged in none of the ordinary business transactions of society, and, as he once told me, he never gave a promissory note in his life. With such an undivided attention to his professional calling, it was not strange that he should reach a high place at the Bar. And he did reach it, and, at the time of his death, no man here stood before him. His example should be a choice model for young lawyers.

Gen. Elisha Sterling, of Salisbury, was a native of Lyme. No one in our profession was more assiduous in its practice than this gentleman. His causes were never neglected in their preparation. The controlling points of every case he discovered quick, and pressed both, in preparation and argument, with zeal. He neglected the study of method and system in his arguments, but, when concluded, nothing had been omitted.

Passing by, on this hurried occasion, a more particular notice of the galaxy of Lawyers, to whom I have alluded, I may be indulged in paying an affectionate tribute to one or two, whose familiar voices still seem sounding in our Court House.

Hon. Jabez W. Huntington earned his high professional character here, where he commenced and continued his practice for several years. He engaged in public life, and returned to his native town of Norwich. He was elected to Congress; afterwards he was elevated to the Bench of the Superior Court, which place he retained, until he was appointed a Senator in Congress, in which position he died in 1847. Having been associated with Judge Huntington at the Bar and on the Bench, I can bear true testimony to his superior abilities in both places.

Of my late brother, Leman Church, Esq., the proprieties of my connexion will not permit me to speak. The deep sensation produced at this Bar, and the grief which tore the hearts of his numerous friends, when he died, is the only eulogy upon his life and character to which I may refer.

I had a young friend, upon whose opening prospects I looked with anxiety and hope. He was of generous heart and liberal hand, and stimulated by an honorable ambition, which seemed nearly at the point of gratification, when death came for its victim. This friend was Francis Bacon, Esq., who died in 1849, at the age of 30 years.

Hon. Oliver Wolcott, the younger, late Governor of this State, was also a member of this Bar, and though he engaged in public life soon after his admission, we are entitled to retain his name on our catalogue. I shall not speak now of his life and eminent services. They make a prominent part of the country's history, and have been, within a few years, faithfully written by his near relative. He died in 1833, and I regret to say that his remains lie in our grave-yard, without a monument to mark his resting place. His bust has been presented, on this occasion, to the Bar of this County.

I make the same claim to retain among the names of our departed brethren, that of Hon. Frederick Wolcott, a son of the elder Gov. Wolcott, of this village. He became a member of this Bar in early life, and with high prospects of professional distinction; but he accepted the proffered offices of Clerk of the Courts and Judge of Probate for this district, in 1793, and soon relinquished professional duties. For several years he was a prominent member of the Council, under the Charter administration. An intimate connexion with this gentleman, both public and private, justifies the high opinion I have ever entertained of his purity of life and character, his public spirit, and his frank and open bearing. I never pass by the venerable mansion of the Wolcott family, in my daily walks about this village, without recalling the stately form and ever honorable deportment of Frederick Wolcott. The duties of his official stations were discharged with the entire approbation of the community for many years, and until a short time before his death, and amidst the conflicts and overturnings in the political revolutions of the times.

Roger and Richard Skinner, were sons of Gen. Timothy Skinner of this town, and members of this bar. Roger commenced business in this village, and gave assurance, by his early talents, of his future standing; but he was here in the most bitter state of Connecticut politics, and, as he believed, was compelled to escape from unmerited opposition. He removed to the State of New York; soon attained a deserved eminence in his profession, and was appointed a Judge of the United States Court, in the Northern District of that State. Richard Skinner removed to Vermont, and afterwards became an eminent Judge of the Superior Court, and ultimately Governor of that State.

In the clerical profession, I have remarked before, that there was early manifested a disposition rather to be good than great. The clergy of this County were nearly all educated men; and many of them ripe scholars and profound divines, and if there were not as many here as in some other regions, whose names have been transmitted to us as among the great ones of New England, it has been because the severer calls of parochial duty, and stinted means, and Christian graces, restrained their aspirations after fame. Divinity has furnished the most common theme, and employed the most pens. We are all theologians in New England.

Rev. Joseph Bellamy, D. D., of Bethlem, was probably the first and most eminent of our writers on this subject. He was eloquent and impressive as a preacher, as well as learned and profound as a scholar and writer. He published several theological works upon practical and controversial subjects, besides occasional sermons, which are found in the libraries of Divines, and have been held in high repute, not only among the disciples of his own peculiar opinions, but among others, as well in Europe as in this country; and a modern edition of them has been recently published. Dr. Bellamy was the grandfather of the late Joseph H. Bellamy, Esq., of Bethlem, a gentleman of great moral and professional worth.

Rev. Jna. Edwards was a pupil of Dr. Bellamy in his theological studies, and, although not a native of this County, he resided among us for several years, as the first settled minister of Colebrook, and until he was called to the presidency of Union College, in 1799. He was the author of several volumes of great merit; and among them, a treatise upon the salvation of all men, in reply to Dr. Chauncey; also, a dissertation on the liberty of the will, in reply to West, and observations on the language of the Stockbridge Indians.

Rev. Chauncey Lee, D. D., who succeeded Dr. Edwards, as minister in Colebrook, was a native of Salisbury, and a son of Rev. Jonathan Lee, of that town. He was educated for the bar, and commenced practice in his native town. This he soon relinquished for the clerical calling. Very early he published a Decimal Arithmetic, and afterwards a volume of Sermons on various subjects. But his most elaborate work, and the one most esteemed by himself, was a poem, entitled "The Trial of Virtue," being a paraphrase of the book of Job. Dr. Lee was a gentleman of some eccentricities, but a very learned divine and impressive preacher.

Rev. Samuel J. Mills, a native of Torrington, and son of the venerable pastor of one of the societies there, is entitled to a more extended notice than I am prepared on this occasion to repeat. Not because he was the author of books, but the author and originator of liberal and extensive benevolent effort. The noble cause of Foreign Missions in this country, is deeply indebted to him as one of its most zealous and active projectors and friends. Another of the most splendid charities of any age or country,—the Colonization Society,—owes its existence to the efforts of this gentleman; and his name will be cherished by the philanthropists of the world, along with those of Howard and Wilberforce.

Rev. Horace Holley, D. D., of Salisbury, was son of Mr. Luther Holley, and one of a highly distinguished and worthy family of brothers. Dr. Holley was first ordained pastor of a Church and Society at Greenfield, in Fairfield County, and was one of the successors of the late Dr. Dwight, in that parish. He subsequently removed to Boston, and became one of the most eloquent pulpit orators among the eminent divines of that metropolis. He afterwards became President of Transylvania University in Kentucky, and died, while yet a young man, on ship-board, when on his return from New Orleans to New England. I am not informed that he left any published works behind him, except sermons delivered on special occasions. He was my class-mate in College, and I knew him well.

The Rev. Dr. Backus of Bethlem, Rev. Mr. Hooker of Goshen, and Rev. Dr. Porter of Washington, are remembered as among the most learned Divines of the County.

Of the Medical Profession and the Medical Professors here, my opportunities of information have not been extensive. And yet I have known enough of them to persuade me that a more learned and useful faculty, has not been found elsewhere in the State. Empiricism has always existed, and will exist; and the credulity of some good men will give it countenance. We depend upon a learned medical influence, more than any thing else, to save us from its death-dealing results.

As early as January, 1767, a Medical association was formed in this County, composed of the most eminent physicians then in practice here. Its object was to establish rules of practice and intercourse;—promote medical science by providing for annual consultations and dissertations, and to protect the reputation of the profession and the health of the community, from the inroads of ignorant pretenders to medical science. Among the names of the gentlemen composing this body, I see those of Joshua Porter, Lemuel Wheeler, Joseph Perry, Seth Bird, William Abernethy, Samuel Catlin, Simeon Smith, Cyrus Marsh, Ephraim Gitteau, John Calhoun, &c. One of the earliest physicians of the County was Oliver Wolcott. He was the son of Hon. Roger Wolcott, of Windsor, a former Governor of the Colony. He had served as an officer in the French war, and settled himself in Goshen before the organization of the County, in the practice of his profession. Whether he continued in practice as a physician after his removal to this town is not known; probably, however, his official duties as Sheriff prevented it. He was subsequently honored with almost every official place which a good man would covet,—he was a member of the House of Representatives, of the Council, a Judge of Probate, a Judge of the County Court, a Representative in Congress, a signer of the Declaration of Independence, Lieutenant Governor, and Governor of his native State, and more than all, the father of an excellent family. He is said to have been a man of uncommon diffidence, and distrustful of his own ability. His public communications display sound judgment, and his more confidential correspondence a warm affection and a pure purpose.

Dr. Seth Bird, of Litchfield, probably held the first place among the early physicians of the County. His reputation was wide-spread. For acuteness of discrimination and soundness of judgment he was not excelled.

Dr. Joseph Perry, of Woodbury, was not only eminent in his profession, but, what was unusual in his day, he excelled as a belles-lettre scholar and was a gentleman well read in various branches of science. Later generations produced their eminent and accomplished physicians. Dr. Nathaniel Perry, son of the gentleman just named; Dr. Daniel Sheldon, of this town; Drs. Fowler of Washington, Rockwell of Sharon, Welch of Norfolk, Ticknor of Salisbury.

Dr. Samuel Woodward, of Torrington, was not only a physician of high repute himself, but he was almost literally a father of the faculty. Dr. Samuel B. Woodward, late of Worcester, Massachusetts, Dr. Henry Woodward, late of Middletown, and Dr. Charles Woodward, of the same place, were his sons,—born and educated in this County. Few men in any community have attained a more eminent and useful position than Dr. Samuel B. Woodward. Under his superintendance the Insane Hospital, at Worcester, was established and for many years conducted, and now sustains a reputation equal with any of the noble charities of this country. The Annual Reports of Dr. Woodward and his other professional writings, and the success of his efforts in the cause of humanity, have earned for him a reputation which will long survive.

Among the Surgeons of note, in earlier times, was Dr. Samuel Catlin, of Litchfield, and at a later period, Dr. Samuel R. Gager, of Sharon.

The medical profession in this County has produced some writers of respectability. Dr. Elisha North was for several years a physician of extensive practice in Goshen, and he afterwards removed to New London. He published an approved treatise on spotted fever, which extensively prevailed in Goshen and its vicinity, while he resided there.

Dr. Caleb Ticknor, of Salisbury, was brother of the late excellent Dr. Luther Ticknor, of that town, and of Dr. Benajah Ticknor, for many years a surgeon in the navy of the United States; and although a young man when he removed to New York City, about the year 1832, he rose rapidly to a high place in his profession. He published several medical works, the most popular of which was, the Philosophy of Living, which constitutes one of the volumes of Harpers' Family Library.

The Chipman family, a numerous brotherhood, removed from Salisbury to Vermont immediately after the Revolutionary War; it produced eminent men. Nathaniel was an officer of the Revolution. He became Chief Justice of Vermont, and a Senator in Congress. He published a small volume of Judicial Reports and a larger treatise upon the Principles of Goverment. Daniel Chipman, a younger brother of this gentleman, was a very prominent member of the Vermont Bar. He was the author of a very creditable essay "On the Law of Contracts"; and besides a volume of Law Reports, he published the life of his brother Nathaniel, and also the life of Gov. Thomas Chittenden.

Hon. Ambrose Spencer, late Chief Justice of the State of New York, was born in Salisbury, the son of Philip Spencer, Esq. He was prepared for his collegiate course under the instruction of Rev. Daniel Fanand, of Canaan; studied the law, I believe, with Hon. John Canfield, of Sharon, whose daughter he married.

Hon. Josiah S. Johnston, late an eminent member of the Senate of the United States, from Louisania, was a native of the same town. He was the son of Dr. John Johnston, who removed early to Kentucky. His academical studies were pursued here.

Samuel Moore, of Salisbury, was a profound mathematician and engaged much in the instruction of young men in what was called the surveyor's art. He published a treatise on surveying, with a table of logarithms. It was the earliest work on that branch of mathematical science published in this country. It introduced the method of computing contents by calculation entirely, without measuring triangles by scale and dividers. It was a valuable treatise, but was nearly superseded by a more finished one by Rev. Abel Flint, in which he borrowed much from Moore.

Ethan Allen is deserving of notice only for his revolutionary services, which are matters of public history. He published a narrative of his captivity as a prisoner of war, and a volume of Infidel Theology. He was a native of this county; the town of his nativity has been a matter of dispute, but it is not a question worth solving.

We have had Poets, too, besides such as I have mentioned, who deserve a remembrance on this occasion.

Hon. John Trumbull, late one of the Judges of the Superior Court of the State, was born in Watertown, in this County, in which his father was a minister. The Progress of Dulness, and McFingal, the most admired of his Poems, were written in early life. They are satyrical productions, and for genuine wit have not been excelled by any modern effort. Judge Trumbull's active life was passed chiefly in Hartford.

William Ray was a Salisbury man, born in 1771, and while a lad developed a taste for poetry, but early destitution and misfortunes pressed upon him and drove him into the Navy of the United States. He was for some time a captive in Tripoli, and in 1808 he published the Horrors of Slavery, and in 1821 a volume of Poems.

Ebenezer P. Mason was a native of Washington. Very few men gave more early promise of literary and scientific distinction than young Mason. His life and writings were published in 1842, by Professor Olmsted, of Yale College.

Washington has been a nursery of eminent men, of whom I cannot now speak without violating my purpose of speaking of the dead, and not of the living.

Mrs. Laura M. Thurston, of Norfolk, permitted to be published by her friends, several poetical pieces of uncommon sweetness and excellence,—the Paths of Life, the Green Hills of my Father Land, and others.

There are but few occasions, and these extreme ones, which call out the qualifications for military life.

Gen. Peter B. Porter was the youngest son of Col. Joshua Porter, of Salisbury, of whom I have spoken before. He was a graduate of Yale College and pursued the study of the law where so many of the noted men of the country have—at the Litchfield Law School. He was among the early emigrants from this County to the Genesee country. He was soon called to occupy places of trust and power in the State of his adoption. He was a member of Congress when the project of the Erie Canal was first suggested, and was one who, with De Witt Clinton, originated that important national work, and is entitled to equal honor with him for its projection. He urged it, when in Congress, as a national work, in a speech of great strength, and asked for the aid of the nation. As a member of the House of Representatives, he was associated with Henry Clay on a Committee to consider the causes of complaint against Great Britain, and drew up the report of that Committee, recommending the declaration of the war of 1812. He thus early ardently espoused the cause of his country, and stood by the side of Tompkins and other patriots, in their efforts to prosecute that war to an honorable result.

He was then a civilian only; but, impatient and mortified at the ill success of our arms upon the northern frontier—his own house pierced by the enemy's shot, on the banks of the Niagara River—he threw off the civil and assumed the military attitude. He raised a regiment of ardent volunteer troops, and at their head, soon contributed to turn the tide of success. His services at Fort Erie and the battles at the Falls, have been repeatedly told by the writers of the country's history. I will not repeat them. So highly were they esteemed by the general Government and the State, that thanks and medals were presented, and before the close of the war he was offered the chief command of the army, by the President. Under the administration of the younger Adams he was offered, and accepted, the place of Secretary of War.

My time confines me to the notice of the most conspicuous of our sons, native and adopted; but there were others, in every town, perhaps of equal merit but with fewer opportunities of display. The list of our members of Assembly, and of men by whose efforts the foundations of society were laid here, and by whom this County has been brought from a repulsive region of mountains and rocks to its present condition of fertility and wealth, would show an aggregate of moral and intellectual worth which no region, equal in extent, has surpassed.*

And by whom were all these eminent and excellent men reared and prepared for the stations which they have occupied in society? By fathers, whose own hands have toiled—by mothers, who were the spinters of the days in which they lived, and who knew and practised the duties of the kitchen as well as the parlor, and to whom the music of the spinning-wheel and the loom was more necessary than that of the piano and the harpsichord.

The spirit of strict economy has marked our progress from the beginning, and by no other could our fathers have left to us this heritage of good! Removed from the profusion, and from what is esteemed the higher liberality of city habits, our County has not fallen behind other kindred communities in encouraging the benevolent operations of these latter days.

A Missionary Society, auxiliary to the Board of Commissioners of Foreign Missions, was established in this County, in the year 1813, and has been in active operation since. This noble charity, since its organization, has received and paid over, as near as I can ascertain, the sum of about $125,000. The benevolent offerings of other denominations—the Episcopalians, Methodists, and Baptists, to the purposes of their respective religious operations, I have no present means of knowing; that they have been equally liberal, in proportion to their means, with their Congregational brethren, I have no reason to doubt.

In the year 1817, the Foreign Mission School was established in Cornwall, with the special object of spreading Christian truth and the means of civilization among the heathen. The origin of this effort, if not accidental, was gradual in its conception and development. Two young natives of the Sandwich Islands were, by the directing, and almost visible hand of Providence, thrown among us and fell under the notice of Mr. Elias Cornelius, in 1815, then a student in Yale College, and since distinguished as a Divine and Philanthropist. The names of these young heathen,

* Here may be mentioned Col. Charles Burrall, of Canaan; Fitch, Nortons, Lee, Johnston, of Salisbury; Pettibone, Battell, and Stevens, of Norfolk; Hon. Aaron Austin, of New Hartford; Sedgwick, Burnham, and Swift, of Cornwall; Whittleseys and Brinsmade, of Washington; Hales, Lymans, and Norton, of Goshen; Mil s and Perry, of Kent: Bostwick, Boardmans, and Merwin, of New Milford; Pardee, Kellogg, and Jewett, of Sharon; Smith and Potter, of Plymouth, and Catlin, of Harwinton; Marshs and Seymours, of Litchfield; Talmadge, of Warren; Rockwells, of Colebrook, and many others in other towns.

as known among us, were Henry Obookiah and William Tenoe. These young men were carefully instructed by Mr. Cornelius, Samuel J. Mills, and Edwin Dwight, with a chief object of preparing them to become Christian Missionaries among their countrymen. They were soon after placed under the care of Rev. Joel Harvey, then a Congregational minister in Goshen; at his suggestion, the North Consociation of Litchfield County, became their patrons. They were, not long after, joined by Thomas Hopoo, their countryman, and all were placed under proper instruction for the great object designed. But a more liberal and enlarged project was conceived; a Seminary in a Christian land, for the instruction of the heathen, joined with the purpose of preparing young men here for missionary service in heathen lands. It was a splendid thought, and the American Board attempted its consummation.

Rev. Timothy Dwight, Hon. John Treadwell, James Morris, Esq., Rev. Drs. Beecher and Chapin, with Messrs. Harvey and Prentice, were authorized to devise and put in operation such a Seminary, and the result was, the Foreign Mission School at Cornwall. Young natives of the Sandwich Islands, and from China, Australasia, and from the Indian nations on this Continent, as well as American youths, were instructed there. The school continued successfully until 1827. The establishment of the Sandwich Island Mission, was one of the important results of this school.

Many years before the modern movement in a temperance reformation was suggested, such a project was conceived in this town, and encouraged by the most prominent men here. A Temperance Pledge was signed in May 1789, repudiating the use of distilled liquors, by 36 gentlemen; and among the names annexed to it, were those of Julius Deming, Benjamin Tallmadge, Uriah Tracy, Ephraim Kirby, Moses Seymour, Daniel Sheldon, Tapping Reeve, Frederick Wolcott, and John Welch—names well known and well remembered here. I believe the first temperance association of modern date, in the County, was formed among the iron operatives at Mount Riga, in Salisbury. The results of this grand effort have been as successful here as elsewhere. If any special cause has operated to retard the final success of this charity, it has been the strangling, death-ensuring embrace of party politicians—the scathing curse of many a good thing. As long ago as 1816, there were distilleries in every town in the County; and in New Milford, as many as 26, and in the whole County, 169! and, besides these, there were 188 retailers of spirits, who paid licenses under the excise laws of the United States, to the amount of $3,760. Whether there be a distillery in the County now, I am not informed; I believe but very few.

I have not attempted to trace the modifications of society here —its progressive changes in modes of opinion and consequent action. It would lead me too far from my object, which has been only to speak of events, and the men who have been engaged in them.

Before the Revolution there was little to excite. There was a common routine of thinking, which had been followed for years—somewhat disturbed, to be sure, by what were called "*new lights*" in religion. But the results of our emancipation from the mother country turned every thing into a different channel, opinions and all. A new impulse broke in upon the general stagnation of mind which had been, and made every body speculators in morals, religion, politics, and every thing else. My own memory runs back to a dividing point of time, when I could see something of the *old world and new*. Infidel opinions came in like a flood. Mr. Paine's "Age of Reason," the works of Voltaire, and other Deistical books, were broad cast, and young men suddenly became, as they thought, wiser than their fathers; and even men in high places, among us here, were suspected of infidel opinions. At the *same time* came the ardent preachers of Mr. Wesley's divinity, who were engaged in doing battle with Infidelity on the one hand, and Calvinistic theology on the other. Here were antagonistic forces and influences, which introduced essential changes, and both have been operating ever since. And it would afford an interesting subject of investigation, to trace these influences to their results. The Methodist preachers first visited this County about the year 1787, and organized their first classes in Salisbury and Canaan. This was their first appearance in the State, and, I believe, in New England. In this County they were received with courtesy, and found many to encourage them among those who did not well understand the old divinity.

I might detain you in speaking of the prevalence and effects of party spirit here; but as this, as well as denominational controversy, is unpleasant to me, I forbear. There was a time, about the year 1806, when this spirit was rife here, and led to prosecutions, fines and imprisonment, and a disturbance of social relations, which has never since re-appeared to the same extent.

I need not say any thing of the present condition of the County. This you see and know. Its Rail Roads, penetrating regions not long since supposed to be impenetrable; villages rising up in the deep valleys, whose foundations have been hidden for nearly a century; and fertility and thrift, where a few years ago were uncultivated forests and wasting water-falls.

Of what shall we complain? Is it that we do not, all of us, make haste to be rich? Ah! is it so, my brethren? Is there nothing but wealth which can satisfy a rational mind and an immortal spirit?

Of the future we may indulge proud hopes, while we doubt and fear. Progress is the word of modern theorists, but of doubtful import. Innovation is not always progress towards useful results. Of this we, who are old, believe we have seen too much, within a few years, and fear much more to come. Our County is but a small part of a State and Nation, and so our fate stands not alone. We can but look to our political institutions as our ultimate protectors, and I urge upon you all, my brethren, their unwavering support. Our Constitution requires no innovating process to improve it. It demands of us more than a mere political respect and preference—almost a religious reverence. Love for it, in all its parts, in every word and sentence which compose it, should be interwoven into all our notions of thinking, speaking and acting. Disturb but one stone in this great arch—but one compromise in this holy covenant—and the whole must tumble into ruin!

MUSIC BY THE WATERVLIET BAND.

POEM,

DELIVERED AT LITCHFIELD, CONN.,

ON THE OCCASION OF THE

CENTENNIAL CELEBRATION, 1851.

BY

REV. JOHN PIERPONT.

POEM.

THE following Poem was then delivered by Rev. JOHN PIERPONT, of Medford, Mass.

ONE hundred times hath this celestial sphere
Marked, on its orbit, a completed year,
Since, with a bandage over both her eyes,
And her scales lifted level towards the skies,
Her drawn sword waiting on her royal will,
Justice first took her seat upon this hill,
In legal form her judgments to dispense,
And make her shield the citizen's defence:—
Justice, the regent spirit that presides
In every hut, where love with peace abides;
In every shop, where thrifty labor delves,
And piles his honest earnings on his shelves;
In every church, whose preacher stands unawed,
Though rich men frown, and no man dares applaud,
And, bold as Paul, and yet as Moses meek,
Speaks out God's truth, as God would have him speak;
In every hall, where righteous laws are made,
Or, of a state, the sure foundations laid;
Where senates counsel wisely for the realm,
Or, with true greatness, monarchs hold the helm

Of the wide empire given to their trust;
Nay! where, in heaven, the Almighty and All-Just,
Over all empires and all worlds supreme,
Weighs kings and culprits with an even beam.

One hundred times hath Winter, drear and chill,
In his snow blanket wrapped this sleeping hill!
One hundred times hath Spring, her naked feet
All red with snowbroth and dissolving sleet,
With snail pace, toiling up her cold sides, crept,
And drawn that blanket off, while yet she slept,
And, blowing hard, to kindle up a flame,
Hath started out some wind flowers, e're June came:
One hundred times hath Summer, bright and brief,
Robed in green grass, in blossom, and in leaf,
This and the sister hills, that, on each side,
Smile on her, as do bride-maids on a bride;
And then, one hundred times, hath Autumn come,
"And that right early," to sing Harvest Home;
And, dreamy Indian Summer being o'er,
Hath given her back to Winter's arms once more.

One hundred years have brought their bloom and fruit,
Since "every one who had a cause or suit,"
Might "come up hither" and present his claim,
With no misgivings, that, whoever came
With a good cause, good witnesses, good men
Upon the bench as judges, and, again,
With twelve good honest jurors; if he saw
That well-fee'd "counsel, learned in the law,"
Had courage, after half a dozen fights,
Would—stand an even chance to get his rights.

And then, at last, the controversy o'er,
The case all settled, to be tried no more,
Those hundred years, as onward they have swept,
Have seen how calm the litigants have slept:—
Judge, jury, counsel, parties have withdrawn,
And to a higher bar together gone,
Where every right decree is ratified,
And every wrong, reversed and set aside.

Those hundred years have seen great changes here,
For changes come with every circling year.
No little change this very hill hath felt;
Time's patient eye can see it slowly melt,
With every rain;—see Bantam River take
Some of its soil to fill up yonder lake,
And, as the wind sweeps o'er it, see each gust
Take on its wings a portion of its dust,
And bear it off forever:—thus this hill
Itself is changed;—nothing on earth stands still.
The earth itself, since from God's hand it came,
Hath never seen two centuries, the same.
Its Alpine "Needles," shooting up, in front
Of melting glaciers, annually grow more blunt;
Some of their cragginess its crags have lost,
Under the power of water and of frost.
Heights grow less high, with every shower, that sheds
Its softening influence on their rocky heads:
And, as the rocks, disintegrating, throw
Their fragments, crumbling into soil, below,

The "water-brooks, that run among the hills,"
To cheer the valleys, and to drive the mills,
On their way sea-ward, bear the mountain's gift,
The river's bed, or sunken plain to lift,
And push old Neptune, though he storm and roar,
Back from the line, that marked his ancient shore.
The Nile, the Mississippi, and the Po,
Bear thus, exulting, as to sea they go,
Each his own burden, to enrich his plain,
Or win, for man, new conquests from the main.
  So, every year, does this, our beauteous star,
Borne round her orbit in her viewless car,
Her smiling face more beautiful display,
As, every year, dark forests melt away,
And, in their stead, glad husbandmen behold
Fields, now all green, now ripening into gold;
While those old central fires, that ever glow
In the deep caverns of the world below,
From age to age, the fossil wealth refine,
That lies, locked up in quarry and in mine,
In God's own time to grope its tardy way,
Up, from eternal darkness, into day;
To bask in sunshine, on a mountain's head,
To roll, with sands, along a river's bed,
To gush, for sick ones, in a mineral spring,
To blush, for fair ones, in a ruby ring,
For orient queens their radiance to throw,
With gold and silver, from a rich trousseau,
To grace a noble, as a star of gems,
For kings to sparkle, in their diadems.

So with the dwellers of this changeful earth;
Birth, growth, maturity, decay, death, birth,
In one perpetual circle roll along;
The strong grow feeble, and the feeble strong;
The children's massy locks grow thin and gray;
Their children take their place, and "where are *they?*"
Thy fathers, Litchfield County, are at rest:
Thy children meet, to-day, to call thee blest.
Honored and loved, as by them all thou art,
They leave their homes, and gather to thy heart,
To see once more thy venerable face,
Once more to feel thy motherly embrace,
Each other's voice to hear, to clasp once more
Each other's hand, still warm, and to implore
God's blessing on thee, for all coming time:—
Me have they asked to bring a gift in rhyme,
To thee, our mother: cheerfully I bring
The best I have;—pray take my offering.

My native County, from thy nursing breast,
Young I withdrew; unpledged I left my nest,
A modest mansion, in a sunny nook,
Tall trees behind it, and a babbling brook
Flowing in front: not that I spurned the spot,
Nor, good old Litchfield, that I loved thee not;
But that, where broader fields before me spread,
With my one talent I might buy my bread.
And now, for more than half the time that fills
The century's circle, since upon thy hills

Hath justice, laying judgment to the line,
Made thee her home, thou never hast been mine;
So that, while many a worthier son hast thou,
To wreath a garland for thine honored brow,
Worthier, since having longer seen thy face,
Lain in thy lap and felt thy kind embrace.
He better knows thee, and might now rehearse,
Our common mother's praise in loftier verse,
Than can the wandering, yet not wayward child,
Upon whose face thou hast so rarely smiled;
None is more happy, at thy knee to stand,
And lay his filial offering in thy hand,
Of all who fill thy halls, and throng thy door,
Who know thee better,—not who love thee more.

When, on a day like this, we come, dear mother,
To honor thee, and welcome one another
To the old homestead, nature bids us look,
To see what names are blotted from thy book,
And what remain, of those we used to see
Honoring themselves, and, in that, honoring thee.
Myself—a stranger, I can only touch
Upon a few,—perhaps e'en that's too much.
O'er once familiar names a shade is thrown,
And names now honored are to me unknown;
Those from my memory I may never blot;—
Will these forgive me if I name them not?
Thy Reverend *Champion*,—champion of the truth;—
I see him yet, as in my early youth;
His outward man was rather short than tall,
His wig was ample, though his frame was small,

Active his step, and cheerful was his air,
And O, how free and fluent was his prayer!
He sleeps in peace and honor; but no son
Upholds his name. His followers, *Huntington*,
Beecher, and all who, since, have filled his place,
Are running yet, and running well, their race.
Collins, who prophesied ere *Champion* came,
Has heirs, to uphold his venerable name;
But other names—names honored more or less,
Known or unknown to me, around me press:
Some were familiar to my childish ear,
Others I knew not till I saw them here;*
A few of them into my verse I weave;
The rest, to fate and tardier Fame, I leave.
This is demanded by the fleeting hour;
And over that, not bards themselves have power.
As thine old *Forests* from thy hill-sides fall,
Thy *Mills* grow rarer, and thou need'st them all.
Thy *Sawyers* have withdrawn to newer lands,
Yet, here and there, a *Boardman* by thee stands;
And with them, close as any woodland tick,
To thy broad skirts thy faithful *Burr-alls* stick.—
That thou, with comfort o'er thy hills may'st ride,
Some of thy *Colts* within thy call abide:
Thou ne'er hast had a *Trotter*, that I know;
Thine aged *Gallup* left thee, long ago:
Yet canst thou ride—way-wise and strong of limb,
Thine *Ambler's* left,—so trust thyself to him.

---

* On the printed list of the several Committees of Arrangement.

No *Seaman* do I find upon thy roll,
To take thy *Northway* towards the Arctic Pole;
No needle guideth thy adventurous tars;
So much the rather may'st thou thank thy *Starrs.*
Not naked art thou by thy children left,
Nor of thy raiment shalt thou be bereft;
For though, as now, for aye should keep aloof,
From thee a *Weaver,* with his gorgeous woof,
Yet, hath the tide of time, that knows no ebb,
Brought for thy use a *Webster* with a *Webb.*
Some of thy *Birds* are flown, I grieve to say,
Scared by thy *Fowlers* and thy *Hunts* away,
Still do thy *Robbins* cheer thee with their throats,
And all thy *Downs* and *Fenns* are gladdened by their *notes.*
Nor, by thy *Hunts* is all thy larger game
Chased from thy soil; for, whether wild or tame,
Unharmed and seeking from no foe to hide,
No arrow quivering in his bleeding side,
When the fierce summer sun upon him looks,
Thy "*Hart* still panteth by the water brooks."
Thou hast an *Adam,*—not "the first," I trow,
Nor yet "the last," as any man may know:—
And, Mother, will thine Adam give me leave
To speak one word of counsel to his Eve?
'Tis simply this—Whene'er you're tempted, madam,
If you *will* yield, do so, but—don't tempt *Adam.*
Mother, I marvel, while thou claim'st to be
The very type of pure democracy,
Through the historian's and the poet's pen
Giving due honor to thy working men—

Thy *Fuller*, *Carter*, *Cutler*, *Taylor*, *Smith*,
Potter, and *Cooper*, with their kin and kith,—
That thou shouldst dandle, on thine aged knee,
The remnants of a by-gone royalty;
That a whole "house of *Lords*" thou shouldst embrace,
Nor, from thy *Nobles* turn away thy face;
Nay, if the truth must out, that thou shouldst cling,
With motherly affection, to a *King*.
Mother, this hint from no unkindness springs;—
No doubt thou art the better for thy *Kings*.

No mines of coal, with its bitumen fat,
Sleep in thy breast—thy granites tell us that;—
Yet have thy laboring *Colliers* done their part,
Thy head to enlighten and to warm thy heart.
Their Sibyl leaves upon the winds were thrown,
For others' benefit, if not their own.
Long since, they left thee;—but do not repine!
If others are enriched by what was thine,
Thou art, in turn, enriched at others' cost;
Thou'st saved thy *Bacon*, whate'er else is lost.

Thy sunny slopes boast not their loaded vines,
Nor laudest thou thy brandies or thy wines;
No golden barley gilds thy round hill-tops,
Nor bend thy poles beneath their weight of hops;
No corn of thine ferments in brewery vats,
Nor foams for thee the cream of murdered cats,*

* On trial of the action, "Taylor *vs*. Delavan," in Albany, it was proved by the defendant that the water used in the brewery of the plaintiff, from which issues so much of the celebrated "Albany Ale," was taken from a filthy pond, into which were thrown the carcasses of cats and other animals.

Bursting from bottles labeled "Brown" or "Pale,"
And sold and swallowed as the best of ale.
Still, when thou standest up among thy peers,
Thou need'st not blush, my County, for thy *Beers* ;—
Not "small," not "ginger," not a medley mass,
With froth redundant, and explosive gas,
But "stout" and "strong" as ever came to hand,
Ne'er growing "stale," however long it stand,
And as well "worked" as any in the land.
We once heard much, though somewhat less, of late,
Of dangerous unions between church and state.
"Stick to thy last, St. Crispin," was the cry;
"Cobble thy shoes! no other business try!"
"Think ye," they questioned, "that your team will draw,
If ye yoke up the gospel with the law?
The State machinery will sadly jar,
If one wheel drives the pulpit and the bar!"
Stand back! ye croakers, we believe you not,
The thing is tried, and now we know what's what.
What danger, pray, in *this* machinery lurks?
How glib it goes! ay, and how well it works!
No wheel, on other wheels, presumes to trench,
Though a whole *Church* is based upon the *bench*.

In the "old school" of truth and honor bred,
Guarding alike the living and the dead,
Thy *Wolcotts*, grave, inflexible, sedate,
Honoring at once the nation and the state;
Before us pass. The Treasury and the Bench,
With moral courage never known to blench,

The one adorned :—the other calmly wore
The robe of righteousness laid up in store,
For him who lives trust-worthy to the end,
The widow's counselor, and the orphan's friend.
  Thy *Holleys*, brothers, shall they be forgot?
Who shall be named, if they're remembered not?
The vigorous off-shoots from a sturdy stem,
Where will you find a brotherhood like them?
Strong as the iron wherein their townsmen deal,
Ay, and as true and springy as the steel,
Their forms as manly as e'er trod a deck,
Their action graceful as a lily's neck,
Their minds as clear as lake ice, and as cold,
With hearts full grown—of nature's manliest mold,
A lustre on the church and state they shed;
Early renowned, and Oh! too early dead;
Two of the brothers in earth's bosom sleep,
While o'er another's bones, rolls the remorseless deep.

  Those legal Titans, who, with earthquake tread,
Met on this hill for battle, and are dead,
Each one a host,—all by each other schooled,—
Strong, *Adams*, *Allen*, *Tracy*, *Reeve* and *Gould*,
Kirby, *Holmes*, *Slason*, ay, and many a *Smith*,
All of them men of marrow and of pith,
Who made illustrious thy golden age,
Another's pen hath touched,—himself a sage,
More competent their merits to rehearse;—
A theme adapted more to prose than verse:—
With him they're left:—no! not now are those names
Entrusted to our keeping,—but to Fame's.

Children, like these, hast thou no cause to curse;
Nor they, in turn, their mother and their nurse.
While thou regard'st them with a mother's pride,
They owe thee much, nor be that debt denied.
Small claim to filial love hath *she* in store,
Who gives her children birth, and nothing more.
In her arms folded, to her bosom prest,
They must be nourished at her loving breast;
Taught pity by her sympathizing sigh
Cheered by the light that sparkles in her eye,
Braced in their arms, as round her neck they cling,
And in their legs, as on her knees they spring,
Then taught to walk, by tottling on the floor,
And to get up, by tumbling out of door,
Till, by her training, hardy, but discreet,
Having acquired the use of hands and feet,
With something in their heads, the little elves
Are turned adrift, and told to help themselves.
So do thy children, Litchfield, owe to thee,
And thy hard treatment, what they've come to be;—
A vigorous race from a harsh nursery.
For, when thy skies have smiled, and wept, and scowled,
And thy winds cut, and sighed, and swept, and howled,
And they have borne the various buffeting,
They've had to bear,—they can stand any thing.
So has it been since first the race began;
So must it be:—the character of man,
Objects around, in nature or in art,
Do much in moulding—each performs its part.

Mountain, lake, forest, waterfall, the sea,
The high or low land where his home may be,
His home itself,—a palace or a shed,—
The air, he breathes, the soil that gives him bread,
The stock he springs from, whether weak or strong,
His early training, whether right or wrong,
His native climate, rigorous or kind,
More or less work, of muscle or of mind,
The state, the church, together or alone,
The ballot-box, the altar and the throne,
All help, the *character* of man to frame,
Yet leave his *nature*, as from God it came.

New England's air, her bleak and rocky hills,
Her crystal springs, cold wells, and babbling rills,
Her soil, that drives her children to their work,
By this most Christian order,—" Starve the shirk,"*
Have not done every thing, but have gone far,
To make New England's children what they are.
Her keen north-westers force the oxygen,
Fresh and condensed, into her growing men;
Her unshod boys, at day-break, are astir,
To pick up chestnuts, beaten from the bur
By those north-westers; and when falls the snow,
And they, no longer, can nut-gathering go,
They, in the snow find exercise and sport;
The snow-ball missile, and the snow-ball fort:
And, as the battle rages, and cold shot
Fly through the air innocuous, let us not

* "If any man will not work, neither let him eat."—St. Paul.

These mimic battles of the boys condemn;
They make the snow-balls, and the snow-balls them.
These forming powers produce a race of men,
Not seen before, nor to be seen again,
On the round world; a stirring, hardy race,
Keen, careful, daring, ready to embrace
Peril for profit,—in each form, or all
The forms encountered by the Apostle Paul.
Perils, that press around the pioneer,—
The fearful antlers of the hunted deer,
The ambushed Indian's arrow, or his slug,
The panther's leap, or Bruin's hearty hug;
Perils that round the full-packed pedler press,
Or in the city or the wilderness;
Perils of robbers, perils on the seas,
Perils from heathens, Tartar or Tongese,
Perils of waters, such as those assail,
Who board an ice-berg, or harpoon a whale,
Perils that throng the Amazon or Nile—
The anaconda or the crocodile;
Perils from famine, perils to his neck,
From Lynch's law or the marauder's deck;
Perils from thieves, while trading at Loo-Choo,
Of getting lost in finding Timbuctoo;
By the Spokanes, of having his head flatted,
By the Typees, of being kept and fatted,
Or, by the Feejees to a jelly beaten,
Or, by New Zealanders, baked crisp and eaten;
Perils by flood and fire; and perils then,
Worse than all these—from his own countrymen:—

These perils *all*, the Yankee will despise,
When he has—"speculation in his eyes."

'T were hard, indeed, exactly to define
The Yankee nation, by a boundary line;
But, draw one north, that on the west shall run,
Of Fairfield, Litchfield, Berkshire, Bennington,
On, towards the polar Bear, till you arrive
At the north parallel of forty-five;
Thence towards the rising sun, until you tread
On the last rock fallen off from Quoddy Head;
Between those limits, and th' indented shore,
Among whose crags th' Atlantic billows roar,
The region lies, of which, if e'er bereft,
The Yankee nation will have little left.
Here dwells a people—by their leave I speak—
Peculiar, homogeneous, and unique,
With eyes wide open, and a ready ear,
Whate'er is going on to see and hear;
Nay, they do say, the genuine Yankee keeps
One eye half open, when he soundest sleeps—
Industrious, careful how he spends his cash—
(Though when he pleases he can "cut a dash")—
Quick at his business, in the field or shop,
He'll traffic with you,—buy, or sell, or "swap;"
And, if you get the better in the "trade,"
You earn your money, and your fortune's made.
Think you to joke him, as you cross his track?
The chance is with him, that he'll joke you back;
And, if your shaft goes nearer to the spot,
Than his, we'll dub you an accomplished shot.

Or, in this wordy war, should it ensue,
That the laugh rests not upon him, but you,
And, feeling galled that, in a bout at wit,
He's given, and you have got, the harder hit,
Should you, in wrath, attempt to tweak his nose,
Or with your boot-heel grind his *bootless* toes;
Or should you, rather, in your fight enlist
A single barrel, than a double fist,
For either job,—a battle or a spat,
The Yankee's ready—if it comes to that.
He loves his labor, as he loves his life;
He loves his neighbor, and he loves his wife:
And why not love her? Was she not the pearl
Above all price, while yet she was a girl?
And, has she not increased in value since,
Till, in her love, he's richer than a prince?
Not love a Yankee wife! what, under *Heaven*,
Shall he love, then, and hope to be forgiven!
So fair, so faithful, so intent to please,
A "help" so "meet" in health or in disease,
A counselor, at once so true and wise,
Bound to his heart by so endearing ties,
The cheerful sharer of his earthly lot,
Whether his home's a palace or a cot,
Whether she glides her Turkish carpet o'er,
Or sweeps, bare-footed, her own earthen floor;
The guardian angel, who shall hold him up,
While passing near the Tempter's couch or cup!—
Not love his wife, so constant, and so true!
Of all unfaithful wives, how very few

Are there, or have there been, who made their bed,
'Twixt Byram River's *mouth*, and Quoddy's *head!*

And then, such house-wives as these Yankees make;
What can't they do? Bread, pudding, pastry, cake,
Biscuit, and buns, can they mould, roll, and bake.
All they o'er see; their babes, their singing birds,
Parlor and kitchen, company and curds,
Daughters and dairy, linens, and the lunch
For out-door laborers,—instead of punch—
The balls of butter, kept so sweet and cool,
All the boys' heads, before they go to school,
Their books, their clothes, their lesson, and the ball,
That she has wound and covered for them—all,
All is o'erseen!—o'erseen!—Nay it is *done*,
By these same Yankee wives:—If you have run
Thus far without one, towards your setting sun,
Lose no more time, my friend,—go home and speak for one!

The Yankee boy, before he's sent to school,
Well knows the mysteries of that magic tool,
The pocket-knife. To that his wistful eye
Turns, while he hears his mother's lullaby;
His hoarded cents he gladly gives to get it,
Then leaves no *stone* unturned, till he can whet it:
And, in the education of the lad,
No little part that implement hath had.
His pocket-knife to the young whittler brings
A growing knowledge of material things.
Projectiles, music, and the sculptor's art,
His chestnut whistle, and his shingle dart,

His elder pop-gun with its hickory rod,
Its sharp explosion and rebounding wad,
His corn-stalk fiddle, and the deeper tone,
That murmurs from his pumpkin-leaf trombone,
Conspire to teach the boy. To these succeed
His bow, his arrow of a feathered reed,
His wind-mill, raised the passing breeze to win,
His water-wheel that turns upon a pin;
Or if his father lives upon the shore,
You'll see his ship, "beam-ends" upon the floor,
Full-rigged, with raking masts, and timbers staunch,
And waiting, near the wash-tub, for a launch.
Thus by his genius and his jack-knife driven,
Ee're long he'll solve you any problem given;—
Make any gim-crack, musical or mute,
A plow, a coach, an organ or a flute,
Make you a locomotive or a clock,
Cut a canal, or build a floating dock,
Or lead forth Beauty from a marble block;—
Make any thing, in short, for sea or shore,
From a child's rattle to a Seventy-four:—
Make *it*, said I?—Ay, when he undertakes it
He'll make the thing, and the machine that makes it.
And, when the thing is made,—whether it be
To move on earth, in air, or on the sea,
Whether on water, o'er the waves to glide,
Or, upon land, to roll, revolve, or slide,
Whether to whirl, or jar, to strike or ring,
Whether it be a piston or a spring,

Wheel, pulley, tube sonorous, wood or brass,
The thing designed shall surely come to pass;—
For, when his hand's upon it, you may know,
That there's *go* in it, and he'll make it go.

See, what has come of this mercurial cast
Of Yankee mind, within a century past;
Nay, within half that time;—come, go with me,
To such a farm-house as we used to see,
Or may see yet, on any of the hills,
That, with his sons, the Litchfield farmer tills.
No wave of wizard's wand, we need to throw
Ourselves back, half a century ago—
Let us go in, then, friend—sit you down there,
On that board stool, or splinter-bottomed chair;—
Beside the blazing fire of hissing logs,
Kept from the hearth-stone by cast iron dogs.—
There, on her lowly seat, the housewife see,
A pair of hand-cards pressed upon her knee;—
"Persall and Pell," upon the back displayed,
Informs the world by whom those cards were made;—
A heap of cotton, lying by her side;—
Cotton that her own hands have washed and dried;
And, as her busy hands their task perform,
White as a snow-wreath, in a Christmas storm,
The pile of rolls swells slowly, as the day,
Wasting her patient spirit wears away.
Then, when, at last, her weary labor o'er,
The raw material taken from the floor,
On her left hand, and by her magic sleight
Laid loosely in the basket on her right,—

Then comes the thought—who doth not with her feel?
"These rolls must now be spun upon the wheel!"
The spinning wheel! ne'er was that monster dumb!
Early and late, you heard its doleful hum;
E'en from the rising to the setting sun,
Early and late, the weary woman spun,
With only this, to help her bear the curse—
"A fearful looking for" of something worse.
Yes:—for although you may have held it hard,
Day in and out, that cotton thus to card;—
Though you might almost hold it as a sin,
Day in and out that cotton thus to spin;—
We must insist upon it, with your leave,
'T were worse, that cotton in a loom to weave.
And could that woman, as she sat so meek,
Carding her white rolls,—or as, week by week,
Her spindle's dull, premonitory hums
Were heard, have failed to think of spools, and thrums?
Have failed to see, amid the gathering gloom,
The reed and treadles of the approaching loom?
  Let us be just. That true devoted dame—
We need not name her here, nor fear to name
Her labor lay in no ignoble line:
She may have been your mother;—she *was* mine—
Let us be just;—that faithful woman had
One thought, amidst her toils, to make her glad.
Her mother's lot, compared with hers, was hard:—
Her mother *had* no cotton wool, to card;
And, to her mother's lot it never fell,
To use the cards, made by Persall and Pell.

Her mother's wheel—it may have been as big
As was her own,—it was not, yet, so trig:—
She'd seen such progress, in the arts of life,
As much to aid the mother and the wife,
Where'er the husband or the child might roam,
In making, for them both, a happy home.

O, had that house-wife as, fatigued with toil,
She sat and watched to see the kettle boil,
For evening tea, observed the iron crown
Of her tea-kettle bobble up and down,
And seen the vapor, as it issued out,
Snow-white, and hissing, from the heated snout;
Wreathe itself up, all spirit-like and warm,
Into the semblance of an angel form;
Seen it unfold its wings, and heard it say—
"Woman, fear not, for thou shalt see the day,
"When I, yes I, the vapor that I seem,
"Of fire and water born, and baptized *Steam*,
"Will save you all this labor: I will gin
"Your cotton first,—then will I card and spin,
"Reel, wash, dry, spool the filling, size the warp;
"Nay if with both your eyes you look out sharp,
"You'll see me fling it so that both your eyes
"Shall fail to see the shuttle, as it flies.
"And, as the shuttle shoots, the reed shall strike:—
"I'll drive them both, and drive them both alike,
"And, when the web is through the loom, by dint
"Of my own power, I'll calender and print!
"Ay, madam, through these labors will I go,
"And give your daughters printed calico,

"For less than half the money, by the yard,
"Now paid, per pound, for cotton, that you card.
"Nay, ma'am, that boy, who, as I tell you this,
"Hears, in my voice nought but the kettle's hiss,—
"That boy,—by spinning, from his towy head,
"And reeling off lines about cotton thread,
"Shall buy more cotton shirting, in one even,
"Than you can card and spin, this side of heaven":—
Had the Steam Spirit then and thus addressed
Her who loved me,—whom I loved first and best,
Would she not, starting up, have "screamed a scream,"
And cried—"I know thee, thou foul spirit of steam!
"I see thou risest from the fires below:—
"Both who thou art, and what thou wouldst I know;
"I know thou liest! I'll have no part with thee!
"Devil, avaunt!—I will not taste thy TEA!"
Yet, have we seen the Power that we suppose,
To have spoken thus from the tea-kettle's nose,
More than make good what, first, appeared to be
At once a boastful and false prophecy.

The wings of Time, who ne'er suspends his flight,
Will not allow, although your patience might,
Your bard to note the multitude of things,
That Time has brought us, on those sweeping wings,
From Yankee genius, industry and skill,
Since Justice took her seat upon this hill:—
Innumerable things, contrived as means
Of saving labor:—multiform machines,

Impelled by wind, by water and by steam,
By sheep, by horses, by the tardier team
Of bullocks,—nay, for labors very nice,
Mills and machinery that are worked by mice!—
A lathe, that turns, out of a wooden block,
A last, an ax-helve, or a musket-stock,
Nay—if you'll stand so, that it can get at you,
It will turn *you* into a marble statue!*—
A printing press, that, by hot water power,
Prints twenty thousand volumes in an hour!
A car, that, if you wish to run away,
Will carry you three hundred miles a day!
But, think not, that, when in that car, you've fled, you
Are "off" so fast that nothing else can "head" you.
If so you've thought, without your host you've reckoned;
The news shall run a thousand miles a second,
Along a wire, by Yankee genius given,
To make a tell-tale of the fire from heaven;
And, if your friends are anxious to restore you,
The lightning starts next day, and gets there long before you!

'Tis not my purpose to appropriate
All that is clever to our native State:—
The children of her sister states, our cousins,
Present their claims:—allow them—though by dozens;—
We're not like dogs, all fighting for a bone,
And every snarler growling o'er his own:—
Not like the runners that enrolled their names
For wreaths of laurel in the Pythian games;

* This is no fiction:—it is strictly true;
'Twill turn a marble 'duplicate' of you.

For, there, though all ran well, who ran the best,
Alone bore off the crown from all the rest.
We would be just, and, so, divide the bays ;—
The wit is common—common be the praise.
But, when we've weighed them, in a balance true,
And given our cousins *all* that is their due,
Will not themselves acknowledge that the weight
Inclines in favor of "the Nutmeg State"?
That, true and fine as is their razor set,
Ours has an edge a "*leetle*" finer yet;—
That, though theirs leaves the visage very sleek,
Ours hugs, a trifle closer, to the cheek?
So that, in all that gives the Yankee place
In the front rank of the whole human race,—
Among her sisters,—"when all's said and done,"
Our little Mother must rank, Number One.
What if her faith, to which she clings as true,
Appears, to some eyes, slightly tinged with *blue?*
With blue *as* blue, aside from any *ism*,
We find no fault;—the spectrum of a prism,
The rainbow, and the flowers-de-luce, that look,
At their own beauty, in the glassy brook,
Show us a blue, that never fails to please;
So does yon lake, when rippled by a breeze;
In morning glories blue looks very well,
And in the little flower, they call "blue bell."
No better color is there for the sky,
Or, as *I* think, for a blonde beauty's eye.
It's very pretty for a lady's bonnet,
Or for the ribbon that she puts upon it;

But in her faith, as also in her face,
Some will insist that blue is out of place;
As all agree it would be in the rose,
She wears, and, peradventure, in—*her hose.*
  Still, for her shrewdness, must the "Nutmeg State"
As Number One, among her sisters rate;
And which, of all *her* counties, will compare,
For size or strength, for water, soil or air,
With our good mother county?—Which has sown
Her children, broad-cast, o'er a wider zone,
Around the globe? And has she not, by far,
Out-done the rest, in giving, to the bar,
And to the bench,—for half of all her years—
The brightest names of half the hemispheres?
Nor have "Creation's *lords*" engrossed her care;
Creation's *ladies* have received their share:—
For, when to Reeve and Gould the former came,
To Pierce the latter:—Pierce, an honored name!
Yea, thrice and four times honored, when it stands
Beside *his* name, who comes, with bloody hands,
From fields of battle; though the applauding shout
From myriad mouths—and muskets—call it out;
Though by him, armies were to victory led,
And groves of laurel grow upon his head!
  Bloodless the honors that to Pierce are paid:
Bloodless the garlands on her temples laid.
To them, reproachful, no poor widow turns;
No sister's heart bleeds, and no mother mourns
To see them flourish. Ne'er shall they be torn
From off her honored brows. Long be they worn,

To show the world how a good Teacher's name
Out-weighs, in real worth, the proudest warrior's fame!—

Our mother county! never shalt thou boast
Of mighty cities, or a sea-washed coast.
Not thine the marts, where Commerce spreads her wings,
And to her wharves the wealth of India brings:
No field of thine has e'er been given to fame,
Or stamped, by History, with a hero's name;
For, on no field of thine was e'er displayed
A hostile host, or drawn a battle blade.
The better honors thine, that wait on Peace.
Thy *names* are chosen, not from martial Greece,
Whose bloody laurels by the sword were won,—
Platea, Salamis, and Marathon;—
But from the pastoral people, strong and free,
Whose hills looked down upon the Midland sea,—
The Holy Land. Thy *Carmel* lifts his head
Over thy *Bethlehem*,—thy "house of bread"—
Not Egypt's land of *Goshen* equaled thine,
For wealth of pasture, or "well-favored kine;"
While many a streamlet through thy *Canaan* flows,
And in thy *Sharon* blushes many a rose.

But, mother Litchfield, thou hast stronger claims
To be called holy, than thy holy names
Can give thee.—Reckon as thy jewels, then,
Thy saintly women, and thy holy men.
Scarce have thine early birds from sleep awoke,
And up thy hill-sides curls the cottage smoke,
When rises with it, on the morning air,
The voice of household worship and of prayer;

And when the night-bird sinks upon her nest
To warm her fledglings with her downy breast,
In reverent posture, many a father stands,
And, o'er his children, lifting holy hands,
Gives them to God, the Guardian of their sleep;
While, round their beds, their nightly vigils keep
Those Angel ministers of heavenly grace,
Who "always do behold their Father's face."
And, when the day returns for toil to cease,
With the disciples of the Prince of Peace,
The voice responsive of thy village bells,
From hill and valley, on the clear air swells,
And up thy hills, and down thy valleys go
Thy sons and daughters, reverently slow,
To eat the bread of life, their pastor brings,
And pay their homage to the King of kings.

Land of my birth, thou *art* a holy land!
Strong in thy virtue may'st thou ever stand,
As in thy soil and mountains thou art strong!
And, as thy mountain echoes now prolong
The cadence of thy water-falls,—forever
Be the voice lifted up of Time's broad river,
As on it rushes to the eternal sea,
Sounding the praises of thy sons and Thee!

SECOND DAY.

At half past ten, A. M., a procession was formed in the same order as the first day, and marched to the Tent, escorted by the "Bacon Guards."

The exercises were then opened by vocal music from the County Musical Association, singing the following hymn to the tune of China; the audience uniting: The fine effect of which, from thousands of voices, can be better imagined than described.

1.

O Lord, thy covenant is sure
To all who fear thy name;
Thy mercies age on age endure,
Eternally the same.

2.

In Thee our fathers put their trust;
Thy ways they humbly trod;
Honored and sacred is their dust,
And still they live to God.

3.

Heirs to their faith, their hopes, their prayers,
We the same path pursue;
Entail the blessing to our heirs;
Lord! show thy promise true.

A prayer was then offered by the Rev. Rufus Babcock, D.D., of Philadelphia, a native of Colebrook.

PRAYER.

Almighty God, our Heavenly Father, beneath the opening skies, we, Thy not ungrateful children, would devoutly bow before Thee in this solemn and joyous hour, recognizing that parental love and care which Thou hast exerted towards us, and calling upon our souls, and all within us, to praise, and bless, and honor Thee, our Maker, our Preserver, and our gracious Benefactor, for the bestowment of infinite, varied, and constant bounties, ever since we had a being.

We rejoice in Thee, as the source of every good and every perfect gift. With humble and adoring thankfulness, we recognize Thee as our fathers' God. Thou didst lead them to this waste, howling wilderness. Thou didst cast out various impediments from before them, and grant them the enjoyment of this favored land, where, in the exercise of a hardy industry, they were enabled to "provide things honest in the sight of all men" for themselves and their households, and not only to see growing up around them, as plants of righteousness, their own favored offspring, but Thou didst enable them to send off to the right hand and to the left, many a promising offshoot, on whom Thy favor has also rested. In their wide dispersion, Thou hast led them like a flock, and multiplied and blessed them; and many of them are now uniting with us in heart, though not in presence, in sending up ascriptions of praise to that All Gracious Benefactor, by whose kind guardianship we and our fathers have been established, directed and blessed.

We thank Thee that the religion of Jesus Christ imbued the mind and heart of those parents, making them what they were to us and the world. Oh, let not their favored children cast away that entire dependence on Almighty God, that humble, grateful recognition of his gracious Providence, which characterized those who have gone before. Oh, let us remember that it will fare ill with us, if we cast aside a dutiful regard of the God of our fathers; if we seek from any other source, blessings that can come from Him only.

We rejoice that among the appropriate exercises of this occasion, we are met here to-day, as our fathers were wont to meet before their Heavenly Father, to give heed to the instructions of Thy most holy word. May Thy rich blessing rest on the speaker and hearers, that we may be instructed, as well as delighted, on this occasion; and that our hearts may be drawn forth in grateful adoration for Thy guardian providence, which has so watched over and prospered and blessed us, and by whose favor we are gathered at this time, and from whom we have been permitted to receive so many gracious tokens of parental care and love, while we trust Thee for thy future care and love.

May the like blessings which have so richly distinguished us, be extended throughout our State, and throughout our States, that each community, on appropriate and fitting occasions, may have an opportunity to meet as we are met, rejoicing in peace and universal prosperity. May we rejoice always in true humility before God; and while praising and blessing Thee for Thy favors, may we humble ourselves because of the ill-requital which has been made for the bestowment of such mercies. In deep humility, it becomes us to confess this day, that we have erred and strayed from Thy ways. Oh, Lord, be merciful and heal all our backslidings, turn us from our perverse ways, and establish us in Thy truth. May the Holy Scriptures be still our blessed guide, and may they instruct us in the duties of industry, frugality, integrity, and benevolence: may they prompt us to extend a helping hand to the needy throughout the length and breadth of the land. Wherever the sons and daughters of this County have gone forth, there may streams of salvation, as from the purest fountain, extend to every parched and desolate place, so that one song may break forth throughout the land: and to the Father, Son and Holy Spirit, we will ascribe praises everlasting. Amen!

THE REV. HORACE BUSHNELL, of Hartford, a native of Litchfield County, then delivered the following Discourse.

The Age of Homespun.

A DISCOURSE,

DELIVERED AT LITCHFIELD, CONN.,

ON THE OCCASION OF THE

CENTENNIAL CELEBRATION, 1851.

BY

HORACE BUSHNELL.

DISCOURSE.

It has often occurred to others, I presume, as to me, to wish that, for once, it were possible, in some of our historic celebrations, to gather up the unwritten part, also, of the history celebrated; thus to make some fit account of the private virtues and unrecorded struggles, in whose silent commonalty, we doubt not, are included all the deepest possibilities of social advancement and historic distinction. On this account, since the Historical Address of yesterday presented us, in a manner so complete and so impressive to the feeling of us all, the principal events and names of honor by which our County has been distinguished, I am the more willing to come after as a gleaner, in the stubble-ground that is left; nor any the less so, if, in gathering up the fallen straws of grain, I may chance to catch, in my rake, some of those native violets that love so well to hide their blue in the grass, and shed their fragrance undiscovered. I think you will agree with me, also, that nothing is more appropriate to a Sermon, (which is the form of my appointment,) than to offer some fit remembrance of that which heaven only keeps in charge, the un-historic deeds of common life, and the silent, undistinguished good whose names are written only in heaven. In this view, I propose a discourse on the words of King Lemuel's mother :—

Prov. 31 : 28. "*Her children arise up and call her blessed.*"

This Lemuel, who is called a king, is supposed by some to have been a Chaldee chief, or head of a clan; a kind of Arcadian prince, like Job and Jethro. And this last chapter of the Proverbs is an eastern poem, called a "prophecy," that versifies, in form, the advice which his honored and wise mother gave to her son. She dwells, in particular, on the ideal picture of a fine woman, such as he may fitly seek for his wife, or queen; drawing the picture, doubtless, in great part, from herself and her own practical character. "She layeth her hands to the spindle and her hands hold the distaff. She is not afraid of the snow for her household; for all her household are covered with scarlet. Her husband is known in the gates, when he sitteth among the elders of the land. She openeth her mouth in wisdom, and in her tongue is the law of kindness. She looketh well to the ways of her household, and eateth not the bread of idleness." Omitting other points of the picture, she is a frugal, faithful, pious housewife; clothing her family in garments prepared by her industry, and the more beautiful honors of a well-kept, well-mannered house. She, therefore, it is, who makes the center of a happy domestic life, and becomes a mark of reverence to her children:—"Her children arise up and call her blessed."

A very homely and rather common picture, some of you may fancy, for a queen, or chief woman; but, as you view the subject more historically, it will become a picture even of dignity and polite culture. The rudest and most primitive stage of society has its most remarkable distinction in the dress of skins; as in ancient Scythia, and in many other parts of the world, even at the present day. The preparing of fabrics, by spinning and weaving, marks a great social transition, or advance; one that was slowly made and is not even yet absolutely perfected. Accordingly, the art of spinning and weaving was, for long ages, looked upon as a kind of polite distinction; much as needle work is now. Thus, when Moses directed in the preparation of curtains for the tabernacle, we are told that "all the women that were *wise-hearted* did spin with their hands." That is, that the accomplished ladies who understood this fine art, (as few of the women did) executed his order. Accordingly, it is represented that the most distinguished queens of the ancient time excelled in the art of spinning; and the poets sing of distaffs and looms, as the choicest symbols of princely women. Thus, Homer describes the present of Alcandra to Helen:

"Alcandra, consort of his high command,
A golden distaff gave to Helen's hand;

And that rich vase, with living sculpture wrought,
Which, heaped with wool, the beauteous Philo brought,
The silken fleece, impurpled for the loom,
Recalled the hyacinth in vernal bloom."

So, also, Theocritus, when he is going to give a present to his friend's bride, couples it with verse:—

"O distaff! friend to warp and woof,
Minerva's gift in man's behoof,
Whom careful housewifes still retain,
And gather to their household gain,
Thee, ivory distaff! I provide,
A present for his blooming bride.
With her thou wilt sweet toil partake,
And aid her various vestes to make."

If I rightly remember, it is even said of Augustus, himself, at the height of the Roman splendor, that he wore a robe which was made for him by Livia, his wife.

You perceive, in this manner, that Lemuel's mother has any but rustic ideas of what a wife should be. She describes, in fact, a lady of the highest accomplishments; whose harpsichord is the distaff, whose piano is the loom, and who is able thus, by the fine art she is mistress of, to make her husband conspicuous among the elders of the land. Still, you will understand that what we call the old spinning-wheel, a great factory improvement, was not invented till long ages after this; being, in fact, a comparatively modern, I believe a German or Saxon, improvement. The distaff, in the times of my text, was held in one hand or under one arm, and the spindle, hanging by the thread, was occasionally hit and twirled by the other. The weaving process was equally rude and simple.

These references to the domestic economy of the more ancient times, have started recollections, doubtless, in many of you, that are characteristic, in a similar way, of our own primitive history. You have remembered the wheel and the loom. You have recalled the fact, that our Litchfield County people, down to a period comparatively recent, have been a people clothed in homespun fabrics—not wholly, or in all cases, but so generally that the exceptions may be fairly disregarded. In this fact I find my subject. As it is sometimes said that the history of iron is the history of the world, or the history of roads a true record, always, of commercial and social progress, so it has occurred to me that I may give the most effective and truest impression of Litchfield County, and especially of the unhistoric causes included in a true estimate of the century now past, under this article of *homespun;* describing this first century as the Homespun Age of our people.

The subject is homely, as it should be; but I think we shall find enough of dignity in it, as we proceed, even to content our highest ambition—the more, that I do not propose to confine myself rigidly to the single matter of spinning and weaving, but to gather round this feature of domestic life, taken as a symbol, or central type of expression, whatever is most characteristic in the living picture of the times we commemorate, and the simple, godly virtues, we delight to honor.

What we call History, considered as giving a record of notable events, or transactions, under names and dates, and so a really just and true exhibition of the causes that construct a social state, I conceive to be commonly very much of a fiction. True worth is, for the most part, unhistoric, and so of all the beneficent causes and powers included in the lives of simply worthy men; causes most fundamental and efficient, as regards the well being and public name of communities. They are such as flow in silence, like the great powers of nature. Indeed, we say of history, and say rightly, that it is a record of *e-vents*—that is, of turnings out, points where the silence is broken by something apparently not in the regular flow of common life; just as electricity, piercing the world in its silent equilibrium, holding all atoms to their places, and quickening even the life of our bodies, becomes historic only when it thunders; though it does nothing more, in its thunder, than simply to notify us, by so great a noise, of the breach of its connections and the disturbance of its silent work. Besides, in our historic pictures, we are obliged to sink particulars in generals, and so to gather, under the name of a prominent few, what is really done by nameless multitudes. These, we say, led out the colonies, these raised up the states and communities, these fought the battles. And so we make a vicious inversion, not seldom, of the truth; representing as causes, those who, after all, are not so much causes as effects, not so much powers as instruments, in the occasions signalized by their names—caps only of foam, that roll conspicuous in the sun, lifted, still, by the deep under-swell of waters hid from the eye.

Therefore, if you ask, who made this Litchfield County of ours, it will be no sufficient answer that you get, however instructive and useful, when you have gathered up the names that appear in our public records, and recited the events that have found an honorable place in the history of the County, or the republic. You must not go into the burial places, and look about only for the tall monuments and the titled names. It is not the starred epitaphs of the Doctors of Divinity, the Generals, the Judges, the Honorables, the Governors, or even of the village notables called Esquires, that mark the springs of our successes and the sources of our distinction. These are rather effects than causes; the spinning wheels have done a great deal more than these. Around the honored few, here a Bellamy, or a Day, sleeping in the midst of his flock; here a Wolcott, or a Smith; an Allen, or a Tracy; a Reeve, or a Gould; all names of honor—round about these few, and others like them, are lying multitudes of worthy men and women, under their humbler monuments, or in graves that are hidden by the monumental green that loves to freshen over their forgotten resting place; and in these, the humble but good many, we are to say are the deepest, truest causes of our happy history. Here lie the sturdy kings of Homespun, who climbed among these hills, with their axes, to cut away room for their cabins and for family prayers, and so for the good future to come. Here lie their sons, who foddered their cattle on the snows, and built stone fence while the corn was sprouting in the hills, getting ready, in that way, to send a boy or two to college. Here lie the good housewives that made coats, every year, like Hannah, for their childrens' bodies, and lined their memory with catechism. Here the millers, that took honest toll of the rye; the smiths and coopers, that superintended two hands and got a little revenue of honest bread and schooling from their small joint stock of two-handed investment. Here the district committees and school mistresses; the religious society founders and church deacons; and, withal, a great many sensible, wise-headed men, who read a weekly newspaper, loved George Washington and their country, and had never a thought of going to the General Assembly! These are the men and women that made Litchfield County. Who they are, by name, we can not tell—no matter who they are—we should be none the wiser if we could name them; they themselves none the more honorable. Enough that they are the king Lemuels and their queens, of the good old time gone by—kings and queens of Homespun, out of whom we draw our royal lineage.

I have spoken of the great advance in human society, indicated by a transition from the dress of skins to that of cloth—an advance of so great dignity, that spinning and weaving were looked upon as a kind of fine art, or polite accomplishment. Another advance, and one that is equally remarkable, is indicated by the transition from a dress of homespun to a dress of factory cloths, produced by machinery and obtained by the exchanges of commerce, at home or abroad. This transition we are now making, or rather, I should say, it is already so far made that the very terms, "*domestic manufacture*," have quite lost their meaning; being applied to that which is neither domestic, as being made in the house, nor manu-facture, as being made by the hands.

This transition from mother and daughter power, to water and steam power, is a great one, greater by far than many have as yet begun to conceive—one that is to carry with it a complete revolution of domestic life and social manners. If, in this transition, there is something to regret, there is more, I trust, to desire. If it carries away the old simplicity, it must also open higher possibilities of culture and social ornament. The principal danger is, that, in removing the rough necessities of the homespun age, it may take away, also, the severe virtues and the homely but deep and true piety by which, in their blessed fruits, as we are all here testifying, that age is so honorably distinguished. Be the issue what it may, good or bad, hopeful or unhopeful, it has come; it is already a fact, and the consequences must follow.

If our sons and daughters should assemble, a hundred years hence, to hold another celebration like this, they will scarcely be able to imagine the Arcadian pictures now so fresh in the memory of many of us, though to the younger part already matters of hearsay more than of personal knowledge or remembrance. Every thing that was most distinctive of the old homespun mode of life will then have passed away. The spinning wheels of wool and flax, that used to buzz so familiarly in the childish ears of some of us, will be heard no more forever--seen no more, in fact, save in the halls of the Antiquarian Societies, where the delicate daughters will be asking, what these strange machines are, and how they were made to go? The huge, hewn-timber looms, that used to occupy a room by themselves, in the farm houses, will be gone, cut up for cord wood, and their heavy thwack, beating up the woof, will be heard no more by the passer by—not even the Antiquarian Halls will find room to harbor a specimen. The long strips of linen, bleaching on the grass, and tended by a sturdy maiden, sprinkling them, each hour, from her water-can, under a broiling sun—thus to prepare the Sunday linen for her brothers and her own wedding outfit, will have disappeared, save as they return to fill a picture in some novel or ballad of the old time. The tables will be spread with some cunning, water-power Silesia not yet invented, or perchance with some meaner fabric from the cotton mills. The heavy Sunday coats, that grew on sheep individually remembered, more comfortably carried, in warm weather, on the arm, and the specially fine-striped, blue and white pantaloons, of linen just from the loom, will no longer be conspicuous in processions of footmen going to meeting, but will have given place to showy carriages, filled with gentlemen in broadcloth, festooned with chains of California gold, and delicate ladies holding perfumed sun shades. The churches, too, that used to be simple brown meeting houses, covered with rived clapboards of oak, will have come down, mostly, from the bleak hill tops into the close villages and populous towns, that crowd the waterfalls and the rail roads; and the old burial places, where the fathers sleep, will be left to their lonely altitude—token, shall we say, of an age that lived as much nearer to heaven and as much less under the world. The change will be complete. Would that we might raise some worthy monument to a state which is then to be so far passed by, so worthy, in all future time, to be held in the dearest reverence.

It may have seemed extravagant, or fantastic, to some of you, that I should think to give a character of the century now past, under the one article of homespun. It certainly is not the only, or in itself the chief article of distinction; and yet we shall find it to be a distinction that runs through all others, and gives a color to the whole economy of life and character, in the times of which we speak.

Thus, if the clothing is to be manufactured in the house, then flax will be grown in the plowed land, and sheep will be raised in the pasture, and the measure of the flax ground, and the number of the flock, will correspond with the measure of the home market, the number of the sons and daughters to be clothed, so that the agriculture out of doors will map the family in doors. Then as there is no thought of obtaining the articles of clothing, or dress, by exchange; as there is little passing of money, and the habit of exchange is feebly developed, the family will be fed on home grown products, buckwheat, Indian, rye, or whatever the soil will yield. And as carriages are a luxury introduced only with exchanges, the lads will be going back and forth to the mill on horseback, astride the fresh grists, to keep the mouths in supply. The meat market will be equally domestic, a kind of quarter-master slaughter and supply, laid up in the cellar, at fit times in the year. The daughters that, in factory days, would go abroad to join the female conscription of the cotton mill, will be kept in the home factory, or in that of some other family, and so in the retreats of domestic life. And so it will be seen, that a form of life which includes almost every point of economy, centers round the article of homespun dress, and is by that determined. Given the fact that a people spin their own dress, and you have in that fact a whole volume of characteristics. They may be shepherds dwelling in tents, or they may build them fixed habitations, but the distinction given will show them to be a people who are not in trade, whose life centers in the family, home-bred in their manners, primitive and simple in their character, inflexible in their piety, hospitable without show, intelligent without refinement. And so it will be seen that our homespun fathers and mothers made a Puritan Arcadia among these hills, answering to the picture which Polybius, himself an Arcadian, gave of his countrymen, when he said that they had, "throughout Greece, a high and honorable reputation; not only on account of their hospitality to strangers, and their benevolence towards all men, but especially on account of their piety towards the Divine Being."

Thus, if we speak of what, in the polite world, is called society, our homespun age had just none of it—and perhaps the more of society for that reason; because what they had was separate from all the polite fictions and empty conventionalities of the world. I speak not here of the rude and promiscuous gatherings connected so often with low and vulgar excesses; the military trainings, the huskings, the raisings, commonly ended with a wrestling match. These were their dissipations, and perhaps they were about as good as any. The apple-pearing and quilting frolics, you may set down, if you will, as the polka-dances and masquerades of homespun. If they undertook a formal entertainment of any kind, it was commonly stiff and quite unsuccessful. But when some two queens of the spindle, specially fond of each other, instead of calling back and forth with a card case in their hand, agreed to "join works," as it was called, for a week or two, in spinning, enlivening their talk by the rival buzz of their wheels and, when the two skeins were done, spending the rest of the day in such kind of recreation as pleased them, this to them was real society, and, so far, a good type of all the society they had. It was the society not of the Nominalists, but of the Realists; society in or after work; spontaneously gathered, for the most part, in terms of elective affinity—foot excursions of young people, or excursions on horseback, after the haying, to the tops of the neighboring mountains; boatings, on the river or the lake, by moonlight, filling the wooded shores and the recesses of the hills with lively echoes; evening schools of sacred music, in which the music is not so much sacred as preparing to be; evening circles of young persons, falling together, as they imagine, by accident, round some village queen of song, and chasing away the time in ballads and glees so much faster than they wish, that just such another accident is like to happen soon; neighbors called in to meet the minister and talk of both worlds together, and, if he is limber enough to suffer it, in such happy mixtures, that both are melted into one.

But most of all to be remembered, are those friendly circles, gathered so often round the winter's fire—not the stove, but the fire, the brightly blazing, hospitable fire. In the early dusk, the home circle is drawn more closely and quietly round it; but a good neighbor and his wife drop in shortly, from over the way, and the circle begins to spread. Next, a few young folk from the other end of the village, entering in brisker mood, find as many more chairs set in as wedges into the periphery to receive them also. And then a friendly sleigh full of old and young, that have come down from the hill to spend an hour or two, spread the circle again, moving it still farther back from the fire; and the fire blazes just as much higher and more brightly, having a new stick added for every guest. There is no restraint, certainly no affectation of style. They tell stories, they laugh, they sing. They are serious and gay by turns, or the young folks go on with some play, while the fathers and mothers are discussing some hard point of theology in the minister's last sermon; or perhaps the great danger coming to sound morals from the multiplication of turnpikes and newspapers! Meantime, the good housewife brings out her choice stock of home grown exotics, gathered from three realms, doughnuts from the pantry, hickory nuts from the chamber, and the nicest, smoothest apples from the cellar; all which, including, I suppose I must add, the rather unpoetic beverage that gave its acid smack to the ancient hospitality, are discussed as freely, with no fear of consequences. And then, as the tall clock in the corner of the room ticks on majestically towards nine, the conversation takes, it may be, a little more serious turn, and it is suggested that a very happy evening may fitly be ended with a prayer. Whereupon the circle breaks up with a reverent, congratulative look on every face, which is itself the truest language of a social nature blessed in human fellowship.

Such, in general, was the society of the homespun age. It was not that society that puts one in connection with the great world of letters, or fashion, or power, raising as much the level of his consciousness and the scale and style of his action; but it was society back of the world, in the sacred retreats of natural feeling, truth and piety.

Descending from the topic of society in general to one more delicate, that of marriage and the tender passion and the domestic felicities of the homespun age, the main distinction here to be noted is, that marriages were commonly contracted at a much earlier period in life than now. Not because the habit of the time was more romantic or less prudential, but because a principle more primitive and closer to the beautiful simplicity of nature is yet in vogue, viz., that women are given by the Almighty, not so much to help their husbands spend a living, as to help them get one. Accordingly, the ministers were always very emphatic, as I remember, in their marriage ceremonies, on the ancient idea, that the woman was given to the man to be a help, meet for him. Had they supposed, on the contrary, what many appear in our day to assume, that the woman is given to the man to enjoy his living, I am not sure that a certain way they had of adhering always to the reason of things, would not have set them at feud with the custom that requires the fee of the man, insisting that it go to the charge of the other party, where, in such a case, it properly belongs. Now exactly this notion of theirs, I confess, appears to me to be the most sentimental and really the most romantic notion possible of marriage. What more beautiful embodiment is there, on this earth, of true sentiment, than the young wife who has given herself to a man in his weakness, to make him strong; to enter into the hard battle of his life and bear the brunt of it with him; to go down with him in disaster, if he fails, and cling to him for what he is; to rise with him, if he rises, and share a two-fold joy with him in the competence achieved; remembering, both of them, how it grew, by little and little, and by what methods of frugal industry it was nourished; having it also, not as his, but theirs, the reward of their common perseverence, and the token of their consolidated love. And if this be the most heroic sentiment in the woman, it certainly was no fault in the man of homespun to look for it. And, in this view, the picture given of his suit, by a favorite poetess of our own, is as much deeper in poetry as it is closer to the simplicity of nature.

"Behold,
The ruddy damsel singeth at her wheel.
While by her side the rustic lover sits,

Perchance his shrewd eye secretly doth count
The mass of skeins that, hanging on the wall,
Increaseth day by day. Perchance his thought
(For men have wiser minds than women, sure,)
Is calculating what a thrifty wife
The maid will make."

Do not accuse our rustic here too hastily, in the rather homely picture he makes; for sometimes it is the way of homely things, that their poetry is not seen, only because it is deepest. The main distinction between him and the more plausible romantic class of suitors, is, that his passion has penetrated beyond the fancy, into the reason, and made the sober sense itself a captive. Do you say that a man has not a heart because it is shut up in the casement of his body and is not seen, beating on the skin? As little reason have you, here, to blame a fault of passion, because it throbs under the strong, defensive ribs of prudence. It is the froth of passion that makes a show so romantic, on the soul's surfaces—the truth of it, that pierces inmost realities. So, I suppose, our poetess would say that her young gentleman of homespun thinks of a wife, not of a holiday partner who may come into his living in a contract of expenditure. He believes in woman according to God's own idea, looks to her as an angel of help, who may join herself to him, and go down the rough way of life as it is, to strengthen him in it by her sympathy, and gild its darkness, if dark it must be, by the light of her patience and the constancy of her devotion. The main difference is, that the romance comes out at the end and was not all expended at the beginning.

The close necessities of these more primitive days connected many homely incidents with marriage, which, however, rather heighten the picturesque simplicity than disparage the beauty of its attractions. The question of the outfit, the question of ways and means, the homely prudence pulling back the heroics of faith and passion, only to make them more heroic at last; all these you will readily imagine.

I suppose many of my audience may have heard of the distinguished Christian minister, still living in the embers of extreme old age, who came to the point, not of a flight in the winter, but of marriage, and partly by reason of the Revolution then in progress, could find no way to obtain the necessary wedding suit. Whereupon, the young woman's benevolent mother had some of her sheep sheared and sewed up in blankets to keep them from perishing with cold, that the much required felicity might be consummated.

But the schools,—we must not pass by these, if we are to form a truthful and sufficient picture of the homespun days. The school-master did not exactly go round the district to fit out the children's minds with learning, as the shoe-maker often did to fit their feet with shoes, or the tailors to measure and cut for their bodies; but, to come as near it as possible, he boarded round (a custom not yet gone by,) and the wood for the common fire, was supplied in a way equally primitive, viz.: by a contribution of loads from the several families, according to their several quantities of childhood. The children were all clothed alike in homespun; and the only signs of aristocracy were, that some were clean and some a degree less so, some in fine white and striped linen, some in brown tow crash; and, in particular, as I remember, with a certain feeling of quality I do not like to express, the good fathers of some testified the opinion they had of their children, by bringing fine round loads of hickory wood to warm them, while some others, I regret to say, brought only scanty, scraggy, ill-looking heaps of green oak, white birch, and hemlock. Indeed, about all the bickerings of quality among the children, centered in the quality of the wood pile. There was no complaint, in those days, of the want of ventilation; for the large open fire-place held a considerable fraction of a cord of wood, and the windows took in just enough air to supply the combustion. Besides, the bigger lads were occasionally ventilated, by being sent out to cut wood enough to keep the fire in action. The seats were made of the outer slabs from the saw-mill, supported by slant legs driven into and a proper distance through augur holes, and planed smooth on the top by the rather tardy process of friction. But the spelling went on bravely, and we ciphered away again and again, always till we got through Loss and Gain. The more advanced of us, too, made light work of Lindley Murray, and went on to the parsing, finally, of extracts from Shakspeare and Milton, till some of us began to think we had mastered their tough sentences in a more consequential sense of the term than was exactly true. O, I remember, (about the remotest thing I can remember,) that low seat, too high, nevertheless, to allow the feet to touch the floor, and that friendly teacher who had the address to start a first feeling of enthusiasm and awaken the first sense of power. He is living still, and whenever I think of him, he rises up to me in the far back ground of memory, as bright as if he had worn the seven stars in his hair. (I said he is living; yes, he is here to day, God bless him!) How many others of you that are here assembled, recall these little primitive universities of homespun, where your mind was born, with a similar feeling of reverence and homely satisfaction. Perhaps you remember, too, with a pleasure not less genuine, that you received the classic discipline of the university proper, under a dress of homespun, to be graduated, at the close, in the joint honors of broadcloth and the parchment.

Passing from the school to the church, or rather I should say, to the meeting-house—good translation, whether meant or not, of what is older and more venerable than *church*, viz., *synagogue*—here, again, you meet the picture of a sturdy homespun worship. Probably it stands on some hill, midway between three or four valleys, whither the tribes go up to worship, and, when the snow-drifts are deepest, go literally from strength to strength. There is no furnace or stove, save the foot-stoves that are filled from the fires of the neighboring houses, and brought in partly as a rather formal compliment to the delicacy of the tender sex, and sometimes because they are really wanted. The dress of the assembly is mostly homespun, indicating only slight distinctions of quality in the worshippers. They are seated according to age, the old king Lemuels and their queens in front, near the pulpit, and the younger Lemuels farther back, enclosed in pews, sitting back to back, impounded, all, for deep thought and spiritual digestion; only the deacons, sitting close under the pulpit, by themselves, to receive, as their distinctive honor, the more perpendicular droppings of the word. Clean round the front of the gallery is drawn a single row of choir, headed by the key-pipe, in the centre. The pulpit is overhung by an august wooden canopy, called a sounding-board—study general, of course, and first lesson of mystery to the eyes of the children, until what time their ears are opened to understand the spoken mysteries.

There is no affectation of seriousness in the assembly, no mannerism of worship; some would say too little of the manner of worship. They think of nothing, in fact, save what meets their intelligence and enters into them by that method. They appear like men who have a digestion for strong meat, and have no conception that trifles more delicate can be of any account to feed the system. Nothing is dull that has the matter in it, nothing long that has not exhausted the matter. If the minister speaks in his great coat and thick gloves or mittens, if the howling blasts of winter blow in across the assembly fresh streams of ventilation that move the hair upon their heads, they are none the less content, if only he gives them good strong exercise. Under their hard and, as some would say, stolid faces, great thoughts are brewing, and these keep them warm. Free will, fixed fate, foreknowledge absolute, trinity, redemption, special grace, eternity—give them any thing high enough, and the tough muscle of their inward man will be climbing sturdily into it; and if they go away having something to think of, they have had a good day. A perceptible glow will kindle in their hard faces, only when some one of the chief apostles, a Day, a Smith, or a Bellamy, has come to lead them up some higher pinnacle of thought, or pile upon their sturdy mind some heavier weight of argument—fainting never under any weight, even that which, to the foreign critics of the discourses preached by them and others of their day, it seems impossible for any, the most cultivated audience in the world, to have supported. O, these royal men of homespun, how great a thing to them was religion! The district school was there, the great Bellamy is here, among the highest peaks and solitudes of divine government, and between is close living and hard work, and they are kings alike in all!

True there was a rigor in their piety, a want of gentle feeling; their Christian graces were cast-iron shapes, answering with a hard metallic ring. But they stood the rough wear of life none the less durably for the excessive hardness of their temperament, kept their families and communities none the less truly, though it may be less benignly, under the sense of God and religion. If we find something to modify, or soften, in their over-rigid notions of Christian living, it is yet something to know that what we are they have made us, and that, when we have done better for the ages that come after us, we shall have a more certain right to blame their austerities.

View them as we may, there is yet, and always will be, something magnificent, in their stern, practical fidelity to their principles. If they believed it to be more scriptural and Christian to begin their Sunday, not with the western, but with the Jewish and other eastern nations, at the sunset on Saturday, their practice did not part company with their principles—it was sun down at sun down, not somewhere between that time and the next morning. Thus I remember being dispatched, when a lad, one Saturday afternoon, in the winter, to bring home a few bushels of apples engaged of a farmer a mile distant; how the careful, exact man looked first at the clock, then out the window at the sun, and turning to me said, "I can not measure out the apples in time for you to get home before sundown, you must come again Monday;" then how I went home, venting my boyish impatience in words not exactly respectful, assisted by the sun light playing still upon the eastern hills, and got for my comfort a very unaccountably small amount of specially silent sympathy.

I have never yet ascertained whether that refusal was exactly justified by the patriarchal authorities appealed to, or not. Be that as it may, have what opinion of it you will, I confess to you, for one, that I recall the honest, faithful days of homespun represented in it, days when men's lives went by their consciences, as their clocks did by the sun, with a feeling of profoundest reverence. It is more than respectable—it is sublime. If we find a more liberal way, and think we are safe in it, or if we are actually so, we can never yet break loose from a willing respect to this inflexible, majestic paternity of truth and godliness.

Regarding, now, the homespun age as represented in these pictures of the social and religious life, we need, in order to a full understanding, or conception of the powers and the possibilities of success embodied in it, to go a step farther; to descend into the practical struggle of common life, and see how the muscle of energy and victory is developed, under its close necessities.

The sons and daughters grew up, all, as you will perceive, in the closest habits of industry. The keen jockey way of whittling out a living by small bargains sharply turned, which many suppose to be an essential characteristic of the Yankee race, is yet no proper inbred distinction, but only a casual result, or incident, that pertains to the transition period between the small, stringent way of life in the previous times of home-production, and the new age of trade. In these olden times, these genuine days of homespun, they supposed, in their simplicity, that thrift represented work, and looked about seldom for any more delicate and sharper way of getting on. They did not call a man's property his *fortune*, but they spoke of one or another as being *worth* so much; conceiving that he had it laid up as the reward or fruit of his deservings. The house was a factory on the farm, the farm a grower and producer for the house. The exchanges went on briskly enough, but required neither money, nor trade. No affectation of polite living, no languishing airs of delicacy and softness in doors, had begun to make the fathers and sons impatient of hard work out of doors, and set them at contriving some easier and more plausible way of living. Their very dress represented work, and they went out as men whom the wives and daughters had dressed for work; facing all weather, cold and hot, wet and dry, wrestling with the plow on the stony-sided hills, digging out the rocks by hard lifting and a good many very practical experiments in mechanics, dressing the flax, threshing the rye, dragging home, in the deep snows, the great wood pile of the year's consumption; and then, when the day is ended, having no loose money to spend in taverns, taking their recreation, all together, in reading, or singing, or happy talk, or silent looking in the fire, and finally in sleep—to rise again, with the sun, and pray over the family Bible for just such another good day as the last. And so they lived, working out, each year, a little advance of thrift, just within the line of comfort.

The picture still holds, in part, though greatly modified by the softened manner of in-door life, and the multiplied agencies of emigration, travel, trade and machinery. It is, on the whole, a hard and over-severe picture, and yet a picture that embodies the highest points of merit, connects the noblest results of character. Out of it, in one view, come all the successes we commemorate on this festive occasion.

No mode of life was ever more expensive; it was life, at the expense of labor too stringent to allow the highest culture and the most proper enjoyment. Even the dress of it was more expensive than we shall ever see again. Still it was a life of honesty and simple content and sturdy victory. Immoralities, that rot down the vigor and humble the consciousness of families, were as much less frequent, as they had less thought of adventure, less to do with travel, and trade, and money, and were closer to nature and the simple life of home.

If they were sometimes drudged by their over-intense labor, still they were kept by it in a generally rugged state, both of body and mind. They kept a good digestion, which is itself no small part of a character. The mothers spent their nervous impulse on their muscles, and had so much less need of keeping down the excess, or calming the unspent lightning, by doses of anodyne. In the play of the wheel, they spun fibre too, within, and in the weaving, wove it close and firm. They realized, to the full, the poet's picture of the maiden, who made a robust, happy life of peace, by the industry of her hands.

> "She never feels the spleen's imagined pains,
> Nor melancholy stagnates in her veins;
> She never loses life in thoughtless ease,
> Nor on the velvet couch invites disease;
> Her homespun dress, in simple neatness lies,
> And for no glaring equipage she sighs;
> No midnight masquerade her beauty wears,
> And health, not paint, the fading bloom repairs."

Be it true, as it may, that the mothers of the homespun age had a severe limit on their culture and accomplishments. Be it true that we demand a delicacy and elegance of manners impossible to them, under the rugged necessities they bore. Still there is, after all, something very respectable in good health, and a great many graces play in its look that we love to study, even if there be a little of "per-durable toughness" in their charms. How much is there, too, in the sublime motherhood of health! Hence come, not always, I know, but oftenest, the heroes and the great minds gifted with volume and power and balanced for the manly virtues of truth, courage, persistency, and all sorts of victory.

It was also a great point, in this homespun mode of life, that it imparted exactly what many speak of only with contempt, a closely girded habit of economy. Harnessed, all together, into the producing process, young and old, male and female, from the boy that rode the plough-horse, to the grandmother knitting under her spectacles, they had no conception of squandering lightly what they all had been at work, thread by thread, and grain by grain, to produce. They knew too exactly what every thing cost, even small things, not to husband them carefully. Men of patrimony in the great world, therefore, noticing their small way in trade, or expenditure, are ready, as we often see, to charge them with meanness—simply because they knew things only in the small; or, what is not far different, because they were too simple and rustic, to have any conception of the big operations, by which other men are wont to get their money without earning it, and lavish the more freely because it was not earned. Still this knowing life only in the small, it will be found, is really any thing but meanness.

Probably enough the man who is heard threshing in his barn of a winter evening, by the light of a lantern, (I knew such an example,) will be seen driving his team next day, the coldest day of the year, through the deep snow to a distant wood lot, to draw a load for a present to his minister. So the housewife that higgles for a half hour with the merchant over some small trade, is yet one that will keep watch, not unlikely, when the school-master, boarding round the district, comes to some hard quarter, and commence asking him to dinner, then to tea, then to stay over night, and literally boarding him, till the hard quarter is passed. Who now, in the great world of money, will do, not to say the same, as much, proportionally as much, in any of the pure hospitalities of life?

Besides, what sufficiently disproves any real meanness, it will be found that children brought up, in this way, to know things in the small, what they cost, and what is their value, have, in just that fact, one of the best securities of character and most certain elements of power and success in life. Because they expect to get on by small advances followed up and saved by others, not by sudden leaps of fortune that despise the slow but surer methods of industry and merit. When the hard, wiry-looking patriarch of homespun, for example, sets off for Hartford, or Bridgeport, to exchange the little surplus of his year's production, carrying his provision with him and the fodder of his team, and taking his boy along to show him the great world, you may laugh at the simplicity, or pity, if you will, the sordid look of the picture; but, five or ten years hence, this boy will like enough be found in College, digging out the cent's worths of his father's money in hard study; and some twenty years later, he will be returning, in his honors, as the celebrated Judge, or Governor, or Senator and public orator, from some one of the great States of the republic, to bless the sight once more of that venerated pair who shaped his beginnings, and planted the small seeds of his future success. Small seeds, you may have thought, of meanness; but now they have grown up and blossomed into a large-minded life, a generous public devotion, and a free benevolence to mankind.

And just here, I am persuaded, is the secret, in no small degree, of the very peculiar success that has distinguished the sons of Connecticut and, not least, those of Litchfield County, in their migration to other States. It is because they have gone out in the wise economy of a simple, homespun training, expecting to get on in the world by merit and patience, and by a careful husbanding of small advances; secured in their virtue, by just that which makes their perseverance successful. For the men who see the great in the small, and go on to build the great by small increments, will commonly have an exact conscience too that beholds great principles in small things, and so will from a character of integrity, before both God and man, as solid and massive as the outward successes they conquer. The great men who think to be great in general, having yet nothing great in particular, are a much more windy affair.

It is time now that I should draw my discourse, already too far protracted, to a close. Some of you, I suppose, will hardly call it a Sermon. I only think it very faithfully answers to the text, or rather to the whole chapter from which the text is taken; and that sometimes we get the purest and most wholesome lessons of Christian fidelity, by going a little way back from matters of spiritual experience, carrying the wise Proverbs with us, to look on the prudentials of the world of prudence and watch the colors that play upon the outer surfaces of life and its common affairs.

I have wished, in particular, to bring out an impression of the unrecorded history of the times gone bye. We must not think on such an occasion as this, that the great men have made the history. Rather is it the history that has made the men. It is the homespun many, the simple Christian men and women of the century gone by, who bore their life-struggle faithfully, in these vallies and among these hills, and who now are sleeping in the untitled graves of Christian worth and piety. These are they whom we are most especially to honor, and it is good for us all to see and know, in their example, how nobly fruitful and beneficent that virtue may be, which is too common to be distinguished, and is thought of only as the worth of unhistoric men. Worth indeed it is, that worth which, being common, is the substructure and the prime condition of a happy, social state, and of all the honors that dignify its history—worth, not of men only, but quite as much of women; for you have seen, at every turn of my subject, how the age gone by receives a distinctive character from the queens of the distaff and the loom, and their princely motherhood. Let no woman, imagine that she is without consequence, or motive to excellence, because she is not conspicuous. Oh, it is the greatness of woman that she is so much like the great powers of nature, back of the noise and clatter of the world's affairs, tempering all things with her benign influence only the more certainly because of her silence, greatest in her beneficence because most remote from ambition, most forgetful of herself and fame; a better nature in the world that only waits to bless it, and refuses to be known save in the successes of others, whom she makes conspicuous; satisfied most, in the honors that come not to her, that "Her husband is known in the gates, when he sitteth among the elders of the land."

Assembled here, now, as we are, from all parts of this great country, most of us strangers heretofore to each other, it is yet our common joy and pride that so many of you return from stations of honor, which are the tokens of your success, appearing among us in names to which you have added weight and luster abroad, and so reflected praise on the home of your nativity and nurture. Our welcome to you is none the less hearty, none the less grateful I am sure to you, that we give you not all the credit of your successes. We distinguish in you still the seeds you carried away. We congratulate you, we honor those who made you what you are. Or if we say that we honor you, we bow our heads in reverence to those fathers and mothers less distinguished in name, it may be, and those virtues of common life and industry which have yielded us both you and all the social honors we rejoice in, on this festive occasion. In this latter sentiment I think you will join me, wishing, if possible, to escape the remembrance of yourselves, and pay some fit honors to the majesty of worth, in a parentage ennobled in yourselves and sanctified by the silence of the places where they are resting from their labors. It will be strange, too, when your minds are softened by these tender remembrances, if your thoughts do not recur instinctively, to what is the tenderest of all sentiments, that which remembers the lessons and the gentle cares of a faithful motherhood. Then let this voice of nature speak, and let the inward testimony of our hearts' feeling hail the witness of the concourse here assembled, as a welcome and sublime fulfillment of the word—"Her children arise up and call her blessed." Or if we exult, as we must, in reviewing the honors that have crowned the one century of our simple history as a people, let our joy be a filial sentiment, saying still, in the triumphant words that close our song—"Give her of the fruit of her hands, and let her own, works praise her in the gates"!

Men and women of Litchfield County, such has been the past; a good and honorable past! We give it over to you—the future is with you. It must, we know, be different, and it will be what you make it. Be faithful to the sacred trust God is this day placing in your hands.

One thing, at least, I hope; that, in these illustrations I have made some just impression on you all of the dignity of work. How magnificent an honor it is, for the times gone by, that when so many schemes are on foot, as now, to raise the weak; when the friends of the dejected classes of the world are proposing even to reorganize society itself for their benefit, trying to humanize punishments, to kindle hope in disability, and nurse depravity into a condition of comfort—a distinction how magnificent!—that our fathers and mothers of the century past had, in truth, no dejected classes, no disability, only here and there a drone of idleness, or a sporadic case of vice and poverty; excelling, in the picture of social comfort and well-being actually realized, the most romantic visions of our new seers. They want a reorganization of society!—something better than the Christian gospel and the Christian family state!—some community in hollow-square, to protect them and coax them up into a life of respect, and help them to be men! No, they did not even so much as want the patronage of a bank of savings, to encourage them and take the wardship of their cause. They knew how to make their money, and how to invest it, and take care of it, and make it productive; how to build, and plant, and make sterility fruitful, and conquer all the hard weather of life. Their producing process took everything at a disadvantage; for they had no capital, no machinery, no distribution of labor, nothing but wild forest and rock; but they had mettle enough in their character to conquer their defects of outfit and advantage. They sucked honey out of the rock, and oil out of the flinty rock. Nay, they even seemed to want something a little harder than nature in her softer moods could yield them. Their ideal of a Goshen they sought out, not in the rich alluvion of some fertile Nile, but upon the crest of the world, somewhere between the second and third heaven where Providence itself grows cold, and there, making warmth by their exercise and their prayers, they prepared a happier state of competence and wealth, than the Goshen of the sunny Nile ever saw. Your condition will hereafter be softened, and your comforts multiplied. Let your culture be as much advanced. But let no delicate spirit that despises work, grow up in your sons and daughters. Make these rocky hills smooth their faces and smile under your industry. Let no absurd ambition tempt you to imitate the manners of the great world of fashion, and rob you thus of the respect and dignity that pertain to manners properly your own. Maintain, above all, your religious exactness. Think what is true, and then respect yourselves in living exactly what you think. Fear God and keep his commandments, as your godly fathers and mothers did before you, and found, as we have seen, to be the beginning of wisdom. As their graves are with you, so be that faith in God which ennobled their lives and glorified their death, an inheritance in you, and a legacy transmitted by you to your children.

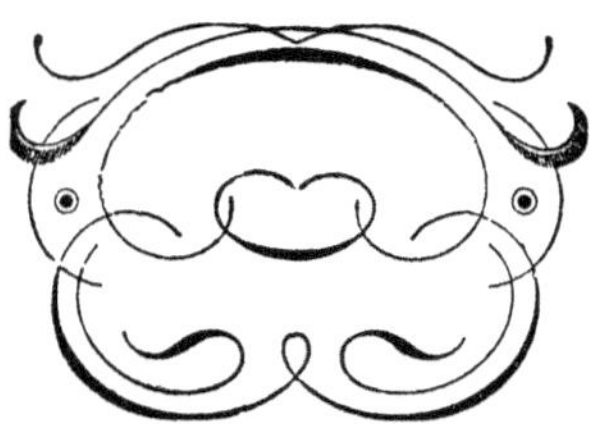

LETTERS,

ADDRESSES, SPEECHES,

AND

Concluding Exercises.

LETTERS, &C.

After Music from the Band, the following letters of apology for non-attendance, from gentlemen residing in other States, natives of the County, addressed to the Central Committee, were read to the audience by George C. Woodruff, Esq.

From Junius Smith, Esq., LL. D., of Greenville, South Carolina, the original projector of Atlantic Steam Navigation—a native of Plymouth :—

Greenville, S. C., July 22d, 1851.

Gentlemen :—

I received yesterday, the Litchfield Circular of March 22d, you were kind enough to send me. I have not seen a single Connecticut newspaper since I have resided in South Carolina, and therefore could have no knowledge that any such meeting was in contemplation. It would afford me singular pleasure to be present at the celebration proposed, but my Tea labors, at this season of the year, will not admit of my absence, and I am, with great reluctance, compelled to forego the gratification.

Pray remember me kindly to those who survive the vicissitudes of nearly half a century.

Your obedient servant,

Junius Smith.

Seth P. Beers, Esq., and others of the Central Committee of the Centennial Celebration of the County of Litchfield, Connecticut.

From Hon. Elisha Whittlesey, Comptroller of the Treasury Department, Washington—a native of Washington in this County.

TREASURY DEPARTMENT, COMPTROLLER'S OFFICE, August 7th, 1851.

Gentlemen:—

Your Circular of March 22d, giving notice that a Centennial Celebration of the County of Litchfield would be held at Litchfield, on the 13th and 14th of this month, was duly received.

Until recently, I intended to have been present, and during my visit, to have entered for the last time the house in New Preston, in which I was born; to have sought for the associates of my childhood, if any survive; to have visited the graves of my ancestors and relatives there, at Salisbury, and in other parts of the State; to have seen again my surviving sister and brother, and other dear relatives and friends; to have listened to the address of Judge Church, the poem of the Rev. Mr. Pierpont, and the sermon of the Rev. Mr. Bushnell—which will be worthy of the occasion, and of the gentlemen selected. But circumstances, beyond my control, deny me the enjoyment of my anticipations.

Fidelity—unyielding fidelity in all business, and in every trust, was enjoined upon me by my parents, in early childhood, and by that eminent divine and Christian, Jeremiah Day. I can not leave here, to attend the Centennial Celebration, to which, by your kindness, I am invited, without violating what I deem to be my duty to the public. I say this with the deepest regret, for I had fondly cherished the hope, I should add one to the number of the assemblage.

Most sincerely and respectfully yours,

ELISHA WHITTLESEY.

Messrs. Seth P. Beers, &c.

From Hon. George B. Holt, late Judge of the Circuit Court of Ohio, and State Senator—formerly of Norfolk, Connecticut.

DAYTON, OHIO, August 6th, 1851.

Gentlemen:—

I received your letter of invitation to attend your Centennial Celebration, to be held on the 13th and 14th inst.; and anticipated, with some hope, until to-day, the pleasure of being with you on the occasion; more especially, as I have a venerable father, rising four score and ten years, also brothers, sisters, and other relatives, still living in your County. My desire to visit my native State and County, is strengthened by the superadded invitation of several valued friends, from whom I have received letters of a complimentary character.

Gentlemen, for any respectability which may have attached to my name, and for any usefulness of which I may have been instrumental, I am indebted to the institutions of New England, as they exist in Litchfield County; instruction in childhood by one of the pious mothers of that land, followed by such advantages as were afforded by the common school, and a professional education in the Law School at Litchfield, when under the direction of Judges Reeve and Gould, now deceased.

It may, perhaps, be supposed, that during a period of more than twenty years in public life, eighteen of those years in the Legislative and Judicial departments of the government, followed by a membership in the Convention which formed the constitution of civil government lately adopted in Ohio, I may have "made my mark," as we say in the west—left some impress of New England institutions upon the character, morals, and manners of the mixed population with whom I have resided for more than thirty years. So far as I may have done so, I feel that I have done some good in my day and generation.

Gentlemen, I am among the sons of New England, proud of the *genuine* Yankee character, proud of their industrious habits, their honesty, their intelligence, their enterprise, and that controlling sense of religious obligation, which make up the character of New Englanders.

I pray you, gentlemen, to accept, for yourselves and those whom you represent, my sincere thanks for your kind invitation, and let me take leave of you by expressing a wish, deep from the heart, for your prosperity and happiness.

Truly yours,

GEO. B. HOLT.

Hon. Seth P. Beers, and others, Committee.

From Hon. Julius Rockwell, of Pittsfield, Mass., late member of Congress—a native of Colebrook.

PITTSFIELD, MASS., August 11th, 1851.

My Dear Sir:—

I have received the Circular of the Committee, informing the native citizens of the good County of Litchfield, of the preparations for the Centennial Anniversary. I have cherished the hope, until now, of being present, but circumstances which I can not control, will prevent my attendance.

The fact, that I am a native of that County, is a source of an honest pride and gratification to me. It would give me the greatest pleasure to be present on this interesting occasion, to listen to the sentiments of the eminent men who are to address the citizens, and emigrants from the County, to enjoy the society of my relatives and friends, and to make new acquaintances.

I can only express a sincere and ardent hope, that every circumstance attending your celebration may be propitious, and that to all present, the occasion may be full of interest and enjoyment.

Those of us, who are compelled to be absent, will look with great interest for the published accounts of the proceedings. We shall be with you in spirit, upon the occasion, and will not fail, as long as we live, to cherish sentiments of affectionate respect for the noble County of our nativity.

With my best respects to yourself and your associates upon the Committee,

I am, very truly yours,

JULIUS ROCKWELL.

William Beebe, Esq., Litchfield, Ct.

From Orsamus Bushnell, of New York—a native of Salisbury.

NEW YORK, August 12th, 1851.

Dear Sir:—

I have received a kind invitation to attend the celebration at Litchfield, on the 13th and 14th inst., and had made my arrangements to attend, and am at the last moment sadly disappointed by the occurrence of professional business which will prevent my attendance. I should rejoice to be with you, but as I can not, permit me to forward a sentiment—to be used, or not, as you may please.

My native State.—If the people do not, *may Heaven* preserve it from a "Code of Procedure," and its Judiciary from the Polls.

Very respectfully and truly yours,

ORSAMUS BUSHNELL.

Hon. Samuel Church.

From Charles J. Hill, Esq., of Rochester, former Mayor of that City—a native of Bethlem.

CITY OF ROCHESTER, Aug. 4th, 1851.

Gentlemen:—

I have the honor to acknowledge the receipt of your invitation to attend the Centennial Celebration of Litchfield County. I exceedingly regret that my onerous business engagements must prevent my attendance; but, although "absent in *body*, I shall be present in *spirit*," and when the day arrives, shall find my soul fired with a thousand recollections of the localities and scenes of my childhood.

It is now thirty-five years since I commenced my permanent residence in this city, an adventurer from my native Litchfield County. At that time, this city, now numbering over *forty thousand* inhabitants, contained *three hundred* souls. *No* churches, no public buildings—except one school-house of very diminutive dimensions, in which was the only meeting on the Sabbath—no *brick* or *stone* dwellings, nor the luxury of *paint* yet applied to any of the few crude wooden dwellings. But a few young *New Englanders* had *marked* the spot, and their indomitable enterprise gave significant indications of the future importance of Rochester.

Among the early *Pioneers* of Rochester, the sons of Litchfield County were not only respectable in *numbers*, but in point of *enterprise and moral worth*, they were generally men of whom their native County need not be ashamed, and are now enjoying the highest esteem of their fellow citizens.

Very respectfully, your obedient servant,

CHARLES J. HILL.

Hon. Seth P. Beers, Jonathan Lee, and others, Central Com.

From Augustin Averill, of New York—a native of Washington.

New York, August 9th, 1851.

Gentlemen :—

I have received the Circular forwarded some time since, and it was my intention, had circumstances permitted, to have attended the Centennial Celebration at Litchfield, on the 13th and 14th inst., but finding it impossible to do so in person, I will, through your Committee, in writing, join my sympathies and good feelings with my friends, relatives, and other inhabitants of my loved native County, and unite with them in congratulations on the auspicious event; very much regretting my inability to meet, rejoice, and give thanks with them on this very interesting occasion.

I am, gentlemen, very respectfully,

Your obedient servant,

Augustin Averill.

Hon. Seth P. Beers, Jonathan Lee, and others, Central Com.

From Gen. James R. Lawrence, of Syracuse, United States Attorney, for the Northern District of New York, a native of Norfolk.

Syracuse, N. Y., August 11th, 1851.

Dear Sir :—

I received your letter of the 31st July, by due course of mail, and have delayed an answer till this time, in the hope that I should be able to attend the Centennial celebration at Litchfield, to which you, as one of the Committee, have so kindly invited me. I now find that my duties as United States Attorney, for this District, will prevent my attendance, which I very much regret.

It always give me pleasure to visit my native State, and and especially the town (old Norfolk) and County where I was born, but that pleasure would be greatly enhanced could I unite with the sons of that time honor'd County, many of whom are now scattered over the different States of the Union, on the occasion referred to.

I shall be with you in spirit. I can easily imagine the happy state of feeling which such an occasion will call forth among such a generation of men; born and brought up in such a place, many of whom, I trust, inherit the sterling virtues of their ancestors. Methinks I can also anticipate some of the topics which will there be discussed. The first emotion should be that of devout thankfulness, for that preserving mercy which has spared the lives and health of so many, and enabled them, from various parts of the country, to revisit their native County, the land of their fathers' sepulchres, on such an occasion.

Gratitude for the intellectual, moral and physical training, which our fathers gave us in our childhood and youth, will doubtless be felt by all.

The prominent characteristics of our ancestors, were economy, frugality, industry, and energy; and these, they taught their children, which laid the foundation, in the first place, for good physical constitutions, without which, little can be accomplished. And most favorably, I apprehend, will the hardy sons of Litchfield County, compare with any other race of men in this respect.

I almost tremble sometimes, when I see so many young men at this day, growing up in luxury, extravagance, and indolence, and as a natural consequence, with impaired health and weak intellects;—better a thousand fold, go back to the simplicity of former times, when every man lived within his income, and taught his children that labor was not only necessary, but honorable for all.

The interests of our common country, cannot fail to be a subject for serious reflection on the occasion. One hundred years ago, your County was incorporated. What wonderful changes have taken place in that time, and what trying scenes did our ancestors pass through! Their energy and patriotism, however, were equal to the occasion, and nobly did they sustain the best interests of their country;—lovers of law and lovers of order: always to be relied upon, under all circumstances.

However much they may have differed as to questions of policy in the administration of the Government, yet ever true to the best interests of the whole country,—ready to sustain the arm of the government in maintaining the rights and honor of the nation. It cannot be disguised that our country, within a short period, has passed a crisis, which, at one time, was full of danger. Questions of a most delicate character, and about which men, and even wise men, differed in opinion, were discussed with great freedom, and sometimes with much bitterness; yet we may now congratulate ourselves on a settlement of these exciting questions, without impairing our glorious Constitution, and without injustice to any portion of our country: and although we may not all think that every thing has been done as we could wish, yet we have great reason to rejoice in the restoration of that fraternal feeling among the great mass of our people in all parts of our beloved country, which has resulted from the recent measures of our national government.

Already do we feel their tranquilizing effect, and if faithfully carried out, we may still look for long years of continued prosperity and happiness as a nation, under our glorious Constitution. I hold it to be the first duty of every good citizen, to obey the laws of the government. Why should he not? every man is a part of that government in this country, where all power is vested in the people. I think we may rely with confidence upon the staid men of old Litchfield, wherever they are, to maintain the laws—whenever the time shall come, when the laws of the land are set at defiance by the people, we shall have no government at all. All will be anarchy and confusion.

In this connection I cannot refrain from alluding to an honored son of old Litchfield, who will be with you at your Jubilee. I refer to the Hon. Daniel S. Dickinson of this State. I know him well; have been associated with him in the Legislature of this State; and although we have always differed politically, yet it gives me pleasure to bear testimony to his integrity, talents, and patriotism: and when I speak of his patriotism, I speak of it in that enlarged sense which embraces the whole Union, and consists in a zealous support and defence of it and its interests. I have seen him on great occasions shake off the shackles of party, and come to the rescue of his country, regardless of all personal considerations. In what I have said of him, I feel that I am only doing simple justice to a political opponent.

I should like to indulge in referring to some of the individuals of other times, who have lived and died in your good old County, but who have now gone to their rest and their reward, not, however, without leaving their impress upon the institutions where they lived, and upon the character of those they left behind;

this, however, can be better done by those who have had better opportunity to know their worth and excellence than I have.

Old Litchfield, I love thee! What other County in the whole Union has produced abler divines, lawyers, patriots, or statesmen? What county has produced a hardier or more intelligent race of farmers? It has indeed been a nursery from which have been scattered broadcast through the Union, men who, carrying with them the energy they inherited, the industry they learned to practice, and the morality of their sires, have been useful citizens and done honor to the place of their birth. Inhabitants of old Litchfield, you have not yet fulfilled your destiny; go on in the walks of usefulness, keep steadily in view the example of your ancestors; let their piety, their intelligence, their energy, their patriotism, their temperance, their sterling virtues, be your guide and example, and when another Centennial Jubilee shall occur, may our posterity have the same reasons for gratitude which we now have, and less to regret. So may it be. *Esto perpetua.* I have the honor to be,

Very respectfully, your obedient servant,

JAMES R. LAWRENCE.

R. Battell, Esq.

From Theron R. Strong, Esq., of Palmyra, New York, late member of Congress—a native of Salisbury.

PALMYRA, August 8th, 1851.

Gentlemen:—

I regret to have to inform you that the severe illness of my children renders it imperative upon me to relinquish my purpose of attending the Centennial Celebration, at Litchfield, on the 13th and 14th inst. Until within a few days past I have confidently expected to attend, and had nearly completed my arrangements for so doing. No ordinary circumstances would have been allowed to defeat my intention, but I must yield to the Providential interposition named.

The celebration has been looked forward to, by me, with very great interest. I have desired to embrace the opportunity to testify, by my presence and participation in its proceedings, my continued affection for the Town, County, and State of my birth,—

that neither time nor distance nor new attachments have been able to sever my love from the place of my origin and the home of my childhood. I have anticipated, on that occasion, the rich pleasure of meeting again some of my kindred, many of the associates of my early years, many valued friends and acquaintances, and reviving and meeting some of the most interesting associations and recollections of my youth. I have also anticipated, what will no doubt be there afforded, a rich intellectual as well as social entertainment; one calculated to improve the minds as well as gladden the hearts of all present.

Nothing could be more proper than this celebration. It will be but a just tribute of respect and regard for the County—a suitable acknowledgement for the virtue, intelligence, good order, prosperity and happiness which have there always prevailed. No community has been more largely blessed in those respects, none has ever existed, whose history in those particulars is more bright or honorable. Even in New England, to which our country is so largely indebted for its renown;—it occupies a proud position and enjoys an honorable fame. It is right to stop at this point in its progress—the termination of the first and the commencement of the second century of its existence, and take a survey of it in the past, to review its leading features and events—to render appropriate honors to those who participated in them, and indulge in the congratulations which such a survey is calculated to inspire.

In such a retrospect, abundant cause for gratitude and praise on the part of those who reside, or were reared there, will at every step be brought to view. Providence has most highly favored the County. Its early settlers were remarkable men. Like their brethren, who, associated with them, founded New England and gave it all the elements of its greatness, they were men of strong moral and religious principle—men of cultivated minds—men of industrious and frugal habits—full of enterprise and perseverance. They established and set in motion and gave direction to a state of society, singularly perfect. Their own character they impressed upon their descendants. The result has been that the County has long been the happy home of a large population, intelligent, virtuous, refined, possessing in an unusual degree, pecuniary independence, and all the privileges, social, moral, educational, and religious, which can promote the benefit and happiness of a community. Amid its magnificent scenery, surrounded by happy influences, and enjoying the advantages there afforded, have been trained numerous sons and daughters, who have emigrated to other portions of the country, most of whom have been prosperous and successful in whatever business they engaged. Many of them have attained high distinction and great usefulness. Go where you may over this extended Union, and we rarely fail to find some of them occupying respectable positions and bearing prominent parts in society.

It is to their early education, and those influences and advantages that these emigrants are largely indebted for whatever they have accomplished. A broad foundation was thereby laid for their prosperity, usefulness and honor. This, in respect to most of them, constituted their sole inheritance, and their career has illustrated that such an inheritance is immeasurably superior to any other.

Twenty-five years have now elapsed since I emigrated from the town of Salisbury, where I was born, during which period I have been a resident of the State of New York. Although proud to be a citizen of the Empire State, and deeply attached to its honor and prosperity, and having reason to be grateful for favors I have experienced in the community where I reside, I am also proud of the State of my nativity, and especially of the County and town of my birth, and bear towards them a regard and affection which will last through my life. With my native town, are identified many of the most interesting remembrances and associations of the past. It is still the residence of some of my early friends, and of a few of my beloved kindred. There are the graves of my parents, and of many friends and relatives.

In connection with this reference to my native town, I must, in justice to my own feelings, briefly allude to two valued friends, now in their graves, who emigrated from it shortly previous to myself, who were long inhabitants with me of the County where I reside, pursuing like myself the practice of the law;—Graham H. Chapin and John M. Holley. They were men of talent, of education, of many noble and excellent qualities, and an ornament to their profession and society. I shall ever cherish their memories with affection and pride.

Again expressing my regret that I cannot be present at the celebration, and tendering my acknowledgments for the honor of the invitation which has been extended to me, I am,

Yours very respectfully,

T. R. STRONG.

To Rev. Jonathan Lee and others, Committee of Salisbury.

From Ebenezer W. Bolles, of Delphi, Ind., a native of Litchfield.

DELPHI, IA., August 8th, 1851.

To the Committee of the Town of Litchfield:—

Happening by chance to see the circular addressed to all who had emigrated from the County of Litchfield, to attend a Centennial meeting at its County seat, and some remarks thereon, my heart warmed to be with you, to see and hear you relate what our fathers were and what they have done for us, their children; to again bring up before our eyes those honorable fathers who bequeathed to us, their children, all they had that was of real value. What was it they left us? was it riches? It has vanished away. Was it poverty? It has turned into riches, to again vanish.—Was it honor? was it liberty? was it love of country? was it love of our religious institutions, and its privileges? was it love of our God? Yes, that which our fathers received from their fathers—that which God in his mercy gave them, and enabled them to keep—that which is better than riches, than gold or silver—that which the more it is used, the greater it grows—that which extends its influence from the Atlantic to the Pacific, and bids fair to still spread, by the blessing of God, throughout the world:—it was that which proceeds from Him—that which He enabled our fathers to defend—that which they cherished as their best gift, and that which I hope their sons, wherever they are, will ever remember to keep and transmit to their descendants.

Methinks I see that old man, with cocked hat, breeches, knee buckles, shoe buckles broad as my hand, with staff in hand; and now I see that old lady, with large calash-bonnet, red cloak, high-heeled shoes, stays, etc.;—now she is on horseback, behind her husband, with a large velvet pillion; now, there are all the little boys, hats off, ready to bow to age and honor; there, the little girls have stepped out of the path, ready with a courtesy:—there goes that old man and woman—they are *town poor*; they, too, are honored, and their descendants are as likely to be as honorable as the rich man's. The blood that goes from the heart goes through all the members from the head to the foot, and from the foot again to the head, and then again through the heart;—all are honorable members in their place, and all contribute more or less to keep and continue that love of those institutions which they have received from Him who first gave it to our fathers. It may degenerate and grow sickly in some members, but it is again renovated, and now flourishes. May all those who have descended from such noble stock, never forget their birthright, but wherever they are, still cherish and keep it pure. May the memory of our fathers ever be blessed.

E. W. Bolles.

P. S. Oh, what a crowd there is of those same old people; they are without number; like Jacob's ladder they extend from earth to heaven!

From Amos Seward, of Tallmadge, Ohio,—a native of Warren; enclosing a list of the names of sixty-one persons, natives of Litchfield County, now living in the town of Tallmadge.

Tallmadge, Ohio, August 5th, 1851.

Gentlemen:—

I shall make no apology for addressing you on the present occasion. Your century celebration, about the middle of the present month, will be interesting to all that may meet with you. Presuming that you would be gratified to know the number who, by birth, were citizens of Litchfield County, and are now located in every State of the Union, I have, at some pains, collected the names, together with the date of their birth and date of their leaving your County, of those now living in this township, *Tallmadge*—named after one of your prominent citizens, Col. Benjamin Tallmadge, late of your place. The township is five miles square, and was first settled by Rev. David Bacon, father of Rev. Leonard Bacon, D. D., in the year 1806. Possibly there may be some inaccuracy in the date of their birth, and of their leaving the County.

Should any one say, that none of this list have shone conspicuous in science, military or politics, I would reply that, neither have we in crime. Our criminal courts have never been troubled with those from your County, settled in this township. We aim to be an industrious and law-abiding people.

I close by giving the following sentiment.

The citizens of Litchfield County in the coming century; may they faithfully copy the virtues, and carefully shun the errors of their predecessors.

The enclosed list contains the names of sixty-one persons, all *natives* of Litchfield County, now residing in the *single township* of Tallmadge, Ohio.

Respectfully yours,

AMOS SEWARD.

Committee of Arrangements for the Century Celebration in Litchfield County.

MEETING AT RICHLAND.

PROCEEDINGS of a meeting of residents of the town of Richland, in the County of Kalamazoo, Michigan, who emigrated from Litchfield County, were next read:—

At a meeting of those citizens of the township of Richland, in the County of Kalamazoo, and State of Michigan, who emigrated from the County of Litchfield, in the State of Connecticut, held at Richland, the 8th of August, 1851, for the purpose of preparing a statement to be presented at the Centennial Celebration, to be held in Litchfield, on the 13th and 14th of August:

On motion, Samuel Woodruff was chosen Chairman, and Eli R. Miller, Secretary.

Whereupon, the following 49 persons, heads of families, citizens of the town of Richl nd, and emigrants from said County of Litchfield, were found now to reside in this place; together with their 98 children and 109 grand-children.*

* The list of names are omitted.

On motion,

Resolved, That we would ardently desire personally to attend the Jubilee, to be held on the 13th and 14th, in the land of our fathers and County of our birth, and that we do hereby appoint and constitute E. R. Miller, Esq., our representative in said convention.

SAMUEL WOODRUFF, *Moderator*.

E. R. MILLER, *Secretary*.

RICHLAND, August 8th, 1851.

SPEECH OF HON. D. S. DICKINSON.

The President then introduced the Hon. Daniel S. Dickinson, late Senator in Congress from New York, a native of Goshen, who addressed the audience as follows :—

Mr. President, Ladies, and Gentlemen :—

Few recollections, indeed, are of deeper or holier interest, than those associated with the home of our childhood. When the mind, like the Patriarch's dove, seeks repose from its wanderings, and returns to the place of its nativity, how many emotions rise up where pleasing, painful memories struggle for the empire of the heart! How is the perilous journey of life, from its cloudless morning, with its joys and sorrows, its lights and shadows, its smiles and tears, made to pass in rapid yet serene review before us. The parts we have severally been called to act upon the great theatre of life,—the relations we have formed and the bereavements we have experienced, all rush in with their attending joys and sorrows and swell the heart too full for utterance. I am proud to boast myself a native of the town of Goshen, in this County, though removed to another state by the varying currents of fortune, while still a child. Yet, by the favor of Him, "who doeth all things well," I have been permitted, after forty-four years absence, to stand upon the threshold of what was once my happy home, and to realize the imaginings of poetic beauty in—

> "The orchard, the meadow, the deep-tangled wild-wood,
> And every lov'd scene, which my infancy knew."

The emotion which the occasion inspired, deepened by peculiar circumstances, are too sacred to pass beyond the heart where they were so painfully felt, and the fragment of the little domestic circle who lived and loved upon that cherished spot, and are yet of earth.* We have assembled here, my friends, in obedience to one of the strongest laws of our nature,—one of the best and loftiest impulses of the human heart. When we have attained the meridian of life, and see age approaching, though yet in the distance—when the passions and impulses are subdued and chastened—when we cease to believe that the "deficiencies of the present day will be supplied by to-morrow," and Hope, that terrestrial charmer, no longer promises her after-growth of joy, we turn with a feeling of devotion which the heart has never before experienced, to cherish that holy love of home which God, for benevolent purposes, has established in the deep well-springs of the heart,—to repose our head, throbbing with the busy cares of life, upon which time, perchance, has written his untimely furrows, like a wayward child, upon that pure and holy altar of domestic love—a mother's knee—saying in the language of a native poet—

"Oft from life's withered bower,
In sad communion with the past I turn,
And muse on thee, the only flower,
In memory's urn."

The children of New England, of which this State, and especially this County, has furnished her full and honorable share, have been thrown broad-cast upon the great battle-field of life, where they have been pre-eminently distinguished for their practice of the sterner virtues of manhood, and their disregard of ease, indolence, and sensual enjoyment. Though proverbial for religious veneration, and their devotion to religious observances, they have never been idle waiters upon Providence, but have acted upon the suggestion of Frederick the Great, who declared that, *Heaven always favored the course of the best disciplined troops!* But the excellencies of our common mother, have been too truthfully portrayed by others, to permit one further word of eulogy. Her sterling virtues have been traced in sober narrative, and her brow garlanded with the choicest

* Mr. Dickinson received intelligence at the celebration that an elder brother was dying.

specimens of poetry and eloquence, which modern times can furnish. All that is left me, is to cast my humble chaplet at her feet, and to declare that, though she has many sons who can bring her choicer offerings, she has none who love her more.

From the life-like delineations of the New England character, in the inimitable productions to which we have listened, we have seen that it is no extravagance to say that her sons have virtually climbed every hill-side, threaded every mountain-pass, explored every valley, fathomed every cave, analyzed every mineral, classed every plant and shrub, and "wrung their shy, retiring virtues out," passed over every lake and river, and navigated every sea; they lasso the wild horse of the Pacific border with the Indian hunter, gallop by the side of the natives upon the ponies of the Pampas, and are first and last in the mines of California. Nor is their enterprise confined to one element alone, but they pursue with success the monsters of the deep, and achieve that which in the days of the patient but afflicted Idumean was regarded so formidable, and *draw out leviathan with a hook.* In short, such is their manly independence and characteristic self-reliance, that if cast naked and helpless upon the banks of the Ganges, instead of becoming objects of charity or commiseration, they would be sure to gain a livelihood and accumulate wealth, by furnishing fuel for the Hindoo Suttees by contract. And what, it may well be enquired, is the secret power by which they move the moral, and change the face of the natural world? It is knowledge,—knowledge, industry, and virtue. What enables one hundred thousand Englishmen, in India, to cast down the temples, overthrow the idols, uproot the heathenism, and play the tyrant and tax-gatherer over seventy millions of savage black-heads, glittering in barbaric wealth, abounding in all the terrible elements of war, and burning with wild ferocity to expel the intruders from their soil? Alas! with all their natural elements of power the answer is given in this :—

> " But knowledge to their eyes her ample page,
> Rich with the spoils of time, did ne'er reveal."

Connecticut has sent forth her children, armed with a good common school education, which, like the battle blade of Fitz

James, the Saxon, has been both "sword and shield," and carved out for them success wherever it has pleased Providence to cast their lot. But it is not to the success of ordinary temporal enterprise, or the accumulation of material wealth alone, that its benefits have been limited. Its teachers and those who minister in holy things, have been forth upon their mission of light throughout the habitable globe. It has gone down to the cottage of the lowly and abject, and led its humble inmates, if deserving, to the most distinguished stations. It has triumphed in the halls of legislation, and shed a lustre upon the pathway of the most illustrious of its votaries. By its light our mothers, sisters, and daughters have fixed their gentle yet mighty impress upon our social structure, as noiseless as the dews of evening fall upon the vegetable world, and have adorned it with all that is virtuous, refined, and elevated. It has served to bind together, in ties of amity and interest, in singleness of heart and sympathy of soul, a great family of states, whose hearts throb responsive to the pulsations of liberty throughout the world,—glowing, like beacon lights upon the mountain, to warn mankind of the dangers of ambition and despotism, and to beckon them onward, through liberty and intelligence to the temple gates of happiness and peace.

The sons of New England who have participated in this system of popular beneficence, comprise a large class in the Empire State, which has generously adopted them as her own, and cast her choicest laurels upon some of the most humble; they mingle numerously with the staid and sturdy yeomanry of the Keystone; they brush the earliest dew-drops from the vast prairies of the West, and mingle their voices with the hum of the Pacific's waves. In the sunny South they stand "like men"—high minded men—like men who know their rights, and knowing, dare maintain, invoking the constitution as the ark of their political safety, and guarding their own institutions, as the vestals preserved the sacred fire. And they all, whether from the north, the south, the east, or the west, love, with the deep, pure, gushing love of sinless childhood, their dear native New England still;—love to gaze upon her cloud-cap'd hills, her fadeless sky, her sunny slopes, her smiling vales, her laughing streams; and to contemplate, with filial reverence, the condition of her refined, joyous, and happy people. But the institutions from which these blessings, under a beneficent Providence, spring, are not ours to sport with, jeopard, or destroy. We hold them in sacred trust, during the pleasure of Him who conferred it, for the benefit of those who shall come after us, to guard and preserve at the cost of life, fortune, and honor. The states of this confederacy were united to "form a more perfect union,—establish justice, insure domestic tranquility, provide for the common defence, promote the general welfare, and ensure the blessings of liberty to ourselves and our posterity." In a few years, we who are assembled here shall all be laid in the dust. When we go hence, we shall separate, many of us for years—most of us forever; but the same blue heavens and beauteous earth will be here; the same rugged hills will remain, and the same streams will dance along as merrily as now, at the music of their own rippling. Our children and children's children will be here, too, for weal or for woe,—basking in the sun-light of our heaven-favored freedom, invigorated, perfected, and beautified by the tests of time and experience, or torn by the conflicts of rival states, and despoiled by domestic violence.

Oh! what modern Erostratus shall seek to hand down an execrable name to undying infamy, by raising his parricidal hand against institutions such as these. Are we not all brethren of one tie upon this great question, which so deeply concerns our integrity and being? Let us, then, by all the bright memories of the past, by the present fruition, by hope of the future, by the spirits of just patriots made perfect, invoke all to preserve, entire, a fountain from which so much goodness flows.

SPEECH OF HON. A. J. PARKER.

Hon. AMASA J. PARKER, of Albany, Judge of the Supreme Court of New York, a native of Sharon, was next called upon, and addressed the meeting.

MR. PRESIDENT:—

WE have come from afar, to revisit the graves of our fathers and the homes of our childhood. The sentiment that prompts us lies deep in the human heart. It is akin to that which impels the faithful mussulman to visit the tomb of the Prophet, and urges the pious pilgrim on his way to the Holy Sepulchre. We stand among the weather-beaten tombs of the Puritans. Our memories recall their stern virtues, their devoted patriotism, their indomitable perseverance. Who is not proud of such an ancestry? We are indeed upon sacred ground. Our tongues refuse to give utterance to the emotions that swell our hearts, and to the recollections that crowd our memories.

We have been wanderers from our early homes. In the great living tide of emigration, we have been borne onward to other States and other lands, seeking our fortunes among strangers, mingling in all the exciting and busy and various scenes of life; and now, after many—many long years of absence, we turn our faces once more towards the place of our birth. We come to greet with delight those so long separated from us,—to gather around the ancient hearth-stone,—to rejoice in the remembrance of early associations,—to recount the various adventures of our lives, and to pay a sad tribute of respect to the memory of the departed. Can any pilgrimage be more sacred than this?

The homes of our childhood! Our hearts throb at the mention of it. Among all the labors, successes and reverses of life, it has been a green spot in our memories. It was the proof-impression of early life—ever distinct—ever bright—ineffaceable. We think of it with love and gratitude, and with a feeling of reverence that belongs only to sacred things. The home of our childhood!

> "Where'er I roam, whatever realms I see,
> My heart untrameled fondly turns to thee."

We think of it—we dream of it—we return to it. It is still home—in miniature. The fields, the buildings, the rooms, seemed much larger to our childish vision, and we recollect them as they seemed to us then. That was then our world, and of course it seemed large to us. We gaze at them, and their proportions change. Yes—they are indeed the same. They are old friends, silent but true—immoveable at least. That old stone-wall has grown a little more gray and moss-covered. It was my early friend,—my defense,—my fortification in my boyish sports and contests. It has stood, many a time, between me and harm. It looks as if it would like to speak to me now; but it is eloquent, even in its silence. And that tree, too, near by, that I climbed so often in my boyhood, and whose spreading branches furnished me a grateful shade in summer, and pockets full of chestnuts in the autumn, who will say that it is not a kind hearted old tree still? Though hollow, I am sure it is not false; and that is more than we can say of all the world. If time has made some inroads on the house, it has only kept pace with myself in that respect.

And there is the dear old hearth-stone, around which we were all gathered, as soon as it was sundown, on Saturday night; for in those days the Sabbath, with commendable promptness, was made to begin thus early. From around that hearth, ascended the morning and evening prayer: instruction, admonition, advice, affection, kindness and hope—all were centered there.

If the sons of Litchfield, who emigrated to other lands, have generally been successful in the battle of life, the reasons are obvious. While the pure atmosphere of these rugged hills, and their simple and active habits of life, gave them vigorous constitutions and physical strength, there were implanted in their hearts a high toned morality, a respect for religion and a love of good order, such as could be no where better taught than in the New

England homes of their childhood. The effect of this teaching has been felt throughout the Union:—its influence will last for ages to come.

The young man of New England,

"indocilis pauperiem pati,"

tempted by the more dazzling prospects in newer States, with a sad heart, but full of hope, leaves the comfortable roof of his father, and turns his face westward. He bears with him a good education, habits of industry and frugality, and an energy and firmness of purpose characteristic of his race. In whatever pursuit he engages, he never doubts, and rarely fails of success. Educated in the practical science of self-government, he is ready to draft constitutions and enact laws; and new States spring up along his pathway. He never forgets the institutions of his early home; and churches and common schools and colleges cluster around him. New England morals and character, though somewhat modified by a change of circumstances, are thus transmitted to the prairies and forests of the west and south. While the emigrant loses none of his attachment to the place of his birth, and none of his allegiance to his native State, he loves too the State of his adoption, and glories in the growing prosperity of the Union. With him it is no sectional feeling, but all is absorbed in his love of country. The stars and the stripes are his banner, and under them he is ready to do battle against the world. He sheds his blood freely in their defense, whether it be on the plains of Mexico or the heights of Bunker Hill. The New England emigrant is ubiquitous. You find him in every State of the confederacy, upholding the principles, the constitution and the flag of the Union, and ready, if needs be, to die in their defense. Can a Union, so bound together, be severed? Never! never! The New England emigrant has already reached the shores of the Pacific, and is looking out for a foothold beyond it; and it is certain he will be satisfied with no resting place till he has planted on it the flag of his native land. Astronomers have discovered several new planets within the last few years, but unless they rub up their glasses and keep busily employed in their observations, Jonathan will beat them in adding stars to our national galaxy.

But, ladies and gentlemen, I should do great injustice to my own feelings, if I failed to speak of Litchfield as it now is. I know that no one has gone out from this County, who does not feel most deeply his obligations to Litchfield; and every returning emigrant, who has traveled, as I have done for the last few days, in different parts of the County, looking at the monuments of the past, enjoying the beautiful prospect every where presented to the eye, and admiring the beneficent changes that enterprise and industry have accomplished, must feel that he has much more reason to be proud of you than you have of him. For I believe there is not to be found, any where within the same extent of country, more real happiness and true comfort, than in the County of Litchfield. The neat looking farm-houses, the well cultivated farms, the beautiful stock scattered upon the hill-side, the mountains cultivated to their very tops, and the vallies vocal with the hum of industry, present a picture so beautiful, that it seems the realization of a poet's dream. The very streams dance gaily along, as if rejoicing in their successful labors at the water-wheel. Here property seems to be enjoyed by its possessor—not squandered in extravagance—nor its use denied by parsimony. Here are neither the extremes of wealth or poverty; but competence, health, thrift and happiness; the just and sure reward of industry and virtue every where abound. And then, to pass from these scenes into the presence of such an assemblage of intellect and intelligence as I see before me, I may well ask, where else on the habitable globe, except among such a population, can so much happiness be found?

Though the New England emigrant marries abroad, his influence is still felt in forming our national character. But he more frequently comes back and takes a New England wife to his home in the West. Who can estimate the value, to the community in which she lives, of such a wife and such a mother? I have no occasion here, in this assemblage, to enlarge upon the virtues and graces of the women of New England.

I have often had reason to be proud of the emigrant sons of Connecticut, and never to blush for them. A few years ago, a Page came to all the members of the National House of Representatives at Washington, and asked them to write down their names, and ages, and the places of their birth. I was gratified to find that nine of the members from the State of New York, were born in Connecticut. I have had a right, sir, to be proud of the sons of Connecticut when I have found them every where distinguished as much for their integrity and industry, as for their intelligence and success in life. They are prominent alike in the cabinet and in the field,—in arts and in commerce,—in the halls of science, and in the various departments of literature.

But, Mr. President, while I speak thus proudly and truly of Litchfield—of Connecticut—of New England,—let me say a kind word for the State of my adoption. We love our native State with a feeling like our love for parents; it is mixed with profound respect and veneration. But the love for the State of our adoption is like that we feel for our wives and our children. We are part of it, and our highest pleasure is to advance its progress and promote its interests. Sir, I have a right to be proud of the great State of New York,—first in population, in wealth, in commerce, in means of internal communication, and in all the elements of greatness. She may well claim the distinguished appellation of the "Empire State." But while she moves majestically on, under her glorious motto, "*excelsior*," and looks confidently forward to the high destiny in store for her country and her race, she seeks for no glory, she will rejoice in no elevation that is not shared by her sisters of the confederacy.

SPEECH OF HON. F. A. TALLMADGE.

Hon. Frederick A. Tallmadge, Recorder of the City of New York, a native of Litchfield, being next called, addressed the audience as follows:

Mr. Chairman:—

Having but just arrived in the village of my nativity, I did not anticipate being called upon to address you, and I assure you that I should much have preferred being a silent listener, to being a speaker upon this occasion.

But, sir, since I have been placed upon the stand by the kind partiality of my fellow citizens, it appears to be expected that I should say something to you; and indeed how could I be silent when amidst the hills and valleys that surround the place of my nativity?

The very trees that adorn your streets, and the residences of our fathers, appear like old friends, and recall the pleasures and sports of childhood. I see myself surrounded by many who in my youth, I thought venerable, and I thank God that they are still spared to participate in the festivities of this day, and as evidences of the salubrity of your climate.

Gentlemen who have preceded me have spoken with just enthusiasm of the political institutions of good old Connecticut, and of the laws applicable to our common schools; they no doubt deserve all the laudation that they have received; but, Mr. President, when I cast my eye at that old school house where I was taught my alphabet, when in a warm afternoon I sat upon a bench without any support to my back, with one eye almost closed with fatigue, and my intellect was aroused and brightened by the application of my master's ratan, I confess that my reminiscence are not of any agreeable character; and when I come to Litchfield and cast my eye at that old school house, I look upon it with any other feeling than that of pleasure. I am the more impressed with this feeling when I see upon this stand, that Rev. gentleman, (Rev. Dr. Robbins,) who taught me my Latin and Greek, and whose exhortations to me, when I had been derelict in my studies, are quite fresh in my recollection. I look upon him indeed with veneration for his patient efforts to instruct me, and reverence him as the last of the "white tops."—(Referring to the white top boots worn by the Rev. Dr.)—Laughter.

But I have no doubt that the public schools have been useful, and so have been many such gentlemen as Dr. Robbins, who have prepared us to be placed under the care of the distinguished President of Yale College who has honored this occasion by his presence.

But, Mr. Chairman, why have we not reason to be proud of a County which has presented the great State of New York some of its most distinguished sons; which has, indeed, sent its children into every State of this glorious Union, and thereby diffused those principles of honor and morality, which our forefathers instilled into their youthful bosoms? Proud am I that the distinguished Senator from New York, Mr. Dickinson, whom I am proud to call my friend—imbibed his first principles, and received the first rudiments of his education amongst the hills of Litchfield; and I have no doubt, Mr. President, that the enviable elevation that he has attained, has been attributable to your common schools, and especially to the free use of the birch and ratan, that he experienced in his youthful days.

[Mr. Dickinson. I had a fair chance afterwards, when I was a teacher, and I paid off the old score.] Laughter.

Mr. Tallmadge. I have no doubt of that, but to recur to Litchfield and its sons.

I see with pride and pleasure on your platform, another distinguished son of our County, the Hon. A. J. Parker, who, with *three* others, natives of this County, occupy seats upon the bench of the Supreme Court, of your sister State, New York.

Sir, how could it be otherwise, when they sprung from the soil that is consecrated by the memories of the Wolcotts, a Kirby, a Reeves, a Tracy, a Gould, an Allen, and many others equally distinguished, whose names and whose characters would afford me a delightful theme for remark—gentlemen whose influence was not limited to our native State, but whose wisdom and characters aided much in controlling the destinies of our common country, and in establishing that happy government under which this nation is attaining such an enviable position among the nations of the earth. But, Mr. Chairman, when alluding to some of those individuals who have been so much distinguished in the history of our County, it will not be regarded as invidious if I allude to one who will be remembered by some of you, and whose excellence of character must be known to all: I allude to the Rev. Mr. Champion, whose venerable appearance is deeply impressed upon my youthful recollection; short in stature, with a head adorned by a massive wig, a countenance that indicated that sincerity and purity of purpose, that characterized his clerical conduct in life; during the revolutionary war, this venerable pastor presided over the flock that worshiped in yonder church, and I shall be pardoned in relating an incident which was given to me by my venerable father, (Col. Tallmadge,) illustrative of that fervent zeal and stirring patriotism, that characterized the clergy of Connecticut, during that momentous struggle.

It was at that period of the revolution, when the whole country was in a state of great alarm, in anticipation of the arrival of Cornwallis, with a formidable army upon our shores, my father was passing through Litchfield with a regiment of Cavalry; they attended church on the Sabbath, when the reverend divine addressed the God of battles thus: " Oh Lord, we view with terror and dismay, the approach of the enemies of thy holy religion; wilt thou send storm and tempest, and scatter them to the uttermost parts of the earth; but, peradventure, should any escape thy vengeance, collect them together again, Oh Lord, as in the hollow of thy hand, and let thy lightnings play upon them."

This was the patriotic feeling that inspired our forefathers, and this spirit, which the Clergy of New England breathed from their pulpits, contributed largely to secure that independence which we now so richly enjoy:—blessed be their memories!

Mr. Chairman,—while participating in the festivities of this day, while recurring to the scenes of our youth, and while many of us, who have strayed far from our native hills, are permitted to recall those scenes, and look upon those hills again, it is pleasurable indeed, but that pleasure is commingled with some sad thoughts. In the meridian of life, I return to you almost a stranger here. When I cast my eyes about this vast assembly, how little am I known to you, and how few of you are known to me ; although born but a short distance from this very spot, I look about, and enquire, where are the ashes of my ancestry, and family connexions whom I left here ? all deposited in yonder churchyard. Where are those distinguished citizens and excellent neighbors, that constituted a society in this County, of which their descendants can ever speak with pride and pleasure? They, too, are in the silent tomb. It is pleasant to refer to their memories. It is sad to know that we cannot recall them.

I will close, Mr. Chairman, with the expression of the hope, that, while the canvas that covers us this day will soon decay, may *we* meet again at the next Centennial Celebration, and that you may preside over us.

SPEECH OF DAVID BUELL, ESQ.

MR. BUELL, of Troy, N. Y., a native of Litchfield, was requested by the Chair to address the audience, and made a few remarks to the following effect.

MR. PRESIDENT :—

I feel much embarrassed at your unexpected call upon me to address this assembly at so late an hour, and after the topics most appropriate to the occasion have been effectually used up by the series of addresses which have enchained the attention of this assembly for the last two days. What can he do, who comes after the King? Indeed, I find myself too much affected in my spirits by what I have witnessed since I came here, and by the recollections of my earlier years, to attempt to interest you by any thing which I could say.

Standing within a few rods of the spot where I was born, after having been a truant from the village of my nativity for fifty-four years, and surrounded by natives of the same town and County, I find myself amidst strange faces;—men and women of Litchfield, but of another generation. I look around this large assembly, to find some of the countenances which were once so familiar, and whose looks are so vividly impressed on my memory. I have recognized but two individuals, among the present residents of Litchfield, who resided here in 1797, when my father's family removed from this town. Many of the descendants of those who then resided here, still occupy these hills, and many objects remain, which forcibly recall the scenes of childhood to my recollection.

Most of the dwellings of the families who resided in the village at the period of my removal, yet remain, and bring to my remembrance the names and looks and characters of those who then occupied them.

At the head of the North street stands the mansion then occupied by the Catlin family. A few rods south, and on the west side of the street, stands the mansion which belonged to Andrew Adams, then Chief Justice of the Superior Court. The dwelling next south, was the residence of Lynde Lord, who long filled the office of Sheriff of the County. The next dwelling south of Sheriff Lord's, was the residence of the Misses Pierce—still the abode of the venerable and much respected lady who founded the Litchfield Female Seminary, which, although one of the earliest institutions for the education of females, was long and widely celebrated. Few, if any female seminaries, have been better conducted, and more successful in elevating the standard of female education in our country. I doubt not that many ladies in this assembly could bear their testimony to the excellence of this pioneer seminary. Next south, stands the dwelling in which Dr. Daniel Sheldon resided, who long held a very high rank among the physicians of this State. A few rods further south, I recognize the mansion of Gen. Uriah Tracy, and which, at a later period, became the residence of the late Judge Gould. Of the eminence of the former as a lawyer and statesman, and of the latter as a profound jurist, it can not be necessary to speak in this place. The next house south, was the residence of Col. Benjamin Tallmadge, a distinguished officer of the Revolution, and long an influential Representative in Congress. Nearly opposite to the mansion of Col. Tallmadge, was that of Julius Deming, for many years a successful and honorable merchant. The house next south of the Square, on the west side of the street, was the residence of Major Seymour, another veteran of the Revolution. A few rods further south, stands the venerable mansion, long occupied by Tapping Reeve, a great and good man, the founder of the Litchfield Law School, long celebrated through our land. Nearly opposite to the mansion of Judge Reeve, was that of the Wolcotts, father and son; and a few rods below, was that of Ephraim Kirby.

The names of all whom I have mentioned must be familiar to a Litchfield audience, even of another generation. I confine my remarks to reminiscences of the village, then called, "*Town Hill.*"

I left the County at too early an age, to have been much acquainted in other towns. Town Hill always charmed all who beheld it, by its beautiful native scenery, and was greatly distinguished for the high intellectual and moral character of its inhabitants.

The admirable Addresses and Poem to which this gratified assembly have been listening, have brought to the recollection of the old, and the knowledge of the young, the names of many, both in the village and through the County, whose memory will be cherished by the generations who will occupy these hills when other centuries shall have rolled away. But, Mr. President, I forbear to trespass further upon ground already so well occupied.

SPEECH OF EDWARD TOMPKINS, ESQ.

THE President next introduced EDWARD TOMPKINS, Esq., of Binghamton, N. Y., whose parents were natives of Watertown.

MR. PRESIDENT, LADIES AND GENTLEMEN :—

I NEED not say to any business man here, that there can be no greater embarrassment in life, than to be unexpectedly, and with empty pockets, called upon with a *sight*-draft. That happens to be my case now; and the embarrassment which the draft now made upon me causes, is aggravated beyond measure by the fact, that, sitting here since yesterday morning, I have learned that I can neither beg nor borrow any thing with which to pay it. Every thing that would be appropriate here, has been already spread before you. Would I go for incidents to the history of Litchfield County? The distinguished jurist who, yesterday, so eloquently bound us, has told us all, and I must repeat, not half so well, a twice-told tale. Would I seek with wit, or fancy, to amuse and instruct you? The brilliant Poet, whom we honor and revere with every fibre of our Litchfield hearts, has exhausted the language, and the whole vocabulary of wit was here used up by him forever! (Laughter.) Would I go further on; and in the domestic relations, so dear to our hearts, so fondly prized, find aught with which, for a moment, I could hope to enlist your attention? The truthful, courageous, heroic divine, who has this morning illustrated them here so well, has again made me bankrupt, and the draft which I would so wish to honor, must yet be protested, unless I can find some claim upon your indulgence that will induce you to release me now. I think I have found it.

Each of the gentlemen who have addressed you, is a *son* of Litchfield: and while the relation is a very dear one, let me tell you that good old mother Litchfield, as they affectionately call her, has yet a dearer. It is a principle in human nature, which we all discover very early in life, and which, as our children grow up around us, we usually see developed in a still more striking manner, that however stern parents may be with their own children, they are, invariably, quite indulgent enough to their grand-children. Applying that principle here, I incur no hazard in assuming, that however severe old Litchfield may have been with her children, yet when she comes to her grand-children, she will spoil them, every one. That is my position now; I am one of, and speak for *the grandchildren*; and I claim here, and now, the fullest measure of indulgence, which our good old grandmother can bestow. The principle upon which I now rely so confidently, was taught me when on my first visit, in childhood, to my Litchfield grandmother; she sweetened the new milk she gave me, when had it been for her own children, she would have churned it before she would have let them taste it; and the lesson I then learned, has stood me in good stead this day.

I would not, willingly, disturb the harmony that prevails here, by any personal grief, yet there has been one occurrence of which I am compelled to complain. I listened yesterday afternoon, with as broad and open-mouthed an interest as any one of you here; and how was I, beyond measure, astonished, when the reverend gentleman—he who has filled the earth with melodies which we could almost fancy, would be sung in heaven—who has shown us that he, like the divine alluded to this morning, can unite two worlds on earth, who charmed us by his brilliant wit, and melted us with his eloquence; when he, a stranger as I supposed to me and to my household, actually painted, at full length before you, and before all Litchfield, feature by feature—even to the color of her hair and of her eyes—saying nothing of the unpardonable allusion to the *color of a portion of her dress*, upon which none but the most heterodox of divines would ever have ventured;—my own Yankee wife. (Laughter.) Think of my surprise—three hundred miles from home, thus unexpectedly to encounter such a picture! Would the gentleman tell me that it was only a general picture? That is the way Clergymen always escape, when their *general* sketches become so personal, that every body applies them! (Laughter.) I had not supposed the reverend gentleman was acquainted with her; and I should have been proud beyond measure, if he had come *openly*, *when I was at home*, to have welcomed him there. *It may be*, he has never been there; (Laughter.) Yet an idea suggests itself to me which, I am afraid, will convince you and *me* that there is, at least, *some* doubt about it. There are no two persons, it is said, who look *exactly* alike. If this be true, it follows that no one description will *exactly* describe them, and inasmuch as I know that this is true, in every line and letter, the reverend gentleman stands convicted beyond the hope of escape, of having resorted to personalities in the portrait he has painted before you. (Great laughter.) I can only say that I am not, naturally, distrustful, or suspicious; and I hope, in the ways of Providence, *if all is right*, (laughter,) that the reverend Gentleman may yet be led to cross my threshold, and that I may have the pleasure, and the honor, of introducing to him the original of the portrait he has so brightly and beautifully drawn.

But, ladies and gentlemen, this is not the tone in which I should address you now. Thoughts of too much moment press upon us,—interests as extensive as our lives. We all feel deeply, that while we have listened, till we can afford to spare the repetition, to eulogiums upon our lofty hills and bracing atmosphere, we have not heard enough, even, to satisfiy our cravings of the domestic relations, the rich social worth which has made Litchfield County what it is. It has been said, over and over, and cannot be too often repeated, that it is these that have made the great men of Litchfield; these that have sent her sons abroad to be crowned with honors and to fill the high places of our land, to explore every recess of creation and return laden with the trophies of their peaceful victories, only to lay them in triumph at the feet of their common mother. But when we look around us to determine—and our attention has been already called to it—what it is to which Litchfield County owes the great results her sons have accomplished, we find we must go back to the dead to seek it; and it becomes us, not sadly—not sorrowfully—but triumphantly, to keep them ever before us, and to recall them from the graves where they are buried. The dead of Litchfield County! That mighty army! Oh think of it, of the host innumerable that would be called forth here and now, if the graves where the sons of Litchfield lie buried could give up their dead. Oh think of the mighty lessons they have taught—the mighty labors they have wrought! The dead of Litchfield! Lost, yet found forever,—absent, yet present now and always,—dead, but living in that glorious life, which, commencing on the confines of time, spreads onward and ever onward, through the endless ages of eternity.

SPEECH OF GEORGE W. HOLLEY, ESQ.

George W. Holley, Esq., of Niagara Falls, a native of Salisbury, was introduced to the meeting and said :—

Mr. President, Ladies, and Gentlemen :—

If the gentleman who last addressed you was in danger of bankruptcy, on account of being compelled to repeat a twice told tale,—if he was a *two story*, I am a *three story* bankrupt; for there is nothing to be said, appropriate to the occasion, which has not already been *well* said. But before proceeding to address you, in a more serious strain, permit me to follow the high example already set, and relate to you an anecdote. When I was a boy I went to see a menagerie. The whole menagerie consisted of an elephant, who was exhibited upon a barn floor. Among those who came to see him, was a tall, lean, wiry, six foot Yankee, who soon became particularly interested in the animal. After walking around him with his hands in his pantaloons pockets, and scrutinizing him closely, and remarking that he was "the curioustest critter that ever he seen," he began to ply the keeper with questions about him. After getting through with his color, his thick hide, his big legs, and his "queer feet," which "didn't have shoes on 'em like a hos," and "wasn't split up like a cow's," he came at last to the *trunk*, which the keeper told him he used mainly as a weapon of defence. "Weapon!" said Jonathan; "weapon! I shouldn't think it was good for any thing for sich use. Why, it's a limber thing, he can't du any thing with it." The result of the parley was, that Jonathan wanted to *hold the elephant* by the trunk, and the keeper was willing he should try the experiment. Accordingly, the keeper kept the elephant quiet, while Jonathan got his trunk under his left arm, seized his own coat collar with his left hand, and put his right arm around the big post next to the "big bay." After Jonathan got himself fairly fixed and settled in his hold, he told the keeper to "let his critter go." After getting the spectators all into one corner of the barn, the keeper stepped aside and told the elephant to take care of himself:—whereupon, he proceeded to give his trunk a twist and a jerk, and Jonathan went across the barn—as a big boy near me said—"all sorts of ends fustwards." But with one particular end he struck the little barn-door, knock'ed it off the hinges and rolled nearly across the barn-yard. Being, fortunately, but little hurt, he got up, and while brushing off the straw and dirt from his vest and pants, (for his coat was all torn off him,) he exclaimed: "Well, I swow, *he is putty stout!*"

There is nothing, from *holding an elephant* to counterfeiting nutmegs and cucumber seeds, that some Yankees will not undertake.

Mr. President,—as an immigrant from this County, I have the honor to be one of those who represent that portion of it included within the limits of the town of Salisbury. That town, through her material and inanimate representatives, has, heretofore, often been heard on public occasions, speaking for herself in tones of thunder;* and the effects of her shots have been often seen and felt in the wasting ranks and sinking ships of her country's enemies. But roaring cannon and booming shot are entirely alien to the voice with which she would address you on this most interesting occasion. She would mingle her warm congratulations, her warmer sympathies, her warmest welcome, with those of her sister towns, on this day. She would unite with them in coming up, with filial pride, affection, and respect, to offer new homage to their common mother, to weave new wreaths for her brows, to lay fresh garlands upon her altars, to sing new praises to her honored name, to exchange heart-felt greetings with others of her children gathered here, to talk of the past and to pray for the future. This occasion is full of interest to every one who hails from Litchfield County.

* Most of the cannon and shot for the Revolutionary War were made in this town.

The rattling thunder in her rocky hills;
The silver music of her gushing rills;
The cold and piercing wintry winds wild wail;
The sweeping cadences of the rushing gale;
The green hill-sides' cool, refreshing shade;
The tinkling cow-bell in the wooded glade;
The bleating flocks and the lowing herds;
The hum of insects and the songs of birds;
The solemn tunes he sung at singing school;
The school house, where he taught the man a fool
Who taught, and questioned much his right to rule;
The merry *dance*, in merry ranks arrayed,
Which still he danced as still the fiddle play'd,
When sleep had settled on his drowsy head;
The boat in which the tugging oar he plied;
The snow-clad hill down which he used to slide;
The gleeful music which the sleigh-bells made,
While the sleigh-shoes, a running octave play'd;
The impressive sound of the old church bell
In the joyous peal or the solemn knell;
The house of God—the good man's prayer,
The good man's warning which impressed him there.

It is pleasant to look again on these familiar scenes, which are daguerreotyped on all our hearts; it is music to our ears to hear again these familiar sounds and voices—it is gladness to our hearts to mingle again with the kindred and friends of life's early day.

But, my friends, you have heard enough of this. Permit me to recall to your attention the closing paragraph of the excellent address to which you listened on yesterday. It referred to the *Union*. And if *my* voice can not have the weight of admonition, let it at least have the force of entreaty, while I pray you to look upon the federal Union of these States as your political ark of the covenant, sacred in your eyes, dear to your hearts, and to be defended and sustained with all your strength. Let not water drown, let not fire burn, let not cart ropes nor chains strangle nor draw out of you; let not principalities nor powers, nor anything else under heaven, take from you your conviction of its necessity, your faith in its efficacy, nor your *determination* that it *shall be* perpetuated. Let us believe that America is, politically speaking, God's present Israel. And though disputes may arise, though local interests may lead to dissentions, though nullification or secession may rear their horrid front, though foul treason may plot to betray us, though unholy factionists, and more unholy fanatics, may seek to embroil us, still let us cling with the tenacity of an unyielding grasp to the faith that our *Union* shall be saved at every hazard—that our institutions shall be preserved through every trial—that the spirit of American freedom shall emerge brighter and purer, from every conflict—that still the chosen Israel shall pass unharmed the troubled Jordan, and pitch its tents in the land of promise and of peace!

MR. GOULD'S REMARKS.

George Gould, Esq., of Troy, N. Y., a native of Litchfield, was next called upon by the President, and spoke as follows.

Mr. President:—

Apologies and themes have all been touched on; and little is left to be said by any one that comes forward now. But twenty years ago I carried away with me a Litchfield *heart*, and I have brought it back to-day: and I will answer to a Litchfield County call, whenever and wherever made.

It has ever been said that those who are born and reared among high hills, have strong local attachments. It should be as truly said, that those reared where high moral principles prevail, likewise have strong *moral* attachments. For me, I profess to nothing above what is common; I claim nothing fabulous; and I trust I am not earth-born,—an Antaeus. But I have this resemblance to the fabled giant;—whenever my feet touch my native soil, I gather new vigor from the contact. Never do I approach these hills, without feeling the exhilaration of a school boy. We, in the valleys and by the river sides, know nothing of your clear atmosphere. You breathe a stronger, purer air; you feel better, live nearer heaven—feel as near heaven as every one of us thought himself, when a boy. Your climate has been objected to; and it is, in winter, dreary and cold. But your State's best poet has said,

— "the wing
Of Life's best angel, Health, is on your gales
Through sun and snow; and in the Autumn time
Earth has no purer, and no lovelier clime."

This is a sentiment to which every one here will respond, and which has been responded to, by those coming from Connecticut, the world over; and no one of them forgets it. The whole air around you is full of every thing beautiful, and bright, and great. Such is your land.

But the *moral* influence, spread abroad in this community, is the great source of its power. One hundred years since, you were organized as a County. And they who composed the County so organized, had come from, been part of, a colony, whose members, at its first organization, were resolved to be governed by the laws of God, till they could make better.

[The speaker was here interrupted by the Rev. Dr. Robbins, who sat on the platform, with "Oh, no; not so!"—the reverend gentleman supposing the speaker to assert,—as has often been jocosely said,—that the founders of the colony at Hartford adopted as part of their municipal code, a *formal resolution* of a purport similar to the words used by the speaker. The speaker continued; first addressing Dr. Robbins.]

You misunderstand me, sir. I did not say that they passed any such formal resolution: though if I did, (as I do not pretend to *remember* the time,) I should but "tell the story as 'twas told to me." Yet "multitude of years should teach wisdom;" and I might be content to be corrected by the lips of age. I said, merely, and mean to say, that at any rate, (whether or not any formal resolution, such, or similar, was passed,) such *was the spirit of the men*. And you stand here, to-day, what you are, as the *result of that spirit*. Governed by those principles and laws, (resolved, or unresolved,) as they are seen to exist throughout this land, and founded on such a moral and religious basis, we see the source of the influence and the honors, of both the homespun and the elegant age.

A people that makes *the Bible* a text-book in schools; that makes that creed and that code the foundation of its political and moral teachings, must ever exert great influence on all within their reach. Among them, a sense "of *duty, God-commanded*, over-canopies all life. It penetrates to the remotest cottage, to the simplest heart. There is an inspiration in such a people: one may say, in a more special sense, 'the inspiration of the Almighty giveth them understanding.'"

As the result of such teachings, years and years ago, Litchfield County was prominent in all those noble enterprises for the benefit of mankind, which have extended their blessed influences over the wide world. I can not better illustrate this, than by the fact, (which I remember to have heard many years ago,) that once, when the great enterprise for civilizing and Christianizing foreign and barbarous nations was halting for want of means, and its wheels had almost stopped, the auxiliaries of Litchfield County sent in a liberal, large supply, and the work moved on. The reverend men of those days, who had charge of the work, then said they "*had reason to bless God for Litchfield County.*" And I have always felt,—as every one here has,—as every one bred where such principles are instilled, and where they remain, must feel,—that we, at least, have always and every where "reason to bless God for Litchfield County."

SPEECH OF HENRY DUTTON, ESQ.

Henry Dutton, Esq., of New Haven, Professor in the Yale Law School, a native of Watertown, was next introduced, and said:—

Mr. President, Ladies, and Gentlemen:—

I shall make no excuse or apology for appearing before you at this time, notwithstanding the displays of eloquence which you have already heard, for I hold that the man who can not say something on such an occasion as this, can have no soul. I never in my life have spent two such days of pleasure and profit, as these, which you, as well as I, have enjoyed. On coming to this place, I passed by the place of my birth, by the hill on which my eyes first opened on the prospect around me; and O, what a prospect! It was no level plain upon which my eyes first opened; but it was a broader horizon than the inhabitants of a plain can ever witness in their lives. And every thing that I have seen, the hills and the valleys, the streams and the wood-lands, have reminded me of the days of my childhood; and especially here have I been presented with a perfect panorama of what passed from the days of my birth, to the time that I entered upon the active duties of life. When we come together here, it is highly important that we should feel gratitude to our common mother; and I have been disposed to look and inquire, what are those things for which I should feel individually grateful. Of these, one is, that I had my birth here, and that in my youth I was one of the farmers of Litchfield County. That gave me strength and vigor, which have enabled me to endure a great amount of labor, both of body and of mind, and I have often thought since, and I presume others have concurred with me in opinion, that it would have been better had I again become one of the "princes of the land." But on returning here and looking at the improvements which have been made, and seeing how much the science of agriculture has gone forward, I have become discouraged from any personal attempts; for I find myself far behind the age;—so I have made up my mind that I will never try to be a farmer again.

This is not the only benefit I derived from being brought up in the County of Litchfield. My first impressions of female beauty and female character are connected with Litchfield County. My ideas of beauty of countenance are associated with the fresh glow of health, which has been heightened by the cool breezes of the north-west, that sweep over these hills; and my impressions of female character are also associated with my recollections of the young ladies of this County. I have had opportunities, since, of seeing grace of motion in a great variety of forms. I have seen ladies move with grace in the dance, in the waltz, and in the polka; but, for real grace of motion, as well as grace of the heart, "O, leeze me on the spinning wheel."

We have been referred to days that are past, and our attention has been directed to those who heretofore have done honor to the County of Litchfield; but I think it may be well to cast a glance, at least, to the present, to see whether the present generation will be able to bear the burthen laid upon them by their ancestors. We have been referred to the bar, and we have been told of the men,—but we need not have been told, for their praises have always rung in our ears,—who distinguished the bar and the bench in this County. Now, I will admit that they raised temples to justice; but I thank God, that at the present day we have at least a Church, and if not quite so large, it is, at all events, quite as well furnished. The days that are past were distinguished for theologians; but we have theologians still. We have had men who were doctors of divinity, who are now laid in their graves; but there are men of the present day, too, who bear that distinguished honor, and although heretofore, in the century that has passed, it has been customary for theologians to go on a pilgrimage to the Lake of Geneva, I think, in the century to come, there will be pilgrimages to Lake Raumaug.

So it is in the political field. It will be recollected, that a short time since there was a general alarm felt, that the Union was in danger, and it became a common question, and a matter of common interest, that the State of Connecticut should be able to do something, and send some man to the seat of government who would be able to render aid in forging chains which would bind the Union together. And when her citizens looked around for the proper person, and searched every other County in the State, they could not find a man who was accustomed to give hard blows enough, until attention was turned to the workshops of Litchfield County, and there they found a Smith; and if the Smiths of Litchfield can not give hard blows, I should like to know who can? The same feeling pervaded every quarter of the State. This was particularly true a few years ago of the western district, comprising the counties of Fairfield and Litchfield. These two counties had a man in Congress in whom they put implicit confidence, and who was every way worthy of that confidence;—one who had managed their affairs well. Every body said he was as good a Butler as had existed since the days of Pharaoh. But here was an alarm about the Union, again, and they wanted somebody to stand guard; they did not care so much about a man to take care of their affairs, but they wanted one who could see danger from afar, and they turned their attention to Litchfield County, and got a man who had always lived on the top of one of the highest hills, and had been looking and looking till he had almost looked his eyes out. He had been accustomed to look so long that many called him *See More*, (Seymour.) And now, so long as we have a Smith to forge chains to bind us together, and a Seymour to stand guard, I think the Union will be safe. (Laughter.)

Mr. President, Litchfield County has done something in another matter. This County was not very much distinguished in its earlier days for poetry; the people then cared more about the realities of life than mere imaginary existences. But at length it was thought desirable that poetry should be brought over from the other side of the Atlantic, and the great question was how it should be done. Here was the sea intervening, and it was feared that before poetry could be got over, it would be lost in the ocean. But they looked for aid to Litchfield County, and she erected a bridge across the ocean, a regular Pierre-pont, over which the genius of poetry passed, and brought with her the sweet "Airs of

Palestine." Litchfield County has done something, too, in the way of the mechanical arts. I should be glad to know how the world could get along, even at the present day, without the aid of Litchfield County clocks? The men might know when to get up in the morning, and go to bed at night; but how in the world would their wives know when to get dinner, if it were not for Litchfield County clocks? Then, again, I suppose the world could have got along as it always had done in years gone by, without those means of communication which exist at the present period. But railroads have come to be a sort of necessity, and I should like to know how we could have had railroads if it had not been for the iron mines in Litchfield County? And after the rails were provided, if one of the sons of that County had not kindly consented to be the President of one Railroad Company, the Secretary of another, and a Director of the rest, so that he might be called the *bear-all* (Burrall,) of the whole concern,—we might have had to travel in wagons still, and instead of there being such a number of sons and daughters gathered here from all parts of the world, there would have been so few here on this occasion, that our friends would have had no reason to spread such a broad tent as this for our accommodation. So we see that our very enjoyments, as well as reminiscences, are owing to our good old mother Litchfield.

Mr. President, the present occasion is not only one of joyousness, but one of seriousness also. We ought not only to look and see to what we are indebted for the present, but we should remember that we stand upon the commencement of another century; we ought to realize and feel that of whatever advantage Litchfield County has been to us, whatever it has made us, there is the higher weight of responsibility resting upon us that when another Centennial is celebrated, our descendants and our successors may come together here and recount with honor and with pride what has been done during another century. If Litchfield County, beginning as we have heard a century ago, a mere waste, a howling wilderness, with here and there a few bright spots, a few settlers in one place and another, has done so much, what ought we to do, and what ought Litchfield County to do in the century, upon which we have entered, starting as we do from where they left off, and commencing with all these advantages thus gathered together and placed at our disposal? Nor is this the only consideration which should weigh upon our minds. We must recollect that the arts, within the last half century, have made man a different being from what he was before. The telegraph and railroads have given man a species of ubiquity; he can speak and his voice will be heard for thousands of miles. The very speeches which these distinguished gentlemen have been making here to-day, will probably be read in St. Louis or New Orleans, to-morrow. Man has now a power to speak to a much greater number of men than ever before, and can exercise an influence upon a far greater number of individuals; and this throws upon him a responsibility, which nothing but the training which Litchfield County has given to her sons would ever enable him to pass through with credit. Let every son of Litchfield County, while he recounts with gratitude what has been done by the County for him, while he recalls with pride what has been done by his forefathers, remember that we who are here now are commencing a new career; and let us so conduct and so exert ourselves in whatever situations we may be placed, that the next century will have more deeds to recount, and the next Centennial will be held with a greater degree of satisfaction and pride.

SONG.

Auld Lang Syne was then admirably sung;—the stanzas by the choir, and the chorus by the audience;—in the following words, prepared for the occasion, by the Rev. H. Goodwin, of Canaan.

1

"Should auld acquaintance be forgot,
And never brought to mind?
Should auld acquaintance be forgot,
And days of Auld Lang Syne?
    For Auld Lang Syne my friends,
    For Auld Lang Syne,
    We'll join the hand of kindness yet
    For Auld Lang Syne.

2

Our Fathers here their dwellings reared,
In social state combined,
These swelling fields their labors cleared,
For Auld Lang Syne.
    "For Auld Lang Syne," &c.

3

Those ancient homes they guarded well,
And stood by freedom's shrine;

And many a fearless warrior fell,
In days of Auld Lang Syne.
"For Auld Lang Syne," &c.

4

And we were nursed amid these hills,
And in these vales reclined;
But we have wandered far away
Since days of Auld Lang Syne.
"For Auld Lang Syne," &c.

5

We've roamed across the prairie wild,
The mountain pass have climbed,
And placed the school-house in the wil d,
Since days of Auld Lang Syne.
"For Auld Lang Syne," &c.

6

We've cleared and reaped the fields of toil;
We've bid the church-bells chime;
And raised the halls of learning high,
Since days of Auld Lang Syne.
"For Auld Lang Syne," &c.

7

We've mingled in the city's strife,
We've delved within the mine,
And braved the ocean's stormy waves,
Since days of Auld Lang Syne.
"For Auld Lang Syne," &c.

8

Hope lured us onward in our course,
While joy around us shined;
But many a cloud of care hath pass'd,
Since days of Auld Lang Syne.
"For Auld Lang Syne," &c.

9

The sturdy men of yore have gone,
And brothers in their prime;
The lov'd and good have disappeared,
Since days of Auld Lang Syne,
"For Auld Lang Syne," &c.

10

We part again to distant scenes,
And leave this hallowed shrine;
But oft we'll think with grateful praise,
Of days of Auld Lang Syne.
"For Auld Lang Syne," &c.

PRAYER.

The following Prayer was then offered by Rev. FOSDICK HARRISON, now of Bethany :—

GOD of our fathers, we rejoice that we may recognize Thee as our God ; that Thou hast kindly brought us together under circumstances of so much interest, and surrounded us with so many testimonials of Thy loving kindness, and that Thou art calling upon us to render our united tribute of gratitude to Thee, the Author and Giver of all our mercies. It becomes us, as descendants of a puritan ancestry, to render thanks to Thy name, for all the mercy manifested to our fathers in days that are past; that Thou didst mercifully sustain them in their days of trial, darkness and peril; that Thou didst enable them to lay broad and deep the foundations of all those institutions, civil and religious, with which we have been blessed. We thank Thee that it was their first care to erect churches, and to provide, by common schools, for the education of the rising generation. We bless Thee, our Heavenly Father, that we had fathers and mothers who early took us by the hand and led us up to the house of prayer, and placed upon us the broad seal of Thine own everlasting covenant, and taught us to remember the Sabbath and reverence the sanctuary. We thank Thee for all the hallowed influences which, through their instrumentality, have come down to us, their descendants, and we bless Thee that from distant parts of this widely extended land, so many sons of this beloved section of our country have been permitted to assemble here, and mingle their congratulations, and repeat their testimonials of respect for each other and their native land. We thank Thee for all the interesting scenes we have enjoyed, and now, our Father, as the hour of separation has arrived, as we part to meet no more on earth, under circumstances like the present, let a deep solemnity pervade every mind ; and while we feel duly grateful for all Thy loving kindness manifested to our fathers in their days, and until the present time, may we humble ourselves for our departures from Thee, and humbly pray for the pardon of our multiplied rebellions against Thee. O give us hearts to appreciate and improve the privileges we enjoy, that it may not be for our greater condemnation that we have been thus exalted in point of privilege; and we pray that Thou wouldst go with us in our various ways, to our several homes. Grant Thy continued care, and smile on the inhabitants of this County in coming time. O let our sons and daughters preserve the principles they have been taught, and let a holy influence descend upon them, and let a wider influence go forth from these hills, combining to bless our widely extended land. And O, make us mindful, our Heavenly Father, that though our present meeting must terminate forever, we are hastening onward to the day when we shall meet in a more august assembly, when the fathers of the generations past, and those of the present, and the multitudes that shall come after us, shall meet before the tribunal of the Judge of all the earth, to render an account for the deeds done in the body. So help us to improve our privileges, that when the summons comes, we may give up our account with joy, and hear the welcome invitation, "Come, ye blessed of my Father, inherit the kingdom prepared for you from the foundation of the world." And now, to the Father, the Son, and the Holy Spirit, be undivided honors, world without end. Amen.

BENEDICTION.

The Rev. Thomas Robbins, D. D., of Hartford, a native of Norfolk, pronounced the Benediction, as follows :—

May the God of peace, who brought our Lord Jesus Christ from the dead, the Great Shepherd of the sheep, make you perfect in every good work to do His will, working in you that which is well pleasing in His sight, through Jesus Christ our Lord and Saviour. Amen.

POEMS.

Several Poems were prepared by different individuals for the occasion, and forwarded to the Committee, among which were the following:

INVITATION TO LITCHFIELD COUNTY JUBILEE.

BY P. K. KILBOURNE.

Long dreaming where "the seat of empire" lay,
Westward the Sons of Litchfield take their way,
And in the regions of the setting sun
Their proudest, noblest victories are won!
They build their cabins on the rushing rills,
Their spires point heaven-ward from a thousand hills,
The wild beast's howl yields to the hammer's clang,
Their songs go up where once the war-whoop rang;
They start the eagle in his mountain eyrie,
Follow the war-path o'er the trackless prairie;
They wander where the cold Nebraska roars,
They plant our standard on Pacific shores,
And in their wake, beneath congenial skies,
New States extend their sway, new cities rise.
And there are orbs of milder light than they,
Radiant with love and gentle as the day,

Waking responsive joys in kindred souls
In some far cot where the Missouri rolls!

Still, truants from our households tho' they be,
Their spirits wing their way o'er land and sea,
And, freed from mortal weariness, in dreams
They climb our hills and wander by our streams—
Revisit each fair scene they loved of yore,
And greet in fancy's realm those they may meet no more!

Oh, all of these, from Life's diverging track,
To their old homes we fain would welcome back,
To share the festive scenes, the joy, the glee,
The life and soul of our great Jubilee!
Come home, ye searchers after fame, come home
From scenes and friends like these why should ye roam?—
Lawyers and statesmen, farmers, merchants, teachers,
Doctors, dealers in stocks, tin pedlers, preachers—
Come, from 'mid northern snows and tropic flowers,
From prairie-land, and blooming orange-bowers,
From California's realm of gold and graves,
From mountain land, and from the mountain-waves;—
Men, matrons, maidens, children—come ye all,
And share the glorious BANTAM FESTIVAL!

A CALL TO THE CENTENNIAL CELEBRATION.

BY A NATIVE OF WOODBURY.

Brothers! from each laughing valley,
From our hill-sides, rough and bold,
Round our common center rally,
Like the Jewish tribes of old!

Fathers, come! your locks will whiten—
Mothers! ye are young no more;
But your fading hopes will brighten,
With the memories of yore!

Come ye sons, so sturdy, growing,
Strong and tall, as freemen should;—
Bring your sisters, fluttering, glowing,
Like rose-laurels in a wood.

We will tell you, if you listen,
How an hundred years ago,
Pilgrims saw our waters glisten
In the valley, far below;

Where the forest, grand and lonely,
In primeval beauty stood,
And the wandering red men, only
Knew the windings through the wood;

Where our household fires are burning,
Wild deer bounded, far and free,

Streams, our busy mill-wheels turning
Idly, sang a song of glee;

Where our fathers sat beside them,
After travel long and sore—
Fearing nought that could betide them,
Might they find a *home* once more!

For a home, they fronted danger—
Wrought with rifle lying near:
To all luxury a stranger,
Was each dauntless Pioneer.

Noble Fathers! silent lying
In your graves rest, stern and cold,
Still ye preach, with voice undying,
To your children, from the mould!

And ye tell us, "Love each other;"
"Guard the homes, we toiled to win,
Let no hatred of your brother,
Doubt or malice, enter in!"

"Chiefly, on each household altar,
Keep devotion burning bright,
Then, ye will not pause or falter
In the doing of the *right!*"

"Firm in purpose and endeavor—
Tireless, till the goal be won,
Men shall know you, wheresoever
There is labor to be done."

Ye are freemen! Ye may glory,
In your union, firm and strong;—
Let *no future* tell a story,
Of dissension, or of wrong.

Look into each others faces—
Ye will meet again no more!
Then depart and fill ye places
Better than you did before.

FOR THE CENTENNIAL.

BY REV. J. LEE.

I.

UPON our hills no moss-clad castles rise,
No massive towers and turrets pierce the skies,
To tell of lordly chiefs of ancient fame,
Their fallen power and greatness to proclaim,
And call our thoughts to distant ages fled,
To wars of kings and mighty princes dead:
No dark monastic walls and gloomy cells,
Here show the seats where superstition dwells,
Where sweet domestic ties are burst in twain,
And joys of home will ne'er be known again.

II.

Green fields, and flocks, and herds, and harvests fair,
And fallows furrow'd by the burnish'd share,
And forests waving on each mountain height,
Dear memories wake, and scenes of pure delight,
In by-gone days, while yet these hearts were young,
And all their chords to nature's joys were strung,
When near the sacred fane the school-house stood,
Where first our minds to learning's paths were woo'd,
And from each spire rang clear the Sabbath bell,
To call our thoughts on themes divine to dwell

III.

No triple crown here wields the sword of state,
To doom our conscience to the felon's fate,
To shut the book of God from vulgar eyes,
And guard the holy portals of the skies;
The open page of truth divine we scan,
And learn the grace that saves apostate man,
The gospel for the poor, of price untold,
With pardons full, unbought with bribing gold—
For boons so rich we humbly bow the knee,
And bless the hand divine that made us free.

IV.

Religion, here, has shone with purest ray,
To guide our footsteps in the "narrow way,"
And righteous law o'er loyal subjects reigned,
Our hearths protected and our rights maintained—
For this fair heritage, so dearly bought,
With tears and toils and bloody battles fought,
Thy name, our fathers' God, alone we praise;—
To Thee with one accord loud anthems raise;
And when our dust with dust ancestral lies,
O bless our HOMES, till suns no more shall rise.

THE CENTENNIAL.

BY H. WARD.

A century's flight hath marked the age,
Since Justice with her sword and scales,
First took her seat, with counsel sage,
Amid these quiet hills and vales.

Through that long vista o'er the stream
Of Time, that flows with rapid tide,
What visions in the distance gleam,
To tell how vain is human pride!

The blast of war—the clang of arms,
Have oft resounded loud and long:
And warriors, fired by Freedom's charms,
Have listened to her thrilling song.

They fought and bled;—Columbia rose
Sublime above the stormy vale,
The joy of friends, the dread of foes,
With glory that can never fail.

And far beyond the ocean's waves,
Contending nations have gone down;
The ivy twines around their graves,
Where perish sceptre, throne and crown.

These quiet hills, these gentle vales,
  Now richly clothed in summer's green,
Have smiled as now, when balmy gales
  Swept o'er the undulating scene.

No rude alarms of hostile foes
  Have echoed 'mid these green retreats!
But calm as yon bright lake's repose,
  Peace reigned o'er all these rural seats.

Heaven bless the friends of early years,
  And all who meet once more in joy,
Where Friendship here her altar rears,
  To greet her sons without alloy.

THE FLAG.

BY J. L. WADSWORTH.

Fling out the flag of Liberty!
  The summer winds should play
With its unfolded stars and stripes,
  Upon this festal day.
Our fathers cared not for their lives,
  So it might freely wave;—
Tis meet that it should float above,
  The children of the brave.

The banner of Saint George's cross,
  Was wont its shade to throw
Upon the pilgrim's refuge land,
  A hundred years ago;
But praises to the pilgrim's God,
  A freer banner now,
Floats o'er the land where rests in peace
  The weary pilgrim's brow.

Still be its stars for the oppressed
  A cheering, guiding light,
Its stripes, the bond of brotherhood
  That freemen still unite.
And, till the centuries cease to roll,
  Still fluttering on the sky,
Be it the standard of a race
  Whose freedom ne'er shall die!

A CALL TO THE CENTENNIAL CELEBRATION.

BY J. L. WADSWORTH.

From northern homes, from southern climes,
  From mart and lonely mead,
From where the red man fades away
  Before the white man's tread;
Who wanders from his native land,
  Who loves this highland shore,
We bid you gather here again;
  Come to your home once more!

The graves are green ye left behind,
  And many a later mound,
Within the field of sepulchres,
  Those ancient graves surround;
But none will e'er return again,
  Those gloomy portals through;
So come to us and shed a tear
  Upon the old and new.

We cannot say, to win you back,
  That we are growing great;
We cannot boast of mighty deeds,
  Of pomp, or show, or state.
But we dwell among those green old hills,
  A quiet, noiseless band,
And from your olden haunts we call—
  Come to your father land!

CENTENNIAL ODE.

BY J. L. WADSWORTH.

GATHERED amid the scenes of yore,
The honored and ancestral hills,
Where hope's young pinion, wont to soar,
Did triumph o'er lifes future ills;
We come from forests of the west,
Or where Atlantic billows flow,
From homes our fathers footsteps pressed,
Pilgrims, an hundred years ago.

Glad greetings for the olden friends
Of childhood's free and joyous hour!
Fond memories for each tree that bends,
Each home-like bird, each home-like flower!
But worship, to the shrines we bring,
Where er'st our sires, in homage low,
Were wont their hymns of praise to sing
To God, an hundred years ago.

The wing of time, with tireless might,
Hath borne the century day by day,—
Unequal to the ceaseless flight,
Wearied, we soon shall sink away.
Then let us choose the truth as those
Who humbly walked with God below,
And from these hills, we trust, arose
To heaven, an hundred years ago.

EPISTLE TO POSTERITY.

ADDRESSED to those who shall meet to celebrate the *Second* Centennial Anniversary of Litchfield County, August 14th, 1951.

BY P. KENYON KILBOURNE.

OUR Jubilee is over! Far and wide,
Through lane and turnpike, pour the living tide;
Each homeward hies, with pleasure-beaming eye,
And heart all redolent with purpose high.
Erewhile, another race, in strange array,
Will welcome to the world YOUR festive-day;
O, when it dawns, "may I be there to see,"
Though strown through every land my dust may be!

Hail, unborn brothers! from these heights of time,
I fain would greet you with the voice of rhyme,
And send my greeting down the vale of tears,
Through the long windings of an hundred years.
Think not my toast a lifeless thing, even though
It cometh from the grave of long ago:
"A health to each, and joy be with you all,
Who gather here at your great Festival!"

O, could the bard but claim the prophet's eye,
And read for you a glorious destiny,
What pride would mingle in his cup of bliss,
To be your Poet on a day like this!

'Twere more than fame, if down through storms and tears,
These lines shall reach you in the far-off years,
For other hands must weave your civic crown—
New names must grace your ensigns of renown.

Conjecture all! No glass can penetrate
The unknown void that hides the scroll of fate;
No still small voice, no charioteer of flame,
Hath told us of your glory, or your shame.
Perhaps, as ye shall read of us, ye'll boast
Your parents were of "that enlightened host;"
Perhaps in sackcloth mourn, that ye must trace
Your lineage to our wild barbarian race!

It may be yours to seal your faith in blood,
Martyrs for God, or for your country's good;—
Soldiers in that dread war of death with life,
When Gog and Magog mingle in the strife.
It may be yours to hail that promised day,
When truth shall hold her universal sway—
When war, and want, and wrong, and crime, shall cease,
And nations own thy sway, O, Prince of Peace!

If true, as hath been said by saint and sage,
The world shall grow in wisdom as in age,
Ye, who have soar'd to heights we cannot see,
Will need no teachings from such worms as we.
If you, like us, must tread life's weary way,
Where clouds and storms may close the fairest day—
Where friends must die—where love's bright chain must sever
In weal—in woe—God be your guide forever!

However MAN may change for good or ill,
The years will roll, their cycles to fulfil;
Tired nature sleeps but to revive again;—
These hills, and streams, and mountains, will remain;
Bold *Prospect* still will lift his brazen brow,
Mount Tom will frown majestic then as now,—
The *Bantam* waters roll their silver tide,
Nor heed the generations that have died.

LITCHFIELD, Thursday Eve., Aug. 14th, 1851.

PORTRAITS.

AGREEABLY to the request of the Central Committee, in their Circular of the 22d of March, and in conformity to a vote of the Central and Town Committees, at their meeting on the 19th of July, repeating the request, the following Portraits were forwarded to the Committee and arranged in the Court-room, where they were open to the inspection of visitors, and attracted much attention through the days of the Celebration, viz :—

A Bust of Oliver Wolcott, Governor of this State from 1817 to 1827 ; by Clerenger.

An elegant full length portrait of Hon. Frederick Wolcott, of Litchfield, Clerk of the Courts for forty years; taken by Waldo & Jewett.

Col. Benjamin Tallmadge, of Litchfield, for many years member of Congress ; by Stuart.

Col. Wm. F. Tallmadge, son of Benjamin T., and an officer in the War of 1812.

Hon. James Gould, of Litchfield, Judge of the Superior Court and Court of Errors; by Waldo.

Wife of Hon. James Gould, taken when 19 years old, and four years after her marriage ; by Waldo.

Major Moses Seymour, of Litchfield, taken in the uniform which he wore at Burgoyne's defeat; by Ralph Earle, in 1789.

Mrs. Moses Seymour, and son Epaphro ; by Earle.

Moses Seymour, Jr., son of Major Moses S. ; miniature.

Wife of Moses Seymour, Jr. ; miniature.

Ozias Seymour, Esq., for many years Sheriff of Litchfield County ; by Snyder.

Rev. Truman Marsh; by Earle, in 1789.
do. by Snyder, about 1842.
Mrs. Truman Marsh; by Earle, in 1789.
Nathaniel Church, of Salisbury, father of Chief Justice Church.
Nathaniel Smith, of Woodbury, Judge of the Superior and Supreme Courts.
Mrs. Nathaniel Smith.
Rev. Noah Benedict, of Woodbury, father of Mrs. N. Smith.
Dr. John S. Wolcott, son of Gov. Wolcott; by Snyder.
Daniel N. Brinsmade, of Washington, Judge of the County Court.
Rev. Ammi R. Robbins, of Norfolk.
William Battell, Esq., of Torrington.
Hon. Augustus Pettibone, of Norfolk, Chief Judge of County Court.
Samuel Forbes, of Canaan.
Alpha Rockwell, the first person born in Colebrook.
Mrs. Rockwell, mother of the above.
Gen. Morris Woodruff, of Litchfield; by A. Dickinson.
Col. Perry Averill, of New Preston.
Rev. N. W. Taylor, Professor in Yale College.
David Bellamy, Esq., of Bethlem, son of Rev. Dr. Bellamy.
Hon. Joseph H. Bellamy, grandson of Rev. Dr. B.
Daniel Bacon, Esq., of Woodbury.
Gen. Chauncey Crafts, of Woodbury.
Rev. Azel Backus, Pastor of Church in Bethlem, President of Hamilton College, Clinton, N. Y.
Gen. David Bird, of Bethlem.
Dr. Daniel Sheldon, of Litchfield; by George Catlin.
Rev. Isaac Jones, of Litchfield; by Snyder.
Mrs. Uriel Holmes, of Litchfield, daughter of Judge Austin, New Hartford.
Major General Francis Bacon, of Litchfield.
Lieut. Frederick Bacon, of U. S. Navy, lost in the "Sea Gull."
E. C. Bacon, Esq., of Litchfield.

Upon which the editors of the New Haven Register remarked, that "one of the most interesting features of this festival, was the display of family portraits at the Court House. We were struck with their resemblance to the children of the third and fourth generation."

The editor of the New Haven Journal observed, that "among the most interesting exhibitions, at the Litchfield Jubilee, was the gallery of pictures at the Court House, where the sons and daughters of the County assembled to celebrate its birth-day, could look upon the portraits of their fathers and mothers of the 'homespun age,' whose wisdom, purity and virtue, contributed so much to the glory of the place of their nativity. There were pictures in every style of art, from the highest excellence to the daub of the traveling painter. Many of them were taken in the latter part of the last century, by Earle; and the quaint dresses of many of the ladies, represented to our eye something more of the aristocracy of the Court, than the simplicity of Dr. Bushnell's 'Kings and Queens of Homespun.' There were the old illustrious names of the County, looking down upon their descendants from the walls of the ancient Court House, where many of them had been wont to assemble during life, when its bar and bench possessed a greater array of talent than any other in the land, and where were their children looking with honest pride, on the noble and intellectual faces of their ancestors."

CONCLUDING REMARKS.

An attempt was made to keep a Register of the names of all who attended the celebration, with a view to publication. And for that purpose, books were lodged at the several Hotels, and at the entrance of the Tent, and a request announced through the village papers, and in handbills, and from the platform, that every person in attendance, would enter his, or her, name, place of residence, and birth. But, owing to the immense crowd, and to the fact that nearly every moment was occupied with the public exercises, very few complied with the request, so that the Register was too imperfect to be published.

Among those in attendance, besides those already named, we noticed Lieut. Gov. Kendrick, of Waterbury; President Woolsey, of Yale College; Col. Amasa Parker, of Delhi, N. Y., a native of Sharon; Wm. Rockwell, Esq., of Brooklyn, N. Y., a native of Sharon; Gamaliel H. Barstow, late Treasurer of the State of New York; Thomas Day, Esq., late Secretary of this State, a native of Washington; David Prentice, late Professor of Mathematics in Geneva College, a native of Bethlem; Hon. D. B. St. John, Superintendent of the New York Banking Department, Albany, a native of Sharon; Lawrence Hull, of Angelica, N. Y., a native of Bethlem; Dr. John Peck, of Vermont, a native of Woodbury; Dr. Goodsell, of Utica, a native of Washington, and E. D. Mansfield, Esq., of Cincinnati, Ohio. Also the following natives of Litchfield, viz.: Hon. Jno. W. Allen, late member of Congress from the Cleveland district, Ohio; Hon. Horatio Seymour, of Utica; Hon. John A. Collier, late Comptroller of New York; Hon. Robert Pierpont, Judge of the Supreme Court of Vermont; J. Huntington Wolcott, of Boston;

H. F. Tallmadge, U. S. Marshal, New York; Jno. Kilbourn, Judge of the Court of Queen's Bench, Canada; Wm. M. Clark, Esq., of New York; Hon. Wm. V. Peck, of Portsmouth, Ohio, Judge of the Circuit Court; Guy, Theodore, and Ashbel Catlin, of Vermont.

Among the venerable men of other days, we noticed on the platform, Daniel Lamson, of Litchfield, aged 97; also, Elisha Mason, of the same town, aged 94—both heroes of the Revolution; also Ebenezer Landon, of Lyons, N. Y., aged 91—having traveled over 300 miles to attend the celebration, accompanied by his son and daughter, and had been absent from Litchfield 46 years.

The early and efficient arrangements of the Central Committee for providing strangers with accommodations, for the preservation of good order, and protection of property, were thoroughly carried out and executed. The Sheriff of the County and his Deputies were constantly patrolling the streets throughout the day, and the detachment from the "Bacon Guards" were constantly on duty through the night. No pocket was picked, no property stolen or injured, no fighting, wrangling or noise, no person intoxicated; indeed, perfect quiet reigned throughout the whole period of the celebration. We have heard of no occurrence which marred the happiness of the Jubilee, or which cast the least cloud over any part of the exercises. Indeed it was a general remark, that on no similar occasion, was a greater degree of good order and harmony observed, than was witnessed here throughout the whole celebration. According to the estimates made by those conversant with large assemblages, there were probably from eight to nine thousand persons present. More than one thousand visitors were lodged in the village the first night, and within seven or eight miles around the village, nearly two thousand more found comfortable lodgings. Every dwelling was stowed with cheerful and happy guests. We have not yet heard of a person who was unprovided with comfortable accommodations.

SECOND

Centennial Celebration

OF THE EXPLORATION OF

ANCIENT WOODBURY,

AND THE RECEPTION OF

THE FIRST INDIAN DEED,

HELD AT WOODBURY, CONN.,

JULY 4 AND 5, 1859.

EDITED BY WILLIAM COTHREN.

WOODBURY:
PUBLISHED BY THE GENERAL COMMITTEE.
1859.

THE ORIGIN OF THE CELEBRATION.

At a meeting of some two thousand persons, from the several towns of "Ancient Woodbury," on the 5th of July, 1858, it was moved by William Cothren, and seconded by Rev. John Churchill:

"That a Committee of two from each of the towns once included, in whole or in part, in the ancient town of Woodbury, be appointed by the meeting, with power to add to their own number, and to appoint all necessary Assistant Committees, for the purpose of making efficient arrangements for the Historical Celebration of the Second Centennial Anniversary of the first Exploration of the Town, and the reception of the first Indian Deed, at Bethel Rock, on the 4th day of July, A. D. 1859, and also to invite gentlemen to deliver the various addresses, &c., of the occasion."

The motion was unanimously adopted, and the following named gentlemen appointed such Committee:

William Cothren, C. B. Phelps,* W. T. Bacon,† P. M. Trowbridge,† *Woodbury;*

R. W. Frisbie, S. H. Mitchell, *Washington;*

T. B. Wheeler, A. B. Downs, Col. C. Hicock,† *Southbury;*

Abraham Beecher, H. W. Peck, *Bethlem;*

H. B. Eastman, F. W. Lathrop, *Roxbury;*

N. J. Wilcoxson, Alfred Harger, *Oxford;*

Dr. Marcus DeForest, Jr., Leonard Bronson, *Middlebury.*

FIRST MEETING OF THE COMMITTEE.

On the 18th day of September, 1858, the General Committee held its first meeting, pursuant to written notice by letter, to each member thereof, from the chairman, William Cothren. This meeting was held at the office of the late Judge Phelps, but the chairman was

---

* Judge Phelps died December 21, 1858.

† Gentlemen since added to their number by the Committee.

absent, attending to professional business in a neighboring town. What the action of the Committee was, will be seen by the following paragraph, which went the rounds of the Connecticut press:

WOODBURY SECOND CENTENNIAL CELEBRATION.

The General Committee having in charge the matter of the second centennial celebration of the discovery of the valley of ancient Woodbury, met at the office of Hon. C. B. Phelps, on the 18th inst., and gave an invitation to William Cothren, Esq., the "Historian of Ancient Woodbury," to deliver the historical address, and to Rev. William Thompson Bacon, the "distinguished native poet of our vales," to deliver the poem on the occasion of the celebration. These invitations have been accepted.

By a vote of the assemblage at the celebration on the 5th of July last, the proposed celebration is to be held on the 4th of July, 1859, at "Bethel Rock." Ample preparations will be made by the Committee to have the celebration worthy of the occasion, and of our historic old town.

All persons having facts or incidents connected with the history of the ancient town, are respectfully requested to communicate them to Mr. Cothren, or Mr. Bacon, who will endeavor to make a proper use of them. W.

On the 17th of December, 1858, pursuant to a like written notice from the chairman to each member of the General Committee, a meeting was held, from which both Mr. Cothren and Mr. Phelps were absent, being engaged in the trial of a cause in which they were opposing counsel. Rev. Wm. T. Bacon, who had a short time previously been added to the General Committee, presided, and Philo M. Trowbridge, Esq., acted as secretary of the meeting. At this meeting, the following votes were unanimously passed, viz:

"*Voted*, That the Centennial Celebration be held at Bethel Rock, in Woodbury, on the 4th and 5th days of July, 1859, pursuant to the vote of the 5th of July, 1858.

Voted, That a sermon be added to the list of exercises already agreed upon for the celebration.

Voted, That we do invite Rev. Henry B. Sherman, of Belleville, New Jersey, to deliver said sermon.

Voted, That there be an Antique Procession on said 4th of July.

Voted, That there be a *Pioneer Encampment* from the several towns of Ancient Woodbury, during said celebration.

Voted, That a committee to carry out the last two votes, and the General Committee of Arrangements for the Celebration, be appointed by the General Committee for Woodbury.

Voted, That a Committee of Invitation for the several towns be appointed by the Woodbury Committee.

VOTED, THAT THE GENERAL COMMITTEE OF WOODBURY BE INSTRUCTED TO SECURE SHORT ADDRESSES FROM RESIDENTS OF THE TERRITORY, AND OTHERS FROM ABROAD, WHO SHALL BE PRESENT AT SAID CELEBRATION.

Voted, That the Committee of Invitation be requested to secure the portraits of early, and other distinguished residents of Ancient Woodbury, for the Antiquarian Portrait Gallery during the celebration.

Voted, That a Committee in each town to collect funds for defraying the expenses of said celebration, including the publication of the proceedings, in pamphlet form, be appointed by the General Committee of each town.

Voted, That every person paying one dollar, or more, towards the expense fund, shall be entitled to a copy of said proceedings, when published.

Voted, That the poets of the territory be invited to furnish odes for the occasion.

Voted, That there be an Antiquarian Pic-nic each day of the celebration."

The substance of these votes was immediately published in the newspapers all over the State, and every body who reads had full opportunity to become informed of the action of the Committee. On their return, Messrs. Phelps and Cothren fully acquiesced in the action of the General Committee. They had left a paper in the hand-writing of Mr. Cothren, requesting action on all the above points.

Pursuant to the above votes, the General Committee of Woodbury appointed the following Committee of Invitation, with power in the Committee to add to its numbers, viz:

Committee of Invitation.

Woodbury—P. M. Trowbridge, Thomas Bull, Lewis Judd, N. B. Smith, Henry Minor.

Southbury—Charles Hicock, Dr. N. C. Baldwin.

Washington—D. B. Brinsmade, H. J. Church.

Bethlem—John C. Ambler, Wm. R. Harrison.

Roxbury—C. Beardsley, N. R. Smith.

Middlebury—Dr. M. DeForest, Jr.

Oxford—N. J. Wilcoxson.

The chairman of the Committee of Invitation immediately drew a circular letter of invitation to the emigrants from Woodbury, submitted it to the General Committee of Woodbury, and it was approved. The first edition of the circular was issued Feb. 1st, 1859. This became exhausted, and a second edition was issued April 1st, 1859, a copy of which is as follows, viz:

WOODBURY, CONN., APRIL 1ST, 1859.

DEAR SIR:—

The citizens of Ancient Woodbury met on Monday, the 5th of July last, and celebrated the Eighty-second Anniversary of our National Independence. Near the close of the exercises of that day, on motion of WILLIAM COTHREN, Esq., it was voted by acclamation to celebrate on the 4th and 5th of July, 1859, the Two Hundredth Anniversary of the exploration of Ancient Woodbury; and to carry said vote into effect, a General Committee of two persons from each of the towns once included in Woodbury, was appointed, with full power to make the necessary arrangements.

The above Committee having appointed the undersigned a Committee to invite all persons who may have emigrated from among us, and all others interested, does hereby extend an invitation to you personally, and solicit you to be present and unite with us in the festivities of the occasion.

It is expected the exercises will occupy two days, and that they will be nearly as follows:

1. Antique Procession.
2. Historical Address by WILLIAM COTHREN, Esq., the Historian of Woodbury.
3. Poem by Rev. WILLIAM THOMPSON BACON, of Woodbury.
4. Sermon by Rev. HENRY B. SHERMAN, of Belleville, N. J.
5. Reading of Letters and Odes, with Speeches from distinguished Emigrants.
6. Mammoth Antiquarian Pic-Nic, both days.
7. Pioneer Encampment on Orenaug Rocks.
8. Amateur Indian Encampment on Castle Rock.
9. "Guards" and Sentinel service on the Cliffs.

The various Committees are now in the active discharge of their duties, and from present indications, the occasion will be an honor to the descendants of the intelligent, virtuous, and noble men who planted the town, and who, in their characters, have left to their descendants a priceless legacy.

Come, then, our "latch-strings are out," our hands are extended to greet you, and around our hearth-stones the "old arm-chairs" are waiting for the absent.

Very respectfully yours.

To this circular were attached the names of the Committee of Invitation, printed above, and one other, which was subsequently omitted for cause.

It had, from the beginning, been the earnest desire of every member of the General Committee so to arrange the parts and apportion the duties necessarily arising out of the celebration, that their action would meet the hearty approval and cordial co-operation of all interested in the objects of the occasion. This was frequently a matter of consultation in the casual meetings of the Committee. Not a word to the contrary was ever heard. It was in this spirit, with this view, after full consultation in the first regular meeting of all the members of the General Committee of Woodbury, which, for this purpose, had been invested with the full powers of the General Committee, that the following action and correspondence took place, viz:

WOODBURY, 25th March, 1859.

REV. J. CHURCHILL,

Dear Sir:—The General Committee were together to-day, arranging a little for the celebration next July, and were desirous of getting some one to make a little opening speech, on the first day of the celebration, after the prayer, and before the other exercises, "Welcoming back the sons of Woodbury, who return to join us in the anniversary." We also wish some Clergyman to speak in reply to the Sentiment—"The early Clergy of Ancient Woodbury." It is proposed that these parts be each twenty or thirty minutes in length, and we desire, thus early, to secure persons to take them, as whoever accepts them would require some time for a preparation satisfactory to himself.

It is our desire that you would take one of these parts, and the one you would prefer. Rev. Mr. Bacon and Mr. Trowbridge heartily join me in inviting and urging you to do this.

We are receiving letters from all parts of the Union, from the sons of Woodbury, who have gone out from us, expressing the greatest interest in the proposed celebration, and promising to attend. We believe that, with a little earnest effort on our part, it will be an occasion we shall long remember with pleasure.

Please write me a line soon, stating whether you will join us in the exercises as proposed.

Yours truly,

W. COTHREN.

Mr. Churchill's Reply.

Mr. Cothren—*My Dear Sir*—I received your letter of the 25th inst., on Saturday afternoon. In reply to it, I would say, that it would have been agreeable to me to have participated, not in any public services, but in such *other ways* as I might, in order to make the occasion to which you refer interesting and profitable. The occasion is one, which for some three or four years past, I have often contemplated, and conversed upon with different individuals in the Town with interest. But no matter for this now. As the programme is widely before the public, and the Gen'l Committee have prepared & sent it out with the Invitation, over the signatures of *another* committee expressly appointed for that purpose, it w'ld to the community at large seem at least much like an afterthought *now* to add two addresses to the occasion. Not only so, but your note gives me to understand that these additional matters are proposed by the General Committee for Woodbury, whereas, I had supposed the Gen'l Com. for Ancient Woodbury consisting of two from each Town to be the proper authority to make the arrangements. It would be *very far* from my wish to speak or to have any public duty on that occasion, & I must respectfully decline your invitation.

Very respectfully,

JNO. CHURCHILL.

Woodbury, March 28, 1859.

On the 16th of April, the Committee had another meeting, and made appointments for the exercises of the second day of the celebration, including the parts refused by Mr. Churchill, he having been the first man applied to after Mr. Sherman was appointed to preach the sermon. These appointees, with the exception of three, who were unable to fulfill on account of sickness in their families, were the same as appeared on the final order of exercises, which was as follows, viz:

WOODBURY SECOND CENTENNIAL CELEBRATION.

There will be a Historical Celebration of the Second Centennial Anniversary of the first Exploration of the Town, and the reception of the first Indian Deed, at Woodbury, on the 4th and 5th days of July, A. D. 1859, commencing at 10 o'clock, A. M.

ORDER OF EXERCISES.

First Day.

Antique Procession, escorted by the Band and Roxbury Guards.

Ode, by the Choir—tune, "*Bruce's Address.*"

Prayer, by Rev. R. G. Williams, of Woodbury.

Short Introductory Address, "Welcoming the emigrants from Woodbury home again," by Nathaniel Smith, of Woodbury.

Music by the Band.

Historical Address, by William Cothren, of Woodbury.

Music by the Band.

Recess of one Hour for Refreshments.

Music by the Band.

Song—"The Pilgrim Fathers," by G. S. Minor.

Poem, by William Thompson Bacon, of Woodbury.

Ode, by the Choir—tune, "*Auld Lang Syne.*"

Benediction, by Rev. Thomas L. Shipman, of Jewett City.

SECOND MORNING,—8 o'clock.

PRAYER MEETING AT BETHEL ROCK.

SECOND DAY,—10 o'clock, A. M.

Music by the Band.

Centennial Hymn.

Prayer, by Rev. Friend W. Smith, of Woodbury.

Hymn.

Sermon, by Rev. Henry Beers Sherman, of Belleville, N. J.

Hymn.

Speech:—"The early Clergy of Ancient Woodbury," by Rev. Anson S. Atwood, of Mansfield, Conn.

One Hour for Refreshments.

Music by the Band.

Ode, by the Choir—tune, "*Sweet Home.*"

Speech:—"The early Lawyers of Ancient Woodbury," by Hon. Seth P. Beers, of Litchfield.

Music by the Band.

Speech:—"The early Physicians of Ancient Woodbury," by David B. W. Hard, M. D., of Bethlem.

Music by the Band.

Speech:—"The Founders of Ancient Woodbury," by Hon. William T. Minor, of Stamford.

Ode, by the Choir—tune, "*America.*"

Speech:—"The early Schools of Ancient Woodbury," by T. M. Thompson, Esq., of Woodbury.

Speech:—"Grand-children of Ancient Woodbury," by Hon. Chas. Chapman, of Hartford.

Speech,—"The Cousins of Ancient Woodbury," by Hon. Henry Dutton, of New Haven.

Volunteer Speeches, by distinguished sons of Ancient Woodbury, from abroad.

Reading of Letters and Odes prepared for the occasion.

Concluding Prayer, by Rev. C. T. Woodruff, of Woodbury.

Benediction, by Rev. Philo Judson, of Rocky Hill.

Hon. NATHANIEL B. SMITH, *President of the Day.*

Hon. D. B. Brinsmade, of Washington,	*Vice Presidents.*
" Joshua Bird, of Bethlem,	
S. W. Baldwin, Esq., of Roxbury,	
Cyrus Mitchell, Esq., of Southbury,	
Nathaniel Walker, Esq., of Oxford,	
Leonard Bronson, Esq., of Middlebury,	

HENRY MINOR, *Chief Marshal.*

Assistant Marshals:

R. I. Tolles,	Elijah D. Judson,
George Camp,	Elisha P. Tomlinson,
Robert Peck,	James Stone,
Benjamin Doolittle,	Truman S. Minor,
W. C. McKay,	George P. Crane,
George Saxton,	James H. Minor.

Three other Committees were appointed at the same time with the Committee of Invitation, viz:

Committee on Antique Procession, Encampment, etc.

Woodbury—Nathaniel Smith, S. F. Peck, J. G. Curtiss, S. Hurd, H. W. Shove, Rev. R. G. Williams, Rev. C. P. Woodruff.

Southbury—T. B. Wheeler, A. B. Downs.

Roxbury—Capt. L. Judd.

Bethlem—H. W. Peck.

Washington—D. G. Platt, Russell W. Frisbie.
Oxford—N. J. Wilcoxson, N. Walker.
Middlebury—Frank. Benham.

Finance Committee.

Woodbury—Henry Minor, George P. Allen, Charles W. Kirtland, George Saxton.

Washington—Russell W. Frisbie, Simeon D. Platt, George C. Cogswell.

Roxbury—F. J. Fenn, C. E. Prindle, C. Lewis, F. W. Lathrop.
Southbury—Col. C. Hicock, C. Whitlock.
Bethlem—Dr. H. Davis.
Oxford—Nathaniel Walker, Dr. L. Barnes.
Wm. E. Woodruff, Woodbury, *Treasurer.*

Committee on Antiquarian Portrait Gallery.

C. B. Crafts, Wm. Hicock, Joshua Bird, B. H. Preston, F. W. Gunn, and the members of the Committee of Invitation.

On the 25th of April, 1859, the General Committee of Woodbury appointed the Committee of Arrangements, and the Committee on the Pic-nic, as will be seen below, and subsequently the General Committees of the other towns appointed similar Committees for their several localities, viz:

General Committee of Arrangements and Reception.

WOODBURY.

N. B. Smith,
Walter P. Marshall,
John P. DeForest,
Dr. C. H. Webb,
Wm. E. Woodruff,
James G. Curtiss,
Daniel S. Lemon,
Elisha P. Tomlinson,
D. Chauncey Somers,
J. Knight Bacon,
T. Bull,
Nathaniel Smith,
Rev. R. G. Williams,
R. I. Tolles,
G. P. Allen,
H. Minor,
Calvin H. Downs,
G. Platt Crane,
E. D. Judson,
L. G. Atwood,
Truman S. Minor,
James Stone,
F. Orton,
D. S. Bull,
Enos Benham,
John A. Boughton,
W. S. Curtiss,
P. A. Judson,

James Huntington,
S. Chapin,
S. Clark,
L. B. Candee,
B. Doolittle,
Sidney Hurd,
J. Parker,
J. W. Rogers,
B. A. Sherman,
F. A. Smith,
T. M. Thompson,
J. F. Walker,
H. Tomlinson,
Rev. C. T. Woodruff.

General Committee of Arrangements on the Antiquarian Pic-Nic.

Mrs. N. B. Smith,
" Wm. T. Bacon,
" R. G. Williams,
" F. W. Smith,
" C. T. Woodruff,
" L. B. Candee,
" Jason Parker,
" W. E. Woodruff,
" T. W. Walker,
" W. Cothren,
" E. J. M. Benham,
" T. M. Thompson,
" A. Gordon,
" G. H. Atwood,
" A. Candee,
" H. S. Crane,
" T. Minor,
" Loren Forbes,
" J. P. Marshall,
" T. Bull,
" C. A. Somers,
" J. F. Walker,
" P. M. Trowbridge,
" H. C. Baldwin,
" D. Curtiss,
" H. Minor,
" T. Judson,
" A. Birch,
" B. S. Russell,
" L. G. Atwood,
" R. Partree,
" B. A. Sherman,
Mrs. S. Minor,
" B. M. Stowe,
" Barlow Russell,
" Fred. Bolton,
" S. Clark,
" H. S. Curtiss,
" N. Smith,
" C. H. Webb,
" C. Betts,
" G. Lathrop,
" E. Parker,
" D. C. Somers,
" G. P. Allen,
" C. P. Strong,
" J. P. DeForest,
Miss Julia P. Marshall,
" Helen O. Atwood,
" Julia A. Bull,
" Rebecca T. Bacon,
" Cornelia Betts,
" Cornelia J. Betts,
" Emma F. Betts,
" Sophia E. Benedict,
" Emily A. Curtiss,
" Sarah P. Clark,
" Maria J. Cogswell,
" Lucy A. DeForest,
" Julia E. Downs,
" Sally R. Hotchkiss,
" M. J. Hitchcock,
" C. Lambert,
Harriet E. Judson,

Miss Mary Minor,
" Amanda E. Phelps,
" S. Maria Phelps,
" Mary J. Parker,
" Helen Parker,
" Susan E. Pierce,
" Wealthy A. Root,
Miss Cornelia M. Smith,
" F. C. Trowbridge,
" Maria B. Walker,
" C. L. Webb,
" Clara C. Vaill,
" Edna E. Russell.

WASHINGTON.

Orestus Hickox,
T. A. Bryan,
Turney Odell,
Henry Seeley,
Charles Hickox,
B. P. Beach,
Sherman Woodruff,
S. A. Baker,
Sherman Hartwell,
Herman Baldwin,
R. S. Leavitt,
T. F. Brinsmade,
F. N. Galpin,
T. H. Woodruff,
E. Hurlbut,
Seth Hollister,
J. B. Newton,
Treat Nettleton,
Henry Nettleton,
E. J. Pond,
Gregory Seeley,
Col. I. Hickox,
Daniel Frisbie,
Wm. C. Bronson,
C. L. Ford,
R. W. Ford,
Augustus Smith,
Sheldon Logan,
Seth S. Logan,
John Fenn,
C. Allen,
Sherman Titus,
Samuel Burgess,
Stephen Morehouse,
Albert Sterling,
Dea. David Punderson,
Dea. S. S. Baldwin,
A. W. Mitchel,
J. Kinney.

Ladies' Pic-Nic Committee.

Mrs. Rev. E. H. Lyman,
" Dr. R. M. Fowler,
" F. W. Gunn,
" C. L. Ford,
" S. S. Logan,
" R. W. Frisbie,
" S. Frisbie,
" S. A. Baker,
" T. A. Bryan,
" F. A. Frisbie,
Mrs. F. N. Galpin,
" S. W. Ford,
" E. Seeley,
" Dr. J. Richards,
" R. S. Leavitt,
" N. Gibson,
" A. Gibson,
" E. Hurlbut,
" C. Leeland,
" H. Morehouse,

Mrs. F. Newton,	Miss Kezia Farrand,
" G. Baldwin,	" Amanda Logan,
" C. Mason,	" Celia Nettleton,
" S. H. Calhoun,	" Isabelle Ford,
" J. Kinney,	" Annie Bryan,
Miss Mary M. Brinsmade,	" Fanny Smith,
" Harriet Fowler,	" Sila Frisbie,
" Mary Kinney,	" Elizabeth Seeley,
" Sarah Hubbell,	" Eliza Odell,
" Eliza Mitchel,	" Ellen Hickox,
" Susan Bronson,	" Lora Hollister,
" Abba Vail,	" Eleanor Frisbie,
" Lydia Parish,	" Frances Ludington.

NEW PRESTON.

I. D. Patterson,	Fred. Whittlesey,
Daniel Burnham,	A. C. Lemmon,
Walter D. Sperry,	David E. Meeker,
Walter Burnham,	S. W. Meeker,
Isaac Brown,	Sherman P. Camp,
Wm. C. Wooster,	James Barton,
G. C. Whittlesey,	Elisha A. Whittlesey,
Hiram C. Bennett,	John M. Ford,
George W. Cogswell,	Levi Morehouse,
Medad Goodsell,	Sheldon Wheaton,
J. E. Whittlesey,	Jerome Edwards.

Ladies' Pic-Nic Committee.

Mrs. Daniel Burnham,	Mrs. S. W. Meeker,
" Walter D. Sperry,	Miss Mary E. Bennett,
" Walter Burnham,	Mrs. James Barton,
" Isaac Brown,	Miss Sarah Camp,
" G. C. Whittlesey,	Mrs. E. A. Whittlesey,
Miss Ruth A. Bennett,	" John M. Ford,
Mrs. Geo. W. Cogswell,	Miss Ellen Wheaton,
" Medad Goodsell,	" Minerva Wheaton,
" S. Augusta Whittlesey,	Mrs. Augusta Scott,
" A. C. Lemmon,	Miss Helen Brown.
" David E. Meeker,	

SOUTHBURY.

T. B. Wheeler,
D. P. Whitlock,
H. D. Monson,
W. C. Beecher,
S. G. Goodrich,
C. Whitlock,
C. Hicock,
C. N. Hall,
H. W. Scott, Jr.,
G. W. Smith.

Ladies' Pic-Nic Committee.

Mrs. S. B. Whitlock,
" N. C. Monson,
" H. B. Stiles,
" F. Stiles,
" L. Smith,
" D. R. Hinman,
" C. S. Hinman,
" C. Hinman,
" C. A. Brown,
" H. W. Scott,
" C. H. Hall,
" E. Pulford,
" E. Hine,
" S. G. Goodrich,
" H. C. Hayes,
" A. H. Shelton,
" J. W. Bradley,
" J. T. Munn,
Mrs. C. Oatman,
" E. Wheeler,
" R. G. Curtiss,
" H. Brown,
" W. C. Beecher,
Miss E. P. Whitlock,
" M. A. Ronaldson,
" Helen E. Hinman,
" Ann Hinman,
" A. F. Stiles,
" M. E. Monson,
" Jennie Stiles,
" Sarah L. Smith,
" Julia Lum,
" Mary E. Mitchel,
" Augusta Stiles,
" Mary Hicock,
" Laura Hicock.

SOUTH BRITAIN.

Rev. A. E. Lawrence,
George Smith,
Oliver Mitchell,
Marshall S. Clark,
Samuel L. Tuttle,
James F. Hinman,
George A. Hoyt,
Calvin Lines,
Elliot B. Bradley,
Samuel W. Post,
John Pierce,
Perry Averill,
Reuben Pierce,
Noah B. Tuttle,
Henry W. Guthrie,
Charles B. Smith,
David F. Pierce,
Samuel J. Stoddard,
Nelson W. Mitchell.

Ladies' Pic-Nic Committee.

Mrs. A. E. Lawrence,
" George Smith,
" Oliver Mitchell,
" M. S. Clark,
" S. F. Tuttle,
" E. B. Bradley,
" N. W. Mitchell,
" Emeline Canfield,
" Eliza Smith,
" N. B. Tuttle,
" G. A. Hoyt,
" Charles Allen,
" N. C. Baldwin,
Mrs. S. D. Garlick,
Miss Nancy Mitchell,
" Harriet Canfield,
" L. A. Treat,
" Anna Bradley,
" Sarah E. Smith,
" Anna Judd,
" Hannah A. Bradley,
" Laura A. Mitchell,
" Elizabeth Downes,
" Sarah Allen,
" May Downes,
" E. M. Averill.

BETHLEM.

James Thompson,
Samuel L. Bloss,
C. C. Parmelee,
Theodore Bird,
William A. Hayes,
B. T. Lake, 2d.

Ladies' Pic-Nic Committee.

Mrs. M. S. Todd,
" R. C. Armstrong,
" L. P. Judd,
" E. L. Thompson,
" E. J. Hubbard,
" S. L. Munson,
" John Towne,
" Mariah Humphrey,
Mrs. H. Davis,
" Theodore Bird,
" E. Riggs,
Miss Margarett Kasson,
" Carrie Thompson,
" Carrie Morriss,
" Immogene Bird,
" Bernice Skidmore.

ROXBURY.

Col. P. N. Hodge,
B. S. Preston,
Nathan R. Smith,
A. T. Barnes,
Charles Beardsley,
F. W. Lathrop,
S. H. Addis,
H. B. Eastman,
Rev. Austin Isham,
A. W. Fenn.

Ladies' Pic-Nic Committee.

Mrs. Aaron W. Fenn,
" Orrin B. Seward,
" Mark T. Hatch,
" Henry H. Fenn,
" Austin Isham,
Mrs. Austin D. Burritt,
" Andrew Weller,
" S. W. Baldwin,
" Erastus Castle,
" Albert L. Hodge.

OXFORD.

Nathaniel Walker,
Dr. Lewis Barnes,
Joel Osborn,
Alfred Harger,
Dr. Geo. A. Tomlinson,
John R. Davis,
Milo D. Northrop,
Sterne Candee,
Benjamin Nichols,
Virgil H. McEwen,
Nicholas D. Hinman,
Charles T. Walker,
O. C. Buckingham,
David C. Riggs,
Horace E. Tomlinson,
Samuel P. Sanford,
Homer Riggs,
Eben G. Wheeler,
Lewis B. Perkins.

Ladies' Pic-Nic Committee.

Mrs. Nathaniel Walker,
" Alfred Harger,
" John R. Davis,
" Nicholas D. Hinman,
" Lewis B. Perkins,
Miss Josephine Flagg,
" Anna C. Fairchild,
" Julia A. Fairchild,
" Jane McEwen,
Mrs. Joel Osborn,
" Benjamin Nichols,
" Milo D. Northrop,
" David C. Riggs,
Miss Antoinett Tomlinson,
Miss Fannie A. Wilcoxson,
" Harriet C. Chatfield,
" Lucy A. Perkins,
" Bernice Riggs,
Mrs. Horace E. Tomlinson,
Miss Jane L. Buckingham,
" Sarah J. Topliff,
" Josephine Candee,
" Mary L. Davis,
" A. Elvira Buckingham,
" Mary E. Buckingham,
Mrs. Orrin C. Buckingham,
Miss Elizabeth Hudson,
" Elsie Williams.

MIDDLEBURY.

James Tyler,
Julius Bronson,
Silas Tuttle,
Erastus S. Curtiss,
John S. Way,
Franklin Platt,

Franklin Benham,
Ebenezer Smith,
Whitfield Upson,
Stiles F. Munson,
Henry W. Newton,
William Tyler.

Ladies' Pic-Nic Committee.

Mrs. William Tyler,
" Franklin Benham,
" F. Hine,
" E. Smith,
" W. Upson,
" S. F. Munson,
" J. S. Way,
Miss Mary Tyler,
Miss Ellen Bronson,
" Julia Tuttle,
" Harriet Curtiss,
" Mary C. Hine,
" Elizabeth Platt,
" Martha Newton,
" Helen Townsend.

The following action, which was decided upon in April, 1859, will explain itself, viz:

The *Indian* Deed given to the founders of Woodbury, in 1659, granted

☞ "*A parcell of Land, bounded as followeth; Potateuk River Southwest; Naugatunck River northeast; and bounded on ye northwest with trees marked by me and other Indians.*"

Potateuk river was the Housatonic, and the "marked trees" extended across South Farms west to the Housatonic river. All north of Derby then to this line was included in this deed, including Ancient Waterbury west of the Naugatuck, part of Litchfield and New Milford. The committee, therefore, considering these towns and the towns formed out of them, to be of near consanguinity to us:

Voted: "To invite our cousins, the towns of Waterbury, Naugatuck, Seymour, Watertown, Plymouth, Litchfield, New Milford and Bridgewater, to unite with us in our approaching Centennial Anniversary."

A committee appointed by the citizens of Woodbury, changed the place for the exercises selected by the vote passed a year ago on Orenaug Rocks, and secured the field of Mr. T. M. Thompson, directly east of the First Congregational Church in Woodbury. It was an exceedingly fine location for the celebration. The large tent of Yale College was procured and supplied with seats, speakers' stand, &c., and the still larger tent belonging to the Litchfield County Agricultural Society, was procured for the Pic-Nic provided by the Woodbury Ladies. A large tent was also provided for invited guests, besides a table set out under the apple trees, loaded with the various articles of the Antiquarian Pic-Nic proper, such as bean porridge, baked beans and pork, Indian pudding, &c., served up in the old style, in old pewter and wooden platters, with old pewter spoons, and other antique articles to match. Besides these, the General Committee furnished a tent for each of the other towns in which to hold their Pic-Nic, except Washington, which chose to furnish its own tent-cloth.

On the first morning of the celebration, the Chief Marshal, Henry Minor, Esq., made out the order of procession, as follows, viz:

A single Fifer and Drummer.
Antique Procession.
Masons.
New Milford Band.
Warner Light Guards.
President of the day.
Vice-Presidents.
Orators of the day and Poet.
Clergy.
The various Committees of Arrangements.
Emigrant Sons, &c., of the Territory.
Citizens at large.

The Chief Marshal wore the Revolutionary military undress of a Major-General, and Dr. Davis, of Bethlem, wore a military suit worn by Col. Bellamy in the war of 1812.

A cloudless sun rose over the fair valley of Woodbury, on the morning of the fourth, and the weather was cool and most delightful.

The day was ushered in by the booming of cannon and the ringing of bells, in the various parts of the town, in the most spirited and joyous manner. At an early hour, the people began to fill the town, and at 10 o'clock, A. M., the streets were almost impassable. The people of Washington came under the direction of Sherman Hartwell as Marshal, in a procession of more than a mile in length, escorted by the New Milford Band. In it were one six-horse team, loaded with fifty persons, ten four-horse teams, sixty two-horse teams, and fifty one-horse teams, with flags, banners, and some antique costumes. Much credit is due to Russell W. Frisbie, and Thomas F. Brinsmade, for this fine turn out. Roxbury came out in her ancient strength. Her procession consisted of 217 teams, under the direction of Col. Philo N. Hodge, as Marshal. This procession was rich in antique display, and contained several things worthy of special mention. Among them was a cart, bearing for a motto, "Days of Homespun," drawn by six yokes of oxen, the team of Ira Bradley, containing a flax-breaker, hetchell, flax cards, double flax spinning wheel, and quill wheel, all in operation, worked by ladies in antique costumes. The driver was Le Roy Bradley in corresponding dress. Another wagon bore John A Squire, of Roxbury, and twenty-two of his grand-children, while another still loaded with people in antique dress, bore a flag with the motto, "Times and Seasons continue—Manners and Customs change." This section was escorted by the Warner Light Guards of Roxbury, in a new and elegant uniform, under the command of Capt Lewis Judd, who performed escort and sentinel duty during both days, and by the excellence of their military evolutions, the strictness of their discipline, and the gallantry of their bearing, might be favorably compared with many a veteran company, which had seen years of drilling. Southbury, also, turned out more than 100 teams, under Charles Whitlock, as Marshal. All the other towns came with very creditable processions, besides the numerous conveyances crowded with people, who did not join any procession.

After the several delegations had arrived, the General "Antique Procession" was formed at about 11, A. M., on the green in front of Hon. N. B. Smith's dwelling house, at the location of the First Meeting House in the town. Under the effective arrangements made by N. Smith, Esq., and H. W. Shove, M. D., aided by Rev. Messrs. R. G. Williams and C. T. Woodruff, it became the marked feature of the occasion. It extended, while on its march towards the grounds, at least an eighth of a mile in length, exhibiting all the varying costumes of the last two hundred years. It was headed by an ancient drummer and fifer. Next came the clergy of the several towns, in bands and gowns, the clerical costume of clergymen of all denominations, less than two centuries ago. Among the clergy, Rev. R. G. Williams was particularly noticeable for the perfection of detail in his costume. Then came the Puritan costumes of two hundred years ago, worn by the Minors, the Judsons, the Curtises, the Stiles, lineal descendants of the early settlers of Woodbury, succeeded and contrasted by ladies and gentlemen in the cavalier costumes of the same period. Some of these costumes were magnificent, and all attracted much attention. Succeeding the couples on foot, came others on horseback, the ladies on pillions. One couple attracted particular attention. They were Capt. Judson Hurd, aged 85 years, and Mrs. Harvey Atwood, aged 72, both dressed in ancient costume, and riding a horse thirty years old. Then followed old chaises with couples clothed in the quaint fashion of other days. And here it should be noticed, that some of these antique costumes and dresses were *bona fide* relics of the olden times, descended as heir-looms from father to son. Nothing could be more curious than this procession of ladies and gentlemen; the latter gallanting the former in all the styles, from that of two centuries ago, down to the present time, the former displaying huge bonnets, high head-dresses, and gowns ranging in size from three breadths in a skirt to the ample dimensions of modern crinoline. The Masons and the general procession followed the antique, making a very imposing display. If the various processions as they entered the town, had been extended in one line, they would have reached the distance of three miles. Nothing in the whole course of the day's proceedings excited such general curiosity, conferred so much real pleasure, or gave so clear an insight into the past.

The procession moved directly to the speaker's stand, arriving there about half-past 11 A. M. The assemblage was, in all probability, the largest ever gathered together in Litchfield county, and far the greatest ever convened in the state on a similar occasion, numbering not less than fifteen thousand persons. Not less than five thousand of these were within hearing distance of the speaker's stand, part of them within, but more without the tent, which was open on all sides. The most effective arrangements had been made by the Chief Marshal for the preservation of order, and to his tact, and the aid of his excellent assistants, great credit is due. Everything was under perfect control. This vast multitude observed the strictest order, and there was no accident of any kind to mar the pleasure of the festive occasion.

The exercises of the day at the stand where Hon. N. B. Smith presided in his dignified and excellent manner, were opened by the choir's singing to the air of "Bruce's Address," the

ODE OF INVOCATION.

BY WILLIAM COTHREN.

Spirits of our sainted dead,
Heroes to these valleys led,
Sages of the hoary head,
Kindly o'er us bend;
Smile upon this classic hour,
To us children, give your power,
In this consecrated bower,
Us your glory lend.

Pioneers of Pomperaug,
Dwellers near the Quassapaug,
By meandering Nonnewaug,
Hasten ye along;
Brothers near the Weraumaug,
By the cliffs of Orenaug,
By the falls of old Shepaug,
Help to swell our song.

From the pines on Bantam's shore,
Softly whispering evermore,
Weekeepeemee's verdant shore,
And from Potatuck,
Come we with our offerings,
All our dear and holy things,
From each side the chorus rings,
E'en from Naugatuck.

Here we come with earnest zeal,
Mindful of our ancient weal,
Memories bright to us appeal,
On this glorious day;
Here where Freedom's banner waves,
Here above our fathers' graves,
We, as erst the native braves,
Glad our honors pay.

We revere those holy men,
Soon returned to Heaven again,
But their works with us remain,
On this festive day;
Thankful to our God above,
For their deeds of matchless love,
Their example let us prove,
While on earth we stay.

PRAYER.

A fervent and impressive prayer was offered to the Throne of Grace, by Rev. Robert G. Williams, pastor of the First Congregational Church of Woodbury, in nearly the following words, viz:

O Lord, our Lord, how excellent is thy name in all the earth. Lord, thou hast been our dwelling place in all generations. Before the mountains were brought forth, or ever thou hadst formed the earth and the world, even from everlasting to everlasting, thou art God.

Thou art the maker of Heaven and earth, and the governor of all things. Thou settest up kings and puttest down princes. Thou dost raise up nations and appoint unto them their habitations, and dost execute thy will and pleasure in them and by them. Varied is their lot and diverse are the manifestations of thy goodness unto them. Many have been left in ignorance of that revelation of thyself, made in thy word unto other favored nations.

We address thee, O God, as the God of the Bible, and we praise thy holy name that unto us thou hast been pleased to send thy word, with its accompanying blessings. We thank thee that thou didst entrust it unto our fathers, so that we enjoy the matured fruits of its long possession, that they so esteemed it and so loved to obey it, that they sought where they might worship thee according to the dictates of their own consciences, enlightened by it. As of thine ancient covenant people, so of them we may say, when thou hast brought a vine out of Egypt, thou hast cast out the heathen and planted it. Thou preparedst room before it and didst cause it to take root, and it filled the land. The hills were covered with the shadow of it, and the boughs thereof were like the goodly cedars. She sent out her boughs unto the sea and her branches unto the river. Return, we beseech thee, O God of Hosts, look down from Heaven and behold and visit this vine: and the vineyard which thy right hand hath planted, and the branch that thou madest strong for thyself. So will not we go back from thee. Quicken us and we will call upon thy name.

We hail thy goodness, O God, in the fruitful valley thou didst open here before our fathers, who led hither two hundred years ago, felt at the sight hereof, that they had found a resting place for their feet, and a home for them and theirs. How has a little one become a thousand, and a small one a strong nation. Verily the lines are fallen to us in pleasant places, yea we have a goodly heritage. Here come up the thousands from the little one, to review that history which thou hast so filled with good, to revive the honored memory of our fathers, to thank and praise thee for them and the results of thy guidance of them. Our joy to-day is thus great because of thy great goodness through the long past. These hills and these valleys display the greatness of thy care. Peace and plenty have abounded as the light of thy smile. Thy covenant mercies have descended in all thine own faithfulness. O God, we thank thee for a pious ancestry, for their Christian courage, for their large and liberal views of Christian institutions, and we this day record thy faithfulness in our experience of the mercy thou dost show unto the children of all such as keep thy commandments. They wandered in the wilderness, in a solitary way. They found no city to dwell in. Hungry and thirsty, their soul fainted in them. Then they cried unto the Lord in their trouble, and he delivered them out of their distresses; and he led them forth by the right way, that they might go to a city of habitation. O that men would praise the Lord for his goodness, and for his wonderful works to the children of men.

Let the incense of those prayers, offered by our fathers in this valley, under the shadow of that Rock which was indeed to them a Bethel, still rise before thee and bring down blessings upon us. Let the noble history of the past, the piety of our fathers, through thy goodness, inspire us with stedfast faith in thee, as a God to be owned in all our personal and civil concerns, and never let us depart from thee. That which we have heard and known, and our fathers have told us, we will not hide them from their children, showing to the generation to come, the praises of the Lord and his strength and his wonderful works that he hath done. For he established a testimony in Jacob, and appointed a law in Israel, which he commanded our fathers that they should make them known to their children, that the generation to come might know them, even the children which should be born, who should arise and declare them to their children, that they might set their hope in God, and not forget the works of God but keep his commandments.

We thank thee O God, for our rich national blessings, our civil and religious privileges, freedom from national commotions, war, pestilence, famine, from tyranny and call to war at the will of fellow-men: freedom to worship God as his own word teaches. Make us not only grateful for these rich privileges, but sensible of our responsibility for them. Enable us to improve them aright, and to transmit them unimpaired to those who are to come after us.

We would implore thy blessing upon thy servant the President of these United States and all others in authority. As we enjoy the sweets of liberty, so let our prayers ascend before thee for all who have them not, especially for the enslaved and oppressed in our own land. Where war rages and man hastens to shed the blood of his fellow man, let the peaceful dove of Christianity soon find a resting place, and the Prince of peace have willing subjects.

We now implore thy presence with us, upon this festive occasion. Guide and guard from all ill. Let no accident harm any here present, and nothing occur to mar the happiness we here seek for ourselves, and to impart to others. Let the preparation for the enjoy ment, and the influence of this occasion be for good to us and our posterity. As the people of these hills and valleys have so much in common, let them ever live together as possessing a common heritage and ever seek to promote their own by caring for the common weal.

God be merciful unto us, and bless us and cause his face to shine upon us. That thy way may appear upon earth, thy saving health among all nations. Let the people praise thee O God, let all the people praise thee. O let the nations be glad and sing for joy, for thou shalt judge the people righteously and govern the nations upon earth. Let the people praise thee O God, let the people praise thee. Then shall the earth yield her increase, and God, even our own God shall bless us. God shall bless us, and all the ends of the earth shall fear him. Let thy work appear unto thy servants and thy glory unto their children, and let the beauty of the Lord our God be upon us, and establish the work of our hands upon us, yea the work of our hands establish thou it. That our sons may be as plants grown up, in their youth, that our daughters may be as corner-stones polished after the similitude of a palace. That our garners may be full, affording all manner of store. That our sheep may bring forth thousands and tens of thousands in our streets; that our oxen may be strong to labor; that there be no breaking in nor going out; that there be no complaining in our streets. Happy is that people that is in such a case, yea happy is that people whose God is the Lord. Blessed be the Lord God, the God of Israel, who only doeth wondrous things, and blessed be his glorious name for ever, and let the whole earth be filled with his glory. Amen and Amen.

The Emigrants from Woodbury were then "Welcomed Home again," by Nathaniel Smith, Esq., of Woodbury:

MR. PRESIDENT, LADIES AND GENTLEMEN, WHO ARE HERE AS RETURNED EMIGRANTS:

We have learned, as the preparations for this our Bi-Centennial Celebration progressed, that many of you would to-day revisit the scenes of your childhood; and have feared that among you there might be some, whose old homesteads no longer echoed to familiar voices,—whose relations had gone out from among us, to a newer or a better land. Lest, therefore, any here should be sad for the lack of kindly greeting in their native valley, the citizens of Ancient Woodbury have directed me to bid you in their name, a CORDIAL WELCOME HOME AGAIN!

We have invited you to unite with us in reviewing a history which is our mutual inheritance,—a past whose story is written all over these hills and valleys. Around us, smiling meadows and cheerful homes speak of the patient, unobtrusive toil that has wrought this "Dwelling in a Wood." Moss, gathered and gathering on the tomb-stones in our grave-yards, tells how long ago the early builders began to fall asleep. Their homes are our possession—their memory a legacy to all.

We are happy to see you here, not only on account of the pleasure your presence adds to the general enjoyment; but more especially because your coming assures us that our history, and song, and services, are not the result of mere local pride, but that you esteem them, as we do, a proper tribute to departed worth, an expression of gratitude justly due from us on such an anniversary, to the noble and the good who have gone before. We commemorate no ordinary struggles and necessities of frontier life. We rehearse the fortitude and success of no common adventurers. Were those whose memory we are here to honor, mere first settlers, actuated by no higher motive than usually leads such into the wilderness, our theme would perhaps be unworthy of this occasion. The pioneer is rarely a man of exalted virtue. Hardy, courageous, and uncouth, he resembles those lichens, which, forerunners of vegetation, fix themselves on the barren rock, by their acids disintegrate its surface and assimilate its substance, till the soil adheres, the grasses grow, and waving flowers succeed them. Not such were the Puritan fathers. They were holy Pilgrims, and the place they sought became a shrine.

To such a spot you return to-day—return to meet cheerful faces and hospitable dwellings. How different was their coming!

"The rocking pines of the forest roared,
This was *their* '*welcome* home.'"

They followed God's guidance into the wilderness, and brought His worship with them. Hardships were before, dangers around them; but they encountered all in that spirit, which instead of choosing castles, towers, or beasts of prey, the emblems of conquest and pride, for armorial bearings, placed three vines upon a shield, and wrote beneath,

"Qui Transtulit Sustinet."

Behold to-day how He has "sustained!" See it in these fruitful valleys! Read it in this happy throng! Truly it is not wonderful that a past thus begun and thus resulting, should move us to unite in public rejoicing. Let other and older nations do homage to conquerors and triumph in their battle-fields, New England celebrates her centuries, which bring down the Puritan's blessing to ever increasing thousands in her land of peace.

Welcome, then, sons and daughters of Ancient Woodbury who return as emigrants to-day—welcome to the land of your fathers, to the scene where we unite to do honor to their memory! How longsoever you have been absent, though you meet with few familiar faces, we greet you as old acquaintances, as near relations. And, knowing that the child of New England never forgets his birth-place, though you have your habitations elsewhere, returning here, we bid you welcome HOME.

ADDRESS

DELIVERED AT

WOODBURY, CONN.,

ON THE OCCASION OF THE

Second Centennial Celebration

OF

ANCIENT WOODBURY,

JULY 4th, 1859.

BY WILLIAM COTHREN, Esq.

ADDRESS.

We stand this day upon the grave of two hundred years. We have come with solemn awe and reverent tread to commune with the long buried past. We are assembled, on this anniversary morn, for the first time, in the long lapse of two centuries, to commemorate the deeds of our departed sires. We are come, after years of absence from the old firesides, to recall the memories and renew the associations of former days. Some of us come to look upon the old homesteads among the hills, and breathe a sigh over the moss-grown graves of ancestors long since gone to their rest. Some of us come to view the hallowed spot on which our eyes first saw the light; where we, in the hours of innocent childhood, received a father's and a mother's blessing, and where we, could we have *our* wish, at the close of a well-spent life, would yield our tired spirits up to the Giver of all good. We are this day surrounded with the results of all the labors of the past, and occupy the proud positions, long years ago so nobly adorned by the sainted fathers and mothers who planted this fertile territory, and who, having ceased from their labors, have "ascended into glory." They have passed away to the land of spirits like the dissolving of a sunset cloud into the cerulean tints of heaven—stealing from existence like the strain of ocean-music, when it dies away, slowly and sweetly, upon the moonlight waters. We do well, on this glad day of liberty, to celebrate their lofty achievements, and do meet honor to their deathless names. If those revered spirits, who have so long enjoyed their sacred repose, can look down through the veil that obscures our view of Heaven, they will approve, with a smile of love, the design of our assembling here. And when, on the morrow, you shall leave this place, to revisit it no more forever, you will feel, that it has been good for you to have been here on this glad occasion.

Let us imagine, for a moment, what a scene met the gaze of the first hardy explorers of these pleasant valleys, two hundred years ago. Every thing betokened that the silence of nature had remained unbroken by human voices since those early days, when "the morning stars sang together," save by those of nature's own uncultivated children, the red hunters of the forest. Nature in all its grand magnificence met the enchanted view of the pale face in these sweetly fertile plains and mountain fastnesses. The grim chiefs of the woody wilds alone roamed over these retired solitudes, save the wild beasts, that growled upon the thousand hills. Every year had the Indians set fire to the fallen leaves, thus denuding the trees of their lower branches, and destroying the underbrush, so that the dense woods presented a most magnificent and enchanting appearance. Thus the "eye was allowed to rove with delight from ridge to ridge, and from hill to hill, which, like the divisions of an immense temple, were crowded with innumerable pillars, the branches of whose shafts, interlocking, framed the arch-work of support to that leafy roof, which covered and crowned the whole." On the meadows by our noble river, were scanty patches of maize, beans, and tobacco, the results of the rude husbandry of the untutored savage of the forest. The whole face of nature was one vast solitude uncheered by the benign rays of civilization. From Wyantenuck to Mattatuck, and from Pootatuck to Bantam, were heard the dismal howl of the wolf, and the war-cry of the red man. Amid these secluded wilds, and by the silvery waters of the Quassapaug, sported the timid deer, and coy doves built their lonely nests. Here dwelt a race groping in the shadow of dim imaginings, faintly led by the light of nature. Here desperate fights and deadly ambuscades were planned. Here did the prisoner of war suffer the extreme tortures of his enemies. Here the romantic lover "wooed his dusky mate," with presents and silent attentions, in primitive simplicity. Here, too, the powwow held his dread incantations, and, if tradition is to be believed, offered human sacrifices to appease the wrath of Hobbamocko, the spirit of evil, the author of all human plagues and calamities. Here, too, in the golden days of the Indian Summer, the poor savage mused of the Great Spirit, the benevolent Kiehtan, giver of his corn, beans, and tobacco, who lived far away to the south-west, in whose blest dominions he hoped, at death, to find his happy hunting grounds.

Such was the scene that greeted the eyes of Capt. John Minor, the intrepid surveyor, and his sturdy companions, as they traversed this territory, which was then the farthest point from shore, that had been explored. This was a short time previous to the 20th day of April, 1659, the date of the first Indian deed of the territory. They spent several days in exploring these valleys, climbing the numerous hills that surround us, and tracing these swiftly gliding streams. They found it to be an excellent place for planting a new colony of pilgrims from the father-land. In the quaint language of the Indian recommendation, when they were negotiating with the first explorers for the sale of these lands, "it was a good place for many smokes of the white man."

But how did our fathers come by their title to this now blooming heritage? How did they acquire the fee to the soil, and the right of dominion? How did they obtain rights, which civilized nations, even, fight for, and wade through rivers of blood to secure? How acquire the same right to rule, that Louis Napoleon and Francis Joseph are now turning Europe upside down to determine? The answer to these questions is at hand, and is honorable to our fathers' sense of right and justice. The descendants of the founders of Woodbury can look upon their landed possessions, as having come down to them by fair, honest, and legitimate titles. No fraud, violence, conquest, or stain of blood attaches to the hem of the garments of our forefathers. They not only purchased their lands of the Indians, but, in some instances, several times over, from conflicting claimants, and dishonest pretenders. They were very particular in procuring title deeds, and alienations executed in legal form and with great solemnity. They were extremely careful, that they might, in this manner, more vividly impress on the minds of the Indians, the binding nature of their contracts. Those children of nature, the former lords of the forest, took great interest in the proceedings, and affixed their uncouth, though often ingenious "marks" of a snow-shoe, a fish, a bow and arrow, a war-club, a snake, or some wild animal, to the deeds that were conveying away forever their paternal hunting-grounds to the pale-faced strangers within their ancient borders. They often stipulated in their conveyances, that the "marked trees," or bounds, should be made "*clere and ffayre*," and that they should be carefully kept from destruction or obliteration.

The deed of 1659, in commemoration of the reception of which we are this day assembled, conveyed all the land within the bounds, "Potateuk River South-west, Naugatunck River North-east, and bounded on y[e] North-west with trees marked by me (Tautannimo) and other Indians." This was signed by the Sachem of the Pagassetts, or Derby Indians, and four of his sagamores, and includes a territory in Litchfield and New Haven counties, nearly as large as Litchfield county itself. It extended, as has been seen, from the Naugatuck to the Housatonic, and from the Southernmost point of Southbury to Bantam Lake. It does not appear that our fathers made much use of this purchase, except perhaps for hunting grounds, till thirteen years later; at which time they planted corn upon the river meadows in company with the Indians. The next year, on the 26th of April, (1673,) they made their first, or Pomperaug purchase, of the Pootatuck Indians, the real occupants of the soil, covering the whole town plot from the Eastern hills to "Wecuppeme," and from the North end of East Meadow to the "Bent" of the Pomperaug River at South Britain, taking in "transiluania and rag-land." By this purchase, a large part of the most fertile and arable lands of the town was obtained. The second purchase of land from the Pootatucks, was made on the 17th of March, 1685–6. This was the Shepaug Purchase, comprising two-thirds of the present town of Roxbury, and part of Southbury. On the 18th of May, 1700, the inhabitants of the town, having become numerous for those days, made their fourth, or Nonnewaug purchase. Till this time it seems, that the Sagamore of that name had retained his possessions in the valley of the Nonnewaug, or East Sprain Stream. But now it came his turn to make room, and it seems that he and his companions did it with a good grace, as the deed informs us the sale was made "For valid considerations moving thereto, besides ye desire y^{t} is wthin us of a friendly correspondency wth ye English inhabitants of s^{d} Woodbury." At a very early day, that part of Southbury known as Kettletown, had been purchased of the Indians for the consideration of a brass kettle. It had been bought the second time seven years after the settlement of the town; and on the 25th of October, 1705, it became necessary to purchase it the third time. Something more than a quarter of a century had passed since the last sale, and, by this time, it is probable that they again felt the need of the "consideration." This was the fifth regular purchase of the Pootatucks. On the 28th of May, next year, the town purchased the sixth, or Confirmatory purchase. This covered and confirmed all former grants and purchases, together with a considerable tract of land in Roxbury, and a piece eighty rods in width from Steep Rock in Washington, to the mouth of the Shepaug, on the West side of that river. In this *deed* the Indians reserved a large tract of land in the South-west part of Southbury, called the Pootatuck Reservation. This was bounded on the North by a line drawn from Shepaug Falls to the "Bent" of the Pomperaug, East by that river, or by a line drawn parallel to, and a few rods East of it, from the "Bent" to its mouth, South by the Pootatuck, and West by the Shepaug river. This reservation, now called "The Purchase," contained the principal Indian village, located on the Pootatuck River, South of South Britain village. After this sale, the Indians continued to convey portions of it from time to time, till 1733, when there was left to them only a remnant of their possessions at the South-east corner, in which was located their last remaining village, called the "Pootatuck Wigwams." They retained their title to this last resting place for the soles of their feet for a quarter of a century longer, when, being reduced to a mere handful in numbers, in May, 1759, just one hundred years ago, they parted with their cherished Pootatuck, and the "remnant that remained," took up their abode with the Scatacook Indians at Kent, where a few of the full, and more of the half blood remain to this day. In all their later sales, they reserved to themselves the right to take game on the lands forever;—a right which was always religiously respected by our fathers, whenever a straggling Pootatuck revisited the graves of his ancestors, or wandered in his once wide dominions!

The "marks" with which these Indians signed their deeds, were interesting and unique. Nonnewaug's mark was a snow-shoe, Wecuppeme's, a snake, Momanchewaug's, a rude drawing of the face of a prostrate foe, Punhone's, a warrior's uplifted arm, and that of Tummasseete, the owner of the first orchard in this territory, was a bow and arrow. These "marks" were as truly signatures, and as readily identified as our own. What the mark of Pomperaug was, is not known, as he never was brought to the sad necessity of parting with any of his hunting grounds. He never made *his* "mark," to such a confession of weakness and declining power.

It is many years since the last Pootatuck, an old squaw, came back to the seat of the Pootatuck village, to revisit the graves of her forefathers, whose bones are washed out from the sandy plain, at every sudden overflow of the noble Pootatuck. Looking up to the place where stood, and still stand, the few remaining trees of "Tummasseete's old orchard," "There," she said, the tears streaming down her wrinkled cheeks, "there is Pootatuck, the home of the buried braves!" What a world of sad associations cluster around that simple outburst of nature! After lingering near the graves of her people a few days, she returned to the place whence she came, and the light of the pristine race, in this territory, went out forever!

Thus it is seen, that the early fathers fairly purchased every foot of the ancient territory, and took conveyances with due and proper solemnities. From the known character of the men, it is to be presumed, that these bargains were honestly conducted; and it does not appear that any dispute of any account, ever arose between the parties, in regard to them. Nor were these purchases liable to the criticism of insufficient consideration. The amounts paid were large for those days of poverty; and no doubt, the untutored savages, who, as yet, considered their lands of little or no value, rejoiced greatly over such large prices and rare articles as they received for pay, and probably thought they had, by far, the best of the bargain. They knew not how soon they would be straightened for land, and their people scattered like the leaves of the forest. In the order of Providence, one race had arisen, another had passed away. Sampson's locks were shorn—his glory and strength had departed. The red man with a sad prodigality had parted with his only wealth.

Let us pause a moment to drop a passing tear over the obliterated graves of a buried race. They are all gone to meet the Great Spirit, and, perhaps, as they desired in life, to revel in "happy hunting grounds." By the romantic Falls of his own ever murmuring stream, is the grave of Nonnewaug. In his own orchard at Pootatuck, near the noble Housatonic, rest the remains of Tummasseete. Within the fertile meadows of Weekeepeemee reposes the brave of that name, in his last quiet sleep. And *there*, by that rock, in your very midst, they buried Pomperaug, the renowned chief of your valley, who gave his name to your beautiful meandering river. A hillock of small stones now mark the spot, dropped there, one by one, with a tear to each, by his remaining braves as they sadly passed the hallowed spot, on their hunting and fishing excursions.

And who were the strange people, that occupied these pleasant dwelling places in the woods, when the white man reached these shores? They were, indeed, a strange race, beginning in mystery, and ending in annihilation. Their origin and mission on earth seem to be one of the secrets of the Great Creator. The race found inhabting these new regions, did not live in comfortable dwellings, surrounded by verdant fields, which they cultivated, but semi-nude, or clad in the skins of wild beasts, they wandered, in small clans, in the dense forests, among the lofty mountains, by the murmuring streams, and along the meandering rivers. They were destitute of the arts of civilized life; had strange rites and unheard of customs. They engaged in fierce conflicts and exterminating wars. They were men of iron will, who knew no fear, and whom severest tortures could not move. They never forgot a kindness, nor forgave an injury. They were idolaters, and on our now peaceful and happy plains, they offered human sacrifices to appease the God of evil, created by their own superstitious imaginations. This rude and barbarous people was scattered all over our extended continent, and yet they had hitherto been unknown—insulated from the rest of the world. Our fathers tried to civilize and Christianize them with little success, though they granted them the privilege of attending their schools and religious assemblies. Some of them, indeed, profited by these privileges, gained the rudiments of knowledge, put themselves under the care of the ministers, and became approved members of the Churches. But the great majority adhered to the dark and cheerless faith, and cruel rites believed and practiced by their forefathers. So far as the Indians of this town were concerned, they were always the friends of our fathers, and maintained with them a perpetual peace. There were some Indian conflicts here, but they arose from the incursions of the Mohawks, who previous to the arrival of the settlers, held the Indians of this territory as tributaries, by superior prowess. As early as 1675, during King Philip's war, they made a treaty with the pioneers to these valleys, in which they covenanted to continue in "friendship with the white settlers, and be enemies to their enemies, and discover them timely, or destroy them." This treaty was ever kept, as a perpetual league, with entire good faith, by both the contracting parties, and many were the mutual offices of kindness they performed for each other. Let it be taken for granted, then, as many have asserted, that the Indian was fierce, vindictive, uncultivated and untamable; yet with all his faults and failings, he stood erect, in the midst of nature's leafy temple, God's original freeman. He could never be enslaved. No superior power, intelligence or cunning, could make him wear the bondman's chain!

Wild rovers of Pootatuck, Mattatuck, Wyantenuck, Pomperaug, Raumaug, Bantam, ye have passed away! Your lights have gone out on the shore! Your thin smokes no longer curl faintly amid the thick woods! Well do we love your good old Indian names, and would that more of them, almost the sole relic of your once powerful people, had been adopted by our fathers to designate the places where your lights went out forever!

Such are the simple annals of the unfortunate, and benighted race that once had possession of this fair heritage, and roamed in haughty independence through these sequestered vales. Not a Pootatuck remains in the territory of the ancient town, to revisit, with Indian wail and lamentation, the forsaken, and almost forgotten graves of his ancestors. When the floods, or excavations of the present inhabitants, exhume the bones of the long buried braves, they are gathered up with eager interest, to grace a public museum or private collection of antique curiosities. Their sun has set in darkness and in gloom. Advancing civilization, so fortunate and happy for the white race, brought nothing to the red man but disaster and decay. With a sad infatuation, they embraced its vices instead of its virtues. Before the white man touched these shores, they enjoyed their wild and savage mode of life without molestation. This was "their own, their native land!" Here were their council fires. On the beautiful rivers, they paddled the light canoe, and pursued their game in the unbroken forests. They went up by their mountains; they came down by their valleys; they followed their own desires for happiness in wild, reckless exhuberance. The mossy cliffs, and the dells in the thick woods, echoed back their shrill songs, and fearful cry of war. But the white man took up his abode in their ancient hunting grounds. The strength of civilization met the weakness of barbarism. From that inauspicious hour, the poor natives waned and retreated farther into the wild solitudes. The children of the forest have passed away—faded from the view, and almost from the memory of man. In their low, unnoticed, and unknown graves, they sleep well! Their existence has become a matter of antiquarian research, and oft-told legend. Their brief history has been written in desolation.

> "Alas, for them, their day is o'er—
> Their fires are out from shore to shore!
> No more for them the wild deer bounds,
> The plow is on their hunting grounds."

The settlement of Woodbury was the result of difference in religious opinion, among the inhabitants of Stratford. It was accomplished by one of the most remarkable and brilliant mental conflicts that ever occurred in planting a New England town. There were giants in those days, for the defence of what they believed to be religious truth. The usual reason for settling a new town had ever been, that the parent town had become too full to accommodate all its inhabitants, and that it was necessary to seek new locations for extending the Church of God, and advancing the interests of religious freedom. No idea of mere worldly advantage entered the minds of the stern and earnest men, who planted our beautiful and ever honored town. The first ministers of the colony being dead, and a new generation coming on the stage of action, alterations in respect to Church membership, baptism, and the mode of Church discipline, were imperiously demanded. Great dissensions on these subjects accordingly arose in the churches at Hartford, Windsor, Wethersfield, and other places, and continued in various parts of the Colony, from 1656 to about 1670. It is difficult for us, at this distance of time, fully to understand the exact merits of the controversy. The system in dispute, was called the "Half Way Covenant" system of Church membership. Upon this question there was the gravest difference of opinion among the most learned and pious men in New England. By this plan, a person of good moral character might own or renew the covenant of Baptism, confessing the same creed as members of the Church in full communion, and affirming his intention of becoming truly pious, in heart and in life, have the privilege of presenting himself, children, grand-children, and even his slaves, for baptism, by giving a pledge for their religious education. Persons thus owning the covenant, were considered members of the Church to all intents and purposes, except that they might not come to the communion table. For conduct unbecoming church members, they could be, and were, dealt with, and punished in the same manner as members in full communion. Consequent upon this practice, baptisms followed close upon births, generally in from one to eight days, and if the child was in danger of "non-continuance," it was baptized on the day of its birth.

In those early days, the choice of pastors was confined exclusively to members of the church, though every freeholder was taxed for their support; and nearly all the offices and honors of the Colony of Connecticut, to which Stratford belonged, were distributed to professors of religion, who alone, in the New Haven Colony, possessed the right of suffrage in meetings of a political character. During the lives of the early colonists, little trouble had arisen on these points, nearly all of the first immigrants having been professors of religion. But this generation had passed away, and a new one had succeeded, many of whom, on account of their not belonging to the church, were excluded from their proper influence in the community. Most of them had been baptized, and by virtue of this, it was claimed that they might own their covenant, have their children baptized, and thus perpetuate the church, and themselves attain the rank of perfect freemen. Hence it may readily be seen why our patriotic forefathers, as well as those who were thus excluded from their proper position in the affairs of the town and colony, desired such a change in church government as would overcome this unjust inequality. All New England became interested in this controversy; and in 1657, it was decided by a council of the principal ministers of the colonies, convened at Boston, that it was the duty of those, who had come to years of discretion, baptized in infancy, to own the covenant; that it was the duty of the Church to call them to do it, and, if they refused, they might be censured by the Church. In consequence of this decision, many owned their covenant, and presented their children for baptism, but did not unite with the church in the celebration of the supper, nor in most other duties of members in full communion. Hence it was termed the "Half Way Covenant System."

The Church of Stratford, notwithstanding the Boston decision, would not adopt this practice, although a large and influential part of its members were in favor of it, together with a majority of the voters of the town, who were not church members. Rev. Israel Chauncey, son of President Charles Chauncey, of Cambridge, who was opposed to this practice, was settled over the Church in 1665, receiving ordination in the independent mode. On this account, a large part of the Church and town was opposed to his ordination. It was therefore agreed, that if after hearing Mr. Chauncey for a certain time, they should continue to be dissatisfied with his ministry, the dissenting party should be at liberty to call and settle another minister, and have the same privilege in the Meeting House as the other party. Accordingly, after hearing Mr. Chauncey the time agreed on, and continuing to be dissatisfied with his ministrations, they invited Rev. Zechariah Walker to preach to them, and finally chose him for their pastor. Both ministers performed public worship in the same house, Mr. Chauncey at the usual hours, while Mr. Walker was allowed two hours in the middle of the day. They had been a long time in agreeing upon this arrangement, as will be seen. But it was difficult always to confine the services to the exact time allowed, and it soon happened, that Mr. Walker exceeded the time limited, one day, to such an extent, that Mr. Chauncey and his hearers becoming impatient, retired to a private house, and there held their afternoon services. They were, however, so much displeased, that next day, they went over to Fairfield, and made a complaint against Mr. Walker to Major Gold, one of the magistrates. The Major, upon hearing the case, advised pacific measures, and that Mr. Walker should be allowed three hours for his public exercises. Then begun that remarkable conflict of master minds, conducted on one side by Rev. Mr. Chauncey and Phillip Graves, and on the other by Rev. Mr. Walker, Capt.

John Minor, "the learned and pious scribe," Hon. Samuel Sherman and Lt. Joseph Judson, men of worth and might, whose blood courses through the veins of a larger number of persons in this great assembly, than that of all others put together. I had almost asked, who is there here that does not claim some connection with those early founders, either by birth or matrimonial ties! It was a battle of the "giants!" Time forbids that I should give full details of this remarkable contest. Nor is it necessary, as they are doubtless familiar to you all, being set forth with great particularity, in the late history of this territory. Suffice it to say, that the efforts of the dissenting party, our fathers, for reconciliation, seem to have been earnest and sincere. Their communications to their brethren were couched in respectful and Christian terms, and their arguments were not to be easily refuted, if at all. Little pains, however, seems to have been taken by the first Church, during the whole controversy, to answer the reasoning of the dissatisfied party, or to conciliate them; but it seemed rather to throw itself back on its dignity with an intention of allowing the dissentients to take their own course. The latter had a majority in the town meetings, and Dea. John Minor, one of their leaders, was Town Clerk during the whole time of the controversy, and for several years afterward. This written controversy has been preserved on the colony and town records, and is a model of Christian courtesy and moderation, well worth the study of all future Church agitators and dissenters. Mr. Walker's party earnestly sought an entire union with the members of the first Church. Even those in full communion offered to be again examined in regard to their "fayth and knowledge," in the same manner as upon their first admission, that the Church might be convinced their peculiar views had not, in any manner, undermined their religious principles, or purity of character. When this was denied, and after they had called Mr. Walker, they earnestly desired to unite the two meetings, and hear both ministers, the more especially, as the Meeting House had been built by both parties. To unite the two meetings was evidently not the best way of composing their differences, although they might not be "fundamental," as was admitted by all, for their opinions in regard to church membership, were so diverse, they could hardly have been much edified in being obliged to listen to the defence of what they did not believe. It would be much like the mingling of the worship of the various evangelical churches of the present day. While the ministers might confine themselves to points on which all were agreed, there would be danger of treading, at times, on forbidden ground.

In September, 1668, the church refused to hear the two ministers in joint meeting, and refused further to consider the disputes between them till Mr. Walker's party had "procured the approbation of the General Court, and the consent of neighboring Churches." In November, of the same year, Mr. Walker, for his people, replied to this communication, in a paper of great power, and informed them that they had concluded, "God willing," to occupy their joint property, the Meeting House, a part of each Sabbath, beginning with the next Sabbath, and that they would use it during that part of the day which Mr. Chauncey's party might determine, but if they did not designate, then they would take the latter part of the day. He closed the communication with the desire that the "God of Peace" would guide the parties to such a course of action as would be for their "mutual peace and comfort." The result of this notice was a compromise, by which Mr. Walker was allowed two hours each Sabbath for his services in the Meeting House, in the middle of the day, between the two services of Mr. Chauncey, till the meeting of the General Court in May, 1669. At that session both parties presented petitions in relation to their disagreements, particularly in regard to the manner in which they should "enjoy the Meeting House." Without reflection, one might say that the readiest way out of the difficulty would have been to have built another church. But it must be borne in mind that the country was new, and the inhabitants poor. It was a great undertaking in their wilderness condition, to erect a suitable building, and heavy taxes for years were necessary to be laid to complete one. The Court took the case into consideration, as requested, confirmed the choice of Mr. Chauncey, ordered both parties to choose "some indifferent persons of piety and learning to compose their differences," and gave Mr. Walker's party liberty till the October session, to occupy the church three hours each Sabbath, in the middle of the day, between the two services of Mr. Chauncey. They could not, however, agree upon the points to be submitted to the arbitrators, and at the October session. 1669, a resolution was passed by the General Court advising the First Church to comply with the desire of Mr. Walker's party, to have union services, allowing Mr. Walker to preach one part of each Sabbath to the united congregation. Some communications passed between the parties relative to this advice, but Mr. Chauncey's party, instead of granting them the privilege which they had so long sought, excluded them from the House entirely, after which, they met for public worship in a private house during the remainder of their stay at Stratford. In reply to this indignity, our fathers merely addressed a letter to the First Church, complaining of the injustice done them, and proposed to divide the town into two parts, that they "might go and live by themselves and have no more dissensions." They also notified them that they should apply to the next session of the Court to grant them this indulgence. It was at this juncture that Governor Winthrop, affected by these unhappy controversies and animosities subsisting in the town, advised that Mr. Walker and his people should remove, and that a tract of land for the settlement of a new town should be granted for their encouragement and accommodation. Accordingly, the General Court, on the 9th of May, 1672, granted to Samuel Sherman, William Curtiss, Joseph Judson and John Minor, the leading members of Mr. Walker's Church, "liberty to erect a plantation at Pomperoage," provided that any "other honest inhabitants of Stratford" should have liberty to join them in settling there, and provided they should "enterteine so many inhabitants as the plantation would conveniently interteine."

Thus ended a controversy that had agitated the minds of the early fathers for about eight years. During the whole of that long period of disagreeing opinions, and exciting discussions, it will be found by a careful examination of all the details, the future founders of our town ever maintained an elevated and christian tone, temper and aim. They furnished a model course of action to us, their descendants, on all occasions of conflict of interests and opinion. It might be interesting, did time permit, and it were pertinent to the theme of the hour, to inquire whether, in this regard, the sacred mantles of those revered Elijahs of the early days, have fallen upon us, their descendants, the custodians of their moss-grown graves! Would to God we could truly claim their stern, conscientious motives, and command of passion, in times when "offenses must come!"

It was in the midst of this controversy, early in 1668, that Mr. Walker was called to perform pastoral labors among the people of the 2nd Church of Stratford, now the First Church of Woodbury. For two years he had preached to them without ordination. Among the other difficulties under which his friends labored, they had found no opportunity to accomplish this desirable point. But being taunted by the First Church, on account of their disorganized state, being informed that they would hold no further communication with them till they were duly organized, and there being no longer any hope of arrangement with the other party, they took the steps necessary to "embody in Church estate." This they accomplished on the 1st day of May, 1670, with the approval of the churches of Fairfield, Killingworth, and the "new church at Windsor." Mr. Walker was ordained on the 5th of May, when twenty male members again publicly owned their covenant, the gathering of the church having been done by themselves in private, on account of the great opposition to them. Seven more male members were admitted a few days after, and ten more, six of whom were females, were added previous to the removal to Pomperaug, in 1672, a number fully equal to that of most other churches at their commencement. This was an honored list of names, one to be revered by the dwellers in these fair vales, while time shall endure, and they shall retain an emotion of religious sensibility, or filial gratitude.

The initial point from which dates the existence of Woodbury, was the grant of the General Court, in accordance with Gov. Winthrop's recommendation, in 1672. As this grant was not made till the May Session, it was too late for our forefathers to move their families into the wilderness that year; but the preliminary arrangements were immediately commenced, and it is related that a few of the proprietors came here, and raised some corn, which they stored in log cribs, but when they returned next spring, with fifteen families, they found that the wild beasts or Indians had rifled them of their contents. By some mistake, the pioneer company passed the Pomperaug, in their journey, and followed up the Shepaug some miles till they discovered their error, when they made the best of their way over the hills to this valley. Arrived upon yonder Good Hill, they perceived the valley of the Pomperaug lying below in solitude and silence. Great was the joy of these pioneers of our town, on this discovery, and it is related that Dea. John Minor fell on his knees, leading in prayer that little band of hardy adventurers, invoking the blessing of Heaven upon their enterprise, and praying that their posterity might be an upright and godly people to the latest generation. So far as the good deacon's own posterity is concerned, his prayer seems to have been answered, for it has never since been without a *Deacon* to proffer the same petition! And on the morrow, at that sacred retreat, the "Bethel Rock" of our fathers, you will have the opportunity of listening to the same pious aspirations from one of his lineal descendants, inheritor of his revered surname and honorable office!

The pioneers encamped the first night on Good Hill. The next day they proceeded to the valleys, to examine and take possession of their lands, and encamped the second night beneath the spreading branches of a large white oak, which has given its name to the local-

6

ity, and pieces of its trunk, long since prostrated by the tempest, are now in the possession of many persons, preserved with religious care as mementoes of that historic old tree. After having examined the whole valley from East Meadow to the intervales below "White Oak Plain," following the Indian trail leading from Nonnewaug Falls, nearly in the line of the present Main Street, by Pomperaug's grave, to the Pootatuck village on the Housatonic, they pitched their tents permanently, and prepared to build their first rude habitations. We have full evidence from the Colony records, that the intervales on the Pomperaug had been deprived of their trees, and had been cultivated by the Indians before our fathers removed here. So the land was in some measure prepared for their occupation. All their dwellings, at first, were built of logs, the nearest saw-mill being at the parent town of Stratford, twenty-five miles distant, through the pathless woods. But these habitations passed away with the first generation, and comfortable frame dwellings took their places. The first framed house was located in Judson Lane, a few rods west of the First Congregational Church. They were built in a substantial manner, in the old lean-to style, the back roof running nearly to the ground, and were covered with rent oak clapboards. Even these dwellings of the leading men would be considered rude ones, at least, at the present day. But our fathers came to this wilderness to enjoy the ordinances of God, according to the dictates of their own consciences, and to extend His Church—not to gratify worldly ambition.

Among the preparations which the early fathers made for their removal hither, was a code of laws, or articles of agreement for their government after their arrival at the place of destination, quite as carefully drawn as that written covenant, entered into by the Pilgrims before they left the Mayflower to pitch their tents in this western land, the goal of all their hopes and prayers. This model constitution, containing all the elements of civilization, justice, and religious liberty, has been preserved to us entire. It is the perfect germ, containing all the elements of our later republican constitutions. It was most truly a form of government founded upon the "consent of the governed"—aye, the written consent. It provided that as many persons should be admitted into the plantation, as could be comfortably accommodated, and that all public charges, civil and ecclesiastical, should be borne in proportion to the size of their home-lots, the largest being twenty-five, and the smallest ten acres, while a bachelor's right could be no more than five acres, just half that of the least opulent married man! Poor, old bachelor—unmated specimen of humanity! He was considered of little account in a new community in the forest, where the legitimate increase of the population was a prime necessity! It was further provided, that considerable tracts of land should be set apart for the support of the preaching of the gospel, and also, in the quaint language of the original instrument, "a parsell of land for y[e] Incouriging a Schoole, y[t] learning may not be neglected to children." Each was obliged to pay his pro rata part of the purchase of the plantation, the expenses of removal, and all other public charges, within ten months after his home-lot was laid out to him, in wheat, peas, and pork, in equal proportions. Lastly, and above all, it was stipulated, that for the purpose of remaining in the "peaceable enjoyment of that way of Church discipline which they were persuaded is according to God," they engaged, each for himself, not to disturb the peace of the plantation, but to subject themselves, personally, "to that Ecclesiastical Government, that should be there established, or practiced agreeably to y[e] Word of God."

These articles were subscribed, March 20, 1672–3, by *seventeen* of our forefathers, whose names should be written in letters of living light! Sherman, Judson, Minor, Curtiss, Wheeler, Wyatt, Styles, Hinman, Jenkins, Johnson, Munn, Terrill, Knowles, Fairchild, we fain would call your sainted shades from the regions of the blest, for one brief moment, that we might here and now render appropriate homage to your ever-brilliant and glorious example! But three of your illustrious names have ceased to have living representatives in this fair territory you did so much to improve and bless. Truly has the Scripture been fulfilled, in your former seats—"I have never seen the righteous forsaken, nor his seed begging bread!" Look kindly down upon us, assembled here with filial hearts and fond recollections, and breathe a fervent benison from your celestial homes!

A moment's examination will show the wisdom of the provisions of the first solemn governmental covenant. The committee of principal men composed a Court to judge between man and man, doing justice according to the letter of God's "written word," until a town should be organized under the jurisdiction of magistrates, "who are appointed of God." Imagine to yourselves such a Court of God, sitting in solemn state, in the midst of these virgin wilds and pathless forests!

There was a restriction as to the quantity of land which a proprietor might have. No one could have more than twenty-five acres for his home-lot, and other divisions in proportion, while the poorest married man was entitled to ten; so that a few rich planters could not control the colony. It was desirable in those early days of danger from savage men and wild beasts, for the inhabitants to live near together. Their home-lots were laid out on both sides of the street with narrow fronts, to bring their houses near each other for mutual protection.

From these articles we learn that here, as in all other early New England towns, the settlers had a particular regard for the establishment of religious institutions. It was their design to erect churches in strict conformity to scripture example, and to transmit evangelical purity, in doctrine, worship and discipline, with civil and religious liberty, to their posterity. So great was the attention paid to these interesting points, that they not only made ample provision for the minister, who was to remove with them, but they also sequestered lands for the future support of the ministry, which went under the name of the "parsonage lands."

Another truly New England feature in this their first solemn agreement, is seen in the ample provision made for a school, "that learning might not be neglected to the children." Our fathers, though living under Kingly rule, were republicans, rejecting with abhorrence the doctrines of the divine right of Kings, passive obedience and non-resistance. Upon these principles they formed their civil institutions. They thought the church should be accompanied by the school-house, religious principle by an educated and ennobled understanding. In this way, they judged, intelligence and good morals could best be propagated.

We notice, also, the poverty of our ancestors at this time, and the entire want of a metalic, or paper currency. All the expenses growing out of the purchase and settlement of the plantation, were to be paid in wheat, peas and pork, in equal proportions, as to value, and if any settler was so poor that he could not obtain a surplus of these, beyond the wants of his own family, then he was to pay in other articles to the satisfaction of the committee having charge of the expenses of the settlement.

It might, to the careless observer, seem frivolous to have a celebration, and deliver long addresses in commemoration of so trivial an affair as the founding of a single town. The satisfactory answer is that the limits of our town comprised a whole county, and that the number, worth and standing of the noble men that founded it, and removed here during the first two years of its settlement, was fully equal to that of most of the New England colonies at the date of their settlement. There were but forty-one signers to the articles on board of the May Flower, on the 11th of November, 1620, for the founding of the ever celebrated colony of Plymouth, the pioneer colony to our immense continent, save the failure of Jamestown, Va. The first grant of the entire colony of Connecticut was made to eleven persons, and the first three towns in 1635, were settled by about sixty persons, men, women and children, or twenty to each town, a much smaller number than that which first colonized Woodbury. Roger Williams pitched his tent at Providence, founded Rhode Island, and formed a body politic for the advancement of religious freedom, when his followers, including himself, numbered only eighteen. Massachusetts Bay colony had a still smaller beginning. At first, it was nearly a failure, and for a considerable time was held only by Roger Conant and three other "disheartened companions," and yet in his lofty trust, he believed that "God would make this land a receptacle for his people." Let it not be considered, then, that the founding of Woodbury was an inconsiderable, or trivial affair. The history of an early Connecticut town is the history of a Colony, a State, or the Union, in miniature. In no way can we form so accurate an estimate of the dangers and difficulties that beset our fathers, the hardships borne, and the labors performed, to secure the liberty and unnumbered blessings, which we now enjoy, as by a perfect history of the events and struggles of such a town.

In these days of civilization and refinement, surrounded by the comforts, conveniences and luxuries of life, we can little estimate the hardships and difficulties encountered by the sainted men and women who first trod these smiling valleys, subdued the uncompromising wilderness, and made the howling wastes to "bud and blossom as the rose." Here they came, in their lofty trust, having no cover for their heads but the over-arching heavens, no lodgings for their weary and travel-worn bodies but such as nature afforded. The men of the present day may carelessly smile at the idea of our fathers' thinking so much of a journey to or from the sea-coast, or even from Woodbury to Bethlem, as we are told they did. But they forget the obstacles and dangers they had to encounter. They forget there were no public roads, and no vehicles, that could be employed for the transportation of their goods. There were no railroads, nor steamboats, running in all directions with the swiftness of the wind. The first females, as well as the males, went on foot, or on horseback, through a trackless wilderness, guided by marks upon trees, or feeling their way, wherever they could find room to pass. In the midst of the first drear winter their provisions gave out, and some of the settlers were obliged to take their way through the pathless forests to the older settlements for food to sustain them during the remaining wintry months. Some of those sturdy men went to Stratford, a distance of twenty-five miles, with hand-sleds, and returned laden with corn for their pressing necessities. We can have but a faint idea of the dangers that surrounded those early founders, on such a journey, exposed to all the perils and privations of those interior forests. They were surrounded by numerous red men, fierce and cruel, who could have destroyed them at any hour, in their isolated and feeble condition. Added to their lack of bread, the pioneers had neither dwellings, nor clothing sufficient to prevent suffering. Should any emergency happen, they were cut off from any succor, or effective retreat. What a sad beginning had these now fair and opulent towns on the Pomperaug and Shepaug!

It was necessary to erect and fortify houses, to make roads for their convenience to the parent town, that in times of danger they might fly for safety, and to spend much time in watchings, trainings, and preparation for the defense of themselves and children. Every thing was to be constructed from rude materials, or brought from a great distance, and procured at a dear rate. There could be no safety but in constant preparation, for any emergency that might arise. They were obliged, with little previous knowledge of the art, to break ground on bare creation, drawing their subsistence from an unwilling, virgin soil! That *fifteen* families, in the wilderness, before they had time to provide for their own pressing wants, should undertake to support a minister of the Gospel, shows the enduring confidence, the lofty trust of those men of iron nerve! They had no shipping, and nothing to export. Every thing must be manufactured by themselves, or they must go without the indispensable necessaries of life. They being only tillers of the soil, must become their own carpenters, blacksmiths, shoemakers, clothiers and tailors! And in one respect it was well. They thus learned the dignity of labor, in every department. "The grim present was lowering upon them with all its sharp and angular realities."

But they accepted the chances, with a firm reliance on Providence. Amid all their difficulties they forgot not the reverence due their holy religion. So strict were they in their religious views, and so high was their regard for the Sabbath, that they scrupled even to call the first day of the week by its heathen, or idolatrous name of *Sun-day*, and they always, when they had occasion to allude to the day, called it either the Lord's day or the Sabbath. For the same reason, Monday was called the second day, Tuesday the third day, and so of the rest. That they might not acknowledge, in the least degree, the authority of the Pope, in speaking of the apostles, Peter and Paul, they invariably omitted the prefix, "Saint," and even the poor isle of St. Christopher's had its saintly prefix similarly disposed of, and left in obscurity.

It has been seen that all the ideas of our fathers were essentially religious, and that the pious sentiment entered into everything. Even in the exhibitions of the tender emotions, and in the preliminary ceremonies of a matrimonial alliance, they ever exhibited the same grave countenance, and air of devotion, as when going to a prayer-meeeting. Perhaps they were the only people who treated the subject with the consideration due to that most important and indissoluble union of "Kindred hearts." But the "course of true love" was usually urgent. There was no time for "billing and cooing," much less for vain flirtations! As an instance of the way in which the thing was done, take the following characteristic example: John Minor, Jr., being seriously inclined, by the state of his affections, unto the blooming and comely damsel, Sarah Judson, immediately mounted his horse, with a deer-skin for a saddle, and rode over in front of the house of the fair Sarah's father. Without dismounting, he sent for her to come out to him, and on her complying with the request, he informed her plainly, that the Lord had sent him to marry her. At this startling announcement, the sensible maid, neither fainting in the present fashionable mode, nor asking time to consult her mamma, replied with hearty good will, "Here is the handmaid of the Lord—His will be done!" What else could the maiden do; for John was a good man, and she believed both him and his message! There was nothing more to be done, than to get on horseback the next Sabbath eve, and sitting on a pillion, behind her messenger from the Lord, ride to the parsonage, and be duly joined in the holy bonds of wedlock. Of the fruits of that primitive marriage, there are many representatives here to-day!

Doubtless the question has often occurred to each of us, how did our fathers and mother's dress? What were their costumes and fashions? By the indefatigable exertions of our "Antique Committee," this question has been very satisfactorily answered here to-day, by their actual, not "counterfeit presentment." You have seen an "early father," a fine old English gentleman, in small clothes and coat of brown silk, white plaited rufles, powdered hair, and cocked hat. You have seen an "early mother," in ash-colored brocade, with white damask skirt, open in front, high-heeled shoes, with large buckles, and an enormous bonnet. You have seen the Puritan costume contrasted with that of the Cavalier of the same age. But these were the holiday suits, brought from old England, and belonging only to the more opulent citizens. After the first settlement here, such rich articles for long years were "rarities under the sun." All the garments of both sexes were of homespun, of their own manufacture, from the raw material to the perfected garment. The small clothes, and even the coats of the men were often made of deer-skins and leather. Nothing is more commonly mentioned in the early inventories of estates. And yet, amid all this rigid simplicity, the General Court, four years after the settling of Woodbury, passed an act against the excess of apparel among the people, as "unbecoming a wilderness condition, and the profession of the gospel;" ordering, that any person who should wear any clothing, that should be "apparently beyond the necessary end of apparel for *covering*, or *comeliness*," should, on due conviction, forfeit *ten* shillings for every offence! How great a commotion would be made by the passage of *such* a law, in these days of expanded crinoline, and of lengthened Shanghai coats!

So numerous had the arrivals of our ancestors become in the new plantation of Pomperaug, during the year 1673, that at the May session of the General Court, in 1674, it was made a town, called Woodbury, and exempted from taxes for four years. In May, 1675, a committee was appointed to lay out a road to Derby, and Stratford was ordered to construct a road to the same place. This committee did not report till May, 1677, and it is probable, that it was not completed under several years. So that the settlers remained secluded from all the world for many years.

But far more serious evils awaited the adventurous pioneers in this "dwelling place of the wood." In June, 1675, King Philip's war broke out, and filled this and the neighboring colonies with the gloom and terror, which always accompany Indian warfare. The startling intelligence of a general combination of all the eastern tribes for the utter extermination of the white race, fell with a sad cadence on the afflicted ears of our fathers. Philip with his fierce band of relentless warriors, appeared suddenly on the scene of action, and misery and destruction followed in his trail. Every portion of the colony suffered from the predatory excursions of the savages, and continual alarms.

The frontier towns, like Woodbury, were particularly exposed to destruction. The General Court, deeply affected with the apparent danger, enacted military regulations of the most careful and rigorous kind. It was equivalent to putting the whole colony under martial law. Sixty soldiers were to be raised in each county, places for defence and refuge to be immediately fortified in every plantation, disobedience of orders in time of attack to be punished with death, and no male, between the ages of fourteen and seventy, to be suffered to leave the colony without permission. Each plantation was obliged to keep a sufficient watch from sunset to sunrise, and to keep one-fourth of the town in arms every day, taking regular turns. The watch was directed to call up every man in the town, an hour before day, and each one was directed to arm himself, repair to his appointed ward, and there stand guard, ready to repel any attack till half an hour after sunrise, when the "warders" again took their places. Scouts on horseback were also sent into the woods each day to look for the foe, with directions to go only so far as to enable them to return by nightfall. These orders were carried out with alacrity, by our town. This was then the most remote north-western town in the colony, and one of the most exposed. It was known, both by the whites and Indians, that persons sleep soundest just before dawn, and hence the order that every inhabitant should be awakened by the watch, and called to arms an hour before day. Guards were stationed on Lodge, Orenaug and Castle Rocks, to watch for the enemy, and protect the inhabitants. Fortified houses were erected on Lodge Rock, and near Mr. Nathan Warner's dwelling-house in Judson Lane, to receive the settlers in case of assault. It is more than difficult, at this distance of time, to realize the trials and alarms, which must exist in feeble communities, reminded each morning of their desperate condition by regulations of such severity, as those that had been adopted. Every effort was made for the public safety, but the dangers thickened so darkly around them, that the settlers were obliged, early in the summer, to remove their wives and little ones to Stratford, "a place," as stated in their characteristic language, "of more hopeful security." This was rendered the more necessary, because their men, as often as they went to the "sea-side towns" on their necessary business, were pressed into the service. So that, as we learn from an autograph letter of Rev. Mr. Walker, in October, 1676, a greater number of men from Woodbury, proportioned to its population, was engaged in Philip's war, than from any other town in the colony. Notwithstanding all these discouragements and dangers, our fathers, after having conducted their household flocks to Stratford, returned to Woodbury, raised and secured their crops, and carried them to Stratford in the autumn.

But the plantation was by no means given up. During the year 1677, the inhabitants slowly returned to the new settlement. In May, 1678, the General Court ordered the remainder to return by the 1st of November, on pain of forfeiting their lands in the town. Immediately after this, the town passed a vote, that the order of the court should be strictly enforced, and requested the Town Clerk to write a letter to those who neglected to return, urging them to come back to their lands. In writing this letter, the clerk, Capt. John Minor, urged them to return, saying, "Friends, it is far from our desire, that any of you should be abused by this act of ours. We covet not your lands but your company. We desire not to displease any of you, but if we cannot please you upon lower terms than by undoing ourselves, we assure you that we cannot come to that price." This action of the court and town brought the wandering children home. In June of this year, Mr. Walker came with his family to reside permanently with his people at Woodbury. Previous to this time, his family had resided at Stratford, and he had ministered at both places as occasion required. The house-holders at this time probably numbered about sixty. It is known that there were as many as that four years later. This would show the whole population to be about three or four hundred.

Previous to this date, they had had no corn mill, and had no flour or meal, except such as they could get occasionally at Stratford. Even on wedding occasions, those times of great interest among all nations, the principal dishes, at the marriage feast, were bean porridge for the soup, and for the other courses, an enormous plate of pork and beans. How would such a wedding entertainment suit the notions of our lady friends of the present day? They would, indeed, feel that they had fallen on evil times! There is but one late instance on record, in this town, of keeping up this time-honored custom of our Puritan mothers, and that occurred a few years ago up in Flanders, on the occasion of the marriage of a certain military gentleman, who bears one of Woodbury's early and honored names.

But this deprivation was too great to be borne by our fathers, and accordingly, they procured a set of small mill-stones at Stratford, so diminutive in size, that they brought them here through the forests on horseback. They prepared mill-gearing, built a small shed on Middle Quarter Brook, a few rods easterly from Dea. Eli Summers' house, and set their mill in operation. It is said that when it was in complete running order, it would grind the enormous quantity of one bushel per day. Great was the rejoicing of our fathers, when this vast improvement was achieved. Each settler, in turn, carried his grist to the mill in the morning, set it in motion, and went for the meal at night. And *here*, my friends, is one of those self-same mill-stones !* Here is a highly interesting relic of the early days, which carries us back in memory to the long ended toils and sufferings of our fathers. Long let this rude memorial be preserved as a rare and sacred fragment, which has escaped the ravages of "time's effacing finger!"

The next important event was the erection of a house of public worship. As soon as the settlers were located, and began to have some of the comforts and conveniences of life, their thoughts naturally turned to this prime object in a New England plantation, in which they might enjoy the ministrations of the gospel. In the early years of their settlement, they had worshipped in each others' houses, in the inclement months of the year, and during the summer months, had convened in the stillness of the Sabbath morn, in a beautiful and retired spot, on the East side of the Orenaug Rocks, between the cliffs, with their sentinels placed on the top of the adjacent rocks, to guard against surprise from savage foes, and there made "the sounding aisles of the dim woods" vocal with the high praises of God. By the rude, pulpit-like boulder, still standing in that lonely dell, we may, in imagination, see the faithful Walker addressing his attentive hearers, and delivering to them the words of "truth and soberness." This spot received the name of Bethel Rock from this circumstance, and has ever been held as a consecrated place by the descendants of those early Christian fathers, whither they have, at times, resorted, for meditation and prayer, to the present day.

The first thing to be done was to determine the location of the new house. The church selected Deputy Governor Robert Treat, afterwards Governor of the Colony, and Major Nathan Gold, as a committee to fix the location. They met here 178 years ago to-day, to hear the matter, and to-morrow, we shall celebrate the anniversary of the "pitching down the stake," on the spot now occupied by the carriage-house of our worthy president, where they built the first Meeting House, in which our fathers worshipped for the long period of sixty-six years in the Congregational mode, and afterwards, for

* At this moment the cloth was removed from the speaker's desk, and one of the mill stones was disclosed to view, from which uncovered, the remainder of the address was read, as well as the other addresses of the occasion.

thirty-eight years in the Episcopal mode. The seats in this edifice were raised one above another, on either side of the center of the house, the pulpit being, as usual, at the end of the house opposite the entrance. The people were called to church, on the Sabbath, by the beat of a drum upon the rock on which the Masonic Lodge stands. The same instrument was used to call the people together on other days in the week, and for other purposes. It beat for town meetings, for the assembling of the train-band, and in cases of alarm in time of war. There was a particular beat for each of these occasions; but what was the difference in the roll of the drum ecclesiastical, the drum military, and the drum civil, is not now known. The people carried their arms to church, and some guarded the sanctuary, while the others worshipped the "Lord of Hosts."

Within the walls of this edifice, Mr. Walker continued to labor till his death, which occurred Jan. 20, 1699–1700, or Jan. 31, 1700, according to new style. He was a man of solid attainments, a fervid and powerful preacher, greatly beloved by the people of his charge. He conducted the affairs of his church with commendable discretion, and both that and the infant town flourished during his administration. Under him the church had secured a firm foundation, notwithstanding all the trials and hardships that beset its earlier years. After a life of usefulness, "ye faithful, worthy, beloved Minister of the Gospel, and much lamented Pastor of ye Chh of Christ," was gathered to his fathers, and his remains repose in the Southern part of the ancient burial ground. He sleeps amid the faithful flock to whom he ministered in life. A rude head-stone of native rock, containing only his name and the date of his death, so worn and obliterated by the storms of 160 years, that the name can scarcely be deciphered, is all that remains to mark the place of sepulture of this "early founder." Often, as I have passed with silent, thoughtful feet, the lowly grave which holds his sacred dust till the resurrection morn, I have had a solemn, passing thought, that this hallowed spot deserved a fitting memorial! It may seem strange to the casual visitor within our borders, that the town he so much improved, blessed and honored by his public and private virtues, has not long since erected a fit and filial monument to the memory of its earliest, and most faithful servant. It is to be hoped, that the day is not far distant, when this debt of gratitude shall have been paid.

In 1700, Rev. Anthony Stoddard commenced preaching to the people, and in 1702, was ordained over the church. Rev. Mr. Chauncey, of Stratford, having forgotten all former difficulties, was one of the officiating clergymen on the occasion. The town built him a house, commencing its erection in 1700, and it still stands at the lower end of the village, in the midst of this beautiful valley, with the hoary Castle Rock for a back ground. It is a venerable relic of the early days of the town—one of the few links connecting us with a former generation! It is a thing of history in a historical locality. Long may it remain to remind us of the virtues of the departed, and of all that is valuable in the past.

The ministry of Mr. Stoddard was remarkable for its duration, and the prosperity which attended it. From the date of his first sermon, as a candidate, to his last, immediately preceding the brief illness that terminated his useful labors, he numbered sixty years in his holy calling, and great peace and harmony ever prevailed under his administrations. The number of communicants was always large, notwithstanding four large societies were taken from his limits during his ministry. These were Southbury in 1730, Bethlehem in 1739, Judea in 1741, and Roxbury in 1743. The good work seemed constantly to glow under his hands, with a steadiness rarely equaled. The whole number by him admitted to full communion, was 474, to the half way covenant, 142, and 1540 received baptism at his hands.

To his ministerial labors he joined those of a lawyer and physician. Like many of the early ministers, he prepared himself for the practice of medicine, that he might administer to the wants of the body as well as those of the mind. In this capacity he was often called. He acquired a very good legal knowledge for those early days. This was the more necessary, as at the beginning of the eighteenth century, there were but few lawyers in the Colony, and as late as 1730, an act was passed limiting the number of lawyers, that might practice, to three in Hartford County, and two in each of the other counties. He was Clerk of Probate for a period of forty years, during which time he drew most of the wills of his parishioners, and did the greater part of the business of the office, the Judge for the time being, approving his acts. All the records of the Court, during the time he was Clerk, appear in his hand writing. He was also one of the largest farmers in the town. After a life of arduous and successful labor, the second pastor, at a good old age, entered into his rest. He died, Sept. 6, 1760, in the 83d year of his age, and the 61st of his ministry, after a severe illness of "about two days continuance." He lived and died enshrined in the hearts of his people. He lies buried in the central part of the old burial-ground, and there reposes, surrounded by a numerous congregation, slumbering in death, very many of whom he himself had followed to the grave. As in life he was ever united to his people, so in death, they are not divided. There let them rest together, till the last "great trump" shall call them to a bright re-union around the throne of God.

For a period of more than fifty-seven years after the first settlement of Pomperaug, the inhabitants had formed but one ecclesiastical society. On the day of sacred rest, and on other occasions, the hardy pioneers of this forest town had assembled in the old meeting-house of the "Ancient Society" in this lovely valley, and offered up their devotions to the ever-living God, as an "undivided whole." For six or eight miles in all directions, these men of God descended from the breezy, life-invigorating hills, and emerged from their rural homes in the sweet valleys, hastening "to the temple," to worship the benign Ruler of the universe. In storm and in sunshine, in summer's heat and winter's cold, they "performed their vows," and forgot not the "assembling of themselves together." Amidst the wilds they sung, and the stars heard, and the lea! Their affections, during this long period, had entwined themselves around the "old sanctuary." They loved their old pastor, and scarcely the great inconveniences suffered by the remote parts of the town could induce them to think of forming new societies, and new church relations.

But the time at length came, when it seemed necessary for them to separate, and attempt the formation of new societies, and the burden of supporting other ministers. In addition to the four new societies already mentioned, that had been constituted from the territory of the first society, South Britain was set off and incorporated a society in 1766, and still later, Oxford and Middlebury societies were formed, in part from its territory. All these societies were the germs of new towns. Judea, together with the society of New Preston, was made a town in January, 1779. It was the first town in the State, incorporated after the Declaration of Independence, and was called Washington, in honor of the Commander-in-chief of the American armies. Southbury and Bethlem were incorporated in 1787, Roxbury in 1796, Oxford in 1798, and Middlebury in 1807. All these societies and towns were planted by the good old pioneer stock, men accustomed to the privations of the wilderness. In 1816, another large and flourishing church was formed out of the First Church, and it was incorporated under the name of the "Strict Congregational Society," with the same territorial limits as the first society.

For nearly seventy years after the first settling of the town, there were no churches within its limits, except those of the Congregational, or "Standing Order." Our fathers emigrated to this country to enjoy their religion, not only free from persecution, but without interruption from Christians of different sentiments. They were desirous, as all churches had been before them, of maintaining a uniformity of doctrine and worship. Correct views of religious liberty were not then held in any Christian country, and toleration was not a virtue of that age. But our fathers were far in advance of the rest of the world in learning and adopting that truly Christian virtue. By the very first code of laws ever published in the colony, in 1672, all denominations of Christians were allowed to worship God in their own way, provided they did not commit a breach of the peace. It is true, that all were obliged to contribute to the support of the regular minister; but this was but the carrying out of a contract on the part of the people, for the only price they paid for their lands consisted in bearing their pro rata share of the amount paid the Indians, the joint expenses, of removal, the expense of building roads, bridges, school-houses, churches, and the support of that mode of worship unanimously established by the first founders of the several towns. New comers, who, as soon as they came, were admitted to all the privileges of the original planters, had no right to complain of the necessity of bearing the same burdens as the rest. But at a very early day, even this provision was changed, so that every one paid his tax to the pastor of his choice.

A short time previous to 1740, some few families in this town adopted the sentiments of the Church of England, and at this date were occasionally supplied by the ministers of the "Society for the Propagation of the Gospel in Foreign Parts." Soon after this a church edifice was erected in the town on the hill between Transylvania and the present center of Roxbury. After the erection of the second Congregational Church, in 1747, near Mrs. J. P. Marshall's house, the old church was used by the Episcopalians for public worship, till the erection of their present church, in 1785. In 1771, Rev. John R. Marshall assumed the charge of the parish, having been ordained by the Bishop of London the same year. The parish flourished under his administrations, and by his piety, devotion, address and perseverance, he laid the foundations, deep and sure, of this now flourishing Church. Besides St. Paul's Church, Woodbury, there are, in the ancient territory, Christ Church, Roxbury, St. John's Church, Washington, and Christ Church, Bethlem.

As early as 1790, services of the Methodist Church were held in Woodbury, at first in the open air under Lodge Rock, by Rev. Samuel Wigdon, and afterwards, for about twenty years, in the dwelling house of "Father" Elijah Sherman, till the erection of a church edifice, and two other flourishing churches of this name exist in Southbury. But neither the time, nor the design of this address allows me to give a history of any of the later incidents of the town. I propose to treat only of those great historical events, in which all the constituent parts of the town were interested, and in which all agreed—all bore honorable part.

One of the few luxuries of the early fathers was the fruit of the orchard, and the beverage made from it. The apple-tree was the constant attendant of the early founders of towns, and followed them in all their wanderings. They made haste, not only to "sit under their own vine," but as soon as possible, with equal satisfaction, to sit under their own apple-trees. Nor, with all their stern morality, does it appear that they had the fear of a "Maine Law" before their eyes, for they freely granted the privilege of erecting "cyder mills," even in the highways, the place of greatest notoriety and temptation. These privileges were doubtless granted as a sort of set-off against their prohibitory law, which enacted that if any "Barbadoes liquors, commonly called Rum, Kill-Divell, or the like," should be landed in any part of the colony, it should be confiscated. There had been a still earlier law among the Pilgrims, abolishing the "vain custom of drinking one to another," assigning as reasons for the act, that "it was a thing of no good use," was an inducement to drunkenness, "occasioned much waste of wine and beer," and forced masters and mistresses "to drink more often than they would." I believe that the reasons given hold good to the present day, but *our* sage legislators never give a reason for *their* legislation.

Would you believe that Connecticut was ever a slave State, and that in this sequestered spot, in these religious vales, in this Puritanic "dwelling-place in the wood," have been heard the "clanking chains of slavery"? Without thought, it would appear incredible to us, who now have such a horror of that institution. Yet it is but eleven years since it was formally abolished. It is more than sixty years, however, since the institution in this State had even a "name to live." It is difficult for us, with our present ideas, to believe that there ever was such a state of public opinion here that the sainted Walker, Stoddard, and Marshall could be slaveholders; and yet such is the fact. All the leading men, and men of property, in the early days, owned slaves. The fact is attested by all our records, town, probate, and ecclesiastical. Nothing was more common in the early inventories, than the item of slaves, nor in distributions, than whole or fractional parts of slaves to the heirs. It is true, that they were treated kindly, educated, presented in baptism, their religious interests cared for, standing rather in the light of children of the household, than that of slaves, yet they were such, bought and sold, and at the will and pleasure of their owners. During the whole of the eighteenth century, the institution flourished here, though in a mild form. They became attached, in many instances, to the place where they had been brought up, and some of them lingered around the "old homestead," long after they were entitled to go free by virtue of law. In the war of the Revolution, freedom was granted to all slaves who would enlist and serve during the war. To avail themselves of this provision, some twenty-five of their number in this town enlisted, at various periods of the war, and made good soldiers, fighting valiantly for the liberties of the country. Several of these, having survived the perils of the war, returned and resided in Woodbury, and received pensions from the General Government, in common with others, for their military services.

Thus have we slowly traced our way through the long years of the dim, dusty records of the early fathers, and we cannot leave these communings with the past without regret. We part with the actors and their deeds as with old friends with whom we have journeyed long. There is an interest lingering about the history, sayings and doings of those iron-hearted men, which belongs to no later generation. The most trivial details in regard to them seem important, and we gather them up with ever-increasing admiration. It was they who subdued this wilderness land, and established here our happy homes, and the germ of our enduring liberties. It was they who laid here the foundations, deep and broad, of our religious institutions, and when they themselves had no "temple made with hands" in which to worship the God of their fathers, led their children to that secluded fastness of Bethel Rock, to pour forth their prayers and praise. It was they, who laid the firm foundations of our educational institutions, the sure nurseries of civil and religious liberty, although for the first fifty years, in their poverty, they could sustain but one school in the territory.

The influence of the pastor in the early days was deservedly very great. Many of the clergy, who first came to this country, had property, and assisted their poor brethren in the expenses and difficulties encountered in making the new settlements. The people were far more dependant on their ministers for every thing at that time, than they have since been. The proportion of learned men was far smaller at that time than at the present day. The clergy possessed a large part of the literature of the colony. They fitted the young men for college, assisted them in their studies at the university, and with their advice afterward. They were fellow exiles and sufferers with their people in this new and strange land. All these circumstances combined, gave them a remarkable influence over their hearers, of all ranks and dispositions. Perhaps in no government have the clergy had more influence, or been more rationally and sincerely respected and beloved, by ruler and people, than in Connecticut.

All these influences exhibited their happy results in the habits and character of the people. The huge old meeting-house was always filled with the "great congregation," in summer's heat, or winter's cold. Although the idea of warming a meeting-house with a stove, or a fire-place, never entered the mind of the boldest innovator upon ancient customs, yet the attendance at the house of God was scarcely less in winter than in summer. The Church was almost always built on the highest hill, at the intersection of roads leading to the various parts of the town, as near the geographical center of the territory as possible. But the people "went up to the temple" to worship for many miles around, though storms were in the air, and the cutting wind howled fiercely over the bleak hill of "the tabernacle." On foot, and on the "ride-and-tie" system, they managed to get to the place of worship, where, by the aid of warm clothing, close sitting, and a ruddy fire in their "Sabbath-Day Houses," or at the parsonage, at intermission, they seemed not aware of the cold weather. Here they spent their time in discussing the sermon, and in such a manner as was suitable to holy time. The hours of the Sabbath, after the return from church, were generally spent in employments appropriate to the conclusion of the day of rest, and such as were calculated to fit them for the everlasting Sabbath in Heaven.

But those early fathers have long since departed. Several generations of their descendants sleep with them, and it is to be feared that many of their valuable customs and strict purity of conduct have departed with them. "Ancient Woodbury" has been greatly favored with able, learned and pious pastors. One hundred years ago, and for some years previous, there were laboring, at one time, in our limits, Rev. Anthony Stoddard, of the first society, Rev. John Graham, of Southbury, Rev. Dr. Bellamy of Bethlehem, Rev. Thomas Canfield of Roxbury, and Rev. Daniel Brinsmade of Judea Societies; a galaxy of talent, learning and piety, without its equal, perhaps, at one time, in a single town. The influence of those revered men, and that of the other noble men who have since that day labored in our courts, has not entirely departed. It "still lives," and will go on blessing and improving those within its reach, till the "latest recorded syllable of time."

They labored amid difficulties and dangers, and we have entered into the results of those labors. They sleep well in these religious vales, far from the land of their fathers. "The dark brown years" have passed over the sacred mounds that cover them, for many generations. It is right, then, that their posterity lingers, with a sad interest, over the lightest trace of their doings! Is it strange that we notice with approbation, acts which, at the present day, would be unworthy of remark? None can contemplate the hardships, labors and dangers endured by our ancestors, their self-denial, firmness and perseverence in defending and transmitting to us this fair inheritance, and not highly esteem and venerate their characters.

Under such severe difficulties were these pleasant dwelling places, and the habitations which we now enjoy, prepared. And yet our ancestors were not the paupers, nor the fortune hunters of the old world. They were the sturdy yeomanry, the intelligent farmers, the middle classes, whose independent spirits spurned the yoke of spiritual tyranny. Oppressed and harassed in the old country, our sainted sires sought in the wilds and fastnesses of this wilderness world, a place for that freedom of thought, and of action, which they could not find under the boasted liberty of the British constitution. Thoroughly impressed with the belief that time, faith and energy would accomplish all that could be done in life, the most appalling discouragements were met and overcome. To their enlightened vision, guided by their fervid and simple faith, there beamed from the distant West the light of perfect liberty, which, like "another morn risen on mid-noon," would continue to shine till the "perfect day."

It will be seen, that I have dwelt long upon the events and incidents of the early days. I have taken the more pains in this regard, because our information of the early days is more scanty than of the recent past. I had intended to have paid my tribute of affection and respect to the memory of the revered men who have lived and labored in and out of our town during the last two centuries.* It would be a grateful privilege to linger, for a moment, among the sweet memories of the distinguished dead for ten generations, who have gone before

* Full and extended sketches of the distinguished men of Woodbury will be found in the "History of Ancient Woodbury," published in 1854.

us to the "undiscovered country." Woodbury has been distinguished, from the very first, for minds of the first order, and men of mark. But time forbids that I should tarry in these filial fields, and so I hasten on to the conclusion of my labors. I am the more anxious to do this that I may not longer keep you from the enjoyment of the rich treat which my Rev. friend (and I am proud to call him my friend,) has in store for you. Descended from an honored stock, and long since adopted as a favored son of the Muses, he will surely adorn this memorable occasion with the gifts of poesy!

Glorious, thrice glorious is the day we celebrate! It is the two hundreth anniversary of the exploration of this valley, the one hundred and eighty-ninth of the gathering of the First Church, and the eighty-third of our national independence. On this glad day of liberty, what sacred emotions arise in the patriotic breast! How shall we rightly honor a day consecrated by the deeds of the noble men of all the past—not more the patriots, who fought in the gloomy days of the Revolution, than those, who struggled amid the dangers of defenceless and remote forests. It has taken all the labors of our fathers, from the first hardy pioneer, to make the glorious present. We enjoy the fruits of all the toil and blood of our fathers for two hundred years. It is meet, then, that we greet with enthusiastic joy the smiling morn of the anniversary of that last, most during and sublime of all the acts of our forefathers, the Declaration of Independence. It is well that we hail its annual return with the ringing of bells upon ten thousand hills; by the booming of innumerable cannon and smaller arms; by rockets, fire-works and illuminations; by solemn processions and grateful prayers to God; by stirring orations and patriotic songs! May the hymns of liberty never die out from our breezy mountains, nor the lofty sentiment of patriotism from our happy valleys! Let the glad echoes be repeated from the Eastern to the Western Ocean, and from the icy regions of the North to the sunny climes of the ever-blooming South!

"Ancient Woodbury" has ever been a military town, from the time of King Philip's war, when, as we have seen, it had a larger number of soldiers in the service, than any other town in the colony, in proportion to the number of its inhabitants, to the last war with Great Britain, when we had more than two hundred men in the field. In every war, and on every "alarm," the men of Woodbury have been found at the post of duty, performing feats of valor. For that fruitless and fatal expedition, under Gen. Nicholson, for the reduction of Montreal and Quebec, in 1709, Woodbury, still the frontier forest town, furnished its full quota of men, being nine, two of whom died from the exposures of the camp, at Wood Creek. Among the forces under the American commander, who was obliged to execute that most unrighteous and cruel decree for the dispersion of the unhappy inhabitants of Acadia, among the New England colonies, tearing the unoffending and peaceful people from their loved and beautiful paternal firesides, were soldiers from our old Puritan town, and nine of those sorrowful victims of England's gross injustice were sent into exile upon the outskirts of our town, to be kept at labor under the direction of the selectmen. From 1744 to 1759, our town freely furnished her sturdy sons for all those ill-managed and desolating wars between Great Britain and France. Col. Benjamin Hinman, and Capt. Adam Hinman greatly distinguished themselves in these campaigns, although the regular troops constantly domineered over the provincials. As soon as the drum, at the " alarm post " in our peaceful shades, sounded the note of preparation for the relief of Fort William Henry, near Lake George, that beautiful sheet of water, once so peacefully resting between its rampart of highlands, the gallant captains, Wait Hinman and Ebenezer Downs, the former at the head of his company of ninety-six men, and the latter leading his company of eighty, marched, at a moment's warning, and made their rapid way through many a trackless and weary solitude to succor their English brethren. In Hinman's company marched Hezekiah Thompson, the first regular lawyer in the village, and Dr. Joseph Perry, one of its most distinguished physicians. And in that final and glorious campaign, conducted under the administration and auspices of the energetic, brilliant and renowned Pitt, in those important victories, resulting in the capture of forts Niagara, Ticonderoga, and Crown Point, and in the more glorious event, the surrender of Quebec to the victorious army under Wolfe, who met death in the battle-field, and whose "spirit escaped in a blaze of glory,"—in all these celebrated engagements, the men of Woodbury, both officer and soldier, stood in the first rank. Valuable, indeed, was this school of military services which closed with this campaign, to our fathers, who were so soon to engage in a life and death struggle for their own liberties. Great was the rejoicing in Woodbury when the news of the last great victory arrived, not unmingled with sorrow at the loss of the slain, three of whom had gone forth from their own hearth stones. Like demonstrations of joy were everywhere shown. In the eloquent words of Bancroft, " America rang with exultation ; the towns were bright with illuminations; legislatures, the pulpit, the press, echoed the general joy; provinces and families gave thanks to God."

But in a far more glorious and interesting chapter of our country's history, the patriotic sons of Woodbury acted a noble and distinguished part. Need I tell the youngest listener in this vast assembly, at least on this cherished anniversary of our country's history, that I refer to the memorable struggle for Independence? It had been generally known, that at the end of the war with France, new regulations would be introduced into the government of the American colonies. Connecticut in particular, was said to be but "little more than a mere democracy, most of them being upon a level, and each man thinking himself an able divine and politician;" and to make its inhabitants "a good sort of people," it was supposed, all that was necessary, was to take away its charter, and crush its energies. The mother country had forgotten its experience in the Charter Oak affair, by which it should have learned, that this would not be so easy a thing as might be desirable. So she, in the magnitude of her towering pride said, "Let the colonies be taxed, and let there be no representation." What a world of interests was affected by that stern and unjust decision! Little dreamed he, who spake it, that it would inflame a continent, and rend from Old England her fairest possession. But the word had been spoken—the decree gone forth! With a fatal madness, an unaccountable folly, she took her furious course. Her children, driven by her intolerance into the savage wilds of a distant continent, were pursued with ruthless barbarity. She little knew, and little cared, if far away over the mighty Atlantic, her arbitrary acts were creating the "land of the free and the home of the brave." From this came the War of the Revolution, to blast the dearest hopes of the people of the new world. Yet from its gloomy shades gleamed forth the light of liberty, which to-day shines with such dazzling splendor.

The passage of the Stamp Act aroused the most intense excitement, alarm and indignation throughout the colonies. Absolute resistance to this measure everywhere appeared, and as early as February, 1766, a Convention of Litchfield county was held, in which the noble men of Woodbury were leading spirits. This body of men, feeling within them the true Yankee fire, "Resolved that the Stamp Act was unconstitutional, null and void, and that *business of all kinds should go on as usual.*" The paramount and immediate cause of the great struggle of the Revolution, was the passage of the Boston Port Bill. This outrageous and malicious act excited universal sympathy for that town, throughout the colonies, but nowhere was it manifested in a more lively or effective manner than Connecticut. The universal spirit of resistance broke out in Woodbury, and in September, 1774, a town meeting was held, at which resolutions of sympathy with the afflicted people of Boston and Charlestown were passed, and a considerable amount of donations was collected, and forwarded to Boston with all possible dispatch. This meeting was held just after the "Great Boston Alarm," caused by a report that ships of war were cannonading Boston. During this "Alarm," a large number of the patriotic sons of Woodbury had marched in mad haste, and made a part of that glorious twenty thousand from Connecticut, who, completely armed, put themselves on the route to Boston to relieve their brother sufferers. It was soon apparent that war with the mother country was inevitable, and the great object of our Revolutionary sires was to form public opinion in favor of a contest with England. This was best effected in that day of scarcity of newspapers, by holding town meetings, in which they could publicly read such papers as treated upon the subject of common interest, and discuss their rights and grievances. In this way, the people became highly excited and exasperated, and patriotism glowed in the coldest hearts. The fathers of Woodbury were fully up to the spirit of the times, and held frequent meetings to advise concerning the public weal. In November, 1774, the people of Woodbury held a town meeting, and appointed a committee to observe the acts of the inhabitants in relation to the non-importation, and non-consumption agreement of the United Colonies, with directions to publish in the Gazette the names of all violators of that sacred agreement, to the end, that all such persons, might "be publicly known, and universally contemned," agreeing to break off all dealings with such persons as should be guilty of such violation.

The decisive step seemed to be now taken. Neither party could recede without betraying weakness or cowardice. The Rubicon was passed, and all waited the next move with intense solicitude. Darkness and gloom had settled upon the moral vision—the veil of the future was drawn over the result, and it was impossible for those of the greatest wisdom to raise that veil and penetrate the mystery beyond. By such severe regulations, we can see the urgency of the danger that threatened the colonists, and the extreme, stern measures, judged necessary by the coolest and wisest intellects of the colonies. It shows us, too, the caliber of the men, who settled this new world, and sought here the supreme blessing of freedom. But putting their trust in the God of battles, and in the justice of their cause, they dared every evil that might come upon them, earnestly pledging "their lives, their fortunes, and their sacred honor," on the issue, and sacrificing all the dearest interests of life on the altar of their country's good.

There can be no better way of appreciating the trials, dangers, and difficulties of achieving our independence, than by carefully noting the labors and struggles of a single important town. One furnishes a type of the whole. In that great contest, Connecticut was one of the foremost, if not the very first State in the confederacy, to resist the tyranny of Great Britain, and to lavish her blood and treasure in sustaining the conflict with her oppressors. Her soldiers were frequently applauded by the Commander-in-Chief of the American army, for their bravery and fidelity. The honor of the first conquest made by the United Colonies during the war, belongs chiefly to Connecticut, and, in a distinguishing manner, to the sons of Woodbury. I refer to the capture of Ticonderoga, May 10, 1775, without the loss of a man, one of the most brilliant and daring feats of the war. At least one half of that little patriotic band of eighty-three men, who entered the fort, were natives or inhabitants of Woodbury. They were led by Col. Ethan Allen, Col. Seth Warner, and Capt. Remember Baker, cousins, and natives of Woodbury,* then residing in the "New Hampshire Grants," and on the demand of the former, in the "name of the Great Jehovah and the Continental Congress," the Commander rubbed his eyes in astonishment, and yielded the fortress. Neither the demeanor of the man, the boldness of his message, nor the nature of his authority, could be gainsayed for a moment. This post, and that of Crown Point, which was immediately taken by Col. Warner, being thus acquired, Connecticut was obliged to garrison, and in 1775, sent 1000 men for this purpose, eight companies of whom were from the limits of our ancient town, containing at least one hundred and fifty men, eighty of whose names are still pre-

* On a careful review of the subject of the nativity of Col. Allen, I have seen no cause to change my opinions in regard to it, as indicated in the "History of Ancient Woodbury," p. 411 to 416, notwithstanding the fact, that my learned and ingenious friend, Payne Kenyon Kilbourne, Esq., of Litchfield, has come to a different conclusion.

Since writing this note, Mr. Kilbourne has been suddenly called to enter into his rest. He had been at Hartford some months, printing with his own hands his History of Litchfield, and the task had been too great for his feeble frame. He sacrificed his life to his last great work. He was a learned and estimable man. His example was one worthy of imitation. A patient, laborious, and indefatigable antiquarian, and a Christian gentleman, has passed away.

served. The garrisons were placed under the command of Col. Hinman, of Woodbury. Is it then vain-glorious in her sons, if to-day they claim it to be essentially a Woodbury affair? Truly, to her brave children must be awarded the palm for securing this opening victory to the American Arms!

Woodbury was noted for the vigilance with which it watched the movements of the tories within its borders, of whom it had a few, as well as for its active co-operation in everything necessary to carry on the great struggle, which had now begun in good earnest. A committee of inspection and observation of the conduct of the inhabitants of the town, was appointed, consisting of thirty of its chief men, and undoubted patriots, which exercised its functions during the whole war, vacancies in the board being filled, from time to time, by the town. The duties, which this committee felt itself called upon to perform, were of the most delicate and difficult nature, and constituted such an oversight and interference in men's private affairs, as could only be justified by such a case of emergency as was then existing. But they were men in whom all had confidence, and upon whom entire dependence could be placed in times of difficulty and danger.

During the first two years of the war, the larger part of the militia, which comprised all the able-bodied men from the age of sixteen to fifty, had been called to serve at various posts, and on various expeditions a great part of the time. Early in 1777, enlistments for three years, or during the war, were called for, and the quota for each town was established. It was a severe levy on the already weakened state of the town. But it met the call with a ready zeal, and undaunted perseverance. Large bounties were offered to those who would enlist, and heavy taxes were laid on the inhabitants, who were not liable to do duty, or did not enlist into the army. Another arrangement, besides increased wages held out by the town, to induce men to enlist, was a provision, which required it to support their families during their absence in their country's service, and committees were annually appointed to carry this provision into effect. From a report to the General Assembly, at the close of the war, in 1783, we learn that nearly £3,000 worth of provisions had, in this manner, been furnished to soldiers' families during the war. Woodbury was also a prominent point for collecting supplies of provisions for the army. The streets of the village, from the First Congregational Church to Mrs. Marshall's dwelling house, were often piled high, on either side, with barrels and hogsheads of pork, beef, lard, flour, and other military stores for the use of the army. Nor was the supply of clothing of every kind, less profuse in quantity, for the wants of the soldiers of the town. In March, 1778, clothing to the value of more than $1,000, was forwarded to them at one time. Besides the provisions thus furnished by the town, for the army during the war, large quantities were purchased of the inhabitants by Shadrach Osborn, of Woodbury, who was assistant commissary of purchases, and also issuing commissary. From his accounts, and other sources, we learn that more than half a million dollars' worth of supplies was furnished by this town, towards the grand amount necessary to achieve our country's independence. This is a showing of which any town may be justly proud.

Such was the care of the town to support and defend those nearest and dearest to the brave men, who were manfully fighting the battles, and consecrating with their blood every battle-field of their country. Such was the anxious care for the soldiers themselves. Those who went forth to war suffered extreme hardships, in common with their brethren from other parts of the country; and those who remained at home, suffered hardships scarcely less severe, in the heavy taxes necessary to pay for the soldiers' bounties, and for the support of their families, while their own business was crippled and nearly ruined.

All this was accomplished under the pressure of most unparalleled financial difficulties. The continental money, by means of British counterfeiting, and the unavoidable loss of credit, arising from so long and sanguinary a struggle, constantly depreciated, and, at last, became nearly valueless. So great was the depreciation, that when the soldiers of the continental army were discharged, after the peace of 1783, many of them were forced to beg their way home, their wages for a service, so long and weary, being scarcely sufficient to purchase them a dinner.

But Woodbury, in a far more important manner, contributed towards a successful issue of the dispute with Great Britain. This was accomplished by sending large numbers of her best sons to the field of battle. In the number and value of her troops, it is believed, that few towns of similar territorial and numerical strength, can vie with her. Their heroic deeds should grace a bright page of our country's history. During the course of the war, more than fifteen hundred of her patriotic sons went forth to "do battle for their country." At the commencement of the war, Col. Hinman's, or the 13th regiment of militia, comprised only the three towns of Woodbury, Kent, and New Milford, and all these were within the limits of the original Indian Deed. Ancient Woodbury had eight out of the twelve companies that composed it, and the number of soldiers furnished from them for the continental army, in 1775, exclusive of the company, that marched in the Lexington Alarm, was at least one hundred and fifty, as that was the number whose "Poll taxes" were abated that year by the General Assembly, on account of their service.

The sun of 1776, although our armies had been successful the preceding year, arose clouded and in gloom. The "note of preparation" was sounded through the land. There was a "hurrying to and fro" throughout the country on business of the most solemn import, affecting the dearest interests we know in life. In June, one-fourth of the able-bodied men between the ages of sixteen and fifty years, in the territory, were drafted, or enlisted. In August, after the evacuation of Boston, and the occupation of New York by the British, the entire militia of Connecticut, west of the river of that name, at the request of Gen. Washington, was ordered to New York. The Woodbury companies were called out on the 10th, mustered on the 11th, and marched on the 12th for their place of destination. The number of officers and soldiers on the military rolls, at this time, was 564, all of whom, but 39, marched at the call of their commanders. Besides these, there were 248 men in the continental army by enlistment, making the number of men in actual service, from this single town, at that time, eight hundred and seventy-three. The entire population of "Ancient Woodbury," by a census taken that year, amounted to only 5,325 souls, so that nearly one-fifth of the population, men, women and children, were fighting for the freedom of their firesides. This "raw militia" was present in the unfortunate operations on Long Island, towards the close of this year, and in Washington's retreat from New York, soon after which, the men were discharged. One would think that it would be impossible to arouse and lead forth to battle, at a moment's warning, all the able-bodied men in the militia of a town, in such a manner as this, but the interests at stake were great, and the most prominent and popular men in the community were in the movement, "heart and hand." The officers addressed the soldiers in the most urgent and patriotic language, and even the pulpit lent its powerful aid to the cause by prayers to the Almighty, and by volunteering to go with them on their campaigns in the capacity of chaplain, as did Rev. Mr. Wildman, of Southbury, on one occasion. A passage from the prayer of the Rev. Judah Champion, of Litchfield, on the occasion of the attendance at his church of a company of cavalry, on their way to oppose Lord Cornwallis, who, with a large fleet and armament was approaching the American coast, has been often repeated, and so well exhibits the spirit of the times, it may well be repeated again:

"Oh Lord! We view with terror and dismay the enemies of thy holy religion; wilt thou send storm and tempest, to toss them upon the sea, and to overwhelm them in the mighty deep, or scatter them to the uttermost parts of the earth. But peradventure, should any escape thy vengeance, collect thou them together again, O Lord! as in the hollow of thy hand, and *let thy lightnings* PLAY *upon them!*" Besides these influences, another aided the Revolutionary fathers of this town. Previous to the action at White Plains, the soldiers from Woodbury had been remarkably fortunate. Scarcely one had been killed or wounded, insomuch it had become a common remark, "the enemy's balls could not hit the Woodbury boys." In consequence of this feeling of security, enlistments went on briskly, and to it, in part, is to be attributed the large number of soldiers who volunteered to go into the service. In that scene of misery at the "Sugar House" in New York, and the inhuman cruelties there inflicted, Woodbury had some representatives.* With so large a number of men in the service, it could not fail to be represented in every field of battle of the eventful struggle in which our freedom was secured, and the mother country humbled in the dust.

The campaign of 1777 opened with an invasion of Connecticut, on the part of the enemy—an event long feared by our people. Troops were called for to defend the coasts, and Col. Moseley's regiment marched to Fairfield. In April, there was a sudden call for troops to go to Danbury, as the British were burning the houses, and destroying the property of the inhabitants. The alarm lists and militia of Woodbury were put in motion, and some of the soldiers, including Hon. Wm. Edmond, afterwards a Judge of the Superior Court, and one of the greatest geniuses this State ever produced, were wounded. Col. Joel Hinman was also wounded at the same moment, in which Gen. Wooster received his mortal wound, at a little distance from him. And here is the ball which buried itself in the left groin of Col. Hinman, where it remained for the long period of thirty-three years, when it was extracted by Dr. Anthony Burritt. On its pas-

* I never pass that beautiful monument in Trinity church-yard, at New York, erected by the Corporation of that Church, without stopping to read its touching and impressive inscription: "Sacred to the memory of those brave and good men, who died whilst imprisoned in this city for their devotion to the cause of American Independence,"—and sadly reflecting how many of Woodbury's noble sons lie mouldering there, sad victims of that cruel and unnecessary immolation of humanity.

sage, it hit a bayonet by his side, cutting and flattening the edge, as you see. And here is another Revolutionary relic, aye a relic of the first days of the colony, two hundred years ago. It has been handed down from father to son, from its first known owner, Capt. John Minor, the Indian interpreter, and is known to be at least 220 years old. By closer inspection, I see the manufacturer's date upon the barrel is 1624. It was used in the Pequot war, in all the French and Indian wars, and in the war of the Revolution. It is said to have caused, first and last, the death of forty red men, and from this circumstance, has been familiarly known as the "forty Indian gun." And here is still another relic of two centuries ago—the old arm chair of Col. Benjamin Hinman, brought from Stratford, and formerly the property of Francis Stiles. Here, too, is his pipe of peace, presented to him at the peace of 1783, with a request that he would smoke it as often as the 4th of July should return—a request with which he faithfully complied. Here, my friend, smoke to the memory of the gallant colonel.* Here, too, is a chair used by Gen. Washington at New York.

It was during this attack, as the British were approaching the village, that Mr. Luther Holcomb, entirely alone, rode upon a hill in front of the enemy, and, waving his sword, and turning his head, as though he were addressing an army behind him, gave, in a voice of thunder, the somewhat imposing command, "*Halt, the whole universe! Break off by kingdoms!*" As this was rather a formidable force to encounter in battle array, especially as it had the advantage of position, the army halted, brought forward their cannon, and sent out flanking parties to make discoveries. Upon this, the kingdoms of the universe quietly subsided, and Mr. Holcomb made good his retreat to Danbury. He did not deem it prudent to see whether "one man could chase a thousand, and two put ten thousand to flight!"

In May, one-fourth of the 13th regiment were detached, and ordered to Horseneck, numbering about one hundred and fifty men. In the battle of Bennington, under the brave Col. Warner, of Woodbury, his friends and neighbors did good service. Two hundred and forty men answered Gen. Washington's draft for Peekskill. In September, the regular army being called to reinforce Gen. Washington, one-half of the militia was drafted to go to Peekskill under Gen. Putnam. Not far from three hundred men marched from Woodbury, on

* These several articles were exhibited to the audience by the speaker. The last remark was addressed to a gentleman, who was at the moment personating Col. Hinman.

this occasion, exclusive of the entire company of "Light Horse," under the command of Maj. Thomas Bull, which was also ordered to the same destination. The attentive student of history will see, at a glance, how much greater was the number from Woodbury, than from other towns, when he considers how small was the whole number in the service. The exact number of the three years' enlistments is not precisely known, but is believed to be, at least, three hundred. At the glorious and memorable victory of Saratoga, we had a large body of men, who fully sustained the high character for skill and bravery, which they had previously earned.

In the early part of 1778, it became necessary to draft one hundred and five men to fill the town's quota of three years' men. The fear of the small pox, which prevailed at all the military posts, and other causes, had retarded the enlistments. It was not strange under the painful circumstances and sad reverses of the close of 1777, when the troops under Washington had worn out their shoes and clothing, and could be tracked in their marches by the blood of their feet, that new recruits were obtained with difficulty. It was emphatically the midnight of the Revolution. But the States having, at this juncture framed and accepted "articles of confederation," and being aided by the French, the war was vigorously prosecuted in all directions.

In February, 1779, the whole militia under Col. Mosely, and the regiment of "Light Horse" under Major Bull, were ordered to Norwalk, and in May, one hundred men from the Thirteenth Regiment were ordered to Horseneck, fifty-seven of whom were from Captain Leavenworth's company. It was during these occurrences, that Gen. Putnam made his famous "escape" at Horseneck, by spurring his horse, when hotly pursued, down a steep precipice, at full gallop.

During the winter of 1780, the troops had suffered greatly in their quarters for want of food and clothing. They were paid off in continental money, and with it they could buy neither food nor clothing. In this emergency, the town in its great solicitude, offered a bounty of £45 in silver for each recruit, and dispatched to the suffering soldiers in the "Connecticut Line," nearly seven thousand articles of clothing, of which they had the most pressing need, among which were about two thousand pairs of shoes. At this period of the war, the prospects of the country were gloomy in the extreme. Only the most hopeful and persevering could see relief in the dark aspect of the forbidding future. Successive defeats and rampant toryism disheartened the American people at the South, and the treason of Arnold, the uninterrupted drain of men and money, producing poverty and distress, chilled the hopes of the patriots at the North.

Yet in August of this year, Washington conceived the plan of taking New York from the enemy, and consequently desired a force, that would not be constantly leaving him by expiration of service. He therefore suggested the policy of enlisting a body of "Volunteers to serve expressly till New York was taken," and to be called on for no other purpose. Instantly twenty-two men left their labors, enrolled themselves for this purpose, and reported themselves to their captains. Three of them were cousins of Col. Ethan Allen, of the Revolutionary stock. These are the names of those noble, fearless patriots,* who could forget even the calls of other duties, the ties of affection, the sacred delights of their cherished firesides and household joys, to go to the aid of their country, suffering, bleeding at every pore! Many times before that year, had they responded to the call of their beloved chief, and only a few days before this, they had returned from an arduous tour of service. Four hundred and forty out of four hundred and eighty, the whole number in the regiment, had been on duty. But nothing could crush the indomitable energies of those sturdy, unselfish men, unselfish in the highest sense of the term. History does not show a brighter example of lofty and sublime devotion to the country's weal!

In 1781, thirty men were added to the continental line, and in 1782, twenty-eight more. This proved to be the last time the town was called upon to show its devotion to the interests of the country during the War of Independence. It has been seen that the efforts of our town to subserve the good cause, began to grow weaker and weaker, as the strength of its soldiers wasted away before the pestilence, and the deadly struggle on the field of battle, and its wealth disappeared under the ever fresh levies of supplies for the army, and the support of the troops. It would seem, that overwhelmed with debt, as the country then was, it could hardly have held out much longer. But however that might have been, it seems that a kind Providence had designed, in His wisdom, to spare them the trial. To Him "who tempers the wind to the shorn lamb," it seemed good to say to pride, power and oppression, "Thus far shalt thou go, and no farther." Early next year, just eight years after the battle of Lexington, Great Britain made propositions for peace, and hostilities terminated. Many of the soldiers of Woodbury were present at the surrender of Lord

* The names of these volunteers were here exhibited to the audience, on a placard, by the speaker.

Cornwallis, which virtually closed the war. The eyes of these survivors of a ruthless warfare beheld a glad sight on the morn of the 19th of October, when in solemn silence—not amid the smoke and carnage of the battle-field—they saw the brave Gen. Lincoln receive the sword of Lord Cornwallis,—the strength and glory of the British army, on this side of the water, broken and destroyed. Well might the news of this auspicious event spread universal joy, as it did, throughout the country. Well might all hearts unite in praise and thanksgiving to God, for this signal blessing, which was to terminate our struggle for independence. It was not inappropriate, that Washington ordered divine service to be performed throughout the army; and that Congress proceeded in solemn procession to the House of God, to acknowledge its grateful sense of this special favor.

But this great boon had been obtained by dangers, and toil, and miseries, with scarcely an equal in the annals of mankind! The blood of the dwellers in these fair vales, and in each town and hamlet of our land, was shed like water on every glorious battle-field of our country, from the skirmish at Lexington to the ever memorable siege of Yorktown—from the sad massacre of the fair and poetic vale of Wyoming to the field of honor on the heights of Saratoga. Their worldly goods, so dearly earned, were freely offered on the altar of their country's good. Hunger, cold, privation of every sort, were cheerfully endured. Every tie which nature holds dear, and which binds the hearts of men in conjugal, paternal, or fraternal bands to the well-known hearth-stone, were sundered at the call of our suffering country in her hour of need, and of peril. They went forth with bounding hearts, and athletic, manly forms. Many of them found honored graves in various parts of our land, and many more returned with dire diseases, mutilated frames and shattered health—the merest wreck of what they were—to the firesides that had missed their presence for months and years. But the result of their labors was glorious beyond expectation, or even the dreams of the most hopeful. They wrought well—a redeemed and widely extended people, now rejoices in the result of their toils and sufferings. Many long years have rolled their slow course away, since the thrilling scenes of the Revolution were acted, but they live, engraved on the hearts of a grateful and happy posterity. The heroic events of that important period, the immortal deeds of our fathers, shall live, too, on the brightest page of history, while thought shall endure, or the recollection of human greatness shall remain. If *there be* "a recompense of reward" for those that do well, surely our patriot sires have long since entered on a bright fruition!

Thus have we wandered through the flowery fields of the past, plucking here and there a sweet garland of wild flowers by the way-side, and another in the cultivated gardens of advancing civilization, as best suited our purpose. We have endeavored, in our humble way, duly to reverence and honor the past. We have traced with pious toil the varying tints, the lights and shadows of the pioneer life of our sainted fathers, who occupied these seats before us. We have rendered them a willing and a filial tribute of love, duty and recollection. There is a pure and unalloyed pleasure in wandering amid the scenes and incidents of the long buried past. There is a sad, though ennobling interest, in seeking the faintest recorded trace of the early fathers. The eye has kindled at the ancient glories, and the soul has been warmed with a placid flow of tender heart sympathies. In the wealth of the past, full well have we traced "God's hand in history." No inquiries can be more interesting to the intelligent student, seeking guidance from the light of former days, and desiring above all to emulate that sublime intermixture of the true principles of stability and progress, so happily blended in the history of our forefathers. The feelings that prompt these filial inquiries are just and natural—they give birth to some of the dearest charities of life, and fortify some of its sternest virtues. The principle that prompts them, lies deep within our nature. In the beautiful words of one of the most eminent of living orators*: "The sacred tie of family, which, reaching backward and forward, binds the generations of men together, and draws out the plaintive music of our being from the solemn alternation of cradle and grave—the black and white keys of life's harpsichord; the magical power of language, which puts spirit in communion with spirit, in distant periods and climes; the grand sympathies of country, which lead the Greeks of the present day to talk of 'the victories which *we* gained over the barbarians at Marathon;" the mystic tissue of race, woven far back in the dark chambers of the past, and which, after the vicissitudes and migrations of centuries, wraps up great nations in its broad mantle—those significant expressions which carry volumes of meaning in a word,—Forefather, Parent, Child, Posterity, Native Land,—these all teach us not blindly to worship, but duly to honor the past; to study the lessons of experience; to scan the high counsels of man, in his great associations, as those counsels have been developed in constitutions, in laws, in maxims, in traditions, in great undoubted principles of right and wrong, which have been sanctioned by the general con-

---

*Hon. Edward Everett.

sent of those who have gone before us; thus tracing in human institutions some faint reflection of that Divine Wisdom, which fashioned the leaf that unfolded itself six weeks ago in the forest, on the pattern of the leaf which was bathed in the dews of Paradise, in the morning of creation." While rendering, therefore, due homage to the past, and profiting by all its honored maxims, we would not blindly worship it. In the proud consciousness of manhood, we should not fear the present, or its bold and startling issues, nor should we be distrustful of the future, and of the hidden mysteries it may have in store. We should not fear the rapid march of events across the stage of life. We would not build a fair superstructure on the ruins of former times, nor would we "bind down the living, breathing, burning present," to the mouldering, though honored relics of the past. We would rather imitate all that was glorious in the acts and example of the "men of seventy-six, the boldest men of progress the world has ever seen." We would emblazon their great principles of conservative progress with a pencil dipped in fire. We are proud of the past, glory in the present, and look hopefully forward to the future. We do not even fear enthusiasts and ultraists, as from the collision of extremes comes the ever truthful mean. We would so mingle them, that there "should flow in harmonious procession the cadence of a history chiming on through the centuries, full of faith and praise." We would fearlessly meet the issues we cannot avoid, while the past impels and the future summons us to prompt action, occupying as we do the great middle ground, between the early age of planting and the bright harvest of the future, which stretches towards us its hands laden with ripened fruit. We would hasten to the golden fields and bright realizations of the days to come. Our acts are not for an age, but for all time.

In the spirit of liberty lies the secret of the great advance made by our town, and by the whole country. Our fathers were the champions of rational, conservative progress, which has been the crowning glory of our land. By this effective agency, every thing has become new. The desert waste, that met the first gaze of our pioneer ancestors, has been made to bud and blossom as the rose. Where once were but scattered cabins of a former race, are now enterprising and busy villages. The ceaseless hum of machinery, giving employment, competence and happiness to hundreds of families, is now heard in our valleys, which in the early days but echoed back the growl of the bear, the cry of the panther, or the dismal howl of the wolf. Instead of the wretched orgies of the powwow, and the inhuman sacrifices of the midnight of barbarism, are churches dedicated to the living God, where prayer and praise are wont to be made. Schools and colleges, those great nurseries of cultivated humanity, abound in every nook and corner of the land. Where once were cherished the savage instincts of men, and a taste for war, now are cultivated the arts of peace and schemes for the happiness and advancement of mankind. Intelligence and enterprise now take the place of ignorance and sloth. These hills and vales, that groaned with scenes of violence and blood, are now made vocal with the praises of the Great Creator. Instead of a race groping in the shadow of dim imaginings, we find one filled with hopes of a rational and glorious immortality. Our fathers found a howling wilderness; we behold to-day, as the result of their labors, from which they long have rested, one of the most beautiful of New England's many lovely villages. Change, great and all-pervading, has been written, in every form, on the face of society. Two hundred years ago, there was but a handful of people, scattered in detached bands, along the Atlantic seaboard, and some of the larger rivers; now the borders of this happy republic stretch from the Atlantic to the Pacific, and from the great Lakes of the North to the Gulf of Mexico. During the two centuries that have passed, since our forefathers first traversed these solitudes, more important events, bearing upon the happiness of mankind, have occurred, than in all the ages which preceded it, save *one*, that blessed the world eighteen hundred years ago. Two hundred years ago there was not a single printing press this side the great deep, and *one* hundred years ago there were but four. Now the press is everywhere, and by the magic power of steam, and the perfection of machinery, thousands of copies are thrown off in a single hour. The iron horse takes the traveler hundreds of miles in a day, through the fastnesses of the hills, and over yawning chasms, at a single leap. The lightning now flashes intelligence, with the celerity of thought, all over our extended country, by means of a network of wires, like the nerves of the body, extending in every direction. All these agencies we welcome as the results of the conjoined and patriotic labors of the past for the advancement of civilization and the good of the world.

Great indeed have been the results of the labors of our fathers, especially during the Revolution, not only to our own favored land, but to the world. Since that hour of deadly peril was passed, our nation has gone prosperously on, and we are almost miraculously increased from three to nearly thirty millions of freemen. Liberty and equality are interwoven with every fibre of our institutions.

Freedom of thought and of conscience is the pole-star of our existence. The active and enterprising spirit of the age has given us a vigorous and original literature. The universal diffusion of knowledge is the grand characteristic of our country. By means of this, the most distant member of our population, which surges to and fro like the waves of old ocean, is visited in his home on the broad prairie, or among the everlasting hills, and prepared to act his part in the great system of republican institutions. A bright destiny for us, under God, may be predicted, far more glorious than king or potentate ever gloried in. In the spirit of liberty, inculcated by every act of our fathers, lies the secret of the present condition of our kind. Exalted indeed is the position of us, who live in the nineteenth century. We stand amid the mighty ruins of the far distant past, while the clear light of liberty has just dawned in full effulgence upon the world. Events of the greatest importance succeed each other with electric speed. We must ride out the storm, and control the swelling flood, or be overwhelmed amid its angry waves. "For us has been reserved the glorious, yet perilous task, of remodeling society—for us a vital share in the regeneration of mankind." Our trust is in the lofty patriotism and intelligence of the people, and we are cheered on by the hope, that the perfection of humanity, having sought in vain throughout the whole world for a permanent resting place, may here, in this western land, take up its final abode.

What shall be the developments and improvements in our highly favored territory, a hundred years hence? The answer to this question must depend mainly upon ourselves. Of all this vast concourse, not one will be here to celebrate the next centennial. Long ere another centennial sun shall rise over this lovely valley, we shall have experienced the "last of earth," and passed to join the innumerable company of the dead! "The dead of old Woodbury! Lost, yet found forever—absent, yet present now, and always—dead, but living in that glorious life, which, commencing on the confines of time, spreads onward, and ever onward, through the endless ages of eternity!" Then let *us*, by the nobleness of our conduct, and the purity of our lives, eschewing all low delights and jarring discords, strive to add our mite to the great and good history of our sainted fathers, who have "ascended into glory." Then will our children, as they shall, with wet lids, assemble here, a hundred years hence, to commemorate *our* history, be enabled to say of us, "they wrought well, and have received the reward of their labors." Then shall our fame, as well as that of those glorious men who have already entered into their rest, be perennial with our noble language, in which it is recorded, now "spread more widely than any that has ever given expression to human thought." Let them, in that distant hour of commemoration, be enabled to apply to our memories, our virtues, and our words, that beautiful apostrophe of our most eloquent historian, to the English tongue: "Go forth, then, language of Milton and Hampden, language of my country; take possession of the North American continent! Gladden the waste places with every tone, that has been rightly struck on the English lyre, with every English word, that has been spoken well for liberty and for man! Give an echo to the now silent and solitary mountains; gush out with the fountains that as yet sing their anthems all day long without response; fill the valleys with the voices of love in its purity, the pledges of friendship in its faithfulness; and as the morning sun drinks the dew-drops from the flowers all the way from the dreary Atlantic to the Peaceful Ocean, meet him with the joyous hum of the early industry of freemen! Utter boldly and spread widely through the world, the thoughts of the coming apostles of the people's liberty, till the sound that cheers the desert shall thrill through the heart of humanity, and the lips of the messenger of the people's power, as he stands in beauty upon the mountains, shall proclaim the renovating tidings of equal freedom for the race!"

At the close of Mr. Cothren's Address, after music from the Band, the vast multitude repaired to the tents, provided with an abundance of eatables by the good ladies of the several towns, where they were hospitably entertained. In a brief space, the people were again summoned to the stand, and the exercises were opened by music from the Band, followed by the well-known song, "The Pilgrim Fathers," sung with fine effect by Gilbert Somers Minor, an aged man of silvery locks and long white beard. Then followed a Historical Poem by Rev. William Thompson Bacon, of Woodbury, as follows:—

SIRES AND SONS,

A HISTORICAL POEM;

PRONOUNCED AT THE

Woodbury Centennial Celebration,

JULY 4th, 1859.

By REV. WM. THOMPSON BACON.

POEM.

ARGUMENT.

A band of Pioneers spy out the land—Advent of the first Colony over Good Hill—Descent into the valley, their location, some facts about them, and why they came—Pass a hundred years, with some notices of descendants—Summary of the Puritan character.

Two hundred years ago, as records say,
*Five sturdy settlers left old Stratford Bay,—
Wells, Harvey, Uffoot, Curtiss and John Minor,
The last, of this design the grand designer,—
And, turning to these northern solitudes,
Sought out a home, among the gloomy woods.

But first, as honest settlers ought to do,
They seek a title to the land in view;—
So turning eastward, far as Naugatunk,†
Where dwelt an Indian Chief—not always drunk,—
Of him, and paying large of course, they bought
All the wide-stretching region that they sought.

This region, as I learn by efforts great—
(The muses are exact in what they state)
Was bounded northward by a trail, that lay
Over old Bantam Hill,‡ nine miles each way;
Westward, it came, the parted hills among,
As Ousatonuc rolls his bulk along;

---

* John Wells, Richard Harvey, Thomas Uffoot, John Curtiss, John Minor.
† Paugasset, now Derby.
‡ Section of Litchfield.

Southward, from this, due east, to Naugatunk,
Where dwelt the aforesaid Chief—so seldom drunk,—
And eastward, by that river, till we come
Back to the region that we started from ;—
All this they buy, I dont know for what sum,
Perhaps three hatchets and a quart of rum.

Sharp purchase that, you say—but stop, *I* say,—
What know you of the land's worth in that day ?—
What did it bear, all this wide stretch of land,
That here, in loveliness, we see expand?
Perhaps a little maize, some worthless chief
Scourged his poor wife, to plant for his relief;
Perhaps a plot of beans the white man gave him,
Yet not enough of these from death to save him;
With here and there a vile tobacco weed,
That he might smoke a little in his need ;—
The rest all left where cat or bear might prowl,
Or echo to the desert wolf's long howl ;—
All this wide stretch of land, and we to give
This up, that five old chiefs, like brutes, might live!

Perhaps it were a little more like song,
A little more to romance doth belong,
To picture here this loveliest paradise,
With all its glowing woods and streams and skies,
As sheltering, *blessing*, in its riches rare,
A race of demi-gods, and angels fair!
Imagination, as she loves to paint,
And lay her colors on without restraint,
Might tell us of the bowers here in the wood,
Where once the Sachem and his Shannup stood,—
Of lonely walk in solitary glade,
Of Indian lover with his Indian maid;
Of hero, prophet, sage, and all that throng,
That roll and thunder in the poet's song ;—
But let me tell you—*me*—one of the men,
That *do* this thing, with pencil or with pen,—
That this same ancient race we thus exalt,
And talk and sing about as without fault;

Clothing them with all virtues and all graces,
As if they were indeed earth's godlike races,—
They were, to say the truth, and shun the evil,
But little better than the "very *devil.*"
They never had one true, heroic thought!
Nothing divine from Him divine was caught!
They were an earthly, animal, hard stock,
Somewhere between a crocodile and rock;
Full of revenge, as is a coal with fire,
Full of all passions—but no pure desire;
Mean, grasping, selfish, lying, filthy, too,
A drunken, squabbling, shouting, cursing crew;
Making their women toil, that they might sleep,
Making their women run, that they might creep;
Kicking them from their wigwams when grown old—
In short, to every vice and demon sold,—
Till Nature, tired of this, her favorite quite,
Snapp'd the life cord, and put him out of sight.

I know, these loveliest of our Saxon homes—
With whom all loveliness by birth-right comes,—
Will feel the singer, with rude hand, among
Their fond divinities of Romance and Song,
Is playing harshly,—yet he bids *me* say,
That truth is tru*er* than a poet's lay
And truth is *dearer* to *some* singers, than
These fancy types of Indian maid and man;
And he perhaps will show you, ere we part,
That he can touch the fancy or the heart,
Fired by the beauty that may be abroad,
Amid the grandeur of the works of God!—
Thrill with the grandest, softening with the weak,
Fired by the noble, melting with the meek,
Till *ye* shall learn, the poet's first, best thought,
Comes from no object, where the truth is—*not!*

These five old settlers—we go back to them.
These five old settlers,—you have had each name,—
Two hundred years ago, their title got,
Turn their flint faces for the land they sought.

Up the bright stream, now Ousatonuc call'd,
Then Pootatook, its sides the most part wall'd
So grandly, by tall, perpendicular crags,
Or now again by meadows and pine snags—
They take their way,—each one upon his back
A musket, with his victuals in a pack.
They reach the place where Pomperaug comes out,
Under the arching wood, with noisy shout,
(Down where the river splits the mountain ridge,
And which we vulgarly call Bennet's Bridge,)
And, taking this, they follow it, long whiles,
Leaving behind them half a score of miles;
Passing South Britain, pleasant, sunny place,
Hugg'd by its hill-sides in a close embrace;
Pass Poverty,* White Oak,† and then, soon after,
The rich alluvial plain of Middle Quarter; ‡
Until they reach this central vale, and stand
And look around upon the unknown land!

It is a thought of beauty and of fear,
To look upon those lonely wanderers here,—
The first white men that ever stood upon
This ancient soil, or look'd upon the sun,—
And try an instant to call up the power,
That lay upon their souls in that still hour!
Was it not solemn, as they paus'd to view
The embracing hills, or look'd upon the blue
Broad heaven, that, like a canopy, came down,
And rested on the circling mountains' crown,
They all alone, alone, amid the scene,—
A solemn, silent, wilderness of green?
O, had some power, one little moment then,
Flashed through the minds of these heroic men,
The mighty future, from the distance caught,
With all its splendid wealth of soul and thought,
It's strength and beauty, innocence and truth,
And reverend age, and loving dreams of youth,
Each age successive gathering up the past,
Till the bright present on their souls was cast,—

*† Localities of Southbury. ‡ Locality of Woodbury.

Would there been wanting to that spot and time,
One single element of the grand sublime?—
And would they not have trembled, in each sense,
At God's unfolding, mighty Providence?

These brave men scoured the region all around,
Sought every spot, and all its promise found,—
The gentle valley and the rounded hill,
The winding stream and solitary rill;
Each opening vista through the forest glade,
And every charm by freak of Nature made,—
From the cool grotto, where the brooklets run,
To splinter'd peak, tall black'ning in the sun;—
At last, discovering what they came for, pleas'd
With what they'd purchas'd, not, like robbers, seized,
Back to old Stratford's strand they turn once more,
And tell the wondrous story o'er and o'er.

Roll back the tide of time! and let us stand
Two hundred years ago, with that brave band,
Who, from the hill, that, westering, skirts this scene,
Looked down upon its rolling forests green,
And, gazing, as they might, with strange surprise,
Let the whole mighty landscape fill their eyes!

Roll back the tide! and let us, as we may,
Group, in our thought, the picture of that day,—
Of that brave band along the forests led,
Now climbing steeps, now where the waters spread,—
Startled, how oft, to catch that sound of fear,
The bark of cat, or yell of mountaineer,—
Till where yon mountain rising to the blue,
Gave all this glorious landscape to their view!

Far to the north, hills over hills survey,
Till their blue tops are mingled with the day;
Far to the south the widening vale extends,
Whose wealth of splendor every beauty lends;
Far to the west, in wide succession spread,
Valley and hill, and jutting mountain head;
While right before them, 'neath the morning sky,
Nature's wide wonders all, were in their eye!

I wonder much, if those broad-breasted men,
In that rough age—(it will not come again,—
Should not perhaps)—I wonder if they view'd
As we, this mighty stretch of wave and wood!
The Spring's first bird was whistling in the sky,
The fragrant birch its tassels flaunted nigh;
Through the moist mould, in beauty ever young,
Tall ranks of flowers on every bank were flung;
Far by the streams, as here and there they view'd,
The classic willow, by the brook-side stood,
Trembling all over in the morning's beam,
Or playing with its shadow on the stream;
The young winds bore their fragrance all about,
Mingled with hum of bee and torrent's shout,
And the wide air with all those sounds was filled,
That fancy ever dream'd, or heart has thrill'd;—
I wonder how those men, of stalwart mien,
In that sweet morn looked forth upon the scene!

One mighty purpose all that age had fired,
One mighty aim each swelling soul inspired;
One truth, fást lock'd, in every soul was kept,
That conscience guarded, and that never slept;—
Man came from God, in his own image made,
And by that charter certain rights conveyed;—
Those rights long trampled by an hireling throne,
Had sent them forth, to ways and wilds unknown;
Here on bleak shores, soft breezes seldom press'd,
Here mid rude scenes, gay fancy seldom dress'd,
Alone, mid death, in want of all but worth,
They battled for the noblest prize on earth,—
Man in his native dignity to stand,
Himself a prince and ruler of the land!

Small time had they then for the mere ideal,
Their love was truth, their present life all real;
They walked the world, faith's vision never dim,
Saw not God's *works*, they only gazed on *Him!*

Tell me, ye sons of that imperial race,
Imperial only, as their truth ye trace;—

Those brave men, scorning courts, and kingly crew,
And only daring less than angels do;—
Tell me, if prince or nobleman there be,
Can boast a prouder ancestry than we!

Come down the hill-side with our gallant band,
And let us trace them round upon the land;
Upward and downward, over all they go,
Northward and southward, east and west they flow.

'Tis thought a party pierce to Nonewog,*
Where dwelt a chief, whose name rhymes well with hog;
Another pierce to Weekeepeemee's plain,
And scour that region o'er and o'er again;
Some pierce to Quasapog, perhaps beyond
That sheet with classic name, yclept *a pond!*
Some scour West Side, then south, down Hesky Meadow,
Then over Rag Land hills, till they are lead to
Grim Poverty's hard name, yet not hard soil,
Then they divide, and scour White Oak awhile;
Then coming north, hungry as wolves for slaughter,
They camp upon the plain of Middle Quarter,
Where stands an oak, or did, 'neath which they found
Their first night's sleep upon the cold, damp ground.

One moment pause. What a suggestive rest,
Was that, that night, upon the earth's cold breast?
Home far away, on every side a wood,
And the whole scene impressive solitude!
They had no past, but such as wrung a groan,
They had no future, but they stood alone;
No wealth, no name, possessions, but His power,
On which to lean in such a solemn hour;—
Tell me of heroes in the battle's van,
Earth looking on to call us knave or man;
The genuine, god-like deed by *this* is known—
That which we bear, in silence, and alone!

Records declare the Shermans take their stand,
Just on the edge of that alluvial land,—

---

* This and the following are all localities of Woodbury.

Where they dwell now, or rather, as yankees will,
They've left the *bottom* for the *top* of the hill.
Curtiss and Hinman, moving south, evince
A love for Southbury—they have loved it since;
Aye, and each other too, and matched and mated,
Till the whole township is to them related.
Walkers come north, and drive a stake deep down,
Close by a rock, that, over it did frown,
And which now neighbor Douglass calls his own,—
Not by descent exactly, for he plan'd
To get a jewel first, and then the land.
The Minors westward on a gentle hill,—
Each generation since, by solemn will,
Has ever held it,—and one holds it still.
The Judson's farther north in Judson's Lane,
The Warners, too. Others—but I refrain;
The Muse would tire, to mark the spots and places,
Where sank the tap-root of our mighty (?) races.

Some things, however, records well declare
About these men, we note, to show them fair,
And, what is more, to show them as they were.
They were not then, of such a blear-eyed kind,
As think to buy, or beg, or steal, or find
All a man ought to have in life's mere rind;—
They enter into solemn covenant,
First, to take care, and feed, man's highest want,
That of his mind and soul, God's earnest plan,
That bulwark of all nobleness in man;—
A stake is driven for a house of God,
And then a school-house rises by the road—
Twin facts, that show God did with them abode.

One other fact, as noticeable, I find—
A little like a "kink" in this first mind,—
Yet springing from a well-meant principle,
So let us honor it, or ill or well.
*Each man's home-lot was limited in space.**
It seems they were afraid the human race
Were not all equal in life's steeple chase;

*Fact.

They thought, by such apportionment, to hold
Each one, as if run in a candle mould—
All just alike, lame, halt, or blind, or bold;
A very harmless doctrine that, because
It happens He above, hath fixed some laws,
Which sometimes bring men's follies to a pause;
And it appears, by further searching, that
Not all of our good fathers were so flat,
As they first seem in this by looking at;
For further resolutions come, in course,
To let the bolder few, that had the force,
Go further back, and buy from any source;
So they were equal in the first law's point—
The second knocked the first all out of joint.
It is'nt the first time wise men their laws make,
Then legislate a little more, and break
What they first made, for—common sense's sake.

How came these Pilgrim Fathers on this spot?
We, children, are concern'd in't—are we not?
Came they for pelf? or did some meaner thing
Burn in their souls, the motive and the spring?
The haughtiest breeze that o'er the billows bore
The May Flower shallop to this western shore,
Bore not, on all that wild and devious way,
A truer, nobler, juster band than they,
Who, from our southern shore, came here and stood,
And built their cabins in the gloomy wood.
The self-same principle that nerved the first,
Burn'd in the second, and by them was nurs'd;
Tis strange indeed, how all that age seems fired
By one grand principle, one thought inspired!
Records make plain, that arbitrary* power
Lay on *our* fathers in their trial hour,
Stern and relentless in the first degree,
Abridging what, to them, was liberty!
The struggle then of "Old lights," and the "New,"
Burning New England's churches through and through;

* The careful student of this part of our history finds, that the first Colony that came up from Stratford, were a minority, crowded out of the Old Stratford Church by an unscrupulous majority—a singular parallel to the extradition of the first Puritan stock from old England.

The old, effete, worn matters of the law,
Fed not some souls—'twas famine in their maw;
Our fathers threw the old away, and took
Their own interpretation of God's book!—
Man's great soul there, with its far reaching thought,
This from the future, to his knowledge brought—
Each for himself, to man, or God, should stand,
Each one a priest and ruler of the land!—
A doctrine that, however spurn'd or curs'd,
Still to go on, as by our fathers nurs'd;
Change every church to a Democracie,
Change every throne and state beyond the sea;
Till in dread ruin, from high summits hurl'd,
Power topples down, o'er all the bondage world;—
Prerogative, in State, or *Church*, lets go
Its living grasp upon man's soul below;
Till every soul, unfearing tyrants' rod,
Stands up alone, responsible to God!

If nobler trait in any soul can be,
Of which to justly boast, for you or me;
If e'er from Heaven came down for human kind,
One single element for soul or mind;—
If power descended, dignity, high grace,
Courage from God, to light up form or face,—
Methinks the world's great records ought to show
How, when, or where it is, with man below!

Earth's record has no history like that—*
Rocking three Islands like the throe of Fate;—
Sifting the race, from highest to the low,
That the good seed among the chaff might show;
Then howls them forth, and hounds them o'er the waves,
To lodge 'neath icy crags, in desert caves;
Makes the land drear, to set their feet upon,
Takes all the light away of stars and sun—
Till nought is left, to please, to win, to fire,
Of all earth ever gives, that can inspire;

* Probably the history of the world presents us with no records, either of private or public heroism, surpassing those found in the history of the early settlement of this country.

That their great souls *to* God alone might go,
Dwelling *in* Him, *from* all we love below;
Then plants, mid such intensest misery,
A germ, to lift the future to the sky;—
Where, mid the records of the race, like this,
Doth the true grandeur of man's soul arise?

And these few men, that stood here on that day,
Fresh from the swamps and tangled forest way,
Embrown'd, or pale, or trembling, or still high,
Faith in each heart, and courage in each eye;
And the meek matron, by her lord's proud side,
Or the sweet maid, but yester eve a bride;—
These were the *children* of *that* race, who came,
Out from the land of bondage and of shame,—
Bondage and shame, that, from her sacred breast,
Unpitying, cast her noblest and her best!

Pass a bright century now of rolling years,
And let us see the scene as it appears.
How the plain widens! How the race spreads out!
Over yon* western hill a people shout!
Another from the north-west† thunders on,
Another from the north‡—a Paixian gun!
The eastern fastnesses§ catch up the roar,
And send it back as ocean's beat, his shore;
And the south valley,|| to the line,|| has voice,
Mixed in with this conglomerate, awful noise!
And what are these tall forms that rise up here?
Brinsmades, Days, Porters, for a high career;
And these from Roxbury, live oak, called Smith,
And Southbury Grahams and Wildmen, men of pith;
Curtis, Stiles, Strong, and Hinman, names succinct
With light and force, each lineament distinct;

* Roxbury.
† Washington.
‡ Bethlem.
§ Middlebury.
|| Southbury and Oxford.

Eastward these Tylers,* north in Bethlehem fair,†
There stands a giant in the pulpit there,
Whose eloquence the devil's self might scare!

I see two stars shoot up the western sky,‡
Two forms like Mars, defiance in each eye;
Northward they take their solitary way,
Where the Green Mountains mingle with the day;
Where like twin streams, down to the vale they go,
A perfect thunder-bolt upon the foe!
Crown Points, Ticonderogas, Benningtons,
These tell the story of these gallant sons,
Lost to this valley by their splendid fame,
For who e'er dreamed that *we* their lineage claim?

The Muse, inquisitive, one moment's space,
Pauses, their perfect lineaments to trace,
Just as Tradition gives their form and face.
Allen was terrible to look upon,
Broad, brawny, hard, Roxbury's genuine son;
His red eye burning like a fiery star,
And his front wrinkled like the front of war;
The "Great Jehovah," "Continental Congress,"
Stuck out all over him, in dress or undress;
And his fierce will, that knitted every limb,
Show'd God or devil only, conquer'd him.
Warner, of equal girth and equal span,
Yet a most perfect, gallant gentleman;
Of noble port, and broad and slab-like brow,
Thick, chestnut hair, and eye of heaven's own glow;
Voice like a clarion, echoing wild and shrill,
Like the gray eagle's call from some far hill;
Hither and thither mid the battle's fire,
Louder and louder rung, higher and higher!—
Yet the dread battle done, the cry for peace,
And not a woman's tears fell fast as his.

I wonder if these men have left no stamp
Down to this day, on wise man or on scamp,

---

* Dr. Bennet Tyler was of this stock.

† Dr. Joseph Bellamy; only second, in point of theological acumen and force, of the theological names of this country.

‡ Col. Ethan Allen and Seth Warner, both of Roxbury.

Such as shall let us see the ancient fire
Burn out in son as it burnt out in sire!

Or have our modern, mushroom virtues grown,
Like weeds that kill whate'er they lean upon,
Till our loved vale, sharing the nation's curse,
Goes on from good to bad, and then to worse,
Till all these virtues, from our fathers sprung,
Become the scorn of every wretch unhung!

Ah, for the land, put in the world's wide van,
To teach mankind to view the perfect man,—
Boasting her freedom in the world's full eye,
Bound hand and foot by her venality;
Boasting her freedom from one tyrant's nod,
Baring her back beneath the million's rod,—
(As if dread Bondage had one curse the less,
Whether a man or million may oppress;)
Boasting her knowledge, liberty and law,
When every foreign fool may see the flaw;
With but this virtue, that her Saxon lust
Will have its will, simply because it must,—
(Strange power of stock!—that, like the sun on snows,
Withers and wastes whatever it oppose!)—
Ah, for such land, if faltering when *He* calls,
Double her deep damnation, *if* she falls!

Yet let us hope. Our fathers names still live,
And some of their bright virtues still survive;
Brinsmades* still live, Days,† whose serene decay,
Like the sun's orb, more glorious sink away;
Smith, erst translated from its rocky‡ dell,
Like mountain oak was strongest when it fell;
Yet springs anew, and bears its honors well.
The Wildman name is gone, yet Scottish Graham§
In his new field, achieves a grander fame.
The Curtiss is with double honor crown'd,
Since here we have, and right among us, found,

---

*† Gen'l. Daniel Brinsmade, of Washington, and Jeremiah Day, of Yale College, both enjoying a serene old age, and more than rich in the honors of a well spent life.

‡ Hon. Nath'l Smith, born in Roxbury, died in this place, 1822. No son of Connecticut, in point of native brain force, ever surpassed him.

§ John Lorimer Graham, of New York.

Bank, broker, farmer, merchant, in one bound,
Always in good condition, always sound.
That primitive Stiles, that chose to guide the plow,
Did up his work to order—does so now;
That primitive Strong, that chose to fight *and* plow,
(He was a Captain) *talks*, but don't fight now.
Those eastern Tylers, strong as any ox,
Only grew stronger and more orthodox,
Till bold the man who dared to try the list,
His single arm against their logic fist.
But that big burly brain, that, from the north,
Shot its sharp eloquence like lightning forth,
That is quite gone—ay, dwindled from the earth.

Methinks I see some other names our mother
Yet keeps, nor will she change them for another;—
The Minor,* from that first Diaconate,
Down to the last, a *True* man and a great,—
Great in two senses—for his stalwart form,
And the rude eloquence his lips can storm;
The Sherman, from that first old honest John,
Down to the Rector,† that we look upon;
The Judson, with his mild and pleasing face,
Blue eye, fair hair, the genuine Saxon race;
The Martin, from that first old "Sargent Sam,"
Down to the last immaculate, "I am;"
And scores of others which I cannot name,
Now filling posts of honor, strength, or fame.

But there's one name, we will not let that pass,
No more for what it is, than what it was;
They've turn'd monopolists on Litchfield hill,
And think to keep the credit of it still;
But if they wish to know whence came that stock,
Somewhere between a live oak and a rock,
Its springtime freshness every year renewed,
As if with everlasting youth imbued,—

* This stock can boast an uninterrupted "Apostolic succession" from the first Diaconate. Unfortunately however—that is, for advocates of "succession"—this succession has split in these latter days, and given us two most honored and laborious Deacons of the same name.

† Rev. Henry Beers Sherman, now of Belleville, N. Jersey, the author's most excellent early friend, and who gave us a most acceptable sermon, which is found in another part of this pamphlet.

We tell old Litchfield, spite of boasts and jeers,
We claim the honor of *that sort* of Beers.*

And if I dared, and could escape the shot,
Sure to return, explosive, hissing hot,
Another should be summon'd, a grand-son,
Pleasant to know, and e'en to look upon,—
Keen as a scimitar with its first edge,
Or, if he will, as vigorous as a sledge;
His very eye a pun in its eclipse,
Before it leaps in beauty from his lips;—
Would you his name, abated not one jot?
A very funny *Chap*, and MAN † too—doubt it *not!*

Perhaps t'were well, that our imported shoots
Receive their due, as well as native roots.
Who bids the muse of History‡ unfold
The treasures of the past, or new or old;
By patient industry and work well done,
Holds up the father's portrait to the son;
Wins honor, and should have it, shall do so,
Though ignorance, hatred, envy, all, say no.
And when, with world-wide fame, with honors graced,
The veteran toilsman § from the realms of taste,
Seeks our loved vale, to rest that busy brain,
That it, refreshed, go forth to toil again,—
What heart refuses in this note to swell,
Honor to him who honor wears so well!

Nor shall be pass'd here our plain men that shine,
Have they not come right down the mighty line?
Walkers and Stoddards! ‖—it would puzzle much
Those ancient men, to give the modern touch

---

* Hon. Seth P. Beers, of Litchfield, a genuine son of the olden time, who, though now verging on his ninth decade, has yet all the vigor, intellectual and physical, of his pristine manhood.

† Hon. Chas. Chapman, of Hartford, a grand son of Woodbury, who lent us some of his truest wit and pathos on the occasion of our celebration.

‡ Wm. Cothren, Esq., the author's associate in the celebration, whose discourse precedes this.

§ Hon. S. G. Goodrich, of world-wide reputation under the *nom de plume* of "Peter Parley," who, after his world-wide rambles, has "pitched his tent" in the south part of this beautiful valley.

‖ It is a notable fact, that the direct lineal male descendants of the two first most able pastors of this town, now represent the north and south interests of the

To horse-shoe, or cart-wheel, or wagon tire,
Fresh from the furnace, sputtering round its fire.
And if you want a cart, sound as a knot,
Without a flaw, twist, crack, or one loose spot,
In body, axle, tongue, or either wheel,
Go up the street, and call on "Uncle Bill." ‡
And men of every grade, and every kind,
All arts and trades among us, soul and mind,
T 'is to be hoped the ancient virtue cast
O'er all, round all, through all, by lineage pass'd,
Lives in this age, shall live, till stars expire,
And the world burns in Nature's funeral fire.

The Muse, in curious mood, would picture here,
One or two separate stocks, as they appear.

She's speculated much upon one point,
And still her logic is quite out of joint,—
Whence came that hardy, iron, Atwood race—
Their characters all written in their face;—
A strange, determined, energetic line,
With brains enough in any path to shine;
Yet full of crosses as an egg with meat,
Of inconsistencies, and yet discreet;
Sharp to see things, the wrong are always righting,
And always peaceable—when they're not fighting;
A race to snuggle to, if on your side,
A race to knuckle to, if not allied;
Wise, sober, just and self-denying, prayerful,
Sly, cautious, cute, sagacious, cruel, swearful;
Mixture incomprehensible of kinds,
Their thousand men and maids of thousand minds;—
In short, the Muse declares, though well acquainted,
She can't decide them sinners or the sainted.

One other name perhaps should rise up here,
Nor need the singer blush that it appear;

---

place in the "ancient and honorable device" of horse-shoeing, and both as famous for "beating" iron, as their Rev'd ancestors were for beating the "drum ecclesiastic."

‡ Famous for the manufacture of ox carts—with but the single objection, that they never wear out.

One in whose wondrous potency of soul,
A dozen men might be, nor fill the whole;
Power in each part of him, and nought but power,
Power from his cradle to his dying hour;
A man of that vast business skill, that it
To any bold emergency might fit;
Knew how to evoke large gains in any line,
Now from a spool of cotton, now a mine;
Lands, stocks, rare merchandise, or common things,
No matter where he sought to strike wealth's springs,
He always hit them at the time—wealth roll'd
Around him literally in a tide of gold.
I honor no man,—let the record be
Preserved, and given to posterity,—
For his fat ledger, between whose twin sides,
A million widows' tears have roll'd like tides;
Or orphans' groans have echoed, as they press'd
Like a hot millstone on their bleeding breast;—
But wealth, the proof of power, our praise may claim,
And wealth, so view'd, may give a man to fame;
And fame was his, as wealth was his, who died,
Of our loved valley, once its strength and pride.*

The Muse depicting character thus here,
Pauses to drop one solitary tear.
Where is that sex, amid this world of strife,
That makes up more than half the sum of life?
One such I knew, of loveliest form and face,
Light on her brow, and light in every place;
Gifted with genius like a torch of fire,
Her birth-right mind, and every pure desire;
Borne from our midst to love's own secret bower,
Charm of each circle, joy of every hour;
Her influence widening as the years ran on,
Her soul aspiring nearer to the sun;—

---

*Jabez Bacon, the author's grandfather, a man of almost fabulous wealth, and all the product of his own unaided genius. He began life a poor boy, and died the richest man in the State.

When the dark shadow on that household fell,
And every virtue sighed to say farewell.*

One other picture, clad in grief 's dark stole,
Comes up and presses sad upon the soul;
And yet all light and love that image dear,
As ye shall deem it, as ye see it here.
The Scholar-pastor! through those long bright years,
Working his prayerful work 'mid joyful tears,
Meekness writ o'er his face, and love's own sign,
Lit up ineffably with love divine;
High in each purpose, clear in every thought,
Rich in those truths experience had brought;
Refined, sweet, eloquent, his spirit feeling
Beauty all round him, every fount unsealing;
His soul fill'd full with solemn tenderness,
A lip that could not wound, but yet would bless;
First to discern his step on Calvary led,
Last by the sick and by the dying bed;
He moved among us of such perfect fame,
That not one word did ever soil his name.†

But hark again, that startling, solemn knell,
Round all our valley with its pealing swell;—
The upright judge, the wit, the mind intent,
With the large heart that always with it went;
Not like too many, worser than he seemed,
But always better than himself had deemed;
Passing his years among us, soften'd, sage,
Almost the feature of another age;—

* Mrs. Mary Smith Monell, daughter of Hon. N. B. Smith, of this place, and wife of Hon. John J. Monell, of Newburg, who died Oct. 22, 1858;—a lady as remarkable for her natural gifts, as she was for her perfect unconsciousness of their possession.

† Rev. Samuel R. Andrew, Pastor of the South Church in this place a quarter of a century, and uniting in himself all the imaginable perfections of a gospel minister.

In this place I cannot but pay a tribute to his "twin brother" in the sacred work, Rev. Grove L. Brownell, of the North Church, for about the same length of time. The northern brother possessed less of the softness and affability of the other, but what he lacked in these was made up in the sterner, masculine virtues—perhaps the more needful in his own field. They were together, a rare combination of ministerial excellence, and the town will long reap the advantages of their mutual faithfulness.

In one dread moment, sent to that far shore,
Where praise, nor blame, shall ever reach him more.*

These were our Fathers. We sit down to-day,
To estimate the worth that in them lay;
Let us be just, avoid fictitious hues,
And take the dicta of an honest Muse.
In that far day, it is not hard to find
The springs that move the common heart and mind;
Harder by far to see the springs that play
Beneath the living maelstrom of to-day.
That day society was, most part, free
From complex causes, which to-day may be;
Their means were limited, their wants, therefore,
Fewer in number, simpler in their power.
They had come far from distant lands and fires,
And bade adieu to ancient gods and sires,
'Mid scenes unparalleled in history,
And scarcely dwelling even in fancy's eye.
Those stirring scenes a few bright, solemn truths
Burnt in on each man's mind, and even youth's;
On infants even, we might deem the fire
Left some dread impress, as it scorch'd the sire.
Those truths were first, indignant sense of wrong,
Borne at their hands who for them should be strong;
Conscience t'was dared to hedge in by such bounds,
As makes earth's records shine with martyr's crowns;
And then the natural wants that all men have,
That always help the good and true and brave,
The love of home, the love of child and wife,
The love of ease, instinctive hating strife,
The love to accumulate an honest gain,
That will not labor laboring in vain,
With a true fear of what is in each man,
As God unfolds it in his chosen plan,
And a safe fear of Him, that puts him first,
And not denies him, though by men accurs'd;
And we might add, a lusty, sturdy health,
One of the best securities for wealth;—

* Hon. Chas. B. Phelps, lawyer and Judge of Probate for nearly thirty years, who died Dec. 21st, 1859, while sitting in his chair, and attending the meeting of the Warner Monumental Committee, at Roxbury.

All this, and these, received as facts, and we
Have the whole key to Pilgrim history.
This made men say in that far day—farewell
To home, to country, all that in them well;
Farewell the spot of kindred and of birth,
The dearest, sweetest, loveliest of the earth;
Farewell, old England, greatest of the sons
Earth yet has known of all her ancient ones;
Greatest as civil, greatest moral too,
Greatest, as we her splendid line review
Of heroes, sages, poets, all that move
In the great past, and make it what we love;
And welcome desert waves and far off shore,
Where home's sweet chimes shall never echo more!

Who dares to slander that bold, Puritan band,
That first set foot upon the western land?—
Tell us of restless spirits—so sent forth
To this, the farthest end of hostile earth?—
Tell of an avarice that sent them on,
Or other passion hateful to the sun?
He shuts his eyes on facts, that, bold as light,
Change to bright burning day the darkest night;
Reads history backwards, and philosophy,
As a dull school-boy in his first degree;—
They came *because* they could not stay at home,
For this they dared December's wintry foam;
Dared the rude desert, and the wintry flood,
The barren rock, and solitary wood—
Places where want and all diseases sprung,
And mountain cat yell'd wild above her young!

'Tis said indeed, the boasted Puritan,
Well, after all, was nothing but a man!
Who says he was? or who pretends to find
Ought but a specimen of poor human kind?
Shuns persecution, yet will persecute,
Dwelling in God, yet showing strangest fruit;
Chases the quaker from old Cambridge Bay,
And burns a witch, or hangs her, as some say;—
(Though't's not so plain, the quaker persecuted,
Was not most justly served and justly suited;

When men run naked through the house of God,
Methinks they need the law, or need a rod;)
Yet if one single soul to God went forth,
By fire or cord, to the new Heavens and earth—
And truth declared it was so,—then first find,
This the *disease* of all that day and mind;
Of minds of highest power beyond the seas,
Men of all ranks and races and degrees;
So if one single soul to heaven was sent,
The age bears *that*—*these* only ignorant.

Methinks we must search history o'er and o'er,
Search every land, and clime, and sea, and shore,
Almost call up fictitious days and powers,
Ere we shall find a nobler stock than ours.
Stern it may be, unpolish'd, narrow, borne
Onward too oft, by what they ought to scorn;
Reading truth strangely, and too often led
By what was in themselves, than what they read;
Frowning at joy, God's taper in the soul,
Making their good, too oft, in form, or stole,
Or look, or gesture, or some other thing
That in religion has no sort of spring;—
And yet for brave intent, that dared to view
God in the face, and say "thou know'st me true;"
For honest, godlike energy, to stand
And battle for the truth, with sword and brand;
And, more than this—to offer life up—*so*
Their perfect rectitude the world might know;
Earth offers no superior of her kind,—
And hence we reverence PILGRIM SOUL AND MIND!

At the close of the Poem, which occupied an hour and a half in the delivery, the assemblage united in singing the following

SONG.

BY WILLIAM COTHREN.

Tune—"Auld Lang Syne."

Should early ages be forgot,
As months and years decline?
Should ancient mem'ries wake us not,
"And days of Auld Lang Syne?"
For Auld Lang Syne, my friends,
For Auld Lang Syne;
We'll give the hand of friendship yet,
For Auld Lang Syne.

Our fathers sought this quiet vale,
With noble, pure design;
Their humble prayers rose on the gale,
Each day of Auld Lang Syne.
"For Auld Lang Syne," &c.

And here their lowly dwellings stood,
'Mid chestnut, oak, and pine;
They sought to do their *neighbors good*,
In days of Auld Lang Syne.
"For Auld Lang Syne," &c.

All honor to that early stock,
Whose hearts did them incline
To praise their God at Bethel Rock,
In days of Auld Lang Syne.
"For Auld Lang Syne," &c.

Right soon they built a church to God,
Beneath the tree and vine;
But they've been resting 'neath the sod,
Since days of Auld Lang Syne.
"For Auld Lang Syne," &c.

Our fathers' power is living yet,
In principles divine;
Their counsels wise we'll ne'er forget,
Nor days of Auld Lang Syne.
"For days of Auld Lang Syne," &c.

Then followed the benediction, by Rev. Thomas L. Shipman, of Jewett City, Conn., formerly pastor of the Congregational Church in Southbury:

"Now may the grace of our Lord Jesus Christ be and abide with us, the descendants of the holy men who settled these pleasant valleys, and with our children, for ever and ever. Amen."

SECOND DAY.

On the morning of the second day, at eight o'clock, about one thousand persons convened in that sacred dell in the thick woods, on the east side of the Orenaug Rocks, about a mile from the village, which was consecrated by the prayers and praises of the early fathers, and by them called Bethel Rock. This meeting was held for the special purpose of commemorating this most interesting fact in the history of our revered ancestors, and the occasion was one long to be remembered by every devout heart.

Rev. Robert G. Williams, pastor of the old Pioneer Church, opened the meeting by giving out one verse of the hymn commencing—

"Be Thou, O God, exalted high,"

which being sung with great solemnity, in the ever welcome air of "Old Hundred," Dea. Eli Summers was called upon to lead in prayer, which he did, after making some feeling and appropriate remarks. Then followed the reading of portions of the 28th and 35th chapters of Genesis, which contain the account of Jacob's setting up a stone to indicate the place where God had talked with him, and naming it his Bethel; which passages occasioned the giving by *our* fathers of the name of Bethel Rock to this beautifully wild and secluded place of prayer and communion with God. Then followed, in rapid succession, appropriate remarks by Mr. B. H. Andrews of Waterbury, Rev. Anson S. Atwood of Mansfield Centre, Dea. Truman Minor of Woodbury, and Rev. Philo Judson of Rocky Hill. Mr. Judson became much affected while giving reminiscences of the great and good men with whom he had communed in prayer in this sacred retreat, in former years, and who now rest from their labors till the "Great Day of Accounts." Then followed the hymn—

"Once more, my soul, the rising day," &c.

Rev. Benjamin C. Meigs, late missionary to Ceylon, where he had labored for more than forty years, now led in a beautiful and impressive prayer, after having made the following remarks:

REMARKS OF MR. MEIGS AT THE BETHEL ROCK.

My Friends! I feel that it is good for us to be here. Here is the place where our Puritan fathers assembled to worship God, before they had any sanctuary built for this purpose, and while their savage foes roamed in these forests. In this beautiful ravine, under these sheltering rocks, by setting a watch on yonder point, they could worship in comparative safety. Hence the name by which this place is known—"Bethel Rock." Surely the God of Bethel is here this morning. "This is none other but the house of God, and this is the gate of heaven." May we not suppose that our pious forefathers are now looking down upon us, while we are gathered together in this consecrated place of worship? With what delight will they behold this assembly, while we pour out our hearts before God in prayer!

We have great encouragement thus to draw near unto him, and to pray for his blessing upon ourselves, upon our children, and our children's children, to the latest generation. He is indeed the hearer and the answerer of prayer. What wonderful illustrations of this great truth has he given to the people of this land within the last two years! How ready is he to hear and answer our prayers! "And it shall come to pass, that before they call I will answer, and while they are yet speaking I will hear." And again, "Bring ye all the tithes into the storehouse, and prove me now herewith, saith the Lord of Hosts, if I will not open you the windows of heaven, and pour you out a blessing, that there shall not be room enough to receive it." God is waiting to be gracious, and I feel that we ought not to depart from this hallowed ground this morning, without a special blessing. Let us carry this blessing with us, to our homes. Let us consecrate ourselves anew to the service of God. Let us all henceforth live unto Him, and not to ourselves Then, though we part to meet no more on earth, we shall all meet in yonder world of glory, and sing his praises forever!

A few appropriate remarks by Dea. Judson Blackman were followed by a prayer from Rev. Anson S. Atwood, and the singing of a verse from the ninetieth Psalm. The regular exercises being now closed, a few moments were spent in hearing volunteer remarks, when the audience united in singing the verse, commencing—

"Lord, dismiss us with thy blessing."

Then followed the brief concluding prayer, by Rev. Philo Judson, and the benediction by Rev. Austin Isham, of Roxbury, and this solemn and interesting occasion was numbered with the events of the past, an event never to occur again during the life of any soul present at the revered spot. Many lingered, as if unwilling to separate, and many more procured and carried away portions of the rock and moss, to be treasured as sacred mementoes of a hallowed spot, and a sacred scene.

At ten o'clock, a procession was formed in the same order as the first day, with the exception of the "antique" portion of it, which was omitted, and marched to the Tent, escorted by the Band and Warner Light Guards.

The services were opened by music from the Band, followed by the reading of the following

CENTENNIAL HYMN.

BY REV. WILLIAM THOMPSON BACON.

Supposed to be sung on the spot where the Pilgrim Settlers held their first Sabbath Worship.

Here, then, beneath the greenwood shade,
The Pilgrim first his altar made;
'T was here, amid the mingled throng,
First breathed the prayer, and woke the song.

The sun, which lends his gladness now,
Lay bright upon the Pilgrim's brow;
And this same wind, here breathing free,
Curled round his honored head in glee.

How peaceful smiled that Sabbath sun,
How holy was that day begun,
When here, amid the dark woods dim,
Went up the Pilgrims' first low hymn!

Hushed was the stormy forests' roar,
The forest eagle screamed no more;
And far along each blue stream's side,
The small wave murmur'd, where it died.

Look now upon the same still scene,
The wave is blue, the turf is green;
But where are now the wood and wild,
The Pilgrim, and the forest child?

The wood and wild have passed away;
Pilgrim and forest child are clay;
But here, upon their graves, we stand,
The children of that Christian band.

O, while upon this spot we stand,
The children of that Christian band,
Be ours the thoughts we owe this day,
To our great fathers passed away!

By prayer and contemplation led,
Be ours by their brave spirits fed;
Be ours their efforts and their aim,
Their truth, their glory, and their name!

An exceedingly eloquent, fervid, and appropriate prayer was then offered by Rev. Friend W. Smith, Pastor of the Methodist Church in Woodbury, a copy of which, we were unable to obtain, but the following is a brief synopsis of its leading topics:

Acknowledgment of the power and goodness of God, in the creation and preservation of all things. His rightful sovereignty. Our dependence on, and duty of allegiance to him. Confession and deprecation of sin. Recognition of, and thanksgiving for the goodness of God, in his providential and gracious dealings with mankind, especially in redemption by Christ; of his goodness especially to us, as a people; manifested in his care and protection of the Pilgrims, in their passage over the ocean, and in their early settlements. His interposition in our Revolutionary struggle; the appointment of Washington, a man of prayer, as leader of our armies; and in leading a mere handful of undisciplined men to final victory. His guidance of, and providential kindness to the explorers and early settlers of Ancient Woodbury. An earnest prayer for the continuance of his grace and protection to our nation generally, and to this community and their posterity particularly; that he would graciously take away all bitterness and remove all animosities from among us; that while we honor men, as the instruments of our success, we may never forget Him by whose providential care they are guided; and that we may all be enabled so to discharge our duties, that when this assembly shall all meet at the judgment, we may stand acquitted through him who taught us to pray—Our Father, who art in Heaven, hallowed be thy name. Thy kingdom come. Thy will be done, on earth, as it is in Heaven. Give us, this day, our daily bread; and forgive us our trespasses, as we forgive them that trespass against us. Lead us not into temptation; but deliver us from evil; for thine is the kingdom, the power, and the glory, forever and ever. Amen.

The choir then sung the following

HYMN.

Tune—"OLD HUNDRED."

Before Jehovah's awful throne,
Ye nations, bow with sacred joy;
Know that the Lord is God alone;
He can create, and he destroy.

His sovereign power, without our aid,
Made us of clay, and formed us men;
And when, like wandering sheep, we strayed,
He brought us to his fold again.

We are his people, we his care,
Our souls, and all our mortal frame;
What lasting honors shall we rear,
Almighty Maker, to thy name?

We'll crowd thy gates with thankful songs;
High as the heaven our voices raise·
And earth, with her ten thousand tongues,
Shall fill thy courts with sounding praise.

Wide as the world is thy command;
Vast as eternity thy love;
Firm as a rock thy truth shall stand,
When rolling years shall cease to move.

Then followed a Sermon, by Rev. Henry Beers Sherman, of Belleville, New Jersey, a native of Woodbury:

THESE THREE.

A SERMON

PREACHED AT WOODBURY, CONN.,

ON OCCASION OF ITS

BI-CENTENNIAL CELEBRATION,

JULY 5, 1859.

BY THE

REV. HENRY BEERS SHERMAN, M. A.

RECTOR OF CHRIST CHURCH, BELLEVILLE, N. J.

TO

THE MEMORY OF

THE REVEREND ZECHARIAH WALKER,

THE FIRST MINISTER OF

ANCIENT WOODBURY;

This Sermon,

PREACHED ON OCCASION OF THE BI-CENTENNIAL CELEBRATION

OF THE TOWN,

BY HIS DESCENDANT IN THE SEVENTH GENERATION,

IS REVERENTLY INSCRIBED.

COLLECTS.

Almighty and everlasting God, give unto us the increase of faith, hope and charity; and that we may obtain that which thou dost promise, make us to love that which thou dost command; through Jesus Christ our Lord. *Amen.*

O Lord, who hast taught us that all our doings without charity are nothing worth; send thy Holy Ghost, and pour into our hearts that most excellent gift of charity, the very bond of peace and of all virtues, without which whosoever liveth is counted dead before thee. Grant this for thine only son Jesus Christ's sake. *Amen.*

SERMON.

"Now abideth faith, hope, charity, these three; but the greatest of these is charity."—1 Cor. xiii: 13.

Now—that is, in our present state as a probation—in this world and upon the life we are living in it, these three abide as the constituent elements of its substantial portion. In the work of our salvation, as the central business which employs and occupies us here, each, as an attribute of our forming character, holds its assigned position in a fixed relation

Now—in this present state of our existence as preparatory for the future, (and in regard of the first two, as will be shown, NOW *strictly and exclusively*,) "abideth faith, hope, charity, these three"—each and all of them—jointly and severally, together and distinctly.

1. Faith—in which the Holy Ghost, the Lord and Giver of Life, moves upon the abyss of our fallen nature, and begets us again unto a lively hope in Jesus Christ; and through which, in its operation by love under that ministration of the Spirit of God which the mediation of the Son procures to bring us to the Father, we are justified and regenerated, renewed and sanctified

2. Hope—by which we are incited to rise above the adversities and trials of this present world, and to look beyond it for the soul's true home. And

3. Charity—by which faith and hope are inclined to a heavenly direction, and all the gifts and graces of the Divine life shaped and consolidated and made holy in the sight of God.

4. The greatest of these is charity—because, in distinction from the other two, it is an attribute of God, and constitutes in man assimilation to his Maker—the renewal of that divine image and likeness in which he was created.

It is foreign to our present purpose, under the straitened conditions of our space precluding it, to enter at large into the definition and description of FAITH. The term is variously employed in Scripture, and is expressive of a great variety of meanings. It must suffice, in the present connection, that we follow the distinctive lines of the passage under review, and confine our survey to the specific indications which it furnishes.

1. Now Abideth Faith.

As employed by the Apostle in our text, and in the chapter which includes it, FAITH is the causative or actuating principle by which all our hopes and desires, all our purposes and endeavors, and even our belief, are made effectual. We say *belief*, because there is a distinction with a difference, between intellectual assent to the system of Divine Truth, and that justifying FAITH, which, laying hold upon the hope set before us in the Deliverer, and resting in the promises of God, brings the whole man under a divine dominion and into captivity to the obedience of Christ; and which, in its working by LOVE, demonstrates the great problem of our souls' salvation. As it "now abideth," FAITH is the provisional agency or means through which the restoration of fallen man to the favor of God is potentially effected. Though it is the condition of our justification—and the *indispensable* condition, in that it allies us to the Lord that bought us—still it is a *part* and not the *whole* of "our high calling of God in Christ Jesus." It is a means to the production of Christ *in* us, "the end of the law for righteousness."

It serves the important purpose of introducing us within the circle of divine grace; leads us to an apprehension of the hope of eternal life set before us in Christ Jesus; brings us within reach of the promised salvation which grace provides, and nerves the soul to lay hold upon and appropriate it. Both in its nature and in its function, FAITH is inferior and subordinate to CHARITY. As an instrumentality it brings us *to* the law of our filial duty, while charity embraces it—for "LOVE is the fulfilling of the law." The simple exercise of FAITH brings us *to* Christ: The operation of LOVE makes us *like* Christ, conforming us unto His image in righteousness and true holiness. Thus *with* CHARITY abideth FAITH: but greater than faith is charity.

Let us not be understood in this connection, as seeking or desiring in anywise to lower the due estimate of FAITH: we are far enough from that. We acknowledge and accredit it, as the initial doctrine in the scheme of divine grace—the condition upon which our justification before God depends and hinges. "Without faith it is impossible to please Him." It is only through faith in the atonement effected by Christ, that we can look for any lasting benefit to accrue to us from His mediation.

We are, indeed, (as the Apostle says, and repeats,) "*saved by grace.*" But that "grace of God which bringeth salvation" can only reach us "*through faith*" It is the appointed medium—the way and means through which we fall in with the gracious plan of God concerning us, and work out our own salvation.

"Now abideth faith"—*now*, as the prime essential of our Christian state. Without it, human hope is but a wayward and delusive fancy; and human righteousness, even the highest grade of it, is but an empty show—a form without the substance—a body without the soul. Therefore, (that is, growing out of the necessity of the case,) "now abideth faith:" and every thought and action of our life—every purpose and endeavor which enters into the account of what we are, must proceed and spring from FAITH, or they pass into the portion of "dead works." It is only as the quickening principle of FAITH pervades and hallows what we do, that our service becomes acceptable in the Divine sight, and thus wins for us the Divine favor. "Without faith it is impossible to please God."

But, (for "the end of the commandment is CHARITY,") if we propose FAITH to ourselves as an end which we are to attain and stop at, we grossly mistake both its nature and its office. It is but the means through which our salvation by grace is to be wrought out. And we should always consider it only as a means—the end which it subserves being eternal life, in which FAITH will have no part nor lot. Although, as our text affirms of it, "FAITH abideth *now*," conjoined with CHARITY and operating by it what is holy and acceptable, yet, as all that is heavenly in its nature is comprehended and included in that "greatest of these," which under the term "LOVE" is defined by St. Paul as "the fulfilling of the law," the truth of the affirmation in our text is made apparent: and while now abideth faith *with* charity, greater than faith is charity.

Let us pass to consider the second feature in the Apostle's statement.

2. "Now Abideth Hope."

What we have shown in demonstration of FAITH as inferior to CHARITY, is applicable alike to HOPE. It "abideth now," as part of that law which as a school-master brings us to Christ. It is the great incentive to exertion in the work of our salvation. It is an important element in the entire texture of our present character; aud is interwoven as a golden thread with the whole essence of our moral being. It enters into the very substance of our fearfully mysterious life; and operates upon the whole surface of that twofold relationship in which we stand, as connected with this world, and looking on to connection with another. It makes us what we are, and umfolds to us what we shall be. Whether in things earthly and temporal, or in things heavenly and eternal, HOPE is the quickening principle which nerves to energy the heart of man, and leads him forward amidst fear and doubt to tread with a firm step the ascending path of life.

"Now abideth hope." It is the soul's youthful impulse, by which we are cheered and comforted in the vicissitudes and adversities of our present lot; and through which, as seeking a more enduring substance than it yields, we receive accessions of courage and of strength, enabling us to grasp the realities of an immortal portion, and to "press forward toward the mark for the prize of our high calling of God in Christ Jesus."

"*Now abideth hope.*" It is the light of human life, which else were cheerless to us. It fulfils a blessed ministry upon the present, whilst accomplishing its higher mission for the future. It comes to us like an envoy from the Sun of Righteousness, with healing in its wings and messages of joy upon its half-opened lips. In the exercise of its ministry as shaped to the circumstances of the fallen, and adapted to the conditions of a world sitting in darkness and under the shadow of death, it tracks its path with light, and scatters blessings all along its course. Beautiful are its feet upon the mountains, bringing glad tidings of good. The lanes and valleys of life rejoice in its visitation, and the wilderness and the solitary place are glad for it. It comes to us in our days of darkness, which are many, and cheers us with the indications of a bright to-morrow. It finds the sky of life with clouds upon it, and tinges them with radiant hues; and even when the storm is dark, bursts through its gloom, and spans the firmament with its bow of promise. It finds us sinking, and arrests us ere we fall. It finds us cast down, and stretches out its hand to raise us. Never, but at our bidding word, does it leave us or forsake us. It keeps back the invading pressure of terrible Despair; and when the scenery of life which surrounds our present experience is barren of all comfort, and the heart grows sick, it beckons us away to the green pastures where the still waters which reflect them are radiant with the smiles of God. With unfaltering accents it tells us ever of a better portion; and even when the earthly dependence fails us in our time of need, opens new sources of enjoyment with its revealing power—still tells us that the world has pleasant places, and that "it is good for us to be here." It transfigures the chequered aspects of our life, and makes them one with its own radiant self. Like the Only-begotten who begat it, it seeks the welfare of mankind, and *goes about doing good.* It comes to us when the heart is sick and ready to faint, and enlivens us with friendly words. It invests the spirit of heaviness with the garments of praise. It lifts up the hands that hang down and the feeble knees; and when joy comes not with the morning but heaviness still endnres, it "giveth songs in the night." It transforms itself into Expectation, and inspires us with fresh trust to quietly wait. It invades the domain of disappointment and the chill recesses of deep grief, and peoples them with glad sounds and happy sights It makes the parched ground to become a pool, and the thirsty land springs of water. The crooked ways of life are made straight before it, and its rough ways smooth. It "goeth forth to its work" with man, and its voice is to the sons of men.

It solaces and consoles us, when it cannot incite and cheer. Remembering our frame, it adapts the exercises of its mission to what we are, and whispers "a word in season to him that is weary." It speaks with soothing tones to the ill-fortuned and forsaken brother, shipwrecked and broken hearted in his voyage of life, and encourages him amid "the waves of this troublesome world," to tempt the adventurous way once more. It renews the face of things, and transmutes to a seeming preciousness the crude rough elements it touches. Oh, it has a charmer's power. There is a wilderness before it, and a garden of Eden behind: before it is despair, lamentation, and woe: behind is the renewal of joy, thanksgiving, and the voice of melody. NOW ABIDETH HOPE. Well for our present happiness it should: well for our immortal yearnings that it doth. It is the light that halloweth with blessedness our present lot; and when abiding in companionship with FAITH, it guides us to that higher happiness we long for, but which we find not here. NOW ABIDETH FAITH AND HOPE. They walk together, and proceed upon their path hand in hand. Hope leans on faith, and faith on hope—each imparting to the other, as they advance, increase of energy—giving and taking strength reciprocal, and enabling us under their united ministry to maintain our lot in time, and to work out for eternity our souls' salvation. NOW ABIDETH FAITH WITH HOPE

But, although they enter thus into the present composition of human character, moulding and shaping it in its various conformations, their existent relationship is restrictive and peculiar and limited to the present. For it is only NOW—in this state as a probation, that these two, "faith and hope abide." Their nature and their office are temporary and transient. They are as commissioned servants; and "the servant abideth not in the house forever." Both have their limits, and to each is its allotted period. As FAITH will have at length fulfilled its mission and become merged in knowledge, so HOPE will become absorbed in fruition, and lose itself in the blessedness of experience—even as the Apostle says: "Hope that is seen is not hope: for what a man seeth, no longer doth he hope for." Both, as we have intimated, are only *temporary*, as means to an end; and when they shall have served their purpose, each will cease. In the termination of His mediatorial work, "the AUTHOR of our faith" will be its "FINISHER," and the Inspirer of our hope that "fulness of joy," toward which it verged and tended. Now they abide, but only in this life.

Strictly speaking, there will be neither faith nor hope in that spiritual condition, which, as the eternal portion of the saved and sealed in Christ, is prepared for them in heaven. As the twilight melts and loses itself in the absorbing and exceeding glory of the day on which it neighbors and which it serves to introduce, so faith and hope will be finally absorbed in the effulgence of Divine love, and lose their finite identity in the infinitude of "His fullness who filleth all in all." "When that which is perfect is come, then that which is in part shall be done away."

Thus much as to what is *transient* and *inferior* in the Apostle's statement. Let us pass now to consider what is *permanent* and *pre-eminent* in his declaration.

3. "NOW ABIDETH CHARITY."

CHARITY, which abideth in this world with FAITH and HOPE, enabling them to fulfil their appointed work, ceases not with the termination of their office; but reaching onward into the world to come, abideth there forever. It is "the greatest of these three," both in its *office* and in its *nature*.

Its asserted superiority is apparent, in the first place, from the fact of its *duration*: for "charity never faileth." While faith and hope abide now and only now, CHARITY abideth both now and forever. It has a twofold relation. It is allied to our present state, and connected with the permanency of the heavenly world. "The greatest of these is charity."

Its asserted pre eminence over faith and hope is apparent, in the second place, from the fact that in its nature it embraces and includes all that is of spiritual essence in both.

In a preceding verse the Apostle affirms, "Charity *believeth* all things." There is FAITH. He adds, "Charity *hopeth* all things." There is HOPE. The exercise of each, you perceive, is assigned to CHARITY, as included among its attributes—the attributes of its present character—or, more strictly speaking, the preliminary accompaniments of its indwelling presence.

Let us examine now with a little more of definiteness, the *nature* of this lasting and pre-eminent grace, as distinctively "the greatest of these three." Wherein does its superior magnitude consist? and what is the substantial basis of its distinction?

4. "THE GREATEST OF THESE IS CHARITY"

CHARITY (as every intelligent reader of the New Testament must understand) is but another name for LOVE. It is accordingly one of the attributes of Deity—nay, we might rather say, *the engrossing attribute:* "for God is love; and every one that loveth is born of God and knoweth God." In the abiding of charity, therefore, "the tabernacle of God is with men;" and the in-dwelling of LOVE is the in-dwelling of God. "Hereby know we that we dwell in Him, and He in us."

It is LOVE which recreates us in the heavenly image, transforms us into the Divine likeness, and moulds us into meetness for an inheritance among the holy. It is the beginner and sustainer of spiritual vitality in man. It is, to our heavenly citizenship, that surrounding atmosphere, which the soul, by the affixed conditions of its renewed life, breathes ever when it lives to God. It is placed by the Apostle in a position of leadership when enumerating "the fruits of the Spirit," because it is "the greatest." It controls the motion of the rest, and holds them in subjection to its imperial sway. It is "the very bond of peace and of all virtues." Without infringement of their identity, but as the greater includes the less, it embraces and comprehends both faith and hope. For "now abideth faith, hope, charity, these three," distinctly and together, severally and jointly.

We must "believe all things;" and we must "hope all things;" and in the strength of that indwelling presence of love whereby they work, we must do all things which the Gospel enjoins as well pleasing in the sight of God. We must "walk by faith;" because faith is led on by love, and is "the substance of things hoped for." We must lean unto hope; because "hope is the anchor of the soul," upon which faith depends; and we must yield ourselves to charity, because "love is of God, and every one that loveth is born of God and knoweth God." In the broad, full sense in which it is defined and described in the chapter to which our text belongs, we must accord to "that most excellent grace" the dominion which it claims, and obey the motions of its will: for "the end of the commandment is charity." We must open our hearts to its gracious influence, that it may enter and abide in us. Thus every Christian principle will be ripened into mature development and harmonious action; all "the fruits of the Spirit," every heavenly grace and virtue, and whatever is requisite to that crowning result which draws to itself our desires and endeavors, "*that the man of God may be perfect, thoroughly furnished unto all good works*," will be cultivated and live and grow in us, subduing unto itself the indigenous produce of our depraved nature, and covering the surfaces of our life with what is true and honest, what is just and pure, what is lovely and of good report.

"Now abideth charity"—*now*, emphatically. Its home is in the heavenly places, in the "house not made with hands, eternal in the heavens:" but for the accomplishment of its mission upon earth, it dwells amongst us, and its tabernacle is with men.

NOW ABIDETH CHARITY. Let us not lose sight of this central aspect of our subject. Let us remember that *Love*, which is the element of our enjoyment in the future world, hath its commencement first, and to a measurable extent, growth and progression *here*. It enters into the texture of what we are, as the index to what we shall be. Through the agency of faith that worketh by it, having made us the children of God, it ministers to our growth in grace and our procession from strength to strength, renewing us in His image from glory to glory, and advancing us toward that perfection of Divine manhood, "the measure of the stature of the fulness of Christ."

It is the sign and mark in man of Divine life; and holds a position of pre-eminence, as the central attribute of our present Christian character, around which, as stars around the source of light, all other gifts and graces of the spiritual life revolve. Dark in themselves, like those lesser lights which deck the material firmament, they shine in their several orbits and make life beautiful, only as Love shines upon them, and as they move in mutual harmony obedient to its supreme control. In divorcement from their subordination to the greater light, and beyond the radiant circle of its attraction, they are shorn of their reflected glory and pass back into the portion of darkness.

Even FAITH, leaning unto itself, degenerates to superstition, bows to a base servitude, and becomes the minister of sin, "working all uncleanness with greediness." It only operates with an upward tendency, and "adorns the doctrine of God," when it goes forth to its work with charity and becomes "faith that worketh by love."

Nay, even HOPE, in its independent action, dissevered from FAITH and unconstrained by LOVE—like that Son of the morning, who spurned the conditions of his dependent being, and ventured upon the ambitious desire "to have life in himself," and who, from his high place among the children of light, was "brought down to the sides of the pit," and quenched his brightness in "the blackness of darkness forever"—even HOPE, left to itself, reverses the motion of its aspiration to a grovelling preference, and goes on to recklessness under the impulse of its own desires. It only fulfils its office as the light of life and brightener of our being, when it clings to faith and abideth in a living connection with charity. It loses the peerless glory which invests it, when it wanders from its dependent sphere, and "the light that is in it becomes darkness" and a bewildering shadow, "deceiving and being deceived." It is "the anchor of the soul," sure and stedfast when it clings to the Rock of Ages, and imbeds itself in those promises of God which are YEA and AMEN in Christ. But, loosing itself from the constraint of LOVE, and relaxing its hold upon the one Object of FAITH, it mocks the anxious eye of the voyager, and "the earnest expectation of the creature," which it draws to itself in the manifestation of a great deliverance, and sinks as lead in the mighty waters.

"Now," therefore, as of moral necessity, it must—NOW, as of spiritual necessity, it does—"ABIDETH CHARITY." Without it, all other gifts and graces are vain and nothing worth, and stand in the religious account only as dross and tin.

This is a most important consideration; and there grows out of it a wholesome lesson for the present time to learn.

What we need for a harmonious religious development, is less talk and more action—less ritualism and more earnestness—less "church" and more Gospel—less theology and more LOVE. The prevalent faith of the age, unsettled, wavering, desultory and distracted, is *as it is*, because its reigning spirit has ejected charity. And the only adequate remedy for the existing religious ailment—the only remedy, which, penetrating beyond the superficial symptoms of its aspect, can reach to the inner source of the disease, and restore blooming health and warm-gushing life to the disordered system, is an infusion of that heavenly element of CHARITY which it so sadly lacks. The life of God in the soul of man depends, both for its energies and for its being, upon this supply. It can never thrive upon the dry husks of abstract orthodoxy and theological refinement and religious emotion and ecclesiastical conceit, which have been for long its allotted rations: It must have its meat in due season out of the fulness of God. And that fulness is CHARITY: For "God is LOVE." Without this, it becomes weak and sick. Without this, it must pine and die.

The practical application which attaches itself to this feature of the subject, has cropped out here and there already in our passing review, and for the most part is apparent to observation. For the remainder, as lying now upon the surface with the conclusion of the whole matter, it suggests itself at once; and the lesson which it teaches is direct and plain. We gather it in a brief survey of that aspect of our text which exhibits "faith, hope, charity, these three" as abiding now *conjunctively*. For thus dwelling together in the bond of a mutual relation and operating their effects in a confluent action, they exemplify an obtaining principle which underlies all other gifts and graces of the Divine life, and upon which the effectual working of each depends. It is in this living coördinate union of the several parts of the religious system, and in their conjunctive action, that the great secret of spiritual growth is bound up. Both the individual believer and the church which is His body, "grow up into Him in all things, which is the Head, even Christ," in proportion as their religious history is an exemplification of this fact and an illustration of this principle.

By the same Apostle who hints it in our text, the whole matter is elsewhere distinctly stated, as entering into the conditions of our growth in grace and in the knowledge of God, till we come unto the measure of the stature of THE PERFECT MAN:—"From whom the whole body fitly joined together and compacted by that which every joint supplieth, according to the effectual working in the measure of every part, maketh increase of the body unto the edifying of itself in LOVE."

This, then, let us remember, and remember again: for we are likely to forget it. In discussing religious matters and defining Christian doctrines, we naturally fall into the scholastic lines; and in the adoption of a peculiar dialect, we are very apt to make use of terms and distinctions which serve to disintegrate and exhibit *apart* what the Revelation of Divine Truth clearly presents in a systematic combination and united shape. Under such a regimen theologies have grown and thriven: but Christianity itself has been dwarfed and starved. Divisions in the system of Christian *doctrine* produce and perpetuate divisions in "the household of faith."

In times when LOVE has waxed cold, and as a consequence upon this, dissentions abound, many, warmed with dogmatic zeal and theological conceit, run up and down and to and fro in quest of orthodoxy. And the zeal of the house eats it up. In an engrossing predilection for *certain parts* of the Christian system, whether catholic or peculiar, the remainder of "the faith once delivered to the saints" is practically discarded and ignored; and in this overmuch attachment to certain *features* of the faith or certain *notions* of the Gospel, the *entireness* of "the truth as it is in Jesus," which is the Gospel *itself*, is "passed by on the other side." The unity of the faith is set at nought, and charity seeks in vain for that in which it rejoiceth. The bond of peace is broken, and controversy comes in 'with his rough voice and unmeek aspect,' and divides the Christian household into rival sections and distinctive classes. Each selects, as the all-in-all for importance, some favorite and peculiar doctrine; invests it, as the theological pet, "with a coat of many colors;" makes a catchword even of its name; and enshrining it in a peculiar dialect, rejoices in that, as the shibboleth of Christianity.

To counterwork this prevalent tendency, which, in a polemical and faithless age, many have realized and more are realizing to their spiritual damage and Christian loss, let us cease from Religionism and cleave to what is of Faith: Let us turn aside from "vain jangling," and "follow after charity which is the bond of perfectness"—in which, as it "now abideth," all that is true and essential and important in opinion and doctrine and practice meets and centres and abides. Under the dominion of LOVE, "the foundation of our faith standeth sure," and the impulses of our hope point in the heavenly direction. The exercises of LOVE constitute a basis of unity in the bond of peace, which is always safe to rest upon; and if we prefer one gift or grace above the others, remembering that "LOVE is of God," let it be always CHARITY, because it is Divine, the greatest and the best. We shall thus be established upon *the Gospel* as a platform; cut loose from an overweening attachment to particular *members* of the body, and fall back upon the body of Christianity ITSELF.

In giving free course to the exercises of this greatest grace, this spirit of the Gospel and of its Author, we shall learn to look rather upon the full-face of Christianity as presented in the Bible, than upon its shifting profile as exhibited in the schools; to sink those minor questions which are not essential to religion, and which a healthful and vigorous action of the Christian life absorbs into itself; to think neither of Paul nor of Apollos, but of THE GOSPEL, which one may have planted and the other watered, but of which only GOD pours into the heart where love abides and upon the life in which charity abounds, the blessed increase.

While, on the one hand, we see *faith* unduly magnified and the graces and virtues of a holy life, and "the doctrine which is according to godliness," thrust comparatively into the background—as if the body were all eye—or while, on the other hand, we hear the necessity of *good works* enforced, without a corresponding emphasis upon the indispensableness of *faith*—as if the body were all ear—let us side neither to the one nor to the other. In a separate view each is wide of the mark, and disjunctively both are wrong. They are the two scholastic extremes of the time; and, like the poles af the earth, *always cold.*

Let us turn away from each, to those tropical regions of the Gospel which are sunned by the genial influences of the Light of Light, and rest upon CHARITY, in which the two jarring notes of the age are melted and mingled and flow together in harmony; in which faith is the abiding principle and a life that is according to godliness the standing evidence of a state of grace; and without which, in their joint abiding, under the sway of charity, all religious profession is as sounding brass, and all seeming righteousness but a fond conceit and an empty show.

Finally, if we understand the nature of CHARITY; if we appreciate its excellence, and admit the asserted fact of its practical abiding now, we cannot regard with passive indifference, nor in any way apologize for those reigning divisions and dissensions which scar the present religious aspect and so sadly retard the progress of the Redeemer's kingdom.

Christianity, let us remember, is an abiding unity. There is one *Faith*, even as there is one *Lord*. And we know His will who is its Author, that all who profess it should be one. It is the manifest object of CHARITY as it abideth now, to consolidate the Christian elements and make us one. For this, it plies us with its gentle ministry, embracing every doctrine, receiving every truth, practising every virtue, and living and moving and rejoicing in the culture and growth and increase of every grace; adorning the doctrine of God the Saviour in all things; stamping the impress of its influence upon every separate act of life; infusing more and more of its heavenly spirit into ours; moulding into a Divine likeness the elements of human character to hallow it with loveliness; and fulfilling the remainder of its mission in "endeavoring to keep the unity of the Spirit in the bond of peace."

FINIS.

After the Sermon, the choir sang the following

HYMN.

Tune—Lenox.

Ye tribes of Adam, join,
   With Heaven, and earth, and seas,
And offer notes divine,
   To your Creator's praise.
Ye holy throng | In worlds of light,
Of angels bright, | Begin the song.

The shining worlds above
   In glorious order stand,
Or in swift courses move,
   By His supreme command.
He spake the word, | From nothing came,
And all their frame | To praise the Lord.

He moved their mighty wheels,
   In unknown ages past;
And each his word fulfills,
   While time and nature last.
In different ways, | His wondrous name,
His works proclaim | And speak his praise.

Let all the nations fear
   The God that rules above;
He brings his people near,
   And makes them taste his love.
While earth and sky | His saints shall raise
Attempt his praise, | His honors high.

Then followed a speech from Rev. Anson S. Atwood, of Mansfield Center, Conn., a native of Woodbury, in reply to the sentiment, "The Early Clergy of Ancient Woodbury," nearly as follows:

Mr. Chairman:—I am called upon to occupy the place of another, who has disappointed us—not to fill the gap, *that* I cannot do. I stand here at a short notice, and with no other claim than that I was born in this town, my ancestors sleep here, and I represent in person a *permanent ministry* of forty years, and I come to speak a few words on the ground of a *permanent ministry* in this homestead of our Fathers.

The sentiment to which I am to respond is, "The early clergy of ancient Woodbury." A noble theme—a rich text, and should the exegesis, the commentary on it, entirely fail, you and I shall have the mutual satisfaction left us, that the *text* remains still in all its beauty and loveliness in the character and lives of the departed. Hold fast the sacred, the precious treasure. It belongs to you and yours as the rightful possessors, to be read, studied and loved in all coming time.

Zechariah Walker was the first Pastor of Ancient Woodbury. It is a good name—*Zechariah*—it is a Bible name, and he was a Bible man. The church was organized in 1670, and he assumed the pastorate. And if tradition tells the truth, and the little of history that has come down to us, may be credited, he is not to be numbered among the *minor* prophets of his day and placed on the last leaves of the Bible. He was not an ordinary man, but made of sterner stuff—a man for the times and the work Providence had for him to do; every way worthy to be the minister of that little adventurous band, who came from Stratford to explore and seek a home in the wilderness of Pomperaug; and when they reached the elevation of that western summit, and had gazed and gazed again upon the valley, the object of their search, reposing at their feet in all its primitive beauty and loveliness, they fell on their knees in gratitude to return thanks to God, and John Minor offered that memorable prayer, which your own historian has recorded—a prayer for a divine blessing on their enterprise, and that they might have an upright and godly posterity in all coming generations. A prayer that has proved well nigh prophetic for ten generations of the descendants of some of these pioneers.

Yes, Zechariah Walker was fitted for such an enterprise, casting in his lot with theirs, comforting and cheering them on in their toils, labors, sacrifices and perils in the wilderness, in laying the foundation of a new order of things.

For a few of the first years of his ministry, the place of worship in the winter was the log cabins of his parishioners; in the summer, the *Bethel* rock was his sanctuary and altar, the beat of the drum his bell, the heavens his sound-board, his chorister unknown, but perched on a rocky eminence might be seen the sentinel watching the approach of danger, while they bowed the knee of devotion before God. There, in the solitude of the forest, the glad tidings of the gospel were heard by attentive ears, and the songs of Zion were sung by strong and joyful hearts.

History says of him, that he had a sound mind, was a powerful and pungent preacher, that he lived in harmony with his people thirty years, died beloved, and sleeps in death with those to whom he ministered.

Anthony Stoddard followed in the pastorate in 1702. A part of his name *Roman*, but all the rest of him was *Stoddard*, from the crown of his head to the sole of his foot; and he had a brave, strong, Christian heart, that beat full and clear, as it sent out its pulsations through all the channels of the duties of his sacred office. Who was his father? Whence came he? We have the answer. He had an enviable descent, from one of the ablest divines New England had raised on her soil. Solomon Stoddard, of Northampton, Mass., was that father, who had few equals, if any superior, in the ministry of that day. He was of a liberal heart, and he gave to the cause of Christ some *large donations*. He had a daughter, Esther, much beloved, and he gave her away to be the wife of the Rev. Timothy Edwards, of East Windsor, Conn., and the mother of the immortal Jonathan Edwards. He had a son, Anthony, equally beloved, and he gave him to Ancient Woodbury.

This son honored his parentage. His intellect and furniture of mind were of a high order; and one would think from the amount of labor he performed, his mind must have been kept from rusting. He must have had almost a giant's strength, to have, in no unimportant sense, discharged the duties of *three* professions: that of a pastor, a physician, and a councillor or judge, while, it is said, he neglected no part of the duties of the ministry. It was from a necessity of the times that all these labors devolved upon him. It must be remembered, that education was almost entirely with and in the hands of ministers in the early infancy of our colonial State. Hence, they had to do many things that belong to other professions. To teach schoolmasters, and fit them for their work, draw deeds, wills, keep records, and even be judges, in same cases, of probate. Many of these burdensome duties pressed upon Stoddard, but he met them cheerfully, manfully devoting soul and body and every energy of his being to the advancement of the best interests of his flock, temporal and eternal, and not without blessed results. A long, prosperous and happy ministry of sixty years crowned his labors. The divine approbation set its seal to his ministry, in permitting him to see almost constant additions to the church through the whole period of his ministry, numbering in all four hundred and seventy-four persons.

At an advanced age, having served his generation faithfully, he came to the grave, "as a shock of corn fully ripe," and his record is on high.

Noah Benedict, the third pastor of Ancient Woodbury, was ordained October 22, 1760. We now come within the recollection of living witnesses, to speak of a man whose name is hallowed in the memories of many who have gone before me. You remember him well—remember him as you remember no other minister you ever knew, and loved him as you never loved any other man. Nor can I think you wrong in it. My earliest years were impressed with the godliness, purity and excellency of his character, as I heard it from parental lips with so much adoration and veneration, that I came to feel, long before I knew him, that he was something more than a man. And I am not alone in this impression. I have heard grave and venerable men, in the profession and out of it, say of him, that "he was born a minister, lived a minister, died a minister; and could not, if he would, have been anything else but a minister;" a minister at all times, in all circumstances, in the pulpit and out of the pulpit—a *noble* minister—a Nathaniel indeed, in whom there was no guile.

There are three men, of the good and the great that I have known, that I would like much to hear pray again, of all men I ever heard pray, if they might come back to the world for a brief space. Noah Benedict, his Deacon, Matthew Minor, and Azel Backus. They are better employed. I recall my impertinent wish.

The venerated pastor of whom I am speaking, and Benjamin Wildman of Southbury, were near neighbors, and long tried and intimate friends; very different were they in natural temperament and ministerial gifts and graces. I remember an anecdote I heard in my youth, illustrative of the two men. Said one of their brethren, who well knew them both and their different gifts, in a circle of Christian friends on a certain occasion, "Give me Benedict to pray, Wildman to preach, and I get as near to God and Heaven as I ever expect to while in the body."

Amiable, dignified, prudent, godly, a sound divine, a solemn preacher, a wise counselor, he stood high in the esteem of all that knew him. His, too, was a long and useful life. It closed in peace after a pastorate of fifty-three years, and having gathered into the communion of the church 272 members. Good men carried him to his burial and wept on his grave.

And who is it that I see in this chair? My worthy and much esteemed friend and class-mate, Nathaniel Benedict Smith. I remember he is the son of honorable parentage. On the one hand, descended from a father that dignified the bench of justice in our State with singular ability and grace; on the other hand, that he is the grandson of Noah Benedict, whose blood flows warm in his veins to-day. I behold in you, sir, *Church* and *State* happily united. Whatever honors may have alighted on your head, and whatever may come after, this is a proud day in the history of your life. It has honor enough for one day.

The sentiment, "The clergy of Ancient Woodbury," is not exhausted, but time fails me. The rest of the list of these worthies, I must hastily group together, with only a passing notice. Of these, may be named, John R. Marshall, John Graham, Thos. Canfield, Reuben Judd, Daniel Brinsmade, Jeremiah Day, the father of a son of the same name, the ex-President of Yale College, whom a thousand pupils in the land rise up to-day to call blessed, were settled over churches within the limits of Woodbury. Of them it may be said, they did a good work for Christ.

Last, but not *least*, were the two first pastors of Bethlehem, Joseph Bellamy and Azel Backus. Both living lights in their day. Dr. Bellamy was truly a great man in the pulpit and out of it. His person and his eloquence were attractive and commanding, and when warmed up by his subject, he carried his audience whither he would, and such a torrent of truth would at times burst forth, that it seemed as if "the foundations of the great deep had broken up."

At the age of *thirty*, only a few years after the "Great Awakening" of 1740, in which he labored abundantly wherever there was an opportunity, he produced that masterly work, "True Religion Delineated," that gained him celebrity on both sides of the Atlantic. One of the best books in the English language *on that subject* ever written. His works and his ability to defend the truth and demolish the error, have never been doubted, and his name will live in all coming time, while God's Law is honored on earth and a free and full salvation is preached to men.

No wonder his successor in the pastorate of the church of Bethlehem should feel a deep anxiety for the approval and success of his ministry, as indeed he did. His inquiry of the colored man of the parish, how his ministry was received, showed this. The answer was, "Master Backus, be very good man—preach very well, but no make God half so great as Dr. Bellamy." The colored man showed his training and improvement under the Greater Master in Israel. But had he lived a few years longer, he might have seen that the mantle of Elijah had fallen on Elisha.

What a record this, to embalm in our memories and in our gratitude for our homestead and our mother, of a history of 143 years of a successful, permanent, and happy ministry, crowned with the blessing of God. Ps. xlviii. 12, 14.

Let God and not man have all the glory. These all died in faith, and have received the reward of, "*Well done, good and faithful servant; thou hast been faithful over a few things, I will make thee ruler over many things, enter thou into the joy of your Lord.*"

Then followed a volunteer speech from Rev. Thomas L. Shipman, of Jewett City, Conn., on "THE DEPARTED CLERGY OF THE PRESENT GENERATION," as follows:

MR. PRESIDENT: I must occupy your attention but a moment at this hour. Give me a fair field and I am a match for my predecessor in the gift of continuance. Let me tell a story. Good Brother Brown, of Oxford, now gone to his rest, came up to my house once, on his way to "Ministers' Meeting," early Monday evening. We talked till twelve, and then I held the candle for him an hour. Our conversation was interrupted by "Ministers' Meeting," on Tuesday and Wednesday. We returned Wednesday evening, so late that he concluded to pass the night. Thursday morning, after breakfast, we resumed conversation, till the family began to set the table for dinner. "Upon my word," said he, "is it noon? I intended to have gone home." "You won't go now till after dinner." After dinner we resumed conversation till four o'clock; he suddenly started. "I must go, for I have a meeting this evening." "If you must go, I will get your horse." I led the horse to the door. He stood with his foot on the step of his carriage a moment, when he spoke: "I must go, but Brother Shipman, *I want to come up and have some conversation with you.*"

Having spent the best part of my life within the limits of ancient Woodbury, I esteem it a very kind Providence that I am permitted to be an eye and ear witness of civic and sacred services so full of interest to all the sons of Woodbury, both native and adopted. The grateful privilege is given me of recalling the names of some of the departed clergy of the present generation, who fulfilled their ministry mainly, if not wholly, within the bounds of Litchfield South Association. There is *Hart*, with his keen and piercing eye, his ready wit, and severe logic; there is *Griswold*, with his commanding form and sonorous voice, ever prepared to insinuate Hart's logic with the witchery of his eloquence. *Harrison*, so gifted by nature that he needed not the adventitious aid of a college diploma. *Andrew*, to whom might be extended what was said of Roger Sherman, "A man that never spoke a foolish word," one of the purest spirits that earth ever gave to heaven. *Brownell*, of different natural temperament, but equally an earnest preacher and faithful pastor, though "dead, he yet speaketh." *Gelston*, having his conversation in the world in simplicity and godly sincerity, and keeping the "even tenor of his way," to a good old age. *Butterfield*, his name is as ointment poured forth, and to mention no more, *Smith*, my nearest neighbor, I seem to feel the beatings of his warm heart while I speak; his sun went down while it was yet day, but it went down to him in brighter heavens. Precious men of God. We enjoyed their friendship while living, we will cherish the memory of their virtues now that they are dead. I met Mr. Boardman, of New Preston, several years after he had left the country. I said to him, "Mr. Boardman, have you found another Litchfield South?" "No, and no other man ever found but one Litchfield South." I partly believe it, wholly this side of the river. The people of this region, "to the manor born"—descendants of the old Puritan stock, give strangers, whether clerical or laical, their confidence cautiously, but when they have given it, they grapple you with "hooks of steel." But I must not detain you. The old Spartans were brief in speech, men of deeds rather than words. Hence, our word laconic, from their Laconia, a word which I greatly fear will have in the next edition of Goodrich's Webster, appended to it, *obsolete*, unless one of those "inconsistent"* Atwoods saves it at the death. That *I* may honor this Spartan virtue, I will close, simply expressing my gratitude for the past history of Woodbury, and as the best wish of my heart, that her sons in all future time may prove worthy of their ancient sires.

The exercises of the forenoon were closed by the following Address delivered in behalf of the Old Pioneer Church, by Deacon Truman Minor, of Woodbury.

"The children of this world are in their generation wiser than the children of light."—*Luke* 16 : 8.

BRETHREN: We live in an era which is peculiar for eulogies and praises bestowed on almost every service done to our State and coun-

* In allusion to Mr. Bacon's portraiture of the Atwoods.

try. Every gift and talent thus employed is cheered in trumpet tones from the capital of our confederacy to the extremity of our territories, proclaiming the deeds of those that have lived and now live. Assemblies are convened, resolutions are passed, monuments erected; they are seen on Groton Heights and Bunker Hill, and on Roxbury slopes; they are designed as so many sparkling stars to proclaim the daring deeds of American heroes. Sculpture now comes forward to the rescue, and carves in solid marble the forms and features of those that have been honored and applauded by the men of the world. Atheneums are built, the relics of antiquity are gathered and stored. The camp-chair of him, once the terror of all Europe, is sought and obtained. Bricks from Nineveh are transported. Hartford oaks are immortalized, and fragments of it introduced into the parlors of the fashionable and great, all for the purpose of handing down to posterity the names and deeds of men, not more exmplary in their lives than were the Twelve Apostles, nor more benevolent in their deeds, or patient in suffering, or forbearing an insult, or more inclined to bridle their tongues for fear of giving offence; and yet they are more often quoted and boasted of as the wonder of the world, and so many radiating points that should attract every mortal eye and claim an adoring prayer from every one that passes by, exclaiming: "These be thy gods, O Israel! that brought thee up out of the land of Egypt and out of the house of bondage." And yet, brethren, these are all proper in their place; they have their respective claims, and, so far as we should, we are ready to pay them our respect and sincere homage; we honor those men, we admire their philanthropy, we mark the patriotism which characterize their lives. Brethren, there is still a set of objects and men that have more attracted our attention, nearly eclipsed our vision—men and objects for which we have the highest personal respect, whose memory and moral worth should be embalmed in the heart and practiced in the life of each member of the old honored Pioneer Church forever. Men that entered into covenant wtth God and one another, and took their lives in their hands and left Egypt and came up into this once wide howling wilderness to plant a Church, surrounded with beasts and savages more wild and ferocious than the lions and Hotentots of Africa. Here in this pleasant valley and mountain fastnesses, they commended themselves and their cause to God; they came here under the guide and direction of the Divine hand, in the possession of the promise: "Lo, I am with you alway even unto the end." They came with a charge superior to that given by the Elders of Israel to Boaz and Ruth saying, "Be fruitful and multiply, and let your seed possess the gates of their enemies." They have been fruitful and obedient, they have driven out the heathen, their enemies, and have taken possession of the land which the Lord their God gave them. Their children have multiplied. Lift up your eyes, my brethren, and see what mean these hallowed domes, these public altars on which the fires of devotion have for generations burnt. A little one has, under the blessing of God, almost become a nation. Go with me up and down these valleys, and over these hills, and behold these their covenant children, the legitimate offspring of a covenant wedlock. These ecclesiastical societies, these orthodox churches, are the fruits which the *Old Pioneer* has borne. The Second Congregational Church in this town is but the other half of ourselves. The Episcopal Church here is one of our junior brethren. The Methodist Church is one of our younger, tender sisters; the Church in Southbury is Reuben, the first born, the beginning of strength. The Church of Bethlem is a son of the royal family; the Churches of Washington and South Farms are of kindred blood; the Churches of Watertown, Middlebury, Roxbury, South Britain and a part of Oxford, are the spiritual children of the sacramental pair.

Mr. President, and Brethren, I said in my commencement that "the children of this world are in their generation wiser than the children of light;" this ought not so to be. It is time for the Church to assert her right to her own sons, and exercise her power. Her worldly competitors should not pluck the laurels from her brow and bear them away in triumph! What if we cannot, as do they, boast an uncouth Putnam, or an Ethan Allen, who demanded the surrender of a fort commanded and defended by British foes, with a roughness and profanity that would chill the blood in the veins of the Puritan Fathers, and make the cheek of modesty turn pale:—yet we *can* speak of important service done by the sons of the church to our country. We can boast of their demanding the surrender of a fort in this once wilderness, commanded by old Apollyon and garrisoned by fallen angels, where, in the midst of their fiendish games and their revelry, were heard ever and anon the yell, the savage cry, and the war-whoop. A demand, not like Allen's, made in the name of a Continental Congress, but from higher authority, in the name of Heaven's Imperial King, did those dauntless soldiers of the cross press, till these sons of perdition were compelled to come out of their wretched dens, and, like the regulars of old, harmlessly gnash their teeth on their victors, and as they retired, break up their arms on the stumps and stones in their way. Had I the strength and the power, I would raise my voice to thunder-tones, and from pole to pole proclaim these men and their deeds immortal. We stand here to-day, my brethren, in these mountain gorges, the representatives of a church and a race of men of whom the world was not worthy. What if they did wander about a while in sheeps skins and goats' skins, afflicted, tormented? They bore the marks of Heaven's high approval; they held in their hands a bond for a deed of the land of Canaan. All along the banks of the river of life these men made fast to the rock of ages by the everlasting couplings of a Heaven-imparted faith, secured thereto by the Omnipotent strength of a God-sustaining covenant. They outrode the storms and changes of mortal years, and are now safely gathered in the Paradise above.

But I forbear. The current of my feelings has drawn me out into deep water, beyond the seaworthiness of my boat. I will now return to those families as they came up from Stratford, or "Egypt," as I have called it. Those families brought up the ark, the tabernacle, and the testimony. It was of Divine direction that some order be preserved in the moving, the setting up, and the taking down of the tabernacle; its boards, tenons and furniture. To effect this it was necessary to make a selection from those families. This was done, and the family of the MINORS was taken. Some name by lot must be chosen, and the name of JOHN was taken. And now, Mr. President, and Brethren, we can with truth say of this man, he was faithful in all his house; he was faithful to the trusts committed to his charge; he was a man of faith and of prayer; he trusted in the covenant mercy of a covenant-keeping God, who has said: "I will be a God to thee, and thy seed after thee." That promise has not yet failed. God has not left him without a man of his own name and blood, for one hundred and ninety years, to serve at the table and tabernacle of his and their covenant Lord. Here is the furniture* which he and they have kept and handled. In these did he bear to their brethren and sisters the emblems of the body and blood of their common Redeemer. From these have they communed with God and one another. Hallowed remembrances! Glorious keepsakes! Let them linger around our memories; let them be bound to our hearts forever; let them, and the elements they bear, serve as a golden chain to bind us to God and each other; and had not God, in his inscrutable providence, moved our respected and learned *Historian* †

* The furniture presented to view. † W. Cothren, Historian of Woodbury.

to take up the wondrous tale of these and the old Pioneer Church history, it would doubtless have remained in darkness and forgetfulness forever. I might speak of the succession of officers in this Church, bearing the name of MINOR; I might tell you of SAMUEL, of JEHU, of JONAH, of CLEMENT, of JOSIAH, of MATTHEW, of SETH; these men were renowned for their piety, some of them peculiarly so for their heavenly mindedness, their self-denial, their watchfulness and prayerfulness, their strictness in conversation on the Sabbath, their entire reservedness in word and action on that holy day; their punctuality in the house of God, and their attendance on all the means of grace; their reading and their familiarity with the Scriptures; their strict honesty between man and man; their law-abiding reverence of those set in authority over them; the utter impossibility of bribing them to do evil; their absolute hatred of all that was wrong; their readiness to give and receive of the things that were good; their tenderness and teachableness; in a word, for all that makes up the Christian character in fallen man. Among these mighty men in the Scriptures, perhaps none were more so than the late Dea. MATTHEW MINOR—he had read the Scriptures through by course *sixty times!* He was as familiar with them as the scholar is with his nouns and pronouns; the Bible was his constant companion —he carried it into the field; its sacred pages were his delight. He would often exclaim, "Oh, how love I thy law! it is daily my delight: I esteem thy precepts more than my necessary food." Brethren, although the mighty have fallen, the weapons of their warfare have not perished—they are still mighty, through God, to the pulling down of strongholds. Shall the mantle of such men fall to the ground? Will we not emulate these men? Shall the glory depart? Shall *Ichabod* be written upon us? Shall the house of Eli be cut off here? God forbid! Let us feel to-day, my brethren, that we are covenant children. We are the circumcised of the Lord, the promises are ours, they were made to our fathers and their children. We are a peculiar people—a royal priesthood—a holy nation; and we do to-day acknowledge God before this assembly as the Author of our adoption; we here avouch the Lord Jehovah to be our God, as he has been the God of our fathers. He has shown himself a covenant-keeping God. He gave our fathers and us faithful teachers, godly pastors, holy men, who wrestled like Jacob and prevailed like Israel; they were the anointed of the Lord; the holy anointing oil was upon them; like Aaron, the priest, they wore the breastplate of righteousness before the Lord, on which was engraven the names of the twelve covenant sons of Jacob—a Heaven-appointed token of mercy to us and our children. Those men have stood between the living and the dead; they have turned away wrath from the people; they have been faithful watchmen, trumpets of a certain sound, that men might prepare themselves for the battle! they were instant in season and out of season; they shunned not to declare the whole counsel of God, whether men would hear or forbear. Among the worthies that have prevailed to turn away wrath from our fathers and us, as a covenant people, are the Reverend names of WALKER, of STODDARD, of BENEDICT—of whom it was said, as of the prophet Jeremiah, that he was born holy; of STRONG, his successor, I shall say but little. His ministry was short. He thought to teach the inhabitants of the old town a new theology, which consisted in the amalgamation of sheep, and fowls, and swine—a mixture of warp and woof, all contrary to the law and the commandment, which says: "Thou shalt not sow thy fields with divers kinds of seed." The other men in the pastoral office have been worthy of their predecessors, of whom was the Rev. Mr. ANDREW, Rev. Mr. CURTIS, and Rev. Mr. WILLIAMS, our present beloved and esteemed pastor. Such have been the fathers' and the children's pastors and teachers. We have, my brethren, been dandled in the lap of piety; we have been trained in the school of the prophets; we have been brought up, like Paul, at the feet of Gamaliel;—may we show ourselves worthy of our noble sires and our holy training.

One word more, Mr. President, in relation to the MINOR family, and I have done. It has been tauntingly said that nothing could be *scored* or hewed from that name but *Deacon* timber. Sir, I glory in the reproach, yet I deny the charge. There have been men of this name and race that have filled important offices in the land; one has received the highest gift of the people of this State—he has filled the Executive chair for two successive years, and filled it honorably; the taunt is therefore groundless.

But I am admonished that it is time, high time, for me to close. I will do so, in one word. And now, sir, let mine be the shame, and let it be the shame of my children, if shame it be, that they and I have lived and died the God-appointed, God-accepted, man-approved DEACONS of the OLD PIONEER CHURCH.

After another re-union at the refreshment tents, the booming cannon, and the music of the Band, again called the delighted multitude to the Speakers' tent, where the exercises of the last afternoon were opened, on the part of the choir, by singing with hearty joy, the following

ODE.

BY WILLIAM COTHREN.

Air—"*Sweet Home.*"

Thrice welcome the day which now brings to the mind,
The deeds of our fathers, so noble and kind;
An incense of sweetness breathes out on the air,
The incense of welcome, the incense of prayer.
  Home, home, sweet, sweet home,
   No place like our firesides,
   No place like our homes.

The earth has grown old for full many a year,
Since the people of God came to worship Him here;
And the graves are moss-grown of the sturdy old stock,
Who prayed in their Bethel, the shade of the Rock.
  Home, &c.

Oh! shades of the mighty, most faithful of men,
Will the meed of your virtues e'er greet us again?
A halo of glory surrounds each fair brow,
Which shall shine in yon Heaven forever as now.
  Home, &c.

Then followed a speech in reply to the Sentiment, "THE EARLY LAWYERS OF ANCIENT WOODBUY," by Hon. Seth P. Beers, of Litchfield, Conn., a native of Woodbury, which is as follows:

MR. PRESIDENT, LADIES AND GENTLEMEN:—In the order of exercises arranged for this afternoon, we were to have been favored with an address by John Lorimer Graham, Esq., of New York, on "THE EARLY LAWYERS OF ANCIENT WOODBURY." In the absence of Mr. Graham, I am kindly requested to occupy the time assigned to him in such remarks as I may deem appropriate to the occasion.

In meeting the call thus made upon me, it cannot be expected that I should occupy *the ground* allotted to him, for the subject matter requires some previous preparation. Nevertheless, while expressing my regret that this interesting feature of our commemoration should be passed by without that proper notice which your Committee contemplated, I will so far step into the gap, as to notice and relate an anecdote of the *earliest Lawyer in Woodbury*. Till about a century ago—whether there were occasion for it before, I cannot say—the ancient town was not *blessed* with the services of a resident Lawyer. Its first legal practitioner was *Hezekiah Thompson, Esq.*, who came here about 1757, and built a house in the south part of the town, which he occupied till his death. This house is still owned by his descendants.

He was a sound lawyer, an able advocate, and withal a man of strict integrity, and a peace-maker. He was distinguished also in his time as a man of wit and humor. The anecdote I propose to relate, will show this.

A person from abroad called on Mr. T., introducing himself as a *relative*. After canvassing the genealogy, the relationship was found to be very remote, and Mr. T. was quite disposed to turn a cold shoulder upon his country cousin. The visitor continued his stay, accompanying his host wherever he went, whether invited or not, till his presence became irksome, and the good lawyer determined to shake him off. Meeting one of his neighbors, he introduced his visitor as a relative. The neighbor inquired whether he was brother, or uncle, or nephew, or cousin. "Nearer than that," replied the squire. "From the best information I can gather from him, I find that my grandfather mended a side-saddle for his grandmother." This indefinite hint was definitely taken, and the country cousin made a speedy exit.

Recurring now, Mr. President, to the broad provisions of your invitation, I hardly know what to begin with. Almost every topic appropriate to the occasion has been anticipated and exhausted in the very interesting and elaborate historical address to which we listened yesterday. I am left, therefore, to glean in a very limited and exhausted field, or to seek in some private nook of it which may have escaped the vigilance of those who have preceded me, materials for the few remarks which are asked from me.

Though we have been invited here to celebrate the two hundredth anniversary of the exploration of "Ancient Woodbury," I presume we are not expected to roam over the whole of that inclusive period, but may be allowed to confine ourselves to events within a much shorter space of time. I must presume upon it, that so long as what I may have to say has a *historical* reference, I am free to select my ground, and occupy it pretty much as I choose.

Under this impression, in the few plain remarks which I propose to submit, I shall confine myself to a term of time *within the memory of men now living*—a period which embraces events as important as any which have occurred within these two centuries.

I go back to *seventy-eight years ago;* and from that stand-point glance over the succeeding time.

What great and notable events have occurred in our country within this space of a man's life! It has witnessed the organization of our American Republic, and its happy settlement under the architect of its Independence. It has seen that greatest among great men, the illustrious WASHINGTON, with his successors in the Presidency, ADAMS, JEFFERSON, MADISON, MONROE, and others highly distinguished, who have come in their places, gathered to their fathers. It has seen the brilliant career of such eminent men as Jay, Franklin, Marshall, Clay, Webster, and many other distinguished men of whom this nation has reason to be proud, begun and ended. It has seen the progress of our country from feebleness to strength, and from comparative insignificance to importance among the nations. It has seen villages grown into cities, and territories ripened into States—our western wilderness subdued by the enterprise of industry, and become the granary of the world. It has witnessed an era in the annals of popular education unparalleled in the history of the world. *What has it not seen?*

Within this period of seventy-eight years there have come into use *Canals*, *Steam Engines*, *Railroads*, *Telegraphs*, and (almost) *a trans-Atlantic Cable.* This space of seventy-eight years has been fruitful of great events—of events more important to the welfare of this nation, than any which have occurred since the landing of our forefathers upon this continent.

And yet on the 1st day of July, 1781—or, (if I may be allowed the three days of grace to which the most simple mercantile instrument is entitled,) I will say seventy-eight years ago on the *fourth* of July, an event occurred, *more important to him who now addresses you*, than any other which has taken place during the whole period.

WHAT WAS IT?

In yonder mansion, late the residence of the much lamented and Hon. Charles B. Phelps, on the first *fourth* day of July, 1781, was found *puling in its nurse's arms, a* CHILD—now, the humble individual who addresses a generation that knew not Joseph. Such is the record in his grandmother's Bible, and who claims to question the authenticity of such documentary evidence, whether in the text or notes? In the text of that sacred book you will find from whence (through his grandfather, *Seth Preston*,) that child derived his christian name; and although the original possessor of the name lived nine hundred and twelve of what was then called years, and though some of my good friends suppose that I have a perpetual lease of life,—I assure them that my lease has already expired, and I am now only an occupant upon sufferance.

My coming hither to-day, seems a completion of the circle of my life. It brings me round to the point whence I started, and connects the termination of the line with its beginning; amid the scenery of my early days the experiences of my early life come back to me.

And now while here, a *reminiscent,* with the aid of objects around me, which call to mind the early events of a life which must soon terminate, and of which the present generation possesses little if any knowledge, my thoughts naturally linger upon that early portion of my life, which was passed in this my birth-place.

Whatever opinions may be entertained by others on this subject, so far as it respects myself, there is no part of my life to which I recur with greater satisfaction, or of which I am more proud, than the first chapter of my history. It would deface the rest, if that were obliterated from the account. Some person has said, (I don't remember who—but am willing to stand sponsor to the sentiment,) "*the best and most important section of every man's life is its first.*" I go back, therefore, to my *best,* and begin with the beginning.

I can say of myself, that I am "native and to the manor born;" and if I am entitled to indulgence anywhere, for lingering upon personal details, I may fairly claim it here. As no person will be likely to undertake my biography, I may as well, perhaps, do it myself. The first twenty years of my life were passed in this, my birth-place; and I shall only sketch this quarter of it, as belonging to the town.

My father, in right of my mother, possessed what was considered a handsome estate, in those early days. When I was yet a boy, by losses on Continental bills and mercantile misfortunes, he became what might be fairly called *a poor man.* I may say, therefore, that *self-reliance* was my birth-right. It has often been my boast, that I am descended from *a long line of illustrious tailors;* and in my early career in this latitude, I so far followed in the footsteps of my illustrious ancestry as to attain some knowledge in the mystery and craft of needle and thread—an acquaintance which has been of great service to me through life, especially in those twenty-five years of it which were devoted to the service of the State in travelling through New England and the West. And had a certain distinguished functionary in a sister State possessed the early advantages which I enjoyed in this respect, his government would probably have never been saddled with that notable charge of *fifty cents for mending his inexpressibles.*

I remember also to have served a temporary apprenticeship with a silversmith, whose shop stood just north of the Episcopal Church. It is not unlikely that I should have gone on to eminence in this sterling trade had I persevered in it; but a mishap turned the current of my life. In an evil hour, as I was pouring some moulten brass into a wet mould, my eyes became thoroughly closed for several months—and ever after, upon that avocation.

Like all New England boys, who are bred to face the world, I learned the several mysteries of farming, gardening, store keeping, and "doing chores," and I think I may say it, without boasting, I acquitted myself in all with honor, if not distinction.

When I look on those rocks and mountains at the East, and upon Bare-Hill in the West, they stand associated with recollections of my boyhood in Woodbury—I remember with the vividness as of yesterday, when, in the autumn and winter, with my box traps, I caught two or three rabbits a night, and when, at the close of the trapping season, I marched proudly with my furs to John Clarke, the Hatter. And even in the height of his prosperity, John Jacob Astor never returned from Columbia river to the New York market with his cargo of furs, more elated with success, than I, with my cargo under my arm, to the Pomperaug market.

In gazing upon these mountains and wooded hills, (about the only things around me which continue as they were,) I remember, and it is a pleasant recollection—of having cut and drawn home upon my hand-sled, both from the East Rock, and from Bare-Hill, numerous loads of fire-wood. Thus industrious habits and an active life, coupled with that self-dependence which I learned as an early lesson, enabled me to face my destiny, and to work my way in the world with a fair measure of success.

With the aid and instruction of the best of mothers, and with such educational facilities as the neighborhood afforded, at an early period I entered a College, where in a few short years, I was prepared for my future life, and *graduated with due honors.*

Do you inquire, what was the name of this College—where it was located—and who was its President? Its catalogue, I believe, was never published—or if published, it was like other things of that sort, *in an unknown tongue.* When translated into our modern phrase, it would be called The People's College. Its President in my day was Lemuel Reed. The College edifice, which was about fifteen feet square, more or less, (probably the latter,) was located on the side of the street below us, nearly in front of your historian's residence. After finishing my course at a "Select School" for a short time, I entered the family of Hon. Nathan Preston, where I remained for five years; and your town and Probate records from 1796 to 1801 will furnish you some standing testimonies in black and white, that I rendered the town and its officers some service before I left it.

While in the family of Judge Preston, I read law under Noah B. Benedict, Esq., for about a year, when I emigrated to Litchfield, and there, in the office of Ephraim Kirby, Esq., and of Judge Reeve, completed my legal studies, and was admitted to the Bar in 1805.

As to the subsequent lines of my history, and the record of some things that I have *done*—but not of much that I have *said*, (for I have, especially in modern times, been more of an *acting* than a *talking* man,) behold they are written in the book of *Cothren*, your Historian.

Thus at the risk of worrying your patience, and of incurring the charge of egotism, I have run over that portion of my history which, including the first twenty years of my life, was passed in this my native town, and properly belongs to it.

And now after the lapse of nearly threescore years since my emigration, I return to the home of my youth, and find myself for the most part, a stranger among strangers. I can recognize only here and there a familiar countenance in this spacious sea of faces; and there are very few in this multitude of the sons and daughters of Woodbury, who recognize me.

And now in conclusion, permit me to inquire:

Where are my cotemporaries?

Where are my class-mates of the Pomperaug College?

Where are the twenty-two students of that sister College, which stood at the base of Masonic-Hall-Rock, in which I was preferred to a tutorship in 1798? Your worthy President is the only one now present.

Where are the thirteen young lads, of whom I was one, who in 1796 planted a liberty-pole on that same rock, and celebrated the twentieth anniversary of our National Independence? Here is the original list of their names in my hand, with the bill of expenses amounting to *5s. 2d.*, sterling.

Where are the eighteen young ladies, who, with those young men on the evening of that day, more than sixty years ago, attended the

Ball at Cunningham's Hall? From the original list before me, not one appears to be present.

Where are the many friends and acquaintances whom I left here in 1801?

With the exception of the *Minors*, *Judsons*, and *Atwoods*, who are stereotyped in the town's accounts, where are the ancient families of Ancient Woodbury?

I can answer as to my own family, who were all here in force when I emigrated, that the name of BEERS has become extinct in the town; and all that now remains here of the Beers blood has flowed back into a branch of my mother's family, and the name is lost in that of PRESTON.

The annals of my father's family are for the most part to be found upon the monuments in yonder grave-yard. With the exception of myself, the solitary remainder of a generation that has passed away, and a few descendants of my sister, all are gone. Having reached that extreme point in human life which is close upon fourscore years, though still in the enjoyment of health and strength, and hardly feeling in its full weight the burden of my years—for which I bless God, and am thankful,—I cannot but feel that my coming hither on this occasion is as a bringing together the two ends of the line, and a making up of the circle of my history. FAREWELL.

"THE EARLY PHYSICIANS OF ANCIENT WOODBURY," by David B. W. Hard, M. D., of Bethlem, Conn.

It is a very pleasant thing to pass in review, a succession of kind and benevolent deeds. And if the aspect of human suffering is not agreeable to look upon; yet the efforts made by the benevolent, the kind hearted, and the capable, to mitigate and relieve it, draw involuntarily from the human heart, the aspiration, God bless you!

Such has always been the mission of the physician in ancient times, as well as at the present. But the matter uppermost in our minds to-day is, those ancient men who first peopled this pleasant valley, and who, by degrees, pushed their homes as so many out-posts, among these loveliest of New England hills.

"The early physicians of Ancient Woodbury," is the sentiment just announced in our hearing, and I now purpose making a few observations respecting them.

And I will remark here, that it is to be regretted that there is so little of their particular and individual history left remaining to us.

I have lately made some search in this direction, but without much result. The printed page of their history is brief and general, and oral tradition, which was so rich a store, has within the last ten or twelve years, been almost wholly lost, owing to the successive removal from among us of those old men who had it in their keeping. The current of time has swept it away from us ; but like as other currents that once existed in the natural world, in a former age, long since past, have left behind them their history sculptured in the bosom of the living rock ; so with these men, their history as it has been passing from among us, has worn for itself channels in our memories, which will not be easily effaced. If their particular and individual history is somewhat obscure, their general history remains, and it is of this I shall speak.

Intimately associated with my earliest remembrance, are certain names, which when spoken in my hearing, always at that time impressed me with the profoundest degree of veneration and respect. These were the names of certain physicians, who once lived within the ancient limits of this town ; and truly may it be said of them, " that a man's works follow him ;" for such is the repute they have left behind them, it would clearly indicate that one of two things must be true, either that they were greatly over-rated, or they were truly men of enlarged and elevated attainments in their profession.

If we concede it to be a fact, that the cotemporaries of these men were their best judges, and that that judgment has been expressed in the traditionary history that has come down to us, then we have unqualified assurance, that as physicians, these men ranked in their profession among the first and chiefest men in the Colony or State.

In reviewing their history, we find them prominently employed in the public offices of the town ; forward and public spirited during the revolutionary struggle ; elected to the office of surgeon in the army, and discharging the duties of this office with untiring fidelity, to a degree that attracted the attention of the commander-in-chief, so that on some of them, Washington bestowed tokens of his special approbation ; and in their public, as well as their private calling, these men seem to have filled to the full, the measure of their useful lives.

From the best sources of information extant, it would appear that no physician accompanied the first settlers in the valley of the Pomperaug, and how soon one may have arrived afterward, does not appear. The earliest date of such physician's residence here, set down in Cothren's History of Woodbury, is 1701. And it would appear from whatever information I can gather, touching this matter, that the first settlers resided here without a competent medical adviser, for a period of about twenty years. And it is probable that the early pioneers depended more for their physical well being, upon good constitutions and temperate living, than upon that cunning subtlety of man's invention, known as the science of medicine.

But luxury has ever crept into the most simple and primitive of all civilized communities; and so in this instance, we find it a matter of history, that in 1701, the settlement in Woodbury were indulging in the luxury of a resident physician.

From this time onward, I find an unbroken succession of intelligent, distinguished, and worthy men, regularly trained and inducted into their profession, according to the custom of those times, residing not only in Woodbury, but in Bethlem, Judea, Roxbury and Southbury.

I said they were trained and inducted into their profession according to the custom of those times. Those splendid universities of medical learning at Edinburgh, at London, and at Paris, which, like planets of the first magnitude, shed their light over the civilized world, were too remote, and too expensive, for the poor student of this western wilderness. But their healing streams reached him, and he drank deep from their fountains of wisdom.

The mode pursued at that time to acquire the knowledge and the qualifications, which made the physician, was this: the candidate entered the office of some one already high and distinguished in the profession; an ample library furnished the knowledge; and the student learned to apply that knowledge by accompanying his preceptor when he visited the sick. And in this mode acquiring such a knowledge of the profession, and such degrees of excellence and attainment were often reached in the end, that it frequently occurred that the savans of our own Yale College spontaneously conferred upon him the honorary degree of Doctor in Medicine.

We see then that the standard of learning among the physicians of Ancient Woodbury was not low, but that here in the wilderness, medical learning took root, grew, and flourished like the gigantic oaks it dwelt among.

It was among such men as these, that our Connecticut Medical So ciety had its origin; and this medical society, from its first inception, moved steadily onward, and did not tire, till they had instituted and founded the medical institution of Yale College.

These men felt an inexpressible contempt for that impudent and vulgar pretence, which characterizes the quack, who is too lazy to work, too ignorant to be employed in any of the occupations of mind, but feels within himself a peculiar talent to fatten on the credulity of that portion of the community, whose love of the *wonderful* and the *marvelous*, eclipses their understanding, and obscures their common sense.

I have hitherto spoken of these men collectively, and I feel an unwillingness to individualize them, making distinctions among them, pointing to the excellences of some, and the defects of others. My desire is to pay that tribute to them *all* which is their due. And yet it is difficult to pass silently by such names as Perry in Woodbury, Hawley and Meigs in Bethlem, Fowler in Judea, Eastman in Roxbury, and Graham in Southbury. We have inherited these names, among the cherished traditions that have come down to us from our ancestors. These men were highly appreciated by the cotemporary inhabitants among whom they dwelt. They were all of them men who "went about doing good," sympathizing with the afflicted and the suffering. And their sympathy was of that kind which takes to itself form and action, and which manifests itself in benevolent deeds.

We read in a history of the highest authority, that a man living in an eastern country, started to go to the town of Jericho, that he fell among thieves, was beaten, and left for dead. Sundry persons, one of whom was a priest, even, saw him lying there, bleeding and dying, but they all passed by on the other side. At length a certain Samaritan passed that way, saw him, and had compassion on him, dressed his wounds, sat him on his own beast, brought him to an inn, and took care of him.

A thousand generations since then, have lived and passed away, and the act in the scene just described, has touched the hearts of all; and all have united in bestowing upon him the surname of the "Good Samaritan."

I have alluded to this scene in sacred history, that it might assist us here to-day, to realize the character and practical lives of those, in behalf of whose memory I am endeavoring to gain a hearing. I would draw back the curtain that has fallen between them and ourselves, that we may once more gain a few transient glimpses of these practical Good Samaritans.

Stricken down by disease, or crushed to the earth by accident, man feels in his heart, "alas, what is to become of me!" And while the community at large, engrossed in their own pursuits, pass by on the other side, these good samaritans, the physicians of Ancient Woodbury, did up their wounds, and took care of them.

Did I hear some one say they were paid for it? True, my friend, compensation sometimes followed; but appeals to their charitable offices were unremitted, almost every day in the year, and like good Samaritans, they responded to those appeals. And if they were so well paid, where are those ample estates left behind them after their own decease? Echo answers—where! Let us honor these men, and do justice to their memories; for in doing so, we do honor to our own human nature.

In those days of practical good sense, almost every household had their family physician. Once chosen to be physician of the family, he usually remained so until his own decease occurred. This resulted in an incalculable amount of good, for the physician felt a permanent, a continued, an abiding interest in the family. And he gained an accurate knowledge of those varied peculiarities, which have so much to do in modifying disease. And from the opportunity that was allowed him, these varied peculiarities which will assume different forms in different families, became to him subjects of study and scrutiny; and in consequence of his knowledge thus gained, he would often relieve their sickness as if it had been done by a power of magic.

The confidence between physician and family, was mutual, and the kind feelings reciprocal. Wherever he was called, he felt himself at home; and, in turn, was regarded almost as one of the family.

And in those desperate struggles with acute disease, where all the resources within him were called forth, he felt as much joy in his own success, as the parent did in the recovery of his child. But when disease gained the mastery, and the patient succumbed under it, it was a way this people had, to take an early opportunity to manifest to him that they appreciated the exertion he had put forth, and that their confidence and friendship remained unimpaired. They knew that it was appointed unto man once to die, and that a last sickness must come to each one of them.

The physical features of a country, the climate, and surrounding scenery, have much to do in forming national and individual character. Effeminacy, slothfulness, ease, and luxury, are in a great degree characteristic of the people living between the tropics.

And this is especially the case, in those delightful islands, and Eden-like gardens of the continents, where nature provides spontaneously for the physical wants of man.

Ancient Woodbury, however, did not lie between the tropics; there was no effeminacy here, save that which sat with the most winning gracefulness, upon the persons of our then young and matronly grandmothers.

Neither was there ease here; except that necessary rest and repose which alternated with diligent labor. And their greatest luxury was a good appetite, which enabled them to take that sustenance which sustained them in their unremitted employments.

Ancient Woodbury was then studded, and canopied, with the primeval forest; there was a dignity in its stateliness, and a solemn grandeur in the deep-toned music which accompanied the swaying movement of its waving branches. The streamlets, the rivulets, and the rivers, flowed then with fuller banks in their shaded channels, than they do now, exposed to the direct glare of the solar rays; and their rushing, murmuring echoes, mingled in unison with the woodland music. The Pomperaug flowed then, as now, through this pleasant valley; and as they looked beyond it, on either hand, bold and rugged outlines were elevated to the view. Near at hand, were abrupt and perpendicular cliffs, and where the eye could extend beyond these, more distant summits overtopped the nearer hills.

All this was in unison with the stout hearts that first made themselves a home in this valley; and it was among this people, and among these scenes, that the physician of Ancient Woodbury imbibed those elevated qualities that were so conspicuous in his career. He could not help but *feel* and *think;* and those feelings and those thoughts took their mould and form from the magnitude of the objects which surrounded him. Among an inferior people, and tamer scenery, these physicians would have been inferior in their profession, and inferior as men; for the thoughts and actions of every living man take color and form from their associations, and their surroundings.

But both physician and patient filled here the full measure of their allotted time, and both have passed onward, on the eternal journey. And it would be to us to-day, a matter of interesting speculation, (having in view the signs of the times,) whether it is probable, that after another two hundred years have passed, the descendants of those who now people the territory of Ancient Woodbury, assembled here, perhaps, to celebrate, as we do to-day, will point to us, in our varied callings, and invoke an honor and a blessing on our memories; or, whether they will go beyond where we go to-day, for merit to applaud, and deeds to commend.

Now, perhaps, some will inquire of me, What kind of doctors were these physicians of Ancient Woodbury? Were they steam and Lobelia doctors? Were they Homœopathic, infinitesimal doctors? Were they "Ingin" doctors? Were they Eclectic doctors? Were they Root doctors? Were they Stick doctors? Were they Hygeian doctors? Were they Graffenberg doctors? Were they Mineral doctors? Were they "Apotacary" doctors? Were they Cancer doctors? And did they know how to set bones? And when they cured any body, did not they always do it with Brandreth's pills?

I will endeavor to make answer to these interrogatories, by replying:

That 2320 years ago, a man-child was born in the Island of Cos, whose name was Hippocrates. Eighteen of his ancestors, counting backward in an unbroken line, had been famous in curing disease. At the head of this line of eighteen, stood Æsculapius, his great ancestor, whom the ancients called the Father of Physic. On his mother's side, he was said to have been descended from Hercules. Occupying this advantageous position, and inheriting the hereditary talent of his family, he applied himself with great assiduity, to the observation and study of disease. His efforts were attended with the most marvelous results. Truth seems to have led him by the hand, while he extorted from nature her hidden laws. Previous to his time, what was known of the art of healing, existed in a state of chaos. He brought *order* out of this confusion, and forever established system and method, and for more than six hundred years, the ancient civilized world were cured of their infirmities after the manner taught by Hippocrates. And so deeply sensible were they, of the benefit he had conferred upon mankind, that, after the manner of those times, they exalted him into a Deity, and erected to his honor and his worship, temples, and statues, and altars smoking with incense. And if Æsculapius was the father, Hippocrates was the great founder of the healing art. His was the great nucleus around which, each later century has contributed and garnered a rich harvest of truth; until now, at the present time, the science of medicine comprehends within its boundaries, a knowledge of the natural sciences, unknown to any other calling in civilized life. On every part of this globe, wherever we meet with civilized man, whatever be his nation, or his language, it is by this same science of medicine, that the sick is treated for his disease.

It was, then, to this school of medicine, that the physicians of Ancient Woodbury belonged. They were trained disciples in the school of Hippocrates. This will answer the question, "what sort of doctors they were?" And you will permit me here to remark, that the divers other sorts of doctors are the *mushrooms* and the *toadstools*, growing upon the outside borders of the healing art.

And now, may the mantle of the physicians of Ancient Woodbury descend upon the physicians of modern Woodbury, who, in practical attainment, I hope, if possible, may eclipse even their lustre. May the sympathy uniting them with the people among whom they dwell, be like that which existed in olden time. May Atwood, the Woodbury physician of 1859, remember he is descended from Atwood the Woodbury physician of 1701. And may the Web* of attainment among them all, both practical and scientific, always Shove* forth their curing and healing instincts; and may the usefulness and professional success of each, mark him as a Fairchild* and lineal descendant of their great ancestor, Hippocrates.

"THE FOUNDERS OF ANCIENT WOODBURY," by Hon. WILLIAM T. MINOR, of Stamford, a grandson of Woodbury.

MR. PRESIDENT, LADIES AND GENTLEMEN:

It has given me great pleasure that I have been able to accept the invitation of your committee and be present with you to join in these commemorative services. Since my arrival here last Saturday afternoon, from what I have seen and heard, I have been somewhat disposed to doubt my own identity. I am inclined to the opinion that I ought to have been "Deacon Minor." I rather think I ought to have been. I am certain that if I had been, and discharged faithfully the duties appertaining to that office, I should have been a much better man than at present; but as I am, it has long been a cherished wish of my heart, to visit the home of my ancestors; to look at the spot which gave them birth, at the playgrounds of their childhood, at the old school-houses in which their education was commenced, and in many instances, finished, at the fields cultivated in their middle age, at the houses which sheltered their old age, at the churches where they ever worshipped, and at the grave-yards where now rest all of their mortal remains. Until now the active business of life has prevented the accomplishment of that wish. I only regret now, as I look upon your beautiful hills and valleys, and partake of your generous hospitality, that duty has been so long neglected. One of the most obvious reflections forcing itself upon the mind, as the eye passes over the immense concourse here assembled, is, what numbers

* Names of the physicians at present residing and practicing in Woodbury.

of the descendants of ancient Woodbury, have come together here, from all parts of our common country; the merchant from his counting room, the mechanic from his work-shop, the farmer from his field, the professional man from his office, the authoress from her study, bringing with her poetical garlands all green and fresh—all leaving behind the active stirring scenes of life, some to clasp the hand of living friends, fondly welcoming them; others, to drop a tear over the graves of departed ones—all to commemorate the virtues of the founders of Woodbury.

Although I mingle with you but as a grandchild, of this good old town, yet I doubt not my appreciation of its growth and prosperity will be as true, and my relish for these exercises as keen and hearty, as of the children and immediate heirs; from all of us a tribute of admiration and respect is equally due to the virtues, the true nobility and the undying energy of its founders.

We shall fail properly to appreciate the character of the founders of ancient Woodbury, unless we look at the circumstances under which they were educated and prepared to become pioneers in the settlement of the new world. In the early part of the seventeenth century, the English throne was filled by James I. Under his reign religious persecution was carried to such an extent, that very many of the best citizens of England, to avoid stripes, imprisonment and even death, were driven into exile. At first their attention was turned to Holland, where they went in 1608, and remained until 1620, from whence they sailed, and in the latter part of that year landed "upon the stern and rock-bound coast" of Plymouth. James I. was succeeded by his son, Charles I. Under the latter, the same persecutions which had characterized the reign of the former, were contintinued in a more aggravated form. Tyranny and oppression were used not only to destroy religious freedom but also to blot out from the English constitution, all the guarantees furnished by that instrument to the citizen for the enjoyment of personal liberty and the rights of property. For twelve years, from 1628 to 1640, the sovereign will of Charles I., despotically exercised without a parliament, ruled the kingdom. In 1640, just about the time when that parliament was assembling, between which and Charles I., civil and religious liberty on one side, and despotism on the other, that mighty contest was waged, which terminated in the trial and execution of the monarch. Another band of exiles from England, fleeing from persecution, landed in Massachusetts and joining with some of the old Plymouth pilgrims, turned their faces westward and settled at

Stratford. Here all remained until religious dissensions springing up among them, the smaller number desirous of peace, in 1659, started out into the wilderness to look out new homes. This exploration brought them to Woodbury, and thus, in a short time afterwards, was the settlement of ancient Woodbury effected.

From what I know of their descendants of the present day, I am inclined to think, that in this respect, we differ essentially from our ancestors. I have no doubt, that although very peaceable when not quarreling, we should have remained at the old place, and fought it out, hoping in time to become the majority.

Let us for a moment pause and contemplate the settlers as they took up their march into the wilderness, yet untrodden by the foot of Christian man. They had assisted in the formation of one settlement, by the waters of Long Island Sound. Here they had planted their Church, erected their school-houses, and built the rude log-hut for the protection of themselves and their little ones. A difference of opinion upon some matter of religious doctrine, was about separating them; the small party conceiving that their mission had not been accomplished; feeling that entire freedom of opinion in all matters of conscience were the great aim of their lives; wishing themselves to enjoy that freedom unalloyed by the harsh and discordant jarrings of dissent and disagreement, and willing that all others should enjoy the same freedom unrestricted by any, save the commands of their great Creator. See them starting out to explore the trackless forest! They had been well fitted in the school of persecution, to become the pioneers of settlement; all those traits of character, both mental and physical, so necessary to endure the hardships of frontier life, had been largely developed by the circumstances surrounding their childhood and middle life; some of them fresh from the persecutions which were so rapidly driving their native country into bloodshed, revolution and liberalism; others, among the first settlers at Plymouth, altogether stalwart, stern, high minded, God fearing men and women; they possessed a sturdy independence of character, which caused them ever to hate oppression, an undying energy which prompted them to enter upon the trackless forest, and a faith true and steadfast, that their Almighty Father would lead them by safe paths to their homes afar off in the wilderness. Follow them in their journey, until at last, about thirty miles from their homes on the top of Good Hill, the hardy band first catch a view of the beautiful valley now enriched by the taste and wealth of their descendants. Then first since creation's morn, did the primeval old forests resound with hymns of praise and thanksgiving to the true *God.* Never before had their quiet been disturbed, save by the howling of wild beasts and the song of the ruthless savage, now fiercely exciting passions by their discordant war whoop, again chanting the death-song of some great brave who had gone to the hunting ground of the great unknown. Here then, our ancestors, after a careful examination of the advantages of the country, settled. Their first care, after rudely providing for the safety and protection of their families, was to provide a place for the worship of God. Their first house was a temple not built with hands, whose floor was the broad earth, whose canopy was heaven's high vault, whose altar and pulpit was Bethel rock. Here, until they were enabled to provide another, for Sunday after Sunday, they assembled for worship, carrying in their hearts a certain faith, that their great Father would protect them from all harm, and in their hands the trusty musket, lest perchance, the cunning Indian might attack them. They were the men from whom Cromwell might at any time have recruited his famous regiment of Ironsides ; they ever trusted in God and kept their powder dry. Here upon principles drawn from the Great Creator, given by inspiration from God to man, did the founders of Woodbury establish a government for themselves, making provision also for the education of their posterity. Neither could their own consciences accuse them of having violated the rights of others in making their location and settlement for whatever of right or title the primitive Indian might have possessed to the soil, every portion of that right and title was fairly and honorably extinguished. Oh that some of the same stern hatred of wrong and oppression, and love of right that characterized the early settlers of this good old town, might be infused into the men of the present day, and that the latter would learn and understand, that the great principles of right and justice of that great charter upon which was founded the government of our ancestors, can not be departed from and violated any more by nations than individuals, with safety to themselves and their interests. Long since have the founders of Woodbury gone to their rest. One after another have they obeyed the summons brought by the celestial messenger from the heavenly city, and with them have gone too many of their stern traits of character.

In the historical address given yesterday, your honored historian alludes to a certain social custom with reference to marrying and giving in marriage in the instance of John Minor, Jr., the son of John the settler, an ancestor of mine. Upon this point I can speak with confidence, from experience, and say that no such custom prevails among his descendants at the present day. If you are disposed to doubt, ask a certain lady who accompanied me here, and I have no doubt that she will inform you that an example established more than five thousand years ago by Jacob, who served fourteen years for Rachel, furnished a rule by which a service any where up to fourteen years was required before the hoped-for yes was spoken. But when asking the question, I beg you for all the world not to hint that I have alluded to the matter, lest another term of service should be required.

Let us now look at some of the results of the principles so early established by them.

I doubt if, when the first settlement was made at Woodbury, or at any of the first settlements of New England, the settlers contemplated a separation between themselves and the mother country, and that they were to be the founders, in the new world, of a mighty republican empire. Yet, when from the stand point of the present, we carefully contemplate these men establishing government upon principles of religious toleration, and making provision for common education, exacting in the enforcement of right, stern in the punishment of vice and the putting down of tyranny and oppression, laying the foundations broad and deep of civil and religious liberty. We feel that the American revolution and the establishment of this government, were but the culmination of their principles. Religious toleration, common education, and as a necessary result of these, a free press, are the three main pillars of republicanism. All the acts of the pilgrim settlers of New England were tending to these results, a thousand causes were all along silently at work, so that they can hardly be traced, except in their grand result, a republican empire. If the spirits of those good old men, who, one hundred years ago, stood on Good Hill, surveying the prospect before and about them, could be brought back to-day, and placed upon the exact spot where first they looked upon the valley of Woodbury; if they could look upon these side hills, all luxuriant with vegetation, these valleys all dotted over with beautiful residences; if they could hear the hum of industry from mountain top and valley, and above all, could they look upon this immense concourse of their descendants, prosperous, happy and contented; if their view could be extended over the thirty-three States of this confederacy, teeming with a population everywhere busy and active, just now engaged in commemorating the birth-day of the government whose protecting power guarantees to all its citizens life, liberty, and the pursuit of happiness, they would feel that their first prayer offered up in this then wilderness, had become prophecy, and that their great faith had been more than realized in its results. Such were our ancestors, the founders of Woodbury; they did well the work allotted for them to do, each in his own sphere. Erect for them the monumental stone! Cherish well their memory in your hearts; above all, guard with fidelity their principles which you have inherited, that on our government may be inscribed "*Esto perpetua.*"

A word more, and I have done. It is said that communities, as individuals, when they commence to exist, commence to die. With reference to this, I will close with offering the sentiment—

WOODBURY.—Its head-stones in 1659, may its foot-stones be in eternity.

The whole audience then united in singing, with great enthusiasm, the following

ODE.

BY MRS. ANN S. STEPHENS.

Tune—"*America.*"

All hail our brothers, friends!
Each heart a welcome sends—
Come neighbors, come!
Meet where your fathers dwelt;
Kneel where our mothers knelt;
Think how they toil'd and felt,
In the old home.

Two hundred years ago,
Old men, with heads of snow,
Bared to the breeze,
'Mid a wild Indian band—
By the red council brand—
Grasped the proud chieftain's hand,
Under the trees.

Soon the log cabin stood,
Deep in the hemlock wood,
Hid by its green;
Sons rose to aid the sire,
Red shone the "fallow fire,"
Up rose the rustic spire,
Peaceful, serene.

As forest leaves are shed,
All round a silent bed,
Under the sod;
There follow'd sire and son,
Each when his race was run,
And all his work was done,
Going to God.

If angels wander by,
When hearts beat warm and high,
Our sires are here;
Thankful that liberty
Has set their children free—
Smiling with sympathy,
Gladness and cheer.

Sons of that pilgrim few!
Souls that are firm and true!
Hail ye the day!
Our union is glorious,
Our strength all victorious,
God reigneth over us,
Praise Him alway!

SPEECH.—"THE EARLY SCHOOLS OF ANCIENT WOODBURY," by Thomas Meritt Thompson, A. M., of Woodbury.

Mr. Thompson, on being called, appeared upon the edge of the stage, with a small piece of manuscript in his hand, which he rapidly tore up, saying, if he had a written speech, such should be its fate at the outset; then, turning to the chair, he said:

MR. PRESIDENT:—Three or four days ago there appeared on this ground a tent, and arrangements for public speaking. At about the same time a programme was put into my hands, in which I found, to my dismay, that I was put down for a speech. I know this tent. It is the Yale College tent. Its associations seemed to seal my mouth, and impose on me silence. I have for years been a regular pilgrim to the shadows of this tent. As a devout worshiper at the shrine of my Alma Mater, under it I have long been accustomed to *listen* to words of wisdom as dispensed by wiser, better, older men, in whose presence *I* know only to be silent. I seem to see, near the pole in the center, the venerable and venerated form of President Day; and as if to keep up the illusion, I see before me, on the stage, Professors Knight and Dutton. Under these circumstances, sir, I came up here this afternoon, feeling hopelessly bankrupt for a speech.

But, Sir, our very recklessness sometimes serves us. It is so with me to-day. I think I know why I am wanted here. As my good luck will have it, you want just at this period, a man who can make a speech inside of ten minutes. [Applause.] I am, then, the man for the occasion. I am going to show you how the thing is done, so that at future centennials all may know how to make ten minutes' speeches. [Laughter and applause.] I will not, however, be too boastful. I am still, in more senses than one, overshadowed by this College tent. I observe that it is rent; (pointing to a large *rent* in the canvass.) It is unlike my speech—in that you will find no holes, for it has never been stitched together.

Mr. President; I am not a native of Woodbury. I feel as if I was a trespasser; yet I heartily thank the Committee for assigning me a part here. I am ingrafted stock, but I have taken some root, and once before, I believe, I took occasion to say, that on this very ground I had made a mark that nothing but an earthquake can efface. I am not a native; but like the Irish gentleman who told the elder Adams he liked the country so well he was going to become a native! So I, whatever may have been my previous hesitation, beg to say that I like the looks of the people assembled here to-day, and am going hereafter to be a native. Put me down for a native! Henceforth, my energies, heart and soul, are with the Woodbury people.

I remember the first Woodbury man I ever saw. I shall show him to you before I am through. You will not wonder why I chose Woodbury as a place of settlement when I tell you I took *him* for a sample of the people. He is the man who honors and adorns our noble festival, our glorious centennial as its presiding officer. May I be permitted to say, if I have put forth any diligence that entitles me to stand here to-day in the presence of princes, yea, of kings and more than kings, I owe it to words of encouragement graciously spoken by him long years ago—"Beardsley, what a smart boy you have got!"

Mr. President, it is to me the central point of interest in the whole occasion, to meet you here. I am filled with emotion. The date of the time I allude to scares me. My memory is tenacious of dates, and I will give it. It was in the fall of 1828. Oh! the record of thirty years on me and on you! It has carried me along from the boy of scarce ten summers, to the meridian of life. It has carried you along from the dark hair and bloom of the man of thirty, to the twilight gray of life's evening. God grant that this evening may be as long, as calm, as happy, as your life has been exemplary, beautiful, and useful. [Amen! from all the elderly gentlemen upon the stage.]

But, sir, it was assigned as my part to respond to "The Early Schools of Ancient Woodbury."—Here, sir, at the outset, I take grounds of open rebellion against the Committee who imposed this part on me—I will not make a speech upon it. To speak of the schools of Ancient Woodbury, is to speak of the Puritan schools, a subject, I take it, needing no illustration from me. The Puritan schools have long since gained the acknowledgment of being the main human agency in the immense moral force exhibited by New England throughout her whole past history. Their influence has gone forth like streams in the desert, to make glad, and bless humanity. The noble men and women in all the higher walks of humanity, for long generations, have been a standing comment upon the early schools. Though I decline to go into this question at large, I will add, as a casual remark, that the early schools had vastly the advantage over those of our day. Then they had *few* books, and learned them *well.* The result was a thoughtful, sedate, prudent race of men. In our time, in the huge multitude of school-books, and in our eagerness to learn everything in the shortest time, we learn *nothing* well. The result is, our people are rattle-brained, empty-headed, inconsiderate. [Applause and laughter.] It is time for us to consider, whether as a people we are not wofully the losers, when for the material activity which characterizes our age, we so freely barter intellectual vigor, and moral force.

But, Mr. President, if the Committee did show a weakness in appointing me to speak on the subject assigned me, they have more than compensated for it in the precautions they have taken to guard the audience from the infliction upon them by me, of a dull, prosy speech. This, they have most effectively done. To make all sure on this point, and to have the stage promptly cleared, they have placed behind me, (pointing to Hon. Chas. Chapman,) the *sharpest* man in Connecticut; a warning I shall take good care to heed; for as I came on the stage with a sort of *crawling* sensation, in view of the many reasons why I should not speak, so I already feel a pricking sensation, and hurry off the stage, lest I should be actually *impaled!* [Makes a hasty exit, amidst roars, shouts, and explosions of laughter.]

SPEECH OF HON. CHARLES CHAPMAN, OF HARTFORD, A GRANDSON OF WOODBURY.

Mr. Chapman next responded to the sentiment, "THE GRANDCHILDREN OF ANCIENT WOODBURY," substantially as follows:

Having been called to respond to the toast last announced, I ought perhaps to imitate the example of the politicians, and "define my position." The nearer we can approach to the common grandmother, on this occasion, the better pleased we are; but, truth to tell, I am but a great-grandson of "Ancient Woodbury." The difference, however, may be of *minor* importance, (if the Governor will excuse the use of the word in that sense,) inasmuch as all the grandchildren are *great* grandchildren to-day.

There is in the human heart an instinctive love for the place of one's nativity. The youth who leaves the paternal roof to seek his fortune elsewhere, keeps the old homestead in view, toils on to acquire a competency, and when he has achieved the end for which he has labored many years, returns to the place of his birth, re-purchases the paternal acres, which have passed into other hands, and rears a more expensive edifice upon the spot where the old mansion stood. He adorns and beautifies the old farm, enriches the old fields, plants hedges where the old walls stood, and calls the place by a fancy name.

Of a kindred character is the regard which one feels for the home of his more remote ancestors, the spot where the family took root in the then new world. This sentiment will show itself in various ways. It "crops out," (in the language of the miners, I mean the *miners* in metals,) from time to time, and on this occasion may be observed upon every hand. The remote descendants of the early settlers in this lovely valley are here in great numbers, and others residing in distant regions have sent their contributions to this festival in letters, relics, and touching sentiments.

I have been commissioned by one of these descendants to present to the town of Woodbury some tokens of his regard, which I trust you will carefully preserve in the archives of the town. I will read to you my "Power of Attorney," (excuse the language of the profession,) and when you hear that, and the name of the man from whom it comes, you will regret with me, that he can not be heard from this stand, upon an occasion so well suited to his tastes as this is. You will recognize in him the historian of Hartford, the author of the life and times of the elder Governor Trumbull, who was the "Brother Jonathan" of Revolutionary memory, and the author of the life of Nathan Hale. An accomplished scholar, an industrious antiquarian, and an orator of surpassing ability, he would have added another charm to these festivities.

HARTFORD, JULY 1ST, 1859.

HON. CHARLES CHAPMAN:

DEAR SIR—In compliance with your solicitation, I take pleasure in sending, through you, some memorials for the forthcoming celebration of the settlement of Ancient Woodbury. They are, a piece of the wood of the far-famed Charter Oak, a view of this Monarch Tree as it looked in life, and a view of it as it looked in death, the morning after it fell. It was within the period of the birth of Woodbury—but a few years only after the Stileses, and Curtises, and Skinners, and Judsons, and Minors, first settled there—that Sir Edmund Andros made his impotent attempt to seize and invalidate that noble Charter under whose folds Samuel Sherman and his associates obtained liberty from the General Court "to erect a plantation at Pomperauge"—and those, the early dwellers there—in common with the Colonists of Connecticut at large—rejoiced, then in the olden time, in that gnarled old Oak, which protected their Constitution of government, and saved their liberties—liberties which have never since been overthrown—but which—consecrated by the sacrifices and services of her sons in the councils and on the battle-fields of the Union—are now, thank Heaven, "imperishable and impregnable."

Pleasant, therefore, I have thought it would be to the descendants of the first settlers of Woodbury, to receive the particular memorials which I commit to your charge. A thousand interesting historic associations cluster around them. They vividly renew the Past. They point to an heroic age for Connecticut. They should incite patriotic emotion. They should teach us all to love and honor our State as it has loved and honored us.

I am myself, Sir, a descendant, in the fourth generation, of that worthy and distinguished divine, who, for nearly sixty years, ministered in Ancient Woodbury—the Rev. Anthony Stoddard—and I therefore feel a special gratification in the fact that the birth of this town is to be duly celebrated, and that you Sir—one of its grandsons—are to mingle, actively, in the "high festival." Few municipalities in Connecticut can point to a more historic past than Woodbury. Its Indian, civil, ecclesiastical, and Revolutionary life—so admirably portrayed by its historian, Wm. Cothren, Esquire—place it among the first of our towns, and justify its good repute. That the celebration in which its citizens propose to indulge, may prove gratifying to themselves—may call up gladdening memories—may glow with the spirit of patriotism—and augment their love for their venerable and happy home, is the hearty wish of,

Yours truly,

I. W. STUART.

[Then Mr. Chapman exhibited the block from the Charter Oak—the picture of the tree as it appeared when standing, and after it was prostrated by the storm.]

There are others, and many others, who are neither inhabitants of Woodbury, nor descendants of those who were, who feel a deep interest in its history, and in these festivities, which mark the two hundredth anniversary of the exploration of this valley. Your industrious and talented fellow-citizen, William Cothren, Esq., has done much to create and foster this interest, by his carefully prepared work—a work that does honor to him and to you, and which is a most valuable contribution to the history of our State.

Our own poetess, who is *the* poetess of Connecticut, *par excellence*, has committed to my hands a little "gem of purest ray serene" from her casket of jewels, which she has authorized me to present to you on this occasion. She rejoices in your history, as you do in her well-earned fame. Like another eminent lady who went from among you in her youth, (*Mrs. Ann S. Stephens*,) and who has contributed to this Festival by her presence and by her pen, she has risen to her enviable position in the world of letters by her own merit. Long may she live to entertain us by her works, and teach us by her example.

RETURN TO WOODBURY.

Back to the hills by summer-breezes courted,
  Back to the ancient roof, the shaded plain,—
Back to the play-ground where their fathers sported,
  The summon'd children turn their course again.

And as the Fountain loves the tuneful voices
  Of her far streamlets, whereso'er they tend,
And at the echo of their fame rejoices
  When nobly with the ocean-tide they blend,—

So this fair Region,—rich in vales and waters,
Swells with maternal pride her flowery zone
At this re-union of her sons and daughters,—
And in their well-earned honor finds her own.

L. H. Sigourney.

Hartford, June 28th, 1859.

There is another of the other sex, who is bound to you by no tie, but who has yielded to my request, and sent a sparkling contribution to this intellectual banquet. He may be known to some of you as a regular contributor to the Knickerbocker, and as an occasional correspondent of some of the journals in this State. He would enjoy this scene, were he present, and for his sake and yours, I regret his absence. I suppose I ought to tell you who he is. He is one of my fellow-citizens, who deals in iron for gain, and courts the muses for fun—brimful of mirth and with a wit that is keener than a Damascus blade. He is a living refutation of the truth of a paragraph in Hudibras, to the effect that

"A man of quick and active wit
For drudgery is more unfit,
Compared to those of duller parts,
Than running nags to draw in carts."

Alike a man of business and a poet, success attends his efforts in both departments.

Our friends, the Clergy, who have figured so largely and so successfully in these exercises, will pardon the spice of levity which may, by a careful examination, be detected in the verses which I am about to read. Yes, I know they will. I see it in their benevolent faces, and I remember, too, that the holidays of the Clergy are "few and far between," and I am persuaded that they enjoy this to the very top of their heart.

But it is time I should tell you the name of my friend who has been so kind to us all. It is George H. Clark, and here is what he sends "greeting," as the Lawyers say:

Geo. H. Clark's Woodbury Centennial Poem.

Mysterious notes were abroad on the air—
Significant hints of some weighty affair:
Rumors increased till they rose to a shout,
And now we all see what the stir was about.

Ye modest admirers, who've nothing to say,
Make room—for spread eagle is coming this way,
We stand, as it were, in our forefathers' shoes,
And the time for tall talking's too precious to lose.

Here frolicsome age shall grow young at the core,
And youth shall strike hands with the boys of threescore:
Brim full of good feeling—Oh! call it not folly—
We've assembled on purpose to laugh and be jolly.

Ye attorneys—turn over a holiday leaf;
The facts are before you—and here is the brief!
So give us as much as you please of your jaw,
But don't, if you love us, don't let it be law.

Ye grave Boanerges—who thunder at sin,
Let your features relax to a good natured grin:
Pretermit theological chafing and chat,
And talk about buttercups, birds, and all that.

Forget, O my friends, in this glorified hour,
The Parson who vanquished that dreadful pow-wow-er;
But remember the Backus and Bellamy jokes,
And up and be merry like rational folks.

Sink the shop, O ye trader in dry goods, to-day,—
Just look at the prospect right over the way!
Don't the sight of the Pomperaug hills and green valleys
Beat all your gay patterns on muslins and challies?

Ye medical men—whose dreams are of drugs,
Omit for a while your professional shrugs:
Give the go-by to boluses, blisters, and nux,
And think of the dandelions, daisies, and ducks.

Ye farmers—the nearest to Nature's own breast,
Who draw from her stores what her children love best;
Who irradiate towns with fresh butter and cheese,
And tickle our palates with lamb and green peas;

We remember your haymows so fragrant in June;
Your pumpkins, as large and as round as the moon;
The green corn we roasted and ate on the sly,
And the rye 'n 'ndian bread, and the—Oh! let us cry!

It makes my mouth water to talk of such things,—
The truth is, you farmers are Nature's own kings:
And the queens!—would you see the true test of their worth?
Just look at those boys! aren't they proud of their birth?

Of course, we'll remember, and speak of with pride,
Seth Warner, and others who fought by his side:
And grand Ethan Allen—the hero all over—
Who conquered Fort Ti, in the name of Jehovah!

Historians assert that you 'd only one witch—
But history makes an unfortunate hitch;
For witches still flourish—as witness these groups!
Though for halters and faggots you substitute hoops.

Then a health to old Woodbury—merry or grave—
And long in the land may her progeny wave,
Nor forget where their excellent grandmothers sleep,
While their own little babies are learning to creep.

Now, my friends, I have disposed of all the props upon which I have relied to sustain me in the event, that my own thoughts should fail. I am left to my own resources, and begin to be apprehensive that you may be mirthfully inclined when I am serious, and seriously disposed when I am gay. Topics were plenty, yesterday morning, but in the two days' speaking they have been, for the most part, used up. All the leading features in your history have been passed in review. Those men who have distinguished themselves most among you have also been already noticed. Of some of them too much could hardly be said. First and foremost among the intellectual giants in our State, was the Hon. Nathaniel Smith, who was born and lived, until his death, within the ancient limits of this town. He was indeed a great man. Without the advantages of early culture, he worked his way to the front rank of the legal profession, at a period when the ablest men, who have been known in the courts of this State, were in full practice. He stood among them *primus inter pares*. As an advocate he had great power, and his efforts were attended with marked success. At a later period he was an ornament to the Bench, and has left a record upon the pages of our Reports of which the worthy President here, (his son) may well be proud.

I must be indulged in saying a few words of another member of the profession who has recently passed away. He was one of the originators of this celebration, and one of the Committee to carry out the plan adopted a year ago. The vacant chair upon the stage draped in mourning, reminds us of him, who, had he lived, would have mingled in these festivities with a keen relish. He (the Hon. Charles B. Phelps,) was a man of genius, and a highly respectable member of the Bar. A ready debater, he was always equal to the emergency of an occasion. He had a keen wit and overflowed with humor.

> "A merrier man
> Within the limit of becoming mirth,
> I never spent an hour's talk withal."

He had moreover a kind heart, which displayed itself on all suitable occasions, and long will he be remembered for his many good deeds. You will hardly "look upon his like again."

You will pardon me for speaking a word of another gentleman of another profession, who has long since gone to his rest. I mean the Rev. John R. Marshall, who was the first Episcopal clergyman in this town. He was an eminently good man, and much beloved by those to whom he ministered in holy things. He planted a vine here which he carefully nurtured while he lived, and which flourishes now in full vigor. He closed his ministry here with the termination of his life, leaving behind him many blessed fruits, "Allured to brighter worlds and led the way."

There are many others who have distinguished themselves here in the different professions, and many who have gone from among you, and distinguished themselves elsewhere, who deserve to be mentioned on this occasion did time permit. There have been too, very many equally worthy and estimable men, who never attained to any particular prominence in the eye of the world, men who pursued the noiseless tenor of their way, but who have done their share in building up your institutions, and in making this valley bud and blossom. They were the fathers and grandfathers of many whom I see before me, and this gathering attests the interest which their posterity feel in their memory. While the blood of some of them courses in the veins of their decendants, their names have become extinct among you. This is true of the names of my maternal grandfather and grandmother, (Perry and Beers,) names once well and favorably known here. One of the latter name (*Hon. S. P. Beers,*) has addressed you to-day, but he has resided elsewhere for more than half a century. From his account of himself, nearly seventy years ago he had the ambition to sit cross-legged upon a tailor's bench, but because perhaps (in the language of the old song,) "the money came slowly in," he concluded to pursue the legal profession, supposed by some to be more productive. It would seem from his statement that he is now an old man, which from his full head of brown hair (which I envy,) and his youthful appearance we should all doubt, had we not confidence in his veracity, and did we not know that he had been the popular commissioner of the School Fund since the earliest recollection of the "oldest inhabitant." The sons of many have emigrated to other portions of the country, and thus have their names become extinct here. The daughters, although eminently worthy of trust in all other particulars, cannot be relied upon to bear up a name. In this particular, however honest they may be, they resemble the most practiced rogues. They are with now and then a solitary (not to say melancholy exception,) in search of an *alias*, and are quite sure to find and adopt it. I have always wondered why they mark their linen with their maiden names. Nearly two days have been spent here in glorifying our grandfathers. But there has been, as there now is, a "better half" of humanity, of whom I have heard nothing said. I marvel that such an omission could have occurred in such a presence. A "mutual admiration society," composed exclusively of men, I confess is not to my taste. We have heard much about great men—good men—valiant men—self-taught men, and about "all sorts and conditions of men." It has been from the beginning—men—men—men; nothing but men. Had they no mothers—no wives? Men have indeed fought the battles of the country; felled the forest trees; tilled the earth, and toiled in the different professions and trades. But woman has toiled too amid dangers which appalled the stoutest hearts. She has braved suffering in its countless forms, such as woman only knows, and submitted to privations with a patient meekness of which woman is alone capable. In the early settlement of the country, the mother nursed and reared her own children; was mistress and servant; carded the wool; spun it into yarn, and made it into cloth. She was her husband's and boy's tailor, her own and her daughter's milliner and mantua-maker; and in a word, discharged every domestic duty unaided. It is not strange that such women should have reared such sons as we have been boasting about here for two days.

Let us do fitting honors on this occasion to the female character. Every man who has risen to distinction in any of the walks of life, is indebted to his mother for those traits of genius which he inherited from her, and those habits of thinking and of action, which are the result of her early teaching.

> "The mother, in her office, holds the key
> Of the soul: and she it is who stamps the coin
> Of character, and makes the being who would be a savage,
> But for her gentle cares, a Christian man—"

How dear to us is the sacred name of mother! She it was whose loving care and ceaseless vigilance protected and nurtured us in helpless infancy. We learned from her those earliest lessons which are most deeply impressed upon our memories, and which time does not obliterate. Our recollections of a mother's love, a mother's care, a mother's patience, and a mother's forgiveness of our faults, freshen and become more and more tender, as our shadow lengthens upon the dial. It is to her that we owe all that we are and all we hope to be.

I might speak of woman in the relation of wife, and of the love, respect, and kindness which she deserves as such. She is sought and won, forsakes father and mother, and cleaves unto the husband. With an amazing confidence, she entrusts her happiness, her all, in his hands. She shares his sorrows, participates in his joys, labors for his advancement, and occupies the position in life in which his success or misfortune may place her. If we loved her when seeking an alliance, how much more tenderly should we feel toward her, when she has committed herself to our fostering care, and has become the mother of our children.

There is still another relation in which I might speak of woman. I mean as daughters. None but fathers know aught of the emotions of a father's heart toward them. With what solicitude do we watch their growth and development. With what intense interest do we gaze upon their budding beauty, and varied accomplishments. With what tender affection do we cling to them, and how they wind themselves about our hearts. And then, endeared to us as they are, and in the flush and beauty of their youth, we are called to relinquish them into other hands, as their mothers were relinquished to us. Then we know for the first time, what the yielding to our request cost some few years ago.

Were there time, and were there not some Governors, Lawyers, Doctors, and Clergymen yet to speak, and whom you are anxious to hear, I should be pleased to enlarge upon this *fair* topic; but even at the hazard of standing between you and those gentlemen for an unreasonable time, I could not say less. When I look upon this immense audience, and especially upon this bed of flowers before me, in which I see the spring violet, the summer rose, and the dahlia of autumn, all in bloom at the same time, as if the three seasons had been consolidated, I wish we had another day in which we could say what we feel and think.

Since my earliest recollection, great changes have been wrought in this valley. The stately elms and maples that line the way southward to the western limit of the village of Southbury, were in their infancy fifty years ago; but now they spread their giant arms in every direction, and are models of strength and beauty. This was then a sparsely settled village; but since that period it has undergone such alterations as to change its appearance altogether. Then it was purely an agricultural town; but now it derives its prosperity in a degree from the successful prosecution of some of the mechanic arts.

The men of that day have been for the most part gathered to their fathers; but I recognize in some of those here, the family likeness, and hear on every hand the family names. The names of Stiles, Curtis, Hinman, Sherman, Judson, Atwood, Strong, and many others, are still preserved, and last, but not least, you have "saved your Bacon." We had yesterday afternoon a taste of the attic salt which gives it value.

In conclusion, let me congratulate the originators of this celebration, and all who have been interested in it, upon the singularly fortunate circumstances attendant upon this Festival. The heavens have smiled upon us—no accident has occurred to mar the festivities of the occasion—and the re-union has been one of unmixed enjoyment. We can be present but upon one such occasion in a life-time. Here we have renewed old friendships, and I trust have formed new ones of an enduring character. Many a history will date from this occasion, for it would not be strange if some, who have met here for the first time, will pursue life's journey hand in hand—will "climb life's hill together," and when the journey is concluded, will "sleep together at the foot" the sleep of death. The youth of both sexes, here present, will excuse this public allusion to a delicate subject, which may have found a place in their private thoughts.

Now, my friends, I must take my leave of you. There is a small army of orators behind me, who are waiting for turns, as the first settlers waited at the old mill; and there are many here whose thoughts, radiant with beauty as they are, will not find vent in words. We part with pleasant recollections of this memorable interview, which we shall cherish while we live.

SPEECH OF HON. HENRY DUTTON.

Hon. Henry Dutton, of New Haven, a native of Watertown, within the limits of the Woodbury deed of 1659, responded to the sentiment, "The Cousins of Ancient Woodbury."

Mr. President:—An incident has occurred since I have been on this platform, which has almost induced me to withdraw. The distinguished gentleman from Litchfield related an anecdote, which seemed to reflect upon the honored practice of "cousining." Now as I am here only under that long established custom, and have no right to be heard, except as a remote cousin of Woodbury, had I not felt the utmost confidence in the friendship of that gentleman, I should have been disposed to take offence. I have been somewhat reassured, however, by the course taken by the eloquent gentleman who preceded me. When that gentleman,

"Whose head is silvered o'er with age,"

but whose

"Long experience has [*not*] made him sage,"

and whom I have known for many years as a grandfather, comes here and palms himself off as a *great-grandchild* of Woodbury, I trust I shall be excused if I claim the relationship of only fourth cousin.

Much credit, Mr. President, has been justly awarded to Ancient Woodbury, for what was done by her sons in securing our independence. But it ought to be remembered that the territory embraced in the deed of 1659, not included within the town, lying along its eastern, northern, and western borders, and now embracing the wooded hills and fertile valleys of Middlebury, Watertown, and portions of Litchfield and other towns, furnished their full quota of men and money in sustaining the glorious cause. I regard myself, Mr. President, as peculiarly fortunate, in being able, on the present occasion, to trace my origin to a point west of the Naugatuck—in being able to give testimony on the subject. One of my earliest recollections is of a near neighbor, who went by the name of "Leftenant Ferris," who exhibited the most complete character of a man, that I ever witnessed. He had served in the army during nearly the whole period of the Revolution, and had lost his property, his limbs, and his health, in the cause. He had aided in securing to his country the blessings of freedom, but what to him, in poverty and distress, was the independence of his country? On an occasion like this, I trust a man has a right to speak of the deeds of his own ancestors. My father, though a mere stripling, was for a short time in the army, and witnessed the scene, when a tent in New York was filled with the corpses of soldiers killed by a single stroke of lightning, in the most fearful thunder storm ever known in this country.

He was also at the battle of Long Island, and used to relate to me with thrilling interest, the scenes which he had witnessed.

He also gave me the names of one, and another, and another, of his neighbors who had gone out at the call of their country, never to return.

James Morris, of Litchfield, South Farms, was a gentleman to whom full justice never has been awarded. He was a scholar, as well as a soldier. I have it from high authority, that he served in the army during a large portion of the war; that he was honored by the friendship of Washington, and that he was selected by him to lead one of the columns which scaled the walls at the memorable siege of Yorktown.

I regret that the request that I received to make some remarks on this occasion, were so late that I am unable to speak of others from the same region, whose merits demand a passing notice, But there was a native of Watertown who contributed as much aid to the cause by his pen, as others did by the sword. I refer to John Trumbull, afterward a Judge of the Superior Court. As the author of Mc-Fingal, he ranks among the first poets which this country has produced.

That poem was written at the request of some of the friends of Independence, to cast ridicule upon the tories; and it is said that many of them feared the pointed shafts of his wit more than they did the bullets of other whigs.

Among the instances handed down by tradition of his readiness at repartee, it is said that he was a Tutor in Yale College at the same time with the late celebrated Dr. Dwight. The class of which he had charge had presented to the worthy Tutor a ring, with the motto, "*meruit plus.*"—He deserves more. The younger members of the faculty then, as in later years, frequently visited the ladies of New Haven. Several of them on one occasion gathered round Tutor Dwight, who was a favorite, admiring the ring, and referred to Tutor Trumbull for an interpretation. He examined it, and replied: The motto says, "he deserves more." He deserves yoking as well as ringing."

Another instance of a ready but severe retort upon an antagonist, has sometimes been ascribed to him, and sometimes to another distinguished wit. It was a favorite doctrine of the schoolmen, as our reverend friends will bear witness, that the will is always governed by the strongest motive; and that were motives equally strong presented, the will would remain quiescent. This was illustrated by supposing an ass was stationed between two bundles of hay—those acute metaphysicians insisted that the poor animal would starve to death before he would touch either of them. It happened that Tutor Trumbull was walking between two other Tutors, till they came to a crossing, when one of his friends requested him to go one way, and the other, another way. He hesitated, and acknowledged himself in a quandary, for he said he had an equal regard for both. One of them suggested that he was like the ass between two bundles of hay. "No," said he, "I am like a bundle of hay between two asses."

The father of John Trumbull, who was Pastor of the Congregational Society in Watertown for many years, was a sample of a rare class of clergymen, who would make themselves rich on a salary of one hundred pounds, or a little over three hundred dollars a year. I have heard from his cotemporaries, many anecdotes regarding him. He was a good farmer, as well as preacher, and was particularly a good judge of horse-flesh. He gave full liberty to his parishioners to cheat him if they could in the sale or exchange of horses. He was, though not large, very athletic.

The Pastor of the Church in Waterbury at the time was Mr. Leavenworth. Wrestling was much more fashionable then than it is now, and challenges were given by the wrestlers of one town to those of another. In a number of trials, the champion of the ring of Watertown had been worsted by those in Waterbury. Mr. Trumbull sympathized with his fellow townsmen in their disgrace, and contrived to appear *incog.* at the next wrestling match. The Waterbury men at first were as usual victorious, when the stranger stepped into the ring, and prostrated them, as fast as they closed in with him.

Soon afterward, Mr. Leavenworth, having heard of the defeat of his townsmen, and how it was accomplished, met Mr. Trumbull, and being somewhat piqued, called him to account for his unministerial conduct. Mr. Trumbull excused himself, by saying that he expected to exchange with his brother Leavenworth soon, and thought it advisable to give his parishioners a foretaste of the thrashing which they would get when he did.

The spirit, Mr. President, which achieved our independence, was not confined to any local limits, but fraternized with the whole human race. It was not confined even to this country, but crossed the Atlantic; and the present struggle for freedom in Italy may be traced to our forefathers. It is not easy to estimate the ultimate effect of the examples of such men as Allen and Warner. Indeed, it has struck me that there is a striking analogy between the events in Italy, and those of our own Revolution, with this difference—that they are compressed within much narrower limits of time there. The enterprise and audacity of Garibaldi, remind us strongly of your own Ethan Allen. The battles of Montebello, Casteggio and Magenta, are a counterpart to those of Bunker Hill, Saratoga and Yorktown. May we not hope that the parallel will still be continued.

There has not been a period for many years, Mr. President, when it more behooved the people of this Union, to recall the deeds, and cultivate the virtues of their forefathers, than the present time. We have reason to hope, indeed, that when Louis Napoleon has driven the Austrians out of Italy, as I pray heaven he may, he will, by giving to the Italians the choice of a form of government, place himself on a higher pinnacle of fame, than any monarch who has preceded him.

But we have no assurance that such will be the result. Success may create the love of power, and he may find the Eastern world too small for his ambition. An earthquake in Italy is often felt in America. When the passions of eighty millions of people are excited, and hundreds of thousands borne into collision, it will not be strange if the concussion should be felt on this side the Atlantic. Let us, then, invoke the spirit of '76, and be prepared to meet every invader.

Samuel Minor, Esq., of Sandusky, Ohio, a native of Woodbury, then spoke to the sentiment, "The Emigrants from Ancient Woodbury," as follows:"—

Mr. President: Under a brief notice, I am desired to make a few remarks in behalf of the Emigrants from Ancient Woodbury, those who have left these hills and valleys for distant abodes, and returned to unite in this festive occasion. In their names, we tender most cordial thanks, for the invitation we have received, to visit our paternal homes—to gather again around the domestic hearthstones and to sit again in the old arm chairs of our ancestors.

Personally, this occasion has a special interest, for around the residence near by, and the grounds on which we are assembled, are gathered all the associations of a New England Home. Here were spent my childhood and youth, and here were received those instructions prized higher than any other legacy earthly parents could bestow. The rocks and trees and hills are as familiar as household words. When I call to mind those who have fallen asleep, and look upon those who live; when recollection runs over the reminiscences of the past, and then turn to the present, the soul is filled with emotions which can not be uttered, and I can only exclaim in reference to this loved spot, as can each returning wanderer as to his own :

'Home, home, sweet, sweet home,
There's no place like our old firesides,
There's no place like our good old homes.'

Those of us who have removed from among you, observe with peculiar interest one feature of this celebration, and that is, the presence of so many of advanced and maturing years, so many bright links connecting the past to the present, so many Elishas upon whom have fallen the mantles of the Elijahs that have gone before; and when I speak for myself, I speak for all who reside in the newer States, and assure you, there is nothing we there so much miss as the presence of good old men. Happy is that community which is blessed by many of them. It is for you my aged Fathers, to remember, that, as physical strength diminishes, the fruits of a worthy character are ripening, and the fragrance of useful lives is being shed abroad over the community. Your influence, like gravity, is silent but powerful. To you we look with confidence and respect. We feel that you have imbibed the spirit and principles of our Puritan ancestors, and are manifesting these principles in your lives, and that you have thus become, not only true sons of the past, but fathers of the future. While we shall endeavor to imitate your example, we rejoice to assure you, that these sllver crowns, these crowns of honor which time is placing on the brow, will be succeeded, in eternity, by diadems of glory in that day when the Lord cometh to make up his jewels.

And now as to those of us upon whom is coming the burden and heat of the day. It is for us to preserve the casket committed to our care, and adhere faithfully to the principles thus transmitted. In this manner, and in this only, shall we find true, that beautiful motto of this State, "Qui Transtulit Sustinet," that he who hath established will sustain. Why is it that the roots of the tree of Liberty have taken deeper and stronger hold, and its branches flourished more vigorously amid these comparatively barren rocks of New England, than in the beautiful savannas of the South, yea, than in the rich prairies of the West? It is because that tree was planted by hands which knew no weariness in a good cause, and was watered by the blood and tears of holy men and holy women.

Travelers and scientific men inform us, that the time was, when, in the distant regions of the North, vegetation clothed the hills and valleys, and animal life existed with no want unsatisfied; but, from causes not yet fully understood, the direct rays of the sun were withdrawn, and where all was beauty, desolation reigned. So is it in the moral world. If holy influences from above no longer produce their designed effect, desolation there reigns, and frozen are the genial currents of the soul.

There is a law in the falling leaf and in the springing flower. There is a law in the solid mountain, and a law in the silent spaces amid the stars, and while these and all other physical laws are followed, the course of nature runs smoothly on. Equally true is it, that there is a law in every department of human society enstamped upon it by him who rules above, and it can not be broken with impunity in the one case more than in the other.

Many here present, while school boys, built with me, by yonder school-house, our forts and houses and castles of snow in winter time, thinking that nothing would destroy them, but found, as summer's sun approached, they slowly but surely disappeared. So now, that we have become men, we shall find, no matter what castles we may build or institutions establish, unless they are in accordance with the great higher law, by power from above, they will be melted, melted, melted away.

But time is passing. Again, we thank you for this occasion; we thank you for the hospitality and kindness received, and for the able addresses we have heard. We thank you for the influence your character still exerts, and that, as we wander over the earth, we are enabled to point with pride to New England, with pride to Connecticut, with pride to Woodbury.

Permit me, in behalf of my adopted, and also my native home, without disparagement to others, to close with this sentiment:

OHIO—Noblest of the Western States.

CONNECTICUT—Parent of the best part of Ohio.

Dr. Leman Galpin, of Milan, Ohio, a native of Woodbury, then made the following remarks:

MR. PRESIDENT:—I have been requested to say something on this interesting occasion. Placed, so unexpectedly, in the condition of the chap who, when called on for a speech, arose and gravely said that it was exceedingly embarrassing for him to attempt to say anything just *then* and *there*, inasmuch as he was *wholly unprepared*—at the same time pulling from his pocket a manuscript speech "got up" expressly for that particular juncture, I trust I shall have that indulgence and sympathy which, in all probability, was accorded to him: protesting, meanwhile, that my embarrassment and want of preparation are very much, if not exactly, like his.

To quiet any apprehensions that may arise in your minds, however, let me assure you that you are not about to suffer the *infliction* of a speech. It is a *crime* of which, hitherto, I never was guilty. Yet, the occasion is such as seemingly to *demand* of those, who were reared in this locality, some expression of their attachment to the place that gave them birth.

After an absence of nearly a quarter of a century, I return from Ohio, the State of my adoption, to meet with you on this joyous, and may I not say momentous, occasion. Others like myself, who had wandered from this "our own dear native town," are present from the Buckeye State to participate in this, the Second Centennial Celebration of Woodbury.

Many, no doubt, if indeed not a majority of the different States of the Union, are represented here to-day. For where have not Yankees gone—and *Connecticut Yankees*, in particular? Is it wholly conjectural to suppose that there is not, probably, a State or Territory in our whole country, in which a *live*, *Connecticut Yankee*, is not to be found? And is it any more preposterous or absurd, or one that will more severely tax our credulity, to imagine that there is a country on the face of the globe inhabited by civilized men, or those living in a state of semi-civilization, even, where the sons of Connecticut cannot be found? I repeat the inquiry—Is there a land or nation under heaven where the representatives of our State—if not of our own native Town, indeed, are not to be found? If so, *where?* And "echo" answers, *Where?* I venture the affirmation—*nowhere*—unless it is where wooden nutmegs are at a discount, or money can't be made.

Sir, I presume I utter a sentiment that will meet with a cordial response from all who are similarly situated with myself, when I say "absent, but not forgotten."

No! memory cherishes, and loves to dwell upon the scenes and incidents of childhood. Of every tree and moss-grown rock, of every hill-side and valley, in short, *of every locality* where we were accustomed to indulge in our childish sports may we predicate an attachment, proportioned to the frequency with which we visited them, and the number of years we spent there.

Nothing can make a stronger, or a more permanent impression

upon the mind and heart than the events that occurred in the different localities, in which we respectively resided. We may affirm the same, also, of the instructions, the amusements, and even the follies and foibles of our youthful days. Some of these acts we would fain remember, and we love to ponder upon them.

But alas! Of how large a proportion of our acts, in the aggregate, we may say—would that we could draw the veil of oblivion over them, and forever blot them from the memory. But, impossible! They are written upon the tablet of the heart, and the lines are ineffaceable.

This gathering of the sons and daughters of Ancient Woodbury, is perfectly demonstrative of the sentiment I am about to offer.

Some of you, it is true, occupy patrimonial estates—cultivating the same farms that your fathers tilled, and residing, perchance, in the same dwellings in which they lived and died. Attached to the domain by more than ordinary ties, no other spot is to you so dear. Your dearest associations cluster around, and indeed, center in the old homestead. Familiar with every nook and corner from very childhood, a value attaches to the ancestral home that dollars and cents cannot correctly represent. Should dire necessity—events beyond your control compel you to leave it, how oft would the imagination revert to that place, than which no other is so dear.

Circumstances seemed to necessitate the migration of some of us, though we left somewhat reluctantly. "Very much land remained to be possessed."

Like bees, when the old hive is full, *new swarms* must seek *new homes*. So it was with us. Leaving with the most kindly feelings, and hence with many regrets, our predilections and affinities for the old home have not been dissevered or alienated. Although absent many years, yet there has never been, by any means, a total transference or an essential diminution of the strength of our attachment. Whatever may have been the social position or pecuniary situation of our parents—whether we were born in a palace or a cot—whether every thing that wealth and influence could command were laid under contribution to augment our comfort and happiness, or whether poverty with all its stern imperious necessities was our lot—in either case, we are prepared to endorse and adopt what Daniel Webster said, when he gave utterance to the sentiment, expressed so tersely and beautifully in the following language: "It is only shallow-minded pretenders who make either distinguished origin a matter of personal merit, or obscure origin a matter of personal reproach. A man who is not ashamed of himself need not be ashamed of his early condition. It did happen to me to be born in a log cabin, raised among the snow-drifts of New Hampshire, at a period so early that when the smoke first rose from its rude chimney, and curled over the frozen hills, there was no similar evidence of a white man's habitation between it and the settlements on the rivers of Canada. Its remains still exist; I make it an annual visit; I carry my children to it, and teach them the hardships endured by the generations before them. I love to dwell on the tender recollections, the kindred ties, the early affections, and the narrations and incidents which mingle with all I know of this primitive family abode. I weep to think that none of those who inhabited it are now among the living, and if ever I fail in affectionate veneration for him who raised it and defended it against savage violence and destruction, cherished all domestic comforts beneath its roof, and through the fire and blood of seven years' revolutionary war, shrunk from no toil, no sacrifice, to serve his country, and to raise his children to a condition better than his own, may my name and the name of my posterity be blotted from the memory of mankind." Noble sentiments—worthy of being written in letters of gold.

But it is an interesting inquiry, and one that draws largely upon the imagination and excites, somewhat, our emotional nature; what will be the feelings, and who the participants in the *Third Centennial Celebration?* Will a single one present here to-day, be there? Not one! We shall all have gone to our rewards. When gone, will our names be remembered, and our memories be cherished? Or shall we be forgotten and no record or tradition, even, exist to tell that we have lived—and that we have lived *here?* Let the history of that day, as *it* only can, decide. But thanks to Ancient Woodbury's Historian, Wm. Cothren, Esq., the names of our fathers as well as of many of us *will be perpetuated* and transmitted to generations yet unborn.

Before closing, Sir, I wish to say, briefly, that many with whom we were formerly acquainted, and with whom we were pleasantly and somewhat intimately associated either in the duties or business transtions of life, "have fallen asleep."

While we cherish and *revere* their memories, still our respect and affiliation for the succeeding generation is neither abated nor abatable. And we are ready to say of the State in general, and of Woodbury in particular—*Connecticut forever.*

I am now prepared to offer the following sentiment:

THE TOWN IN WHICH WE WERE BORN.—As soon "can a woman forget her sucking child," as a man can forget the place of his nativity.

Gen. William Williams, of Norwich, Conn., Chairman of the Committee of Arrangements for the Centennial Celebration to be held at Norwich, on the 7th and 8th of September next, being introduced by the President, spoke nearly as follows:

MR. PRESIDENT:—At this late hour, without consuming the time in apologies, I come to respond to your call.

Permit me, Sir, to supply an omission in the address of the Hon. gentleman from Hartford, who so ably and appropriately addressed the audience, in announcing that the Poetess of Connecticut, (Mrs. Sigourney,) of whom he made honorable mention, is a native of Norwich—to them a matter of reciprocal pride.

Yesterday, Sir, I beheld for the first time your beautiful Alpine valley. On my arrival, hearing a person inquire for the Rev. Mr. Williams, and understanding his residence to be quite near, the thought struck me, he must be a cousin, and that on a Centennial Celebration, it was allowable and proper to look them up. I soon made myself known to him, and my reception satisfied me that he belonged to the old stock; and on inquiry, we find that for two generations, in our country, we had a common ancestry, and that in the third generation, where it branched off, the name of his ancestor has descended through the successive generations, in the line to which I belong, and that I bear his name. The Rev. Wm. Williams died at Hatfield, in 1741, in the 76th year of his age, and 56th of his ministry. This gentleman married the daughter of the Rev. Solomon Stoddard, of Northampton, and was consequently brother-in-law to the Rev. Anthony Stoddard, the pastor here of revered memory.

Mr. President, we are all the children of good old Connecticut, and whether we live on this side of the river, or the other, we are one in our love of her institutions. In my native County of New London, repose for six and for seven generations, the ashes of my paternal and maternal ancestors. A tree which has taken such root, may well send out its branches over the river, and thus permit us to commune on this occasion. There is another, and a yet tenderer sympathy, that made me wish to see your rural town. When I read, the last winter, in our local newspaper, the interesting obituary of one who had honored this the place of her birth, as well as her distant home, from whence her spirit went up to heaven, I wished to see Woodbury, and to say, Sir, that I too know the stricken heart of a bereaved father, for I mourn the death of my children.

There is still another tie why I have joined in your bi-centennial celebration. We have in prospect a like occasion in Norwich, on the 7th and 8th days of September, where, Sir, we shall be happy to welcome you with your honorable associates.

Permit me, Sir, in conclusion, to say, honor to Woodbury, and her successful celebration.

Rev. Robert G. Williams then read to the audience the following

PARTING LAY.

BY MISS HORTENSIA M. THOMAS, OF WOODBURY.

Fair "Dwelling in the Wood!" thy ample halls
To-day have opened wide their folded doors
To greet thy children,—their ancestral walls
Shall echo back the songs each glad heart pours.
To-day, no home outvies it, far or near;
Where is the land would claim to be thy peer?

Thy roof is purest azure, and thy walls
The wooded slopes that bound these pleasant vales;
These groves, with rocks enclosed, thy happy halls;
God's benison is on thy hills and dales.
Two centuries since, the hardy pioneer
Found, and rejoiced to find, such dwelling here.

Thousands of dwellings now, that, since those days,
Have reared their walls beneath the one great dome,
Send forth their sons and daughters, and the rays
Of Freedom's sun gild every happy home.
All meet as friends to-day—to-morrow, part:
Breathe, native soil! one blessing from thy heart;
Speak in the breeze that doth these leaflets stir,
And deign to make me thine interpreter.

Soft and low, soft and low,
A whisper comes from the soil:
"What! ask ye a blessing? already blest,
In your evening pleasure's quiet zest,
In the peaceful dreams of your nightly rest,
The meed of your daily toil."

Wildly sweet, wildly sweet,
The tree-tops echo the tone,
Borne aloft by their branches waving high,
And wafted away towards the azure sky,
Enraptured each ear, and enchained each eye,
By Nature, and her alone.

" Truly blest, truly blest,
In the memories of the past;
Ye know that your fathers, a noble race,
Their blessing left to their dwelling-place;
Their names shall the page of History grace,
As long as these mountains last.

" Wake the harp, wake the lyre,
For the men of that earlier day.
They were daring of heart, they were strong of hand;
Their watch-word was 'God and our native land!'
They are now enrolled in the heavenly band;
They are blest, they are blest, for aye!

" Wake the harp, waken lyre,
For their 'children's children' stand
Where in days of old the 'Fathers' trod,
Ye have kept the vows that were made to God,
Where those 'Fathers' knelt on yonder sod—
God bless you, my noble band!

" Wander far, wander long,
My children, it gives me no pain;
For the brooklet that murmurs through this vale
Is like the stream of the southern tale,—
Who drinks of its waters can never fail
To come back for a draught again.

" Childhood's voice, childhood's mirth,
E'er pleasant, thrice pleasant here;
For, when gray-haired men, they'll recall this day,
And I know their children will cease their play,
To learn where the 'Fathers' knelt to pray,
While the olden tales they hear.

" Sunset hour, sunset hour—
It hastens my parting song.
'Twas *a good old custom*, that set of sun
Should smile her last upon labor done,—
I am listening now for the sunset gun:
'Good night!' to this joyous throng."

———

And I, too, bid "Good night!"—I've tried to tell,
What to each heart, I ween, is better told,
By myriad voices, Nature's songs that swell,—
So may it be until the world grows old.
May human hearts thrill to these murmurs sweet,
Till, on the river's brink, the angels' feet
Shall wait to guide them to the realms of light,
And loving lips shall speak the last "Good night!"

Rev. C. Trowbridge Woodruff then read, with admirable effect, the closing poem of the occasion, written by Mrs. Ann S. Stephens, the distinguished authoress of New York, a native of Ancient Woodbury:—

A POEM

By Mrs. Ann S. Stephens, written for the second centennial celebration at Woodbury:

We have met—we have met, by the graves of our sires,
Where the forest once reddened with war council fires,
Where the smoke of the wigwam, while curling on high,
Left its bloom on the hemlock,—its cloud on the sky.

Let us turn from the brightness of this happy hour,
Two centuries back, when the savage held power,
From the Naugatuck, sweeping through gorges and glen,
To the bright Housatonic and onward again.
Here a wilderness spread in its wildness and gloom,
Revealed by the starlight of dogwood in bloom,
And the broad rivers ran in the flickering shade,
Which the pine trees and cedars alternately made.
Here the chiefs gathered wild in their gorgeous array,
And their war-path was red at the dawning of day
Along the broad plain where light lingers clear,
Came the crack of the rifle—the leap of the deer.

When the leaves of the oak were all downy and red,
And the wild cherry blossoms were white overhead,
When the buds and the sap of the maple were sweet,
And the child lay asleep on the moss at her feet,
Here the squaw sat at work in the cool of the trees,
While her lord roamed at will, or reclined at his ease,—
This—this is the picture all savagely grand,
Which our forefathers found when they sought out this land.

The contract was honest our ancestors made
When they found the red warriors lords of the shade;
They came not to wrangle or fight for the sod,
But armed with the law and the blessing of God,
With the gold they had won by privation and toil,
They purchased a right to the rivers and soil.
Then their cabins were built, and they planted the corn,
Though the warwhoop soon answered the blast of the horn,
And the sound of the axe as it rang through the wood
But challenged a contest of carnage and blood.
Still, upward and onward in peril of life
They planted our homesteads with labor and strife,
For labor is mighty, and courage is grand,
When it conquers the foe as it toils with the hand.
While the war-cry resounded from valley and hill,
The smoke of the fallow rose steady and still;
If a cabin was burnt on the hills or the plain,
A score of stout hearts piled the logs up again.
If famine appeared, it was not to one roof,
For charity then had its power and its proof;
No mortar stood empty while one teemed with corn,
For of danger and want is true brotherhood born.
Thus our forefathers worked, and our forefathers won
The wealth we inherit from father to son,
Till their heads grew as white as the snow when it lies
On the pine branches lifted half way to the skies,
And they laid themselves down in the ripeness of years,
While a new generation baptized them with tears.
While the meeting-house, crowned with its belfry and spire,
Takes rose-tints from dawn—from the sunset its fire,—
While our homesteads are built, where the log cabin stood,
And our fields ripen grain to the verge of the wood.—
We ask for no trophies to tell of their deeds,
No thunder of cannon, nor tramping of steeds,
For each wild flower that springs to the smile of its God,
Has written their virtues abroad on the sod.

We have met—we have met in the bloom of the year,
The first glow of summer encircles us here;
The sunshine is warm on the ripening fruit,
And the whip-poor-will sings when the robin is mute;

Our mills as they toil through their burden of grain,
Send over the waters a mellow refrain.
While the wind whispers low as it whispered to them,
And sways the pale rose on its delicate stem,
Our souls as they feel the melodious thrill,
Send up a thanksgiving more exquisite still,
And our fathers might bend from their heaven of bliss,
To smile on a scene of rejoicing like this.

Rev. C. T. Woodruff, Rector of St. Paul's Church, Woodbury, then said the concluding prayer, as follows:—

"Our Father who art in heaven, hallowed be Thy name, Thy kingdom come, Thy will be done on earth as it is done in heaven. Give us this day our daily bread. And forgive us our trespasses as we forgive those who trespass against us. And lead us not into temptation; but deliver us from evil. Amen."

"O Lord, who hast taught us that all our doings, without charity, are nothing worth; send thy Holy Ghost, and pour into our hearts that most excellent gift of charity, the very bond of peace, and of all virtues; without which, whosoever liveth is counted dead before thee: Grant this for thine only Son Jesus Christ's sake. Amen."

"O God, who art the blessed and only Potentate, the King of kings and Lord of lords; the Almighty Ruler of nations; we adore and magnify thy glorious name for all the great things which thou hast done for us.

We render thee thanks for the goodly heritage which thou hast given us; for the civil and religious privileges which we enjoy; and for the multiplied manifestations of thy favor towards us. Grant that we may show forth our thankfulness for these thy mercies, by living in reverence of thy almighty power and dominion, in humble reliance on thy goodness and mercy, and in holy obedience to thy righteous laws. Preserve, we beseech thee, to our country, the blessings of peace; restore them to nations deprived of them; and secure them to all the people of the earth.

May the kingdom of the Prince of Peace come; and, reigning in the hearts and lives of men, unite them in holy fellowship; that so their only strife may be, who shall show forth, with most humble and holy fervor, the praises of Him who hath loved them, and made them kings and priests unto God. We implore thy blessing on all in legislative, judicial and executive authority, that they may have grace, wisdom, and understanding, so to discharge their duties as most effectually to promote thy glory, the interests of true religion and virtue, and the peace, good order, and welfare of this State and nation. Continue, O Lord, to prosper our institutions for the promotion of sound learning, the diffusion of virtuous education, and the advancement of Christian truth, and of the purity and prosperity of thy Church; change, we beseech thee, every evil heart of unbelief; and shed the quickening influences of thy Holy Spirit on this community, and on all the people of this land. Save us from the guilt of abusing the blessings of prosperity to luxury and licentiousness, to irreligion and vice; lest we provoke thee, in just judgment, to visit our offences with a rod, and our sins with scourges. Imprint on our hearts, we beseech thee, a deep and habitual sense of this great truth, that the only security for the continuance of the blessings which we enjoy, consists in our acknowledgment of thy sovereign and gracious Providence, and in humble and holy submission to the Gospel of thy Son Jesus Christ. And, while thy unmerited goodness to us, O God of our salvation, leads us to repentance, may we offer ourselves, our souls and bodies, a living sacrifice to thee, who hast preserved and redeemed us, through Jesus Christ our Lord. Amen."

"O God, whose days are without end, and whose mercies can not be numbered, make us all, we beseech thee, deeply sensible of the shortness and uncertainty of human life; and let thy Holy spirit lead us through this vale of misery, in holiness and righteousness, all the days of our lives: That, when we shall have served thee in our generation, we may be gathered unto our fathers, having the testimony of a good conscience; in the communion of the Catholic Church; in the confidence of a certain faith; in the comfort of a reasonable, religious and holy hope; in favor with thee, our God, and in perfect charity with all the world: All which, we ask, through Jesus Christ our Lord. Amen."

"The grace of our Lord Jesus Christ, and the love of God, and the fellowship of the Holy Ghost, be with us all, evermore. Amen."

Rev. Philo Judson, an aged clergyman of Rocky Hill, Conn., a native of Woodbury, after making the following remarks, pronounced the benediction, and the great assembly broke up, to meet no more on a similar occasion, within our beautiful valley:

Mr. President:—This is a glorious and interesting day to Woodbury. I am proud to say that I am a descendant of the Pilgrim fathers.

I have attended celebrations before, but never one equal to this. It excels all that have been held in this State. I have been informed by those who were present at the Litchfield County Celebration, August 13th and 14th, 1851, that it was not equal to this in point of interest, though that was a *County* Celebration. When Woodbury takes hold of any subject or enterprise, it moves forward, and excels others.

Woodbury, in the reputation and elevation of character of its inhabitants, excels any other town in the State, of the same population. She has produced more great literary men. Her voice, influence, and power have been felt in the halls of Congress, and Courts of justice.

Look at our Smiths, Benedicts, Shermans, Minors, Strongs, Judsons, Phelpses, and Marshalls.

Look at our Beers. An anecdote may show something of his character when a lad.

A lady remarked, when young, she was in the same class at school. When Beers was not there, she could keep the head; but when that plague, Seth P. Beers, came, I knew I must lose it, as he was the best *speller*, and would beat all the others in the school. We might know that he would do something in the world. But he was good in *figures*, and he has figured, as you have seen, here, on Litchfield hills, and all over the United States. Our *Beers* was brewed in Woodbury, and we sent him on to Litchfield Hill, where he *worked* and *foamed*, and did very much to make Litchfield what she was and now is.

In a masterly and skillful manner, he arranged and systematized the school fund, brought order out of confusion, and placed it in a situation to be managed with much less labor and expense than before his accession to office, following the good example of Hillhouse.

Our fathers enacted a law, that made it the duty of all the inhabitants to attend meeting on the Sabbath. If they were absent a particular number of Sabbaths, they must be called to account at the close of the year, and if absent too many Sabbaths, were fined five dollars. Jehu Minor and others were in the habit of riding on each Saturday, towards night, through the neighborhood, and letting the people know the Sabbath was approaching, announcing to them that they must lay aside their work and worldly concerns by sunset, take their Bibles, and on the Sabbath, go to meeting.

I wish we had Jehu's now to go through the length and breadth of our towns, calling upon the people to prepare for the Sabbath, and be in the Sanctuary on the Lord's day.

As soon as the people began to neglect the place of worship on the Sabbath, iniquity increased a hundred fold.

This morning we met for prayer at Bethel Rock. My friends, my feelings and emotions were such as language cannot describe. We stood on sacred and holy ground. There our Pilgrim fathers and mothers worshiped on the Sabbath for about eight years, during the summer season. The overhanging rock, as you saw, is perhaps 300 feet long, and very high. Our fathers, seated by this rock, would to some extent be shielded from the storms. Sentinels were placed on the top of the rock, so as to give the alarm if the Indians approached. There was a stone pulpit, as you saw. O! what prayers were there offered by our fathers. Prayer meetings have been held there, more or less, ever since. In 1811, I attended a prayer meeting with Dr. Azel Backus, Dr. Bennet Tyler, Dr. Lyman Beecher, Rev. Messrs. Clark, Harrison, and others. It was one of uncommon interest and solemnity—we wrestled with God in prayer.

Are we now prepared to receive a blessing from the God of our fathers? And shall we now so look up to God by faith, that our souls shall be baptized anew with the Holy Ghost, the great principles of our fathers be revived, and all of us consecrate ourselves anew unto God? Do we not feel that God is now with us by his special presence and Spirit? We believe that numbers of you feel this. Let us carry from this place the fire of heaven, and the spirit of our Saviour.

Woodbury has produced more great and eminent men than any other town of equal size. Dr. Dwight of Yale College remarked, that Hon. Nathaniel Smith's native talent was superior to that of any man he ever met. He had not his equal in this State—some say, not his equal or superior in New England.

This has been a glorious celebration. Even our friend, Hon. Charles Chapman, of Hartford, comes here to share in the glory, trying to claim some relationship here. We had supposed he had popularity and glory enough in Hartford for any one man.

But he labored very hard, as you have seen, to make out that he was the *great-grandson* of *somebody* in Woodbury! I do not know but he made it out, because he will make out *anything* he undertakes.

But while listening to his spicy, eloquent, and able speech, I believe we should have been willing to adopt him as a *grandson*. At the next centennial celebration, they will probably be willing to adopt him as a *son!*

The Historical Address by William Cothren, your able historian, was very learned, interesting, eloquent, and instructive. He is deserving of much credit, and has done immense service to the community in giving us the History of Woodbury. It is an able work, and must have required much persevering research. It is read with deep interest by those away from Woodbury. Many lay it on their tables, next to their Bibles. It is read by those that are not descendants, with great interest. It is a very popular work among intelligent and literary men. Its interest will increase as time passes on. In fifty or one hundred years from this time, it will be read with tenfold more interest than now, even in Woodbury. It will go down to generations yet unborn, and be considered as one of the most interesting of histories. Cothren's name will be immortal—remembered as long as time shall endure. Many will rise up, and call him blessed!

Philo M. Trowbridge is deserving of much credit for collecting and preserving facts, and assisting in the several historical works. He will receive a blessing, and the community will never forget him.

Woodbury has sent forth more ministers than any other town within my knowledge. Nearly eighty heralds of the cross have descended from the loins of the first William Judson. Many of them have borne his honored surname, and many others have borne the honorable names of the female alliances. They have preached the Gospel far and wide, and their labors have been greatly blessed. None can estimate the great and good results which have arisen from the labors of the ministers who have gone out from Ancient Woodbury. Eternity alone can unfold them.

We are now about to pronounce the blessing. The solemn moment has arrived, and we are now about to part, to meet no more in this world.

Are you all now prepared to receive the blessing of salvation, through the atoning blood of Christ? Will you now all go forth determined to carry out the great principles of your Pilgrim fathers, and make sacrifices to save souls and bless the world wherever you go? What is your response?

Are you now ready to receive the blessing of Heaven?—And now, may the grace of our Lord and Saviour Jesus Christ, the love of God, and the communion and indwelling of the Holy Spirit, be with you all, now and ever. Amen and Amen.

LETTERS, ODES, &c.

Previous to the close of the exercises at the Stand, William Cothren, Chairman of the General Committee, announced in its behalf, that a considerable number of letters, odes and toasts, were in the hands of the Committee, which could not be read for want of time, but that they would all appear in the book of the proceedings of the celebration. In accordance with this promise, they are here recorded with many thanks to their distinguished authors.

From Hon. John Lorimer Graham, of New York, a native of London, England, and grandson of Ancient Woodbury.

NEW YORK, July 2, 1859.

WILLIAM COTHREN, ESQ.,
Chairman of Committee, &c., Woodbury, Conn.

DEAR SIR,—I accepted with great pleasure your kind invitation to be present at the Historical Celebration of the Second Centennial Anniversary of the first exploration of the Town of Woodbury, &c., on the 4th and 5th inst., and it is now a source of deep regret that the sudden illness of one of my family prevents my attendance.

I highly approve of these demonstrations; they are just tributes to the memories of our patriotic and virtuous ancestors; they contribute to perpetuate the knowledge of their energy, enterprise and morals; distinguishing characteristics of the race of men who first peopled "*the land of steady habits;*" they teach to the rising generation a duty which should be constantly inculcated; veneration for our progenitors who, in their eventful lives, portrayed the highest attributes of man.

During fourteen years of my youth, I accompanied my revered father in an annual visit he made to his aged mother, in Southbury. It was my father's custom to take me on the morning after our arrival to the rural spot "where the rude forefathers of the hamlet sleep," and there standing beside the tombs of his venerated father and grandfather, he would discourse of their virtues and piety, and, pointing to the tablets he had himself erected to their memories, he pathetically enjoined it upon me to imitate the example of these excellent sires,—especially adverting to the holy life of that eminent man of God, his noble grandfather, "*John Graham, D. D.,*" whose name he bore, and who for *fifty-four* years had been the spiritual teacher of the people of Southbury.

The impressions produced by these solemn scenes have not been and never can be effaced, and they had a powerful influence, as will your celebration, upon the hearts of all true sons of "Ancient Woodbury," in causing me ever to revere, through life, these departed worthies whom you assemble to honor.

It is nearly half a century since these scenes occurred. You can realize what an intense interest I have felt in again visiting that sacred spot, and how great is my disappointment in not being able to participate in your celebration. I should with pleasure have offered some extemporaneous remarks, as requested by your committee, and, to the extent of my ability, contributed to enliven the joyous occasion.

Let it be remembered that none who here attend your festive scene can be present at another similar celebration; all of us before that time will have passed away; but I trust that while we live we will cherish a fond and reverential recollection of our honored forefathers, and that their memories may be embalmed in the hearts of their latest posterity—who should emulate their noble example and hold it up for imitation to their children's children.

I beg to present to the committee the accompanying sentiment, which I should have offered had I been present at their festival.

With best respects and thanks to your colleagues of the committee, and with renewed assurances of esteem,

I remain, Dear Sir,

Very sincerely your friend,

JOHN LORIMER GRAHAM.

William Cothren, Esq.—The Historian of "*Ancient Woodbury*," whose industry, accuracy and impartiality, have produced a most interesting and faithful narrative and truthful history, entitling him to the lasting gratitude of all the descendants of the first settlers of the soil which is endeared to them by recollections as sacred as they are imperishable.

Given by John Lorimer Graham, of New York.

From Hon. Charles J. Hill, of Rochester, New York, a native of Woodbury.

Rochester, June 28, 1859.

Gentlemen:—With gratitude I received your cordial invitation to attend your interesting celebration, and most sincerely regret that I am now obliged to relinquish the pleasing anticipation I had indulged of being present and responding in person.

I am a native of the *present* town of Woodbury, and trace my paternal and maternal ancestry, all residents of *Ancient Woodbury*, nearly back to its first settlement.

From twelve to sixteen years of age, I was a member of the family of one whose name was honored throughout the State, and whose memory, as my early patron, is embalmed in the deep recesses of my heart.

The lovely valley and grounds, skirted by "Bethel Rock" and the more distant hills, the pleasant streams, and all the delightful scenery of Central Woodbury, were entirely familiar to me, and constituted my *play-ground*.

But what made a more indelible impression on my mind, was the presence of the great and good men who then resided there and within the limits of Ancient Woodbury. Men of strong intellect, high cultivation, eminently pure morals, whose mission it was to *honor* the memory of as honorable and virtuous an ancestry as ever blessed any community; by cultivating their virtues, and fostering the institutions of religion and literature, and handing them down in their purity with their attendant blessings to the present generation.

It is a pleasing reflection, that in the picturesque valley of Woodbury, commenced the first settlement of Litchfield County, so celebrated for the large number of eminent men she has sent out to settle and adorn all our new states and territories, no less than for the preeminent position she maintains at home, in reference to all the institutions which enlighten and bless a people.

Is it strange that the present generation should delight to honor the memory of that noble band of emigrants who first traversed the wilderness to the site of Woodbury; men of indomitable enterprise, lofty patriotism, and devoted piety?

How could I fail to entertain a high veneration for the past generations of that locality, when it was my privilege near half a century ago, although but a lad, to be familiar with the *faces*, and *forms*, and *characters* of such men as the Rev. Messrs. Benedict, Wildman, Backus, Tyler, Porter, and others, in the ministry, and Messrs. Smith, Benedict, Minor, Strong, Phelps, and others, in the legal profession? If such were some of the *professional* men of those days, what was the character of others in the various professions which I cannot ennumerate,—and what kind of men were the *laity* among whom they lived? May I not say as a general remark, that they were the upright, intelligent, good men, who *deserved* the society and intercourse of the eminent men just alluded to?

Ancient Woodbury contributed liberally in men for the defence of our common country. Many of us whose ancestry resided there, back to the early settlement of the town, can say that the lives of not a few of them were sacrificed in the armies of the *old French* and *Revolutionary* wars.

She has done much for other sections of the country, in sending out emigrants, such as are ever wanted to fill places of labor and high responsibility; men to adorn the various professions, to carry forward business enterprises, sustain good institutions, as well as to cope with the severest hardships of pioneer life.

Forty three years ago I came to Rochester a young adventurer. This present city of *fifty thousand*, then had a population of three hundred; among whom I found a small representation from "Ancient Woodbury;" say two men, one of whom lately deceased, the other still living here; both of whom I must refer to again.

Although the numbers furnished by Ancient Woodbury to this locality, have not been large, yet among them have been from the first settlement of the place to the present time, men of high position; some of them in the first rank as professional gentlemen, legislators and *philanthropists*.

One (Ruluff D. Hannahs, from Bethlem,) was among the early pioneers of Western New York and Rochester; the first exporter (it is believed,) of *Genesee Flour* direct to New England by teams; one of the first to transport produce down the Genesee Valley to Rochester by boats; the first to run a boat over Genesee Falls, saving himself by swimming to the shore; and the last person who passed the celebrated "Carthage Bridge," 196 feet high, with a loaded team, just previous to its fall. He is now enjoying a "green old age," with a competency and the esteem of our citizens.

Permit me to express my enthusiastic approval of the action of your citizens on the last "Fourth of July," in resolving to hold a "Centennial Celebration."

The thousands who will be there, and the other thousands whose *hearts* only will be with you, will, I trust, be richly rewarded in the elevating and ennobling inspirations of the occasion.

How can we fail to be reminded of our worthy ancestry by a thousand incidents and mementos; and after long years of absence, looking again upon few of their *faces*, but many of their former abodes, or in silent sadness reading inscriptions upon the monuments which mark the places where their *ashes* repose.

Names of persons highly esteemed in life for varied talents and virtues; others distinguished for their eccentricities; some for their eminent piety; some for their wealth; some for their great intellect; others for their unbending integrity; (I hope none for lack of it,) last, but not least, others for their overpowering eloquence, will be brought back to the memory with impressive vividness.

Thus will the memory, perhaps the concience, be quickened to a retrospect of the instructions, warnings and maxims which multitudes had received from the lips of those to whom the present and future generations are so greatly indebted. Nor is this indebtedness felt merely by the present inhabitants of Ancient Woodbury, but in all sections of our country are to be found emigrants, who, with grateful hearts, and oft with tearful eye, would rejoice in any opportunity to testify to the salutary influence of their worthy ancestors. Many of this class who will not be present at your jubilee, will nevertheless receive the record of your doings, which they will ponder with intense interest, and with unwonted emotions tell the story to their children.

Respectfully and sincerely yours,

CHAS. J. HILL.

P. M. Trowbridge, N. B. Smith, John C. Ambler, Esquires, and others, Committee.

From Hon. John Sherman, member of Congress from Ohio, a grandson of Woodbury :—

Washington, Feb. 24, 1859.

My Dear Sir :—Since the receipt of your circular-note, I have been debating with myself whether I could accept your invitation. If it is possible I will do so. Nothing could give me greater pleasure than to join in the celebration of the Two Hundredth Anniversary of the Exploration of Ancient Woodbury. Though born in Ohio, I have been led to respect and cherish the local history of old Connecticut, the birth-place and home of all my ancestors for two hundred years. If, therefore, other engagements will allow, I will surely attend.

Very truly yours,

W. Cothren, Esq. JOHN SHERMAN.

Sentiment by Hon. Royal Ralph Hinman, of Hartford, a native of Southbury :—

"May the present descendants of Woodbury become as great and good as were their ancestors, the first settlers."

Sentiment by SHERMAN TUTTLE, Esq., of Southbury:—

"Our honored ancestors: may we imitate their virtues, and ever cherish their memories with tender emotions."

From SAMUEL FULLER, D. D., of Andover, Mass.:—

ANDOVER, MASS., Feb. 14, 1859.

My Dear Sir:—I thank you and the Committee for their hearty invitation to be present at your proposed meeting next July. I can only now say, that I shall come if possible, and shall take the liberty of inviting my only sister, Mrs. Lester, of Rensselaerville, who was born on the south side of Judson Lane, a little east of the Pomperaug, to accompany me. Such a gathering I have long desired, and I pray the Lord may allow me to be one of the great assembly.

Most truly yours,

S. FULLER.

From Col. HENRY STODDARD, of Dayton, Ohio, a native of Woodbury:—

DAYTON, June 29, 1859.

P. M. TROWBRIDGE, Esq.,

Dear Sir:—Several years since I addressed a letter to the late Judge Phelps, in answer to one from him, requesting information in relation to Major Amos Stoddard, who was a native of Woodbury, which might enable Mr. Cothren to take some notice of Major Stoddard in his history of Woodbury, which he did in very favorable terms. In my letter to Judge Phelps, (which Mr. Cothren may still have,) I stated the manner in which Major Stoddard's military chest and papers came into my possession, and I alluded to a small manuscript volume of miscellaneous productions of his pen, and amongst others, a sermon in verse.

Under the impression that the novelty of such a production from a man of a military character would not be inappropriate to such an occasion as your Anniversary celebration, and might amuse some of those who may be present on the fourth and fifth of July, and as its tone, and the sentiments it promulgates are not unfavorable to the character of its author, (a native of our old town,) my son has copied, and I herewith send it to you, to be disposed of as your Committee shall think proper.

I have up to this time had a lingering *hope* that I should be able to be with you on the fourth and fifth, but the causes which led me to the expression of the fears which I stated in my note to you on the 11th inst., still exist, and I shall not be able to make the visit to the place of my birth, which would afford me so much pleasure.

I assure you and your Committee, my dear sir, that it would afford me great satisfaction to be with you and the few of my early acquaintances who are still living, though I fear that after an absence of more than half a century, I should find their number so small, I should indeed be a stranger. Your jubilee, and the proceedings indicated in your circular, cannot fail to be interesting to all who shall be permitted to witness them, and especially to those like myself, who have long been absent from the scenes of their childhood.

Accept, dear sir, for yourself and the citizens of our ancient town, my acknowledgment for their kind remembrance of

Yours respectfully,

HENRY STODDARD.

P. M. Trowbridge, Esq., Chairman, &c.

A Sermon. By Maj. Amos Stoddard, a native of Woodbury.

"Why art thou so full of heaviness, O my soul, and why art thou so disquieted within me? put thy trust in God!"—*Psalm* 42 : 6, 7.

Why drops the head? Why languishes the eye?
What means the flowing tear, and swelling sigh?
Where are the lenient med'cines to impart
Their balmy virtue to a bleeding heart?
Fruitless are all attempts of kind relief,
To mix her cordial, and allay my grief.
So strong my anguish—so severe my pain,
Weak is philosophy, and reason vain;
Their rules like fuel make my passions glow,
Quicken each pang, and point the sting of woe.
Imagination strives to please the eye,
While dark'ning tempests skirt the floating sky—
And fancy no sweet thoughts can now suggest
To lull the raging tumult of my breast.
In vain chaste mirth invites—or friendship calls,
Wit dies a jest, and conversation palls;
The works of art and nature dull appear,
And each obtruding thought creates despair—
No scenes amuse me which amus'd before,
And what delighted once delights no more,
The wide creation beautiful appears,
And nature's aspect a rich verdure wears!

Yet still her bloom with sickening eyes I see
And all her luxury is lost to me.
The budding plants of variegated hue,
The blossoms op'ning with the morning dew—
The vernal breeze which gently fans the flowers,
The laughing meadows and distilling showers—
The enamel'd garden where the works of art
Give strength to nature—and fresh charms impart—
Where gaudy pinks and blushing roses bloom,
Rich in array, and fragrant with perfume—
Where Flora smiling sees her offspring vie,
To spread their beauties, and regale the eye—
Alas! all in vain with charms united glow,
To deck the scene, or gild the face of woe.
So when the morning lark ascending sings,
While joy attunes her voice, and mounts her wings—
Tho' to her cheerful notes the hills reply,
And warbling music dances round the sky—
Still in her strains no pleasing charms I find,
No sweet enchantment to compose my mind;
In vain the sun his gaudy pride displays,
No genial warmth attends his fervent rays,
So when his absent light the moon supplies,
And planets glitter to enrich the skies—
No gleam of comfort from their lustre flows,
No harbinger of peace, or calm repose;
But gloomy vapors o'er the night prevail,
And pestilence is spread in ev'ry gale!
Thus weakened by a gradual decay,
With sighs I pass the melancholy day;
Prepare to drink life's bitter draught with pain,
And thirsty still, alas! I taste again!
But stop! O man, thy plaintive strains suppress,
With Christian patience learn to acquiesce—
The instructive voice of reason calmly hear,
And let religion check the starting tear.
What e'er the will of Providence assigns,
'Tis infidelity alone repines,
For those who trust in God disdain to grieve,
And what our Father sends, with joy receive;

Whose sharp convictions testify his love,
And certain blessings in the end will prove,
Who sees how man would err without control,
Afflicts the body to improve the soul;
By power on man he lays what man deserves,
And by chastisement—thus the whole preserves,
So that though low'ring skies and strengthening gales,
Should raise a mighty storm, and rend the skies—
Yet if calm reason at the helm preside,
My little barque will stem the frowning tide—
And adverse currents shall at last convey,
The shattered vessel to the realms of day!
Thus satisfied—how rash it is for man,
When under God's correction to complain!
My soul with sad disquietude opprest,
Directs her flight to heav'n in search of rest—
And refuge take—(which peace at last will bring)
Beneath the shadow of th' Almighty's wing.
On him I fix my mind, and place my trust,
A being infinitely wise and just—
And if his Providence some beams create
To brighten the complexion of my fate—
My thankful tribute to his throne I'll raise,
In joyful hymns of gratitude and praise;
But should indulgence suit not his designs
Who evil into happiness refines—
Let due submission make my burden light,
And constant think—"Whatever is—is right!"
Then be thou not disquieted my soul,
Have lively faith—and that shall make thee whole.
When heav'n inflicts—with calmness bear the stroke,
Since to repine, is only to provoke;
Learn to adore the justice of thy God,
And kiss the sacred hand which holds the rod,
That sacred hand which first the heart explores,
Probes ev'ry wound, and searches all the sores;
Then the right medicine properly applies
To cleanse the part where deep infection lies!
Hear this, thou coward man—nor dread the smart,
Which tho' it stings, will purify the heart;

For resignation will promote the cure,
And tho' the means are sharp—the end is sure.
Since then afflictions are thro' mercy sent,
To be of good the happy instrument;
Since for the noblest ends they are designed,
To form the judgment and improve the mind;
To curb our passions—to direct our love,
To awe mankind, and speak a God above;
O may I view them with religious eye,
Without a murmur and without reply.
Hence shall I taste the sweets which evils bring,
And seek the honey while I feel the sting;
Hence shall I learn the bitter cup to bless,
And drink it as a draught of happiness;
A wholesome potion which—tho' mix'd with gall,
May still preserve my life—my soul—my all!
So though the promis'd fruit should fail the vine,
The fig-tree sicken, and its bloom decline;
The labor of the olive be in vain,
And flocks infested, perish on the plain;
Tho' corn and oil, and wine at once decrease,
The fields grow barren, and the harvests cease;
The baffled hinds their fruitless toil deplore,
And vales uncheerful—"laugh and sing no more,"
Yet still with gladness would I serve the Lord,
Adore his wisdom, and obey his word!
Hear thou, O God! regard a suppliant's prayer,
Soothe all my pangs, and save me from despair.
Illuminate my soul with gladsome rays,
And tune my voice to thy eternal praise,—
Dispel the clouds of darkness from my eyes,
And make me know that to be good is wise.
Let christian precepts all my soul employ,
And be not more my duty than my joy;
Let conscience void of art and free from guile,
Still in my bosom innocently smile;
Her cheerful beams will gild the face of fate,
And make me happy in whatever state.
Hence shall I learn my talent to improve,
If poor by patience, and if rich by love;

If fortune smiles, let me be virtue's friend,
And where I go, let charity attend;
Within my bosom, let compassion dwell,
To soften all the woes which others feel;
T' assuage by kind relief affliction's sighs,
And wipe the bursting tears from widows' eyes;
To feed the hungry—the distress'd to cheer,
The needy succor, and the feeble rear!
Hence shall my mind inflamed with public good,
Unshaken stand where plenty rolls her flood!
Hence shall I scorn temptation's gilded bait,
Look with disdain upon the pomp of state,—
And by humility be truly wise,
Learn vice to shun, and grasp the christian's prize.
But if it be thy blessed will to spread
Clouds of thick darkness, low'ring o'er my head,
Let me have grace to know in my distress
I still to thee may have a free access,—
And be an heir (tho' all the world should frown,)
Of heav'nly glory and a future crown.
From these reflections true contentment flows,—
Contentment such as grandeur seldom knows;
Hence in the lonely cot a relish springs,
Above the taste of courts, and pride of kings!
Thus in the flood of wealth be thou my guide,
And steer my course 'twixt av'rice and pride,
Or in the ebb of fortune teach my mind
To know its duty, and to be resign'd.
Prepare me to receive or good or ill,
As the result of thy almighty will;
Thy will whose chief design and gen'ral plan
Tend to promote to happiness of man!
Be ev'ry sensual appetite suppress,
Nor the least taint be lurking in my breast;
Let steady reason my affections guide,
And calm content set smiling at my side;
Teach me with scorn to view the things below
As gaudy phantoms and an empty show.
But fix my mind upon the things above,
As the sole object of a christian's love!
Make me reflect on my eternal home,
A dying Saviour and a life to come;

Then shall I—as instructed by thy Son,
In ev'ry station say—"thy will be done!"
March 18, 1791.

From Hon. THOMAS B. BUTLER, of Norwalk, Judge of the Superior Court.

BRIDGEPORT, Feb. 11th, 1859.

FRIEND COTHREN:—I thank you cordially for your invitation. I do not expect to be in this section of the country, at the time named. If I am, I will be at Woodbury. Having once resided there, and having warm recollections of kindness and attention from many of its living citizens, I should enjoy the occasion.

Very truly yours,
THOS. B. BUTLER.

From Miss JULIA E. SMITH and sister, of Glastenbury, Conn., friends and ardent lovers of the history of Ancient Woodbury.

To the Honorable Committee appointed for the Celebration of the Two Hundredth Anniversary of the Exploration of Ancient Woodbury.

As daughters of Ancient Woodbury, in right of our late mother, who was born and bred within her limits, and who received an education there, which would do honor to the young ladies of the present age, we would make our most grateful acknowledgments to the honorable committee for their circular of invitation, and programme of the proceedings on that memorable occasion. It is with much regret that under our present circumstances, we cannot avail ourselves of the great privilege of once more meeting beloved friends, and beholding the faces of those we honor and respect, though not of our personal acquaintance. It is also no small sacrifice to our feelings, that we must be denied the pleasure of hearing the living voice of esteemed speakers, particularly of the eminent author of that most interesting History of Ancient Woodbury.

With heart-felt wishes for the prosperous termination of these two illustrious days, and that the sons of the birth-place of our maternal ancestors may so live as to do honor to their noble progenitors, and that her daughters may rise up and become a blessing to their age and generation, is the sincere desire of

Your obliged friends the descendants of Ancient Woodbury,
MISSES SMITH.

Glastenbury, June 27th, 1859.

From Hon. JOHN E. HINMAN, of Utica, New York, a native of Southbury:—

UTICA, May 17, 1859.

Messrs. Trowbridge, Bull, Judd, and others, Committee, &c.:

Gentlemen:—Your kind invitation of the 1st inst. to join your celebration of "The Two Hundredth Anniversary of the Exploration of Ancient Woodbury," by that noble band of pioneers who sought a refuge and a home, and contributed in no small degree to found an empire, was duly received.

Nothing could afford me greater pleasure than to unite with the good people of Woodbury in their proposed demonstration of honor, respect and gratitude for the memory of those who first explored and settled this ancient and favored town—a town renowned in the history of the Colony and State of Connecticut; a town which furnished its just (and I am proud to say, liberal,) quota of men and means in a glorious struggle for civil liberty and national independence.

At the mention of Woodbury, a thousand recollections and associations come upon the mind. There rest the hallowed remains of many generations of my ancestors; and there, too, reside many of their descendants, whom I greatly regard.

Age and infirmity will prevent me from being personally present at your celebration, but in heart and in spirit I am most cordially with you.

With many thanks for your kind attention, and best wishes and prayers for the welfare and happiness of the good people of "Ancient Woodbury," and wishing the world would follow their good example, I am, dear sir, most truly and respectfully yours,

JOHN E. HINMAN.

From R. F. TROWBRIDGE, Esq., of Syracuse, N. Y.

SYRACUSE, 10th July, 1859.

My dear Mr. Cothren:—I regretted that I was compelled to leave Woodbury without bidding you a good-by, although I deputized Mr. Trowbridge to do so for me. The interest and pleasure which it was my happy fortune to find in your classic and beautiful town, not only repaid me all my trouble in reaching that picturesque spot, but, believe me, dear sir, when I say it is the happiest recollection which my memory can present. The many interests and pleasures which were crowded into the brief space of time, and which were so unexpected by me, will serve to brighten many hours of cheerful retrospect in the years to come. I can now scarcely realize that it was not all a dream, a light and happy dream which flitted over my dull, daily working life, and left its ideal impressions upon my memory and my heart. I came among you a stranger; I left with many new tenants in my breast, whose worth and excellence have become already very dear to me.

I shall commence to-morrow to jot down for the compositors up stairs, some of the incidents and impressions which I received of the people, the ceremonies, the character and customs of the Puritan State. There has been hanging for years in my library a portrait of Gov. Trumbull, together with a Second Lieutenant's Commission issued by him; and often when I look at it, the remark of Washington comes to my memory: "That Gov. T. was always his forlorn hope; that he was the only person on whom he could draw at sight for men or munitions, *and the draft was never dishonored!*" I cannot now tell you where I learned it, but read it, or heard it from some authentic source.

I am under many obligations to you for your kind hospitalities, and the friendly interest you manifested toward me, even under the pressure of so much weight upon your attention. Be assured, my dear sir, that I fully appreciate it, and shall expect an opportunity of repaying it, as a matter of *my* right.

Please accept of my most sincere regard.

Very truly yours, R. F. TROWBRIDGE.

WM. COTHREN, Esq.

From JONATHAN KNIGHT, M. D., of New Haven, Conn., Professor in Yale College:—

NEW HAVEN, June 30, 1859.

To WM. COTHREN, Esq., Woodbury:

Dear Sir:—I received, a long time since, an invitation to attend the centennial celebration of the settlement of Woodbury, on the 4th prox., for which I beg to acknowledge my indebtedness. From the time I first learned that such a celebration was to be held, I have intended to be present at it. I might have availed myself of your invitation, and come as a guest, but suppose I can be there of right as one of Woodbury descent. My mother's grandfather was born in Woodbury. He was Rev. Benjamin Strong, the first clergyman of the Parish of Stanwich, where he officiated from 1735 to 1756. I have been able to learn very little concerning him, as the Church records of Stanwich were destroyed by fire a few years ago. I suppose he was the Benjamin Strong whose name is in the history of Woodbury as having been born in 1710.

I judge so merely from the identity of the name, and the correspondence of the time of his birth, with the probable age of the minister of Stanwich. I hope by further inquiries to find out something more about him. With much esteem, yours truly,

J. KNIGHT.

From Hon. ROYAL RALPH HINMAN, of Hartford, Conn., a native of Southbury:—

P. M. TROWBRIDGE, Esq.:

Dear Sir:—I informed you in my previous letter that I w uld write to you again, whether I would attend at Woodbury the 4th day of July, and you know nothing but ill health would prevent my being present at the celebration of so important, as well as pleasing, an event, of our own first ancestors in this country. I do not feel able to attend at Woodbury, which I very much regret.

The performances of the day will restore not to life, but to recollection, the ancient fathers of Woodbury, with their standing and biography, to their fifth, sixth, seventh, and some of the eighth generations; and the old cemetery will confirm the fact that they lived and died there. Rev. Zechariah Walker, who was the first Minister, and a principal cause of the settlement, will figure largely on this occasion, and Hon. Seth P. Beers, and others of his descendants will probably be present to hear the standing of their progenitor.

John Minor, (the son of Thomas, of Pequot,) the Interpreter of the Indian language, and Town Clerk of Stratford and Woodbury, a first settler; Capt. Wm. Curtiss, (Curtice) another important first settler, and a grantee of the town; Hon. Samuel Sherman, of Stratford, will not be forgotten on this day, as well as his son, Worshipful John Sherman, Joseph Judson, Senior, from Concord, Mass., a subscriber at Stratford, of the fundamental articles of the settlement, as was his son, John.

While the foregoing will be noticed at the meeting, as well as Col. Joseph Minor, Titus Hinman, (then young,) Hackaliah Preston, and his son William, and many others too numerous to mention; last, though not least, those of a later date, the Thompsons, Grahams, Benedicts, Stoddards, Smiths, Bacons, Phelpses, and others, will not be forgotten on this occasion. Most respectfully yours,

ROYAL R. HINMAN.

YONKERS, N. Y., June 26, 1859.

From Prof. Harvey P. Peet, LL. D., of New York, a native of Bethlem, and Professor in the Institution for the Deaf and Dumb, New York.

Institution for the Deaf and Dumb,
New York, June 30, 1859.

Gentlemen:—Though strongly tempted to avail myself of your kind invitation to meet with my old neighbors and townsmen, and their worthy descendants, to celebrate the second centenary of the exploration of Ancient Woodbury, I find that imperative official duties will deprive me of that gratification. I will, however, at least be with you in spirit, contributing, for the intellectual fruit of your pic-nic, a few thoughts and reminiscences, which, I trust, you will be in the mood to receive with friendly indulgence. And I anticipate to receive, in return, far better than I send, when I come to read the record of your sayings and doings on the occasion.

The large appetite of our ancestors for intellectual food, in their day hardly accessible except from the pulpit, is strikingly shown by the circumstance that it was the immediate cause of the founding of our ancient mother town. The Rev. Zachariah Walker continued his sermon so long, that he overpassed the two hours allowed for the occupation of the meeting-house in Stratford, by agreement with the other division of the Church. Thus compelled to remove into the wilderness, or stint themselves in spiritual and intellectual nourishment, they took care in their "fundamental articles," to reserve ample "accommodations for ye ministry," and "a parsell of land for ye incouraging a schoole, that learning may not be neglected to children." And let us add our prayers to those of the worthy Deacon Minor, when he kneeled upon Good Hill, just two centuries ago, the grand wilderness temple with its gray pillars and green canopy, towering above him, and before him the lovely valley of the Pomperaug, then first revealing its fertile intervals to Christian eyes—that the posterity of those founders, to the remotest generations, may never neglect the worship of God, their duty to their fellow men, or the training and schooling of their children.

Many and eloquent will be the voices of bards and orators among you, and fitting commemoration will, I know, be given to the rude virtues of the red men who once glided through the woods, not forgetting the love-lorn Waramaukeag, or that "potent prince," the Christian sachem, Weraumaug, at whose death-bed the Rev. Daniel Boardman had his great praying match with an Indian Powwow, by sheer energy and perseverance in prayer, vanquishing the devil-worshiper, and driving him into the Housatonic.

Such were our fathers, sturdy in work, potent in prayer, solicitous as early and as much to have a place of public worship, and provide schooling for their children, as to minister to the temporal wants of their families. Hence the public spirit of the New-Englanders, so largely manifested in churches, schools, and colleges.

As they hewed down the wilderness, its ancient inhabitants, fierce and untamable as they were, vanished after a few short but sharp struggles. The red men are gone, leaving no more enduring monuments than the heap of pebbles that marks the grave of a chieftain; for while degenerate Americans break off and carry away, the red men piously added stones to the monuments of the great, or the bed of shells, where clams and oysters had ministered, during uncounted generations, to the sustenance of a village. If, as some believe, their shades, instead of dwelling in their own happy hunting-grounds, yet linger around the scenes where their lives passed, how must the woods and rocks around you appear to anointed eyes populous with dark forms and mournful faces; and how will their spectral eyes flash up at the sight of your "Amateur Indian Encampment" on one of their ancient seats!

I am tempted to dwell a moment on the unselfish patriotism of our fathers, who, though enjoying peace in their own inland borders, went forth, leaving scarcely an able-bodied man behind, even to gather the corn, to peril their lives in defence of their countrymen in more exposed situations. Who can read, without a thrill of ancestral pride, of the eight hundred able-bodied men from one town of five thousand souls, who, like a Highland clan gathering to the summons of the fiery cross, left their safe and happy homes, to "moisten with their blood every battle-field," in the long and often doubtful struggle for independence? And while the younger and more hardy were bearing aloft the flag of their country at Long Island and White Plains, as afterward with better fortune at Bennington and Saratoga, those whom age or other causes exempted from regular service, enrolled themselves in a volunteer corps, each man providing himself with "a good gun, sword or bayonet, and cartridge box, for the defence of our invaluable rights and privileges, and promise to support the same with our lives and fortunes," as the agreement of the Bethlem volunteers reads,—in the last sentence emulating the lofty spirit of the signers of that immortal Declaration, that had then just gone forth to fill the public mind, and elevate the national feeling with the consciousness of a new nationality, destined to fulfill the famous prophecy of Berkely—

"Westward the course of Empire takes its way."

I will trust yet further to your indulgence, while I say a few words of the peculiar favor which my little native town of Bethlem received from the Great Head of the Church, in the succession of eminent pastors, such as has very seldom been vouchsafed to any one town. From the first formation of the society under Dr. Bellamy, in 1739, to the resignation of Mr. Langdon, in 1825, a period not much less than a century, this little town, among the hills, enjoyed with but brief cessations, the ministerial care of pastors, who, as theologians and preachers, and two of them as teachers, shone as stars of the first magnitude in the bright firmament of New England worthies. To Dr. Backus, the second pastor, I owe a more special tribute of gratitude, as under his ministry my first religious impressions were received, and in his school I took lessons in the art of teaching, in which he was so eminent. Of him it was said, that "when out of the pulpit he ought never to go in, and when in, he ought never to go out." In or out, however, he was as one of David's mighty men, and I may even say, that he "attained to the first three" of his time. The New Haven papers that announced the death of Dr. Dwight, remarked that three great pillars of the Church had just been removed—Dr. Dwight, Dr. Strong of Hartford, and Dr. Backus, whose deaths were all announced in one number of the paper.

The time has long since gone by, when the people of Ancient Woodbury were content with the currants that grew on the increase of a few twigs brought from a distant town by one of our mothers on horseback, or with mortars like the primitive contrivances of their "red brethren," to grind their corn. As our tastes become more fastidious with the means we have of indulging them, and you will be provided with intellectual as well as literal fruit, of the rarest native flavor, improved by scientific culture, and ripened by genial suns, I will offer no more of my crude currants or half-ground grain, but conclude with the hope that the occasion may be one of such unalloyed enjoyment, that the memory of it may endure in the homes of every child of Ancient Woodbury, at least till the time comes for another Centennial Gathering.

Very sincerely and faithfully, your fellow townsman,

HARVEY P. PEET.

Messrs. John C. Ambler, Wm. R. Harrison, Com. for Bethlem.

ODE.

BY MISS HORTENSIA M. THOMAS, OF WOODBURY.

From hill-side and mountain glen, hither ye come,
Oh! earth has no dearer spot,—welcome ye home!
Say, ye who have wandered far 'neath fairer skies,
Say where is the landscape as fair in your eyes?
Home, home, sweet, sweet home,
Oh, earth hath no dearer spot than home, sweet home!

We count none as strangers here, if they can claim
That love for their country, burns pure in its flame,
While mountains or rocky hills echo our song,
All—all the chorus join, the glad notes prolong.
Home, home, sweet, sweet home,
Oh, earth hath no dearer spot than home, sweet home!

Once more for your native hearths make the glad strain,
May peace spread her sheltering wings here not in vain,
And God grant our peaceful homes foster not pride,
But grace that shall lead to a home by His side.
Home, home, sweet, sweet home,
May we all to that mansion fair, be welcomed Home!

From Mrs. BETSEY T. A. WHITING, of Vermillionville, Illinois.

VERMILLIONVILLE, Ill., June 8, 1859.

GENTLEMEN :—Having received your kind invitation to attend the celebration of the exploration of Ancient Woodbury, on the 4th and 5th of July, 1859, I exceedingly regret that ill health and home duties must prevent my being with you. I am a daughter of New England, and although attached to my Western home, I turn with fond recollections to my native hill, (Carmel Hill,) Bethlem, and old associates, many of whom I trust will be with you at the coming Anniversary.

Please accept my thanks for yourselves and those you represent, for your kind invitation, also, my sincere wishes for your continued prosperity.

BETSEY T. AMBLER WHITING.

Trowbridge, Bull, Judd, &c.

From Hon. Henry Booth, of Poughkeepsie, N. Y., recently a Judge of the Court of Common Pleas in Pennsylvania, and now Professor in the Poughkeepsie Law School.

Poughkeepsie, June 11, 1859.

P. M. Trowbridge, Esq.,

Dear Sir:—Your circular and note of invitation came to hand a month since, or thereabouts; and I have deferred answering in the faint hope that I might at length see my way so clear as to be justified in giving a favorable reply. But engagements have thickened on me to such an extent that I am nearly compelled to abandon the idea of being present, even on an occasion so interesting as your anticipated jubilee. I have come to this conclusion with extreme reluctance, and will yet avail myself of any chance that occurs; but the prospect is so extremely unfavorable, that it will not be best *to rely* on me for any thing.

Your recollection is entirely in fault (or else mine is,) with regard to my ever having indulged in rhyme, even in my youthful days; and my occupation and studies for many years past, have been far enough removed from any thing of the kind. Still if anything could inspire poetic raptures, it would be an occasion like the one you have in prospect; and the charms of both eloquence and poetry surely cannot be wanting to grace your jubilee.

I am pleased to observe that the able and indefatigable historian of Woodbury, is to deliver a historical address. Nothing could be more appropriate. His work is one of much merit. I obtained a copy of it shortly after its publication, and I always desired to thank him personally for the pleasure which the perusal gave me, as well as for the zeal, industry, and perseverance with which he prosecuted his work, and which was the more note-worthy and generous, from the fact that he is not a native of the district whose records and local incidents he has taken so much pains to preserve. If he has failed of receiving a suitable pecuniary compensation, (as I fear he has,) he will at least reap a reward in the esteem of the community of which he deserves so well.

I am very respectfully and truly yours,

HENRY BOOTH.

From Rev. RUFUS MURRAY, of Detroit, Mich., a native of Woodbury.

DETROIT, June 30, 1859.

P. M. TROWBRIDGE, ESQ.,

Dear Sir:—I received your letter of March last, inviting me to be present at the Woodbury Centennial Celebration, and I have since been looking forward to the time with pleasure, inasmuch as I had made up my mind to come and socially commingle with my native and fellow townsmen in their festivities and historical celebration of the "two hundredth anniversary of the exploration of Ancient Woodbury," but recent sickness in my family will prevent my being present, which I exceedingly regret, as nothing would have been so gratifying to my feelings to have once more visited my native town, old Woodbury, especially at this time on the interesting occasion anticipated in interchange with those of my boyhood days and youth, who now, with myself, have grown old and gray with the frosts of more than three score years; but though providentially deprived of this happy greeting and pleasure, yet I am not unmindful of the rich legacy left to the descendants of Woodbury, by her ancient and noble sires, and I most cordially congratulate all of you in your joy and most worthy celebration of the exploration of ancient Woodbury; for I feel to express, and can truly say, not only from early associations, but venerated feelings of love, honor and celebrity, old Woodbury, "with all thy faults, I love thee still," indeed she is identified as one of the first of the ancient towns of Connecticut, for her patriotism, zeal and love of country, the noblest sentiments that can warm and animate the human breast. Nothing, therefore, and no time more appropriate than the glorious Fourth, our Nation's birth-day—our country's independence, for your jubilee; when all, of every religious sect, and political creed, whatever their preference or faith, are lost and mingled in one common feeling of love and brotherhood in their celebration of ancient Woodbury, as well as their freedom and independence. We of this nation have been most remarkably favored with the visible interference and protection of heaven; for there are in our own history, so many plain and unequivocal marks of a divine power and assistance, that if we do not acknowledge it, and rejoice that the Lord God Omnipotent reigneth, we are either the blindest or the most ungrateful people on earth. For when we look back upon the American Republic, the theatre of those events which tried men's souls, and the several parts they acted, we cannot but acknowledge the power of him, whose kingdom is the Lord's, and who is governor among the nations. But our fathers, where are they? This question may well be repeated by Americans in this nineteenth century.

The first members, too, of that old Congress, when and where was there ever such another assemblage before, or since, of like sterling worth, profound wisdom, talent energy and firmness of principle, bold patriotism and resolute courage; ready and willing to sacrifice their all on their country's altar.

That small, but heroic assemblage of high-born souls, congregated from the thirteen colonies, determined to be free or die in the sacred cause; all are now reaping the reward of their patriotic labors, in eternity, while we are enjoying the legacy they bequeathed us—freedom and independence—which we fancy will ever be held in lasting remembrance by every true American; for too well does the present generation appreciate the excellence and patriotism of those men, who guided the destinies of our country in those days of darkness and bitter trial; too well does it estimate the glorious events which have exalted these United States to their present elevation and greatness; and too well do they reverence the wisdom and patriotism they boldly espoused and manifested in laying the foundation and platform of our glorious republic, ever to be disregarded, or lost to the remembrance and affections of future posterity. No, while the world shall stand, may the heroic, manly and christian virtues of our fathers, as well as the causes and principles of that memorable event of our country's declaration of independence be treasured up and garnered in the hearts and affections of a grateful people, and the more sacredly regarded, admired, venerated and cherished, the farther we roll down the tide of time; because as we cherish and appreciate the christian Sabbath, the privileges and blessings of the christian religion, so should we esteem and prize our civil liberty, our country's freedom, our nation's birth-day. The legacy is ours, and just is the everlasting law that hath wedded happiness to virtue. In fullness is its worth—in fullness is its glory—in fullness be its praise!

Most respectfully yours, &c.,

RUFUS MURRAY.

From Hon. HILAND HALL, Governor of the State of Vermont, a grandson of Ancient Woodbury.

NORTH BENNINGTON, Vermont, July 1, 1859.

GENTLEMEN:—I had expected, until within a day or two past, to have been able, in compliance with your invitation, to unite with you in the celebration of the Two Hundredth anniversary of the exploration of ancient Woodbury, but I now find it will be impracticable for me to do so.

My father was born in ancient Woodbury, (Roxbury Parish,) in 1763, and remained an inhabitant of the town until 1779, where he, as a member of the family of my grandfather, removed to Bennington, and settled on the farm on which I now live. I have heard much from his lips of Woodbury and its people, and have long had a desire to visit the place. I had fondly hoped to gratify that desire on the approaching anniversary of our National Independence, but find myself compelled reluctantly to forego that pleasure.

Woodbury has also peculiar claims upon my patriotic feelings as a Vermonter. It was the birth-place of men to whom, perhaps, more than to all others, the State of Vermont owes its existence as an independent Commonwealth.

Prior to the revolution, the lands of the territory now comprising the State of Vermont, had been granted, in the name of the King, by the royal Governor of the province of New Hampshire, and the settlers had purchased under those grants, not doubting that their titles were valid. The territory was, however, claimed by the governing authorities of New York, as forming a portion of that province, and the king, from political considerations, without probably designing to interfere with previous grants, decided the controversy in favor of New York, by declaring the western bank of Connecticut river to be the boundary between the two provinces. Mr. Colden, the Lieut. Governor of New York, not satisfied with obtaining the jurisdiction of a territory which had never before been treated by the crown as belonging to that province, coveted, for the benefit of himself and friends, the right of soil in the lands already granted. He accordingly proceeded to grant them anew to the members of his council, the attorney-general and other officers of government and favorites, not forgetting to take prudent care of himself and family.

When the settlers declined to surrender their possessions to the new claimants, writs of ejectment were brought against them before the New York courts, their titles declared to be invalid, and writs of possession issued against them in favor of the New York plaintiffs.

Thus far all had been tolerably smooth work with the New York land speculators. But with the settlers it had now become a question whether they should tamely submit to the unjust oppression of their enemies, or resist them by force. Believing their situation to be one which fully justified revolution, they decided upon the latter, and Ethan Allen, Seth Warner and Remember Baker, all formerly belonging to Woodbury, became their acknowledged leaders. They organized a body of volunteers under the name of "Green Mountain Boys," and forcibly and effectually resisted all efforts of the New York sheriffs and their *posses* to disturb the possessions of the settlers or to establish the New York authority over them. The Green Mountain Boys, under their Woodbury leaders, resorted to such primitive modes of punishment for land-craving intruders as were deemed necessary to deter them from invading the disputed territory. A few of the most obstinate and incorrigible "Yorkers," after a formal trial before a committee of the settlers, were punished, as described in the quaint language of Ethan Allen, by being "chastised with the twigs of the wilderness, the growth of the land they coveted," which mode of punishment was familiarly denominated "*the application of the Beach Seal*," in allusion to the formal land patents of the New York governor, of which the pendent seal formed a distinguishing part. It had the intended effect of terrifying their enemies and of preventing further intrusions.

By the New York governor and council, as well as by the land jobbers, the Green Mountain Boys were assailed with many opprobrious epithets, but they were most usually denominated "the Bennington mob." Various methods were used to overcome them. They were indicted as rioters, repeated proclamations offering rewards for the arrest of Allen, Warner and Baker, and a few others, were issued, and finally they were declared by the New York government to be outlaws, and without a hearing, were adjudged to suffer death, if they neglected to surrender themselves for the space of seventy days. But all these efforts of the New York authorities, as is well known, were vain. The revolt thus begun by "the Green Mountain Boys," was continued until after the close of the revolution, when the titles of the settlers under New Hampshire, were quieted, by the admission of Vermont as a member of the federal union, with the full and free consent of the government and people of New York.

Nor is it alone against the land speculators of New York that the services of Allen, Warner & Baker are deserving of grateful remembrance. They were equally active and successful in their opposition to the oppressions of the mother country. The news of the shedding of American blood at Lexington, had no sooner reached the forests of the New Hampshire Grants, than the Green Mountain Boys were mustered under their Woodbury leaders, and in a few days they were in the triumphant possession for the Continental Congress, of the strong fortresses of Ticonderoga and Crown Point.

The importance of this event in the American Revolution, can now scarcely be appreciated. It was at once seen and felt by the king's high tory executive of New York, Lieut. Governor Colden, who immediately wrote an account of it to Lord Dartmouth, the British Minister, using the following language. "A matter of great importance was carried out in the northern part of this province, no less than the actual taking his Majesty's forts at Ticonderoga and Crown Point, and making the garrison prisoners. * * The only people of this province," he adds, "who had any hand in this expedition, *were the set of lawless people whom your Lordship has heard much of under the name of the Bennington mob.* They were joined by a party from Connecticut, and another from Massachusetts Bay," &c.

But this letter has already grown to a much greater length than I intended, and I must forbear even to mention the numerous other important services of these Woodbury men to the State of Vermont and to the whole country.

The State of Vermont has recently erected a creditable monument at the grave of Allen in Burlington, and I am informed that the people of Connecticut are doing themselves equal honor by placing one over the remains of Warner at Roxbury. He was a hero of whom not only Woodbury, but Connecticut, and indeed the whole country may well be proud.

Again, expressing my regret at not being able to meet and form personal acquaintance the ensuing week with my territorial cousins of Woodbury, I am, gentlemen,

Very respectfully, yours,

HILAND HALL.

To P. M. WOODBRIDGE, THOMAS BULL, and others, Committee of Invitation to the Celebration of the Two Hundredth Anniversary of the Exploration of ancient Woodbury, &c.

ANCIENT PORTRAIT GALLERY.

Agreeably to the request of the Committee of Invitation, and in conformity to a vote of the General Committee, Charles B. Crafts, Esq., of New Haven, aided by Miss Helen Blackman, of New Milfor, Miss Helen E. Hinman, of Southbury, and others, procured and arranged in a tasteful manner, at Academy Hall, the following list of portraits and antique articles, which were visited and admired by thousands. Nothing could better carry the mind back to the early days of the fathers, and give their posterity true glimpses of the past, than these portraits and relics, that had come down to us from a "former generation." The sons and daughters of old Woodbury could look with pride upon the faces of these departed ancestors, who had lived and labored in these valleys, and who by their wisdom, patriotism and virtues, had shed an ever undiminished lustre upon their descendants.

Hon. Nathaniel Smith and wife, taken, 1807.
Phineas Smith and wife.
Hon. Nathan Smith, taken, 1834.
Rev. Noah Benedict and son.
Rev. Samuel R. Andrews, taken, 1826.
Wife of Rev. Lyman Smith.
Rev. Charles Sherman.
Gen. Chauncey Crafts, 1826.
Rev. Grove L. Brownell, 1226.
Dr. R. Abernethy.
Dr. J. R. Eastman.
Elisha Michell, D. D.
Shadrach Osborn and wife.
Dr. Samuel Steele, taken, 1826.
R. C. Steele, taken, 1826.
Willie Steele Cothren, son of William and Mary J. Cothren.
Hon. William Hinman.
Gen. David Bird and wife.
Col. David Bellamy and wife.
Nicholas J. Masters and wife, taken, 1796.
Hon. Charles B. Phelps.
John P. Marshall.
Albert Blackman.
John Pernett and wife.
——— Marshall.
John Blagg.
Jasper P. Blagg.
Wife of Col. Pearse.
Two of Daniel Bacon, Esq., taken in 1795 and 1826.
Two of his wife, " " 1795 and 1826.
Asahel Bacon, wife and two children, 1795.
Elijah Sherman, Esq., and wife.

Jesse Minor.
Norman Parker.
H. J. Lindsley.
John McKinney.
Timothy Terrill.
Rev. Fosdic Harrison and wife.
Mrs. Caroline Camp.
A looking glass 200 years old.
Two paintings over 200 years old.
One painting over 300 years old.
Map of New England 104 years old.
A book of pamphlets, one title page being as follows:

"*The Picture of a Puritane,*"

or a relation of the opinions, qualities, and practices of the Anabaptists in Germanie, and of the Puritanes in England. Wherein is firmly proved that the Puritanes doe resemble the Anabaptists, in aboue four score seuerell thinges. By O. O., of Emmanuel. Whereunto is annexed a short treatise, entituled, puritano-papismus, or a discovery of Puritan-papism.

London.

Printed by E. A., for Nathaniel Fosbroke, and to be sold at his shop at the West End

Of paules, 1605.

One Silver Tea Caddy, purchased with Continental money.
One Table Spoon, 1712.
One set Tea Spoons, 1786.
One pair Knee Buckles, 1781.
One High Heel Shoe, very old.
A copy of the Farmers' Journal, printed at Danbury, Conn., 1790.

Lace Pattern and Bobbin used by the mother of Roger Sherman, signer of the Declaration.

Antique China Shoes, &c.

A Child's Embroidery, 1773.

Antique Shoes, Mrs. N. R. Smith, Roxbury.

Shoe Buckles, worn by Gen. Ephraim Hinman, Roxbury; exhibited by M. L. Beardsley.

Small Brass Tea Kettle, brought from Holland 1656 or 1657; exhibited by Mrs. D. C. Sanford, New Milford.

Silver Spoons, small in size, formerly owned by Mrs. Capt. Truman Hinman.

Silver Pepper Boxes, 1770, owned by Mrs. Capt. Truman Hinman.

Silver Tankard, 1790, owned by Mrs. Anna Hinman.

Gold and Silver Knee Buckles, 1750—Mr. Truman Hinman.

Satin Brocade Dress, worn by Mrs. Capt. Truman Hinman, 1760.

Pictures formerly owned by Edward Hinman, Esq., commonly called "Lawyer Ned," one of the two earliest lawyers in Woodbury, 1760.

Embroidery—Linen Curtains, wrought in colors in worsted, about 1765, by Miss Sarah Hicock, afterwards second wife of Col. Benjamin Hinman, now owned by Mrs. Olive Hinman Laird.

An Indian Belt of Pomperaug, owned by Erastus Osborn, Esq., 1659.

The last list of eight distinct kinds of articles, was exhibited by Miss Helen E. Hinman, of Southbury.

"The Pequot Gun," made and dated in 1624; the "Forty Indian Gun," so called from the alleged fact that it had been the instrument of death to forty redskins; Washington's New York Chair, and that of Col. Benj. Hinman, with his "Pipe of Peace," were also on exhibition. There were many other things of interest in this collection of antiquities, of which the editor, in the hurry of the separation of the great assembly, was unable to obtain.

The following sweet lines, written for the Litchfield Centennial Celebration, in 1851, by a lofty genius of Woodbury, a most lovely and estimable lady, now an angel in the regions of bliss, breathe the sentiments and emotions she would have loved to express, had she been spared to join in the exercises of our interesting festival.* The reader can not fail to be impressed with their beauty, and their adaptation to the circumstances of our celebration. They seem like a voice of the loved and lost, from the spirit land, breathing a spirit of deep affection from the realms of happiness.

A Call to the Centennial Celebration.

Brothers! from each laughing valley,
From our hill-sides, rough and bold!
Round our common center rally,
Like the Jewish tribes of old!

Fathers, come! your locks will whiten—
Mothers! ye are young no more;
But your fading hopes will brighten,
With the memories of yore!

* Mrs. Mary Smith Monell, wife of Hon. John J. Monell, of Newburgh, N. Y., and only daughter of Hon. N. B. Smith.

Come, ye sons, so sturdy, growing,
  Strong and tall, as freemen should;—
Bring your sisters, fluttering, glowing,
  Like rose-laurels in a wood.

We will tell you, if you listen,
  How two hundred years ago,
Pilgrims saw our waters glisten,
  In the valley, far below;—

Where the forest, grand and lonely,
  In primeval beauty stood,
And the wandering red men only
  Knew the windings through the wood;

Where our household fires are burning,
  Wild deer bounded, far and free;
Streams, our busy mill-wheels turning
  Idly, sang a song of glee;

Where our fathers sat beside them,
  After travel long and sore—
Fearing nought that could betide them,
  Might they find a home once more!

For a home they fronted danger—
  Wrought with rifle lying near:
To all luxury a stranger,
    Was each dauntless Pioneer.

Noble Fathers! silent lying
  In your grave-rest, stern and cold,
Still ye preach, with voice undying,
  To your children from the mould!

And ye tell us, "Love each other;"
  "Guard your homes we toiled to win,
Let no hatred of your brother,
  Doubt, or malice, enter in!"

"Chiefly on each household altar,
  Keep devotion burning bright,
Then ye will not pause or falter
  In the doing of the *right!*"

" Firm in purpose and endeavor,
Tireless till the goal be won,
Men shall know you, wheresoever
There is labor to be done."

Ye are freemen! Ye may glory,
In your Union, firm and strong;—
Let no *future* tell a story,
Of dissension, or of wrong.

Look into each other's faces—
Ye will meet again no more;
Then depart and fill your places
Better than you did before.

CONCLUDING REMARKS.

The weather during the two days devoted to the exercises, was clear, cool, and delightful. It was a general remark that Providence seemed to smile on the celebration. The immense concourse of people exhibited very great interest in the proceedings, which never flagged during the extended exercises, and constant sittings of the two days. There was a generous and intelligent appreciation of the intellectual feast prepared for them, on this occasion, never excelled at any similar celebration. Although the labors of the Committee have been severe and painful, beyond the comprehension of many, and might exceed the belief of all, yet its members feel fully compensated for all their pains and toil, by the expression of entire satisfaction and approbation, on the part of the people, which greet them on every side. So far as we know, every hearer, whose voice has yet been heard, declares the celebration to have been an *unbounded success.*

On the Sabbath preceding the 4th, allusions to the approaching celebration were made in several of the Churches in town, and an appropriate welcome to the returned emigrants from the old town extended. In the First, or old Pioneer Congregational Church, the oldest by many years in this county, the pastor, Rev. Robert G. Williams, read a sermon, preached by Rev. Anthony Stoddard, its second minister, on the 6th of July, 1754, to the same Church, in presence of the levies, raised to march against Crown Point, in the old French War. The sermon was written on leaves about three inches square, and showed evident traces of the patriarchal age of one hundred and five years. The historical associations which clustered around it, the place, the identical manuscript, the very presence in which we were assembled, listening to the same words which our fathers, who have been slumbering for generations in the old church-yard, heard on that occasion, so momentous to many hearts, wrought up the imagination to a temporary companionship with the silent shades of the spirit land. It was a fitting introduction to the exercises of the celebration, that was so soon to occur.

It was not a small matter to feed and shelter the vast multitude assembled at the celebration. But the most ample provision to meet the exigences of the occasion had been made by the ladies. Tents had been prepared by the Committee, for each of the towns once included within the limits of Ancient Woodbury, "with ensigns flying," to direct the people to the proper places. There was also a tent appropriated to the use of invited guests from abroad. In these the multitudes united in a mammoth Antiquarian Pic-Nic. No price was demanded, but like the sunshine, all was free. But the antique pic-nic proper was celebrated beneath the deep blue sky, within the shade of some large apple trees, spread on old tables, covered with pewter platters, wooden trenchers, pewter and wooden spoons, and all the antiquarian articles that had been preserved, and handed down to us from "former generations." The viands consisted of bean porridge, baked pork and beans, Indian pudding, hominy, rye and Indian bread, and numerous other primitive dishes. Mrs. N. B. Smith presided over the table arrangements for Woodbury, with that ease and grace for which she is so much distinguished, aided in the most effective manner by nearly all the other ladies of the town. In all the tents the tables groaned with abundance, and were set out with a taste in arrangement, and excellence of viands, rarely equalled on any similar festive occasion. Too great praise cannot be awarded to the ladies for the indispensable aid they furnished at the joyous festival. Where all did well, it would be invidious to mention names.

Among the many pleasing incidents of the celebration, was the reading of the beautiful and thrilling poem, in the preceding pages, by Mrs. Ann S. Stephens, a native of "Ancient Woodbury." There was a soul, and an emotion, pervading the whole of the production, that showed the heart of the writer was in the subject; and so striking was its effect on an audience wearied by the almost uninterrupted exercises of ten hours, that when the reading was concluded, and the "Historian of Ancient Woodbury" advanced to the front of the stand, and moved three cheers for the "Poetess of Ancient Woodbury," it was responded to by the great assemblage, with an enthusiasm which must have been grateful to the distinguished authoress, who was, at the moment, sitting quietly upon the stand.

An attempt was made to keep a Register of the names of all who attended the celebration, with a view to preservation. The request that every person would register his name, was announced from the stand. But owing to the great multitude, and to the fact that every moment was occupied with interesting public exercises, very few complied with the request.

Among the distinguished persons in attendance, besides those already named, we noticed the following named persons; and doubtless there were many others, whom we did not see in the crush and hurry of the occasion:—Hon. John Boyd of Winchester, Secretary of Connecticut; Hon. Origen S. Seymour of Litchfield, Judge of the Superior Court, with his son, Edward W. Seymour, Esq.; Jonathan Knight, M. D., of New Haven, Professor in Yale College; Hon. Ralph D. Smith of Guilford, a native of Southbury; Hon. William B. Wooster of Birmingham; E. B. Cooke, Esq., Editor of the Waterbury American; Rev. J. M. Willey of Waterbury; Hon. Judson W. Sherman, Member of Congress, of Angelica, N. Y.; Hon. Green Kendrick of Waterbury; Nathaniel A. Bacon, Esq., of New Haven; William Nelson Blakeman, M. D., a distinguished physician of New York, and a native of Roxbury; Charles Nettleton, Esq., of New York, a native of Washington; Hon. Samuel G. Goodrich of Southbury, late Consul at Paris, the well-known "Peter Parley;" C. S. Trowbridge, Esq., of Auburn, N. Y.; R. F. Trowbridge, Esq., of Syracuse, N. Y.; Rev. Charles W. Powell of Middlebury; Alexander Frazer, Esq., of New York; Rev. C. S. Sherman of Naugatuck; Rev. Abijah M. Calkin of Cochecton, N. Y.; Rev. Ira Abbott of Southbury; Rev. Jason Atwater of West Haven; Rev. J. K. Averill of Plymouth; Rev. E. Lyman, and Hon. Charles Adams of Litchfield, Editor of the Litchfield Enquirer.

Among the venerable men of other days, we noticed on the stage, Capt. Judson Hurd, 85 years of age, so active and vigorous, that he had ridden on horseback in the morning, with his "lady love" of 72, on a pillion behind him. We also noticed Dea. David Punderson of Washington, aged 86, Nathaniel Richardson of Middlebury, aged 85, and Mr. William Summers, of the ripe age of nearly ninety years, a resident of Woodbury, and the oldest man in town.

The extended and efficient arrangements of the General Committee, for providing strangers with accommodations and protection, were thoroughly carried out. Perfect satisfaction and quiet reigned throughout the celebration. More than fifteen hundred visitors were lodged in the town the first night, and in the other towns of the ancient territory, at least twice that number. All the inhabitants threw open their doors, and from ten to seventy-five persons to a house found quarters for the night. Even our least opulent citizens displayed an extraordinary anxiety to add to the general enjoyment of the occasion. As an instance, Mr. Harry M. Fox, who, certainly, is not much blessed with this world's goods, fed twenty-six persons, and lodged twelve. We have not yet heard of an individual, who was not provided with reasonable accommodations.

To the active field operations of Rev. R. G. Williams, Rev. C. T. Woodruff, James Huntington, Esq., Wm. E. Woodruff, Esq., and John A. Boughton, B. A., the people are, in good part, indebted for the arrangement of the tents, and preparation of the grounds in a comfortable and beautiful manner.

To Philo M. Trowbridge, Esq., for his indefatigable labors for many months, both as chairman of the Committee of Invitation, and as Secretary of the General Committee, as well as for the excellent taste displayed by him in the antique department, the warmest thanks of the public are due.

A very pleasing feature in the "Antique Procession," not before noticed in these pages, was the fine turn-out of King Solomon's Lodge, No. 7, of Free and Accepted Masons, of Woodbury, in the splendid regalia of its mystic brotherhood. This is not only one of the oldest lodges west of Connecticut river, having received its first charter in 1765, from the Provincial Grand Lodge of the Colony of Massachusetts, but it has been one of the oldest and most respectable in the State, both for the number and character of its members. It was with becoming pride, that they joined in the antique portion of the proceedings of the festival, celebrating at once the antiquity of the town, and the establishment therein of their own ancient, benevoolent, and honorable fraternity.

The music on the occasion was furnished by the New Milford Band, in a highly creditable and satisfactory manner. During the evening of the first day, it serenaded the orator of the day, and other residents connected with the active exercises of the occasion. In short, every part of the programme was well performed, and the whole celebration was pronounced by all present to be a perfect success. As it was the largest, so it was more perfect, in all its arrangements, than any similar celebration in this country.

INDEX.

27

Copy of a letter from Wm. Cothren Esq
to S. P. Beers.

"Hon. S. P. Beers

Dear Sir,

I received by Saturday's mail a letter from Hon. J. L. Graham, who resides in New York, in which occurs the following ~~tribute~~ to yourself, so just and appropriate, ~~that~~, at his request, I send ~~the~~ same to you.

I more than ever regret my inability to participate in ~~these~~ joyous festivities; But what was my loss was the gain of the Auditory, from my old friend Seth P. Beers being drawn out by reason of my absence; who made a most happy and admirable speech:— pungent, witty and pathetic. I know him well, and entertain for him great regard. We are related, and when I studied Law at Litchfield with Judges Reeve & Gould, he was my friend and adviser, I being ~~then~~ boy. His whole career has been ~~that~~ of a man of high integrity and great industry, and ~~the~~ State of Connecticut owe him an everlasting debt of gratitude for his fidelity and devotion to ~~the~~ cause of education, in guarding & nursing the School Fund.

"When you see, or write to, Mr. Beers,
"present him my kindest regards, and express
"to him how gratified I am, in having been
"represented at the Celebration by so able
"and worthy a substitute".

This is a very high compliment from our mutual friend, and permit me to add, ~~that~~ it is one very justly deserved.

Yrs. very truly
W. Cothren.

Woodbury Aug. 22. 1859.

www.ingramcontent.com/pod-product-compliance
Lightning Source LLC
LaVergne TN
LVHW021140110826
845150LV00005B/1086